MONARCHY AND THE END OF EMPIRE

This unique and meticulously researched study examines the triangular relationship between the British government, the Palace, and the modern Commonwealth since 1945. It has two principal areas of focus: the monarch's role as sovereign of a series of Commonwealth Realms, and quite separately as head of the Commonwealth. It traces how, in the early part of the twentieth century, the British government promoted the Crown as a counterbalance to the centrifugal forces that were drawing the Empire apart. Ultimately, however, with newly independent India's determination to become a republic in the late 1940s, Britain had to accept that allegiance to the Crown could no longer be the common factor binding the Commonwealth together. It therefore devised the notion of the headship of the Commonwealth as a means of enabling a republican India 'to continue to give the monarchy a pivotal symbolic role and therefore to remain in the Commonwealth.'

In the years of rapid decolonization which followed 1945, it became clear that this elaborate constitutional infrastructure posed significant problems for British foreign policy. The system of Commonwealth Realms was a recipe for confusion and misunderstanding. Policy-makers in the UK increasingly saw it as a liability in terms of Britain's relations with its former colonies, so much so that by the early 1960s they actively sought to persuade African nationalist leaders to adopt republican constitutions on independence. The headship of the Commonwealth also became a cause for concern, partly because it offered opportunities for the monarch to act without ministerial advice, and partly because it tended to tie the British government to what many within the UK had begun to regard as a largely redundant institution. Philip Murphy employs a large amount of previously-unpublished documentary evidence to argue that the monarchy's relationship with the Commonwealth, which was initially promoted by the UK as a means of strengthening Imperial ties, increasingly became a source of frustration for British foreign policy-makers.

Philip Murphy is Director of the Institute of Commonwealth Studies in London.

D1333777

Monarchy and the End of Empire

The House of Windsor, the British Government,
and the Postwar Commonwealth

PHILIP MURPHY

OXFORD
UNIVERSITY PRESS

OXFORD
UNIVERSITY PRESS

Great Clarendon Street, Oxford, OX2 6DP,
United Kingdom

Oxford University Press is a department of the University of Oxford.
It furthers the University's objective of excellence in research, scholarship,
and education by publishing worldwide. Oxford is a registered trade mark of
Oxford University Press in the UK and in certain other countries

First published 2013
First published in paperback 2015

Published in the United States of America by Oxford University Press
198 Madison Avenue, New York, NY 10016, United States of America

British Library Cataloguing in Publication Data
Data available

Library of Congress Cataloging in Publication Data
Data available

ISBN 978–0–19–921423–5 (Hbk.)
ISBN 978–0–19–875769–6 (Pbk.)

For Flo

Contents

List of Plates

17. The Queen speaking at the opening ceremony of the CHOGM in Coolum, Australia, in March 2002. © Commonwealth Secretariat.

18. The Queen at Marlborough House in May 2006 with three Commonwealth Secretaries-General: (from left to right) Chief Emeka Anyaoku, Don McKinnon (the then current Secretary-General), and Sir Shridath Ramphal. © Commonwealth Secretariat.

19. The Queen with Commonwealth Secretary-General Emeka Anyaoku, leaving Westminster Abbey, London, after the annual Commonwealth Day Multi-Faith observance. © Commonwealth Secretariat.

20. Twelve-year-old John Samson from the Jacaranda Foundation, Malawi, presents the Royal Commonwealth Society's Jubilee Time Capsule to the Queen in November 2012. © Capsool/Joe Gardner.

Preface and Acknowledgements

The legacy of Empire continues to haunt British society and remains as contentious a subject as ever. The monarchy, too, seems to have lost nothing of its fascination or its capacity for generating controversy. Nevertheless, despite having lived her life under intense media scrutiny, Queen Elizabeth II remains something of an enigma. What is clear, as Frank Prochaska has noted, is that 'she likes dogs, horses, the Commonwealth and her grandchildren'.[1] This book seeks to explore the relationship between monarchy and Empire/Commonwealth in the post-war era, focusing largely on the Queen's reign. Its model and inspiration is Ben Pimlott's ground-breaking 1996 biography of the Queen.[2] Both in print and in person Pimlott encouraged historians of contemporary British politics to take the monarchy seriously and to incorporate it into mainstream political history. He was particularly fascinated by the interface between the personal and the institutional, a phenomenon that becomes ever more striking as the Queen's reign enters its seventh decade.

Yet this sort of political history has not become very much easier to write than it was in the 1990s. Up until the beginning of that decade, government files relating to the royal family were routinely closed for 100 years. A White Paper on open government, published in July 1993—the so-called 'Waldegrave Initiative'—appeared to signal a more liberal approach to the vetting of 'sensitive' historical documents. It specifically ruled that papers relating to the royal family should normally be subject to the standard thirty-year period of closure.[3] Its impact remains a matter for debate.[4] Ironically, however, many historians would suggest that the implementation from 2005 of the Freedom of Information Act of 2000 (FOI) has represented a major step backwards. Under the Act, access to communications with the royal household was restricted by a special exemption (section 37). This, however, was subject to a public interest appeal. Partly for this reason, it was clearly not regarded by the Palace as a sufficient safeguard for the confidentiality of royal correspondence. They appear to have persuaded government to apply other exemptions to documents relating to the royal family. During the research I conducted for this book in the National Archives, I noticed that government vetting terms were regularly invoking the privacy provisions of the act (section 40, which relates to personal information, and section 41, which relates to information provided in confidence) to withhold historical documents relating to the royal family. These exemptions were not subject to any public interest appeal. Some of

[1] Frank Prochaska, *The Making of a Welfare Monarchy* (New Haven: Yale University Press, 1995), 250.
[2] Ben Pimlott, *The Queen: A Biography of Elizabeth II* (London: HarperCollins, 1996).
[3] *Open Government*, Cmnd 2290 (London: HMSO, July 1993), section 9.22, 68.
[4] Richard J. Aldrich, 'Did Waldegrave Work? The Impact of Open Government upon British History', *Twentieth Century British History*, 9/1 (1998), 111–26.

this material dated from the 1950s and in many cases it was possible to find uncensored copies that had been released to the National Archives decades before. These revealed that the most innocent references to the Queen's views or even simple mentions of communication with her were enough to attract the attentions of the censors.

Nevertheless, this still was clearly not sufficient for the Palace. In October 2007 the government announced the establishment of an independent review of the thirty-year rule, chaired by the editor of the *Daily Mail*, Paul Dacre. This appears to have provided the Palace with a pretext to lobby for a further tightening of the act. The Dacre review, which reported in January 2009, recommended that the thirty-year rule be reduced to fifteen years. In June 2009 the government announced that the period would eventually be reduced to twenty years. Yet it also took the opportunity to announce an extension of the existing exemption from FOI legislation of information relating to communications with members of the royal household. It was explained that this was to ensure 'the constitutional position and political impartiality of the Monarchy is not undermined'. In the cases of the Sovereign and the Heir to the Throne the exemption would apply without qualification until five years after their deaths.[5] A provision to this effect was included in a Command Paper published by the Labour government in February 2010. The following month it was incorporated in the Constitutional Reform and Governance Bill 2009–10 at its report stage. The change actually came into operation under the subsequent Coalition government in January 2011.

The Palace may have been concerned by attempts by journalists to use FOI legislation to investigate recent attempts by the Prince of Wales to lobby government ministers.[6] Yet in tightening the restrictions on access to documents relating to the royal family the British government has now created a climate in which perfectly innocuous correspondence dating from the beginning of the Queen's reign is regarded as unsuitable for release. This sort of censorship also applies to major collections of private papers (such as those of Anthony Eden at the University of Birmingham, and Harold Macmillan and Harold Wilson in the Bodleian Library, Oxford). Meanwhile, the royal archives in Windsor remain closed for the current reign and are likely to continue to be so for the remainder of the Queen's lifetime. In terms of oral history, the subject of the royal family tends to be one which inspires discretion and circumspection on the part of many potential witnesses. As a result of all this, we probably know far less about the way in which constitutional monarchy operated in our lifetimes than our grandparents did in the 1950s when the official biographies of George V and George VI were published.

That is not to say that significant quantities of material, including documentary evidence from official files, are not available (as anyone consulting the endnotes of the chapters below will notice). Partly because of the sort of censorship discussed above, however, the record is patchy and often evidence is at its most elusive when

[5] House of Commons Library, SN/PC/05377, 'Public Records, Freedom of Information and the Royal Family', 9 March 2011.

[6] *The Guardian*, 16 December 2009.

one is particularly curious to learn the Queen's views (for example, over the Suez Crisis of 1956). Scholars specializing in intelligence history have demonstrated how a kind of documentary archaeology—based on fragments of evidence that have escaped the attentions of Whitehall's vetting teams—can build up a revealing picture of their subject. This is, to some extent, the approach taken below. The kind of conventional political history presented here may be somewhat out of step with the focus on culture and representation in much recent academic writing on empire and monarchy. Yet as was also the case until recently with the history of the intelligence community, we lack a body of work which really integrates the story of the British monarchy into broader histories of Britain's post-war international relations. This book leaves many questions unanswered. Yet it will hopefully help to stimulate debate not just about the monarchy itself, but about the laws that currently prevent us from learning about how it operates.

I began writing this book while working in the History Department at the University of Reading. I benefited greatly from discussions with my colleagues there about this subject. Particular thanks are due to Roy Wolfe for his help in locating a number of published sources. In September 2009 I was seconded to the Institute of Commonwealth Studies (ICwS) as its director. This inevitably delayed progress on the book, although it has greatly enhanced my understanding of the contemporary Commonwealth and in the process—I hope—enriched the discussion that follows. Through my association with the Institute I benefited immensely from the advice of many people whose knowledge of Commonwealth affairs far surpassed my own. They included Victoria te Velde, Richard Bourne, Stuart Mole, James Manor, and Daisy Cooper. The late Peter Lyon proved highly encouraging in the early stages of the research for this book. I have learned much from conversations both with my colleagues at the Institute and also with Charles Anson, Chief Emeka Anyaoku, Lord Carrington, Simon Gimson, William Heseltine, Derek Ingram, David McIntyre, and Lord Owen. A number of conferences and witness seminars organized at the ICwS have helped to shape my approach to some of the issues discussed below. A witness seminar held in December 2009 at which William Heseltine and his successors as the Queen's private secretary, Robert Fellowes and Robin Janvrin, discussed the engagement of the Palace with the Commonwealth proved particularly valuable, as did a public interview with Sir Shridath 'Sonny' Ramphal which my colleague Sue Onslow and I conducted in June 2012. David Clover, our specialist librarian at the ICwS, has proved immensely helpful, as has Hilary McEwan, the archivist at the Commonwealth Secretariat. I should also like to thank the staff of the National Archives, the Bodleian Library, Oxford, the Churchill College Archives Centre, Cambridge, the Irish National Archives, and the Royal Archives in Windsor. Incidentally, I decided not to include material from the Royal Archives in this book. Scholars are not able to see material relating to the current reign. They are also required to submit for approval work that cites material from the Archive, something I was not prepared to do. I am extremely grateful to Vanessa Rockel for her invaluable help in selecting the illustrations for this book.

Crown copyright material from the National Archives in Kew is reproduced under the Open Government Licence. I am grateful to its Director for permission to quote copyright material from the Irish National Archives. Excerpts from the Macmillan Papers in the Bodleian Library, Oxford, appear by kind permission of the Macmillan Trust. I am also grateful for permission to quote from material in the BBC Written Archives Centre. The Commonwealth Secretariat kindly allowed me to quote from material in its archives, and to reproduce a number of photographs from its image library. Other illustrations in the book appear by kind permission of Ian Berry/Magnum Photos, *Private Eye* magazine, Steve Bell/belltoons, Capsool/ Joe Gardner, and Express Syndication Ltd.

Some of the material in the manuscript has appeared in print in the following articles: 'The African Queen? Republicanism and Defensive Decolonization in British Tropical Africa, 1958–64', *Twentieth Century British History*, 14/3 (2003), 243–63; 'Breaking the Bad News: Plans for Announcement to the Commonwealth of the Death of Elizabeth II, 1952–69', *Journal of Imperial and Commonwealth History*, 34/1 (March 2006), 139–54; 'By Invitation Only: Lord Mountbatten, Prince Philip and the Attempt to Create a Commonwealth Bilderberg Group, 1964–1966', *Journal of Imperial and Commonwealth History*, 33/2 (May 2005), 245–65; and 'Independence Day and the Crown', *Round Table*, 97/ 398 (October 2008), 667–76.

I owe a huge debt of thanks to Harshan Kumarasingham and David Cannadine, who kindly read through the complete manuscript of this book and made a series of extremely helpful suggestions. I am also grateful to OUP's anonymous reader for their insightful comments, and to my editors and production team at OUP: my editors, Stephanie Ireland and Cathryn Steele; my production editor, Emma Barber; and my copy editor, Charles Lauder. My final word of thanks must go to Christina, Alex, and Nicky, who have dealt with my absorption in this project over many years with characteristic indulgence.

List of Abbreviations

ANC	African National Congress
BDEEP	British Documents on the End of Empire project
BSAP	British South Africa Police
CAB	Cabinet Office
CAO	Central Africa Office
CFD	Citizens for Democracy (Australia)
CHOGM	Commonwealth Heads of Government Meeting
CIO	Central Intelligence Organisation
CA/B	Commonwealth Advisory Bureau
CO	Colonial Office (in TNA)
CRO	Commonwealth Relations Office
DLP	Democratic Labour Party (of Trinidad and Tobago)
DO	Dominions Office/Commonwealth Relations Office (in TNA)
DOHP	The Diplomatic Oral History Project
EPG	Eminent Persons Group
FCO	Foreign and Commonwealth Office (in TNA)
FO	Foreign Office (in TNA)
FOI	Freedom of Information Act of 2000
GCHQ	Government Communications Headquarters
HC Deb	*Hansard*, House of Commons Debates
ICwS	Institute of Commonwealth Studies
IGCCM	Inter-governmental Group on Criteria for Commonwealth Membership
KAU	Kenya African Union
MEPO	Metropolitan Police (in TNA)
MH	Marlborough House
OECS	Organisation of Eastern Caribbean States
PNG	Papua New Guinea
PNM	People's National Movement (of Trinidad and Tobago)
PPP	People's Progressive Party (of British Guiana)
PREM	Prime Minister's Office (in TNA)
PRG	People's Revolutionary Government (of Grenada)
RCS	Royal Commonwealth Society
TNA	The National Archives, Kew
TSO	The Stationery Office
UDI	(Rhodesia's) unilateral declaration of independence
UNIP	United National Independence Party (of Northern Rhodesia)
ZANU	Zimbabwe African National Union
ZAPU	Zimbabwe African People's Union

1

The Holy Family: An Introduction

The most influential examination of constitutional monarchy in modern Britain is undoubtedly Walter Bagehot's *The English Constitution*, which first appeared in book form in 1867. In terms of the pitiless gaze it casts on this institution, its nearest counterpart in the late twentieth century is probably *The Enchanted Glass: Britain and its Monarchy* by Tom Nairn, which originally appeared in 1988.[1] Bagehot and Nairn were writing, respectively, before and after the high point of the monarchy's engagement with empire, and neither had very much to say on the matter. Yet they shared a fascination with the way in which the monarchy was presented, and the illusions it served to generate. These themes are central to the current study.

For Bagehot, writing at the dawn of mass politics, those illusions were justified in terms of securing the support of what he regarded as a dangerously ignorant and unsophisticated population for Cabinet government. Yet he retained a profound suspicion of the royal dynasty and the hereditary principle, concluding that it was only during the current reign that 'the duties of a constitutional sovereign' had 'ever been well performed'.[2] For Bagehot, the key function of the monarchy was that it made government intelligible to ordinary people, particularly through its focus on a family. As he famously noted:

> A *family* on the throne is an interesting idea . . . It brings down the pride of sovereignty to the level of petty life. No feeling could be more childish than the enthusiasm of the English at the marriage of the Prince of Wales . . . But no feeling could be more like common human nature as it is, and as it is likely to be.[3]

In addition to this, according to Bagehot, the royal family sanctified government with the force of religion, provided a focus for pageantry, and set the standard for national morality. Bagehot anticipated many of the preoccupations of the current literature on the monarchy, particularly its emphasis on performance and display in the interests of rallying popular support behind the existing political order. At the same time, however, he was alert to the fact that the monarchy itself continued to be able to exercise genuine influence. In one of the most frequently quoted definitions of the proper role of constitutional monarchs, Bagehot claimed that they had three rights: 'the right to be consulted, the right to encourage, the right to warn'.[4] Yet he recognized that, by the simple fact of having witnessed the inner workings of government over many decades, a monarch could come to exercise considerable sway over politicians and officials. This aspect of monarchy is less frequently explored in the contemporary literature, although it is an important one.

Finally and ironically, when Bagehot did look overseas to the British colonies of North America and Australia, he identified peoples who by virtue of their embrace of education and spirit of equality could reap the benefits of Cabinet government without requiring the vulgar trappings of monarchy to ensure it retained public confidence. In this respect the spirit of Bagehot would live on in those UK diplomatic representatives who from the 1960s onward prophesied the imminent disappearance of the monarchy in those Commonwealth countries which still retained the Queen as their Head of State.

Despite the pivotal part played by the Crown in Imperial/Commonwealth affairs in the intervening century, in *The Enchanted Glass* Nairn, like Bagehot, paid relatively little attention to its global reach. This is despite the fact that in his Introduction to the revised 1994 edition he identified the very peculiarities of the UK's version of monarchical nationalism ('Ukania' in Nairn's lexicon) that are crucial to understanding the Crown's Imperial and Commonwealth role. Like Bagehot, he focused on the idea of the symbolic family. He noted that nationalism is usually constructed around notions of a common ethnic/racial identity, juxtaposed with the 'perception of a mortal threat'. The latter classically manifested itself in terms of either the threat of invasion or the reality of 'foreign' occupation. By contrast, in the British case 'a pure genetic myth—Protestant, aristocratic consanguinity—has been made to stand in for the usual collective ideology of popular nationhood'. Defining identity in terms of allegiance to 'a single symbolic family', Nairn suggested, suited the interests of an 'ex-Imperial and multi-national state' in discouraging the development of mutually exclusive forms of identity politics.[5] A notable exception to this rule was provided by the Ulster Protestants, for whom 'loyalty' to the Crown became a symbol of an embattled form of ethno-religious sub nationalism.

Nairn focused on the specific theme of the Commonwealth only fleetingly in the course of his book, noting tensions between this traditional monarchical nationalism and the forces of the 'new right' as characterized by Mrs Thatcher.[6] He was far more interested in exploring what he regarded as the infantilizing influence of the British monarchy closer to home. Yet the idea that a sense of collective belonging based on allegiance to a family could transcend the conventional markers of national identity was an essential element of British Imperial ideology. As David Cannadine notes, the tendency from the reign of George III to present members of the royal family as paragons of domestic virtue and stability lent itself to a broader conception of the nation as a family. From this,

> it was but a step to envisioning the whole of the British Empire as a great global family, with the monarch at its head—a sovereign who, from the 1930s, made this sense of family and of headship real by speaking to his subjects every Christmas on the wireless in their own front rooms, whether they lived in Cheltenham or Calcutta, Canberra, Cape Town, Calgary or Cairo.[7]

Like so many other elements of that ideology, it also lingered on in the development of the modern Commonwealth. In a bizarre flight of fantasy for a politician not known for rhetorical excesses, the Labour Prime Minister Clement Attlee wrote to his Indian counterpart, Jawaharlal Nehru, in March 1949, begging him to halt his country's progress towards republican status. Attlee noted that, hitherto, the link between Commonwealth members had been the King:

> I say the King rather than the Crown. King George has often stressed this point to me. The Crown is an abstract symbol connoting authority, often connected in the minds of some with an external power. But the real link is a person, the King. At the head of the Commonwealth is a family. This family does in a very real sense symbolise the family nature of the Commonwealth ... Thus not only the British, but French Canadians, Maltese, Africans and others, people of advanced and people of primitive culture, see this family symbol not as something alien, but as something which is their own. It is not altogether fanciful to compare this conception with that of the Holy Family in the Christian world. Christians do not consider Joseph, Mary and Jesus as Jews, but as Dutch in Holland, Welsh in Wales and Chinese in China.[8]

The 'family' was, as we shall see, a motif that appeared regularly in royal speeches and broadcasts, the term broadening out to become a metaphor for the Empire/Commonwealth as a whole. Yet, as Nairn also notes, this protean signifier of collective identity also lent itself to a multi-cultural Britain partly shaped by Commonwealth immigration.

BRITISH SHINTOISM AND THE COMMONWEALTH

Clement Attlee's rather bizarre comparison of the House of Windsor to the Holy Family points to another aspect of the history of the British royal family. Philip Williamson has charted the process by which, in the first half of the twentieth century, the British monarchy became 'the symbol and exponent' of a 'particular set of public values'.[9] Raising the rhetorical pitch a couple of notches, David Starkey has recently argued that one of the factors that has ensured the survival of the monarchy in Britain, alongside its embrace of public spectacle and voluntarism, has been the efforts by its supporters to make it the focus of what was virtually a secular religion.[10] For Starkey, one of the architects of this pseudo-religion was Cosmo Lang, the Archbishop of Canterbury from 1928 to 1942. At its heart was the notion that the members of the British royal family placed duty before personal happiness: the central motif was therefore one of self-sacrifice following in the steps of Christ himself. It was for this reason that the Archbishop was so keen to engineer the abdication of the hapless Edward VIII, who had no intention of becoming a sacrificial victim upon Lang's altar of moral rectitude.

While Starkey's thesis might appear a slightly over-elaborate means of seeking to understand the durability of constitutional monarchy, there is no shortage of examples of 'British Shintoism'. On 14 December 1936, immediately following Edward's abdication, Lang made a remarkable broadcast on the BBC in which he simultaneously launched a startlingly vicious attack on the fallen angel of the House of Windsor and sanctified Edward's successor. His charge against Edward was that the King had 'surrendered the trust' placed in him by God to pursue his 'craving for private happiness'. Lang accused him of having 'sought his happiness in a manner inconsistent with the Christian principles of marriage' within a social set 'whose standards and ways of life are alien to all the best instincts and traditions of his people'.[11] He contrasted Edward with his brother, the newly proclaimed George VI, invoking the familiar image of the Christian family at the heart of the Empire: 'Truly it is good to think that among all the homes of the Empire—the homes from which all that is best springs—none can be more happy and united than the home of our King and Queen.' One of Lang's co-conspirators in ousting Edward VIII was Geoffrey Dawson, the editor of *The Times*. On the morning of the coronation of George VI, an editorial in *The Times* pronounced that kingship relied 'not upon intellectual brilliance or superlative talent of any kind, but upon the moral qualities of steadiness, staying power and self-sacrifice'.[12]

It is almost certainly no coincidence that the principal exponent of British Shintoism in the post-war era was also one of the leading propagandists of the Commonwealth. Dermot Morrah, like Dawson, was a member of the Round Table movement and regular contributor to the group's journal. In a collection of essays compiled by the UK's Central Office of Information to commemorate the Queen's 1961 visit to India and Pakistan, Morrah contributed a brisk survey of the British monarchy from its earliest origins to contemporary times. Injecting a breath-taking element of the supernatural into the usually rather stale conventions of Commonwealth constitutional theory, Morrah wrote:

> The Queen is for all the peoples of the Commonwealth the supreme symbol of unity; and in many aspects she is—like the magical sacrificial kings of the dawn of history— the embodiment of the life of the people, so that what is done for her is done for all. This much is true in a broad sense even of those Commonwealth countries which are republics.[13]

Indeed, the Empire/Commonwealth underwrote British Shintoism. As Williamson has noted, the notion that the Empire depended upon the monarchy was an article of faith in royal circles.[14] It thus became incumbent upon members of the House of Windsor to follow the moral precepts expected of them by Lang and Dawson, lest their prestige be tarnished in the eyes of the monarch's Imperial subjects, and Britain's global power consequently undermined. The question 'What would the Commonwealth say?' remained as powerful as, if not more so than, the views of the established Church in placing constraints on the private life of the royal family. According to Alan Lascelles, who served as private secretary to both George VI and Elizabeth II, it was certainly a key element behind Winston Churchill's objections to the romance between the Queen's sister, Princess Margaret, and Group Captain Peter Townsend. Recording a conversation with Churchill, Lascelles noted Churchill's that Margaret was only 'one motor accident' away from the throne and added:

> Subsequently he agreed with what seemed to me an equally important aspect of the affair—that the contracting of such a marriage by Princess Margaret was not a matter of so much weight as was the possibility that, some day, the Sovereign's subjects all over the British Commonwealth and Empire might have to ask themselves whether or not they were prepared to accept a child of the marriage as their King or Queen.

Indeed, this side of the problem—the Commonwealth's possible reaction to the marriage and its consequences—clearly disturbed Mr Churchill more than did the entirely certain reaction of the Church.[15]

Margaret's subsequent public renunciation of any intention to marry Townsend 'mindful of the Church's teachings that Christian marriage is indissoluble, and conscious of my duty to the Commonwealth' made her a somewhat unlikely paragon of the virtue of self-sacrifice.

On the question of religion there was the added complication that the British monarch inherited the title of 'Defender of the Faith and Supreme Governor of the Church of England' while presiding over an empire and subsequently being head of a commonwealth the population of which was predominantly non-Christian. In April 1943, Alan Lascelles was irritated to hear that Lord Linlithgow, the Viceroy of India, had complained to the Secretary of State for India, Leo Amery, that Muslim opinion would be upset by a recent broadcast by the Queen extolling the importance of Christianity. An exasperated Lascelles wrote in his diary, 'One might as well argue that the Queen ought never to announce the fact (as she does each Sunday) that she has been worshipping in a Christian church, and not a mosque or a synagogue or Hindu temple'.[16] It is beyond the scope of this study to consider this matter in any depth. It will, however, touch on the ways in which Queen Elizabeth II, who—like her parents—is a devout Christian and who regularly includes references to her faith in her speeches and broadcasts, has attempted to reconcile this with her Commonwealth role.

ORNAMENTALISM AND 'DE-DOMINIONISATION'

One of the most significant contributions in recent years to the study of the monarchy in relation to empire, and also one of the most controversial, was David Cannadine's *Ornamentalism: How the British Saw their Empire*, published in 2001. As the title implies, the work playfully subverts the thesis of Edward Said's hugely influential 1978 study *Orientalism*. Said argues that the construction of racial 'others' in the scholarship and literature of the nineteenth and early twentieth centuries served to facilitate and validate the spread of European imperialism by reinforcing notions of Western racial superiority. For Cannadine, by contrast, Britain's rulers in the age of empire were obsessed not by racial difference but by distinctions of rank and class. Aristocratic Imperial proconsuls felt far more at ease in the company of Indian princes than amongst British compatriots of lower social status. Indeed, the British mapped their own particular obsessions with rank and class onto their colonial subjects. Thomas R. Metcalf, for example, talks of 'the larger colonial project of ordering the whole of India's society' following the 1857 'Mutiny' in which 'its princes and landlords, like its castes and tribes, were set into a "scientifically" structured hierarchy . . . Only after they had been properly ranked and labelled, and so frozen into place, so the British believed, could they exercise their "traditional" authority.'[17]

At the apex of this imperial hierarchy was the British monarchy. Cannadine talks of the 'symbiosis between crown and empire' in the nineteenth century, a 'two-way process whereby an imperialized monarchy merged with and moulded a monarchized empire'.[18] Drawing on his earlier contribution to the highly influential collection of essays on the 'Invention of Tradition' edited by Eric Hobsbawm and Terence Ranger, Cannadine demonstrates how imperial trappings provided the tinsel for a reinvented British monarchy with a renewed taste for ritual and display.[19]

In the dying days of the Empire, this obsession with rank lived on in the minds of those responsible for choreographing royal rituals in the United Kingdom itself. In the run-up to the Queen's coronation in 1953, the Colonial Office itself was slightly taken aback to be asked by the Earl Marshal's Office to list in order of precedence the 300 guests from the colonial territories who would be attending the ceremony in the Abbey. This led to a great deal of soul-searching as to where, for example, the Maltese nobility should be placed, or whether bishops should be placed in the same category as missionaries.[20] In its attempt to rank members of the various colonial royal families, the Colonial Office was even forced to consult the Admiralty as to the number of gun salutes their members had received at George VI's coronation in 1937. They learned that the Queen of Tonga and the Sultan of Zanzibar had tied in first place with twenty-one guns, the Sultan of Brunei and most of the Malay Sultans had received seventeen, while the poor Sultan of Lahej had only received nine. On this basis, they were able to divide the rulers into three groups. The tie-breaker used by the Colonial Office to rank the Queen of Tonga in relation to the Sultan of Zanzibar was the stage of constitutional development reached by their respective territories. Since Tonga was judged to have achieved a higher degree of independence than Zanzibar, the Queen won.[21]

The converse of Cannadine's view of empire is that decolonization can be seen 'as witnessing, embodying, portending and meaning the end of hierarchy. . . . In most countries, sometimes rapidly, sometimes more slowly, independence was thus simultaneously a political and social revolution, as empire and hierarchy, indeed empire *as* hierarchy, were rejected.'[22] We will see in Chapter 5 how the choreography of independence celebrations provided the British with one final opportunity to affirm hierarchy—although we will also note that by the time Hong Kong was returned to China in the 1990s notions of hierarchy seem to have decayed very much along the lines Cannadine suggests.

The way in which those hierarchical structures were exported from the UK was one of a broader set of concerns that animated a major series of academic conferences exploring Empire in terms of the creation of a 'British World'. With its focus on notions of loyalty and identity within the empire of settlement, the British World conferences offered further encouragement to studies of the role of the Crown as a symbol of Imperial unity and belonging. Along with Cannadine's work it has helped to spawn a number of micro-studies of Imperial royal ceremonies and royal tours.[23] At the same time, in one of the most stimulating essays that emerged from the conferences, Donal Lowry challenged the idea that loyalty to the Crown in the Empire was the exclusive preserve of settlers of British descent, and more specifically, of those who professed a Protestant faith.[24] As we shall see, the assumption that such loyalty would be strongest among Britain's Imperial 'kith and kin', and would correspondingly weaken as the countries of the 'old' Commonwealth became more ethnically diverse, shaped post-war debates in Whitehall about the likely fate of the Crown in those territories. Yet, as Lowry notes, a variety of communities including, for example, Canadians of French or Irish Catholic descent had their own particular reasons for identifying with and valuing the Crown, a phenomenon which complicated the notion of 'loyalism'.

It is worth bearing this in mind when we consider another important offshoot of the recent interest in Britishness, hierarchy, and the Crown. In a major intervention in the debate about post-war British decolonization, A. G. Hopkins has recently challenged the tendency to exclude the 'Old Dominions' from the standard narrative.[25] Running parallel to the liquidation of the colonial Empire after 1945 was, Hopkins suggests, a process by which the 'Old Dominions' sought to give constitutional and symbolic expression to their independence from Great Britain. While the adoption of new flags and anthems could be regarded as mere window dressing, such moves need to be seen as part of a wider process of material and ideological change beginning in the mid-1950s. Globalization weakened the Dominions' cultural and economic bilateral links with the UK and contributed to 'the destruction of the core concept of Britishness, which had given unity and vitality to Greater Britain overseas'. Reinforcing this process of cultural decolonization was the abandonment of the attempt to exclude from the Dominions non-white immigrants, and the struggle by indigenous peoples to assert their civil rights.

An aspect of this process to which Cannadine has paid particular attention and which relates particularly closely to the position of the monarchy is the disintegration of the Imperial honours system as Commonwealth countries introduced their own national awards. The system had developed from the second half of the nineteenth century, reflecting once again the British obsession with order and rank. As Cannadine notes, by the early twentieth century this system 'tied together the dominions of settlement, the Indian Empire and the tropical colonies into one integrated, ordered, titular, transracial hierarchy that no other empire could rival'.[26] Indian princes, Malay Sultans, and Dominion politicians were all eager recipients of these honours. And at the pinnacle of this system was the British monarch—the 'Fountain of Honour'. Yet, from relatively early on, this was an area in which Dominion governments sought to give symbolic expression to their sense of both their own nationhood and their relationship with the UK. In 1919 the Canadian government formally requested that the King refrain from conferring honours on his subjects resident in Canada (a prohibition that was only lifted during the Second World War and again during the Korean War). The South African government made a similar request in 1925.[27] Finally, in 1967 the Canadians established their own domestic honours system. Australia followed suit in 1975 and New Zealand in 1996.[28] As we shall see in the case of Australia, this was a process in which the Palace, and the Queen herself, displayed considerable interest and not a little concern.

A major theme of this book is that there has indeed, in some senses if not in all, been a gradual decline in the significance of the Crown as a focus of a shared

'Commonwealth identity' and a means of maintaining bilateral ties between Britain and its former territories. Perhaps more importantly, there was a widespread *perception* from the 1960s onwards that affection for the Crown was bound to diminish to a point when even the older Commonwealth realms would steadily adopt republican constitutions. Perceptions often ran ahead of reality. Writing in 1993 on the future of the monarchy in Australia and Canada, David Estep suggested that it was seemingly 'inevitable' in the former that the Crown would be abandoned in favour of a republic.[29] Yet just as observers have long predicted the steady decline of the royal connection, they have also, like Estep himself, commented on the quite differing attitudes across Commonwealth countries to the surviving legal, constitutional, and symbolic links with the UK, including the Crown. The noticeably less pronounced nature of republicanism in New Zealand than in Australia appears to reflect a broader tendency on the part of the former to be more reluctant to dismantle such links. Whereas, for example, Australia abolished appeals to the Judicial Committee of the Privy Council in London in 1968, New Zealand only did so in 2004.[30] Furthermore, as Peter Boyce's comparative study has recently demonstrated, there have been and remain significant local factors binding the older Commonwealth realms to the Crown. In the case of New Zealand, one such factor is a sense on the part of Maori leaders that, since the 1840 Treaty of Waitangi, the Crown has acted as a special guarantor of the rights of their community.[31] In the case of Canada, some provincial governments have cultivated their relationship with the Crown as a means of seeking to buttress their own constitutional authority against the powers of the federal government.[32] As such, there is no simple link between a steady 'de-Dominionisation' and the growth of republicanism. Indeed, as we will see, while it is possible to identify longer-term issues that might make republicanism prevalent in some realms rather than others, the complex interaction of these factors has thwarted the predictions of many would-be Cassandras.

EMPIRE, MONARCHY, AND BRITISH NATIONAL IDENTITY

The pioneering work of John MacKenzie has provided a further framework in which studies of the British monarchy have situated themselves. MacKenzie sought to demonstrate the wide variety of ways in which he believed empire shaped British politics, culture, and society.[33] The emergence of a self-consciously 'imperial' monarchy was part of that process. MacKenzie's most prominent critic in recent years has been Bernard Porter, whose 2004 study *The Absent-Minded Imperialists: Empire, Society and Culture in Britain* provoked a heated academic debate.[34] Porter challenged the assumption, bordering on an article of faith on the part of historians influenced by post-colonial theory and by MacKenzie's more empirical work, that British culture was profoundly influenced by its empire. One of Porter's key arguments was that Empire was administered on such parsimonious and minimalist principles that only a small minority of the British population—mostly drawn from the upper middle classes—had any direct contact with it.

Very much running parallel to the theme of 'de-Dominionisation' in the post-war era is the process by which sections of the British governing elite rejected the idea of an imperial monarchy (in its refurbished Commonwealth guise) in favour of a much narrower sense of national identity for which the monarchy remained a sacred figurehead. Nairn's relative neglect of the Commonwealth dimension to the British monarchy in *The Enchanted Glass* can partly be explained by a determination to maintain a tight focus on the political formation of the UK itself. Yet it may also be because he had devoted a chapter in an earlier collection of essays, *The Break-Up of Britain: Crisis and Neo-Nationalism*, to a figure who in many ways personified that post-war rejection of Empire. This was another fallen angel of twentieth-century Britain, J. Enoch Powell, who placed himself firmly beyond the pale of mainstream British politics with his notorious 'Rivers of Blood' speech on immigration in April 1968. A version of Nairn's piece on Powell had originally been published in the *New Left Review* in 1970. Powell is periodically rediscovered by scholars identifying themselves with the self-proclaimed 'New Imperial History'. This brilliant early work by Nairn, however, anticipates many of the themes explored in subsequent analyses of Powell's career. Nairn quotes a speech delivered in 1964 in which Powell claimed:

> There was this deep, this providential difference between our empire and others, that the nationhood of the mother country remained unaltered through it all, almost unconscious of the strange fantastic structure built around her . . . England underwent no organic change as the mistress of a world empire.[35]

For many readers, Powell's speech will immediately bring to mind the present-day debate between MacKenzie and Porter. In the meantime, however, it is important to note that Powell, while maintaining that the essential elements that constituted the English nation had been little affected by the experience of empire, and displaying an almost fetishistic reverence for what Nairn describes as the 'sacred icon[s] of the great conservative past'—particularly the Crown, Parliament, and constitutional convention—saw all these things as being under threat from the lingering illusions of Imperial ideology.

As the Second World War ended Powell, once a fervent imperialist, underwent a Damascene conversion which roughly coincided with India's headlong rush towards independence. As early as 1946, in a speech at Trinity College Dublin, Powell denounced the 'myth of the British Empire' and particularly its hold over the Conservative Party.[36] Eight years later, he identified the paradox at the heart of the Westminster Parliament's relationship with the colonies: that an institution, the legitimacy of which rested on its representative nature, could claim authority over colonial peoples who were denied representation.[37] By 1957, he was seeking to influence his party's agenda for the next general election, arguing that 'the Tory Party must be cured of the British Empire, of the pitiful yearning to cling to the relics of a bygone system'.[38] In its place, the party had 'to find its patriotism again, and to find it, as of old, in this England'. Those 'English' institutions were not, he believed, easily compatible with Empire. Powell's intervention in the Hola camp debate of July 1959 added a further element to his critique of Empire. He explicitly denounced the view that different moral standards could apply in different parts of the Empire: 'We cannot say, "We will have African standards in Africa, Asian standards in Asia and perhaps British standards here at home."'[39] A clear implication of Powell's speech, although one that he failed to spell out at the time, was that if colonial rule could not be exercised without compromising 'British standards' it would be better not exercised at all.

This sense that a political entity could only function on the basis of a shared set of moral and cultural values also informed Powell's attitude to the Commonwealth and immigration. In an anonymous article in 1964 he described the Commonwealth as a 'gigantic farce', and claimed that the 'open door' policy on immigration which had, until recently, accompanied it, had 'inflicted social and political damage that will take decades to obliterate'.[40] In a clear reference to the headship of the Commonwealth, he spoke of the resentment of British people at seeing their sovereign 'playing an alien part as one of the characters in the Commonwealth charade'. In short, Powell's approach to decolonization was essentially defensive in nature. He regarded the process of shedding Empire as a means of 'cleansing' Britain of influences that were ultimately incompatible with her core values and institutions. He condemned attempts to preserve some vestige of British influence over former colonies not merely because of their ultimate futility but because they continued to leave Britain exposed to some of these dangers. And, for Powell, one of the institutions most vulnerable to being devalued by its complicity in the preservation of Britain's post-Imperial illusions was the monarchy itself.

The project of promoting the Queen as head of the Commonwealth was for Powell a self-delusion that prevented the British from having to confront the realities of imperial retreat, and in the process tarnished the image of the monarchy. Had he read the memoirs of the first Secretary-General of the Commonwealth, Arnold Smith, he would have been interested to note that when, in the 1970s, 'a few African cabinet ministers' asked whether the link between the Crown and the headship should be broken and a rotating headship put in its place, Smith told them that 'such a change would deeply upset British opinion at a time when Britain was still going through the neurosis of diminished relative power in the world'.[41]

Powell's career also provides the starting point for Bill Schwarz's recent study, *The White Man's World*. For Schwarz, Powell exemplifies a shift away from the 'wilfully immortal' monarchical nationalism identified by Nairn, to one based firmly on a 'language of racial whiteness' threatened by 'enemies within and without'. This shift reflected a significant change within the UK itself, coinciding with the process of rapid decolonization overseas. Although essentially a post-colonial phenomenon, the notion of the 'white man' under threat drew on the imagery of the colonial frontier, 'the homesteads on the veld or in the bush, prey to racial assault'.[42] Powell and his follows imagined a lost world of untrammelled Anglo-Saxon supremacy, presided over by the 'sacred icon[s] of the great conservative past' identified by Nairn. And just as they drew on the language of the frontier to characterize the plight of white Britain, they constructed the white settlers of Ian Smith's Rhodesia as the inheritors and guardians of a sort of British patriotism that had almost been extinguished at home. In both cases, the

Commonwealth was the enemy: for having opened the door to non-white immigration and for supporting the cause of Smith's African nationalist opponents. Yet the Commonwealth was among the institutions that mattered most to the Queen and with which she was most closely associated. Hence the post-war New Right, to which Powell played the role of John the Baptist, was deeply conflicted about the monarchy, seeing it as the sacred symbol of British nationhood, and at the same time as the principal player in the 'Commonwealth charade'. As we explore these tensions over the course of the book, we will encounter Powell playing the part of Greek chorus at key moments in the development of the Queen's Commonwealth role.

THE POLITICS OF INFLUENCE

The emphasis in recent academic literature about the contemporary British monarchy on ritual, display, and notions of national identity might distract us from a more practical question which no one considering the monarchy and the Commonwealth can fail to consider: given the extraordinarily detailed knowledge of the Commonwealth that the Queen has developed over her lifetime, is she capable of exerting an influence over this area of policy? Again, Bagehot noted that in his own day constitutional monarchy retained the potential to shape policy and, rather more recently, Peter Hennessy has urged scholars to give more serious consideration to royal influence over post-war British politics.[43] The Queen herself has been privy to the inner workings of government for longer than any other contemporary public figure in the UK. The constitutional conventions that prevailed when she came to the throne in 1952 are set out by the Cabinet Office's 'Precedent Book', drawn up in the early 1950s but only made public in 2006.[44] It makes clear that in the middle of the twentieth century, the role of the monarch continued to be more than purely 'ornamental', and the Palace enjoyed access to a wide range of official documents. In terms of Commonwealth affairs it received Cabinet minutes and memoranda (which formally constituted the Cabinet's advice to the monarch). The monarch also saw the Cabinet agenda, the minutes of a range of Cabinet committees including the Commonwealth Affairs Committee and the Commonwealth Relations Committee, and copies of Commonwealth Relations Office (CRO) telegrams circulated to the Cabinet. As heir to the throne, Princess Elizabeth had received copies of Cabinet minutes and memoranda since June 1950 at the personal insistence of Prime Minister Clement Attlee.[45] During the war, the King had access to highly sensitive operational papers, including situation reports from the Joint Intelligence Committee, and in July 1942 Churchill ruled that the King should always be fully briefed on future operations, however secret. The monarch was—and continues to be—briefed by the Prime Minister in person at regular audiences. In addition to this, in February 1938, at the time of Anthony Eden's resignation from the Foreign Office, George VI asked that arrangements be made to provide him with immediate news of serious developments. It was agreed that the King's private secretary, the Prime Minister's private secretary, and the Cabinet

Secretary should liaise closely to ensure that such news could be rapidly conveyed. This detailed knowledge of government business, accumulated over many decades, has, as we shall see, left the Queen in a position to influence policy, particularly in matters such as the Commonwealth in which she is known to take a special interest.

A FEMINIZED MONARCHY?

In Bagehot's day as in Nairn's, the edifice of royalty was presided over by a woman. Dorothy Thompson's ground-breaking study of Queen Victoria suggests that the fact that she was a woman may have eased Britain's transition to a properly constitutional monarchy. It certainly made it easier for her to be portrayed as in some sense above politics and, as such, the focus of a broader sense of patriotism.[46] Yet Thompson also points to a tension between Victoria's public functions as sovereign and the need to conform to the contemporary notion of 'separate spheres' in which the woman's role was expected to be essentially within the family.[47] At one level, the presence of Victoria's consort Prince Albert made it easier to reconcile those two roles in the public mind. It was possible for the Palace to present Albert as the masculine 'guiding intelligence' behind the Queen's conduct of affairs of state. Conversely, however, satirists were able to portray Victoria as the mere cypher of an interfering husband, nicknaming her 'Queen Albertine'.[48] After Albert's death, critics were even more scathing about men in Victoria's circle who were considered to have an improper degree of influence over her, most notoriously her servants John Brown and Abdul Karim.

During the reign of Elizabeth II, the presence of a woman on the throne has likewise complicated the way in which the monarchy has presented itself. It may, for example, have assisted in reinforcing the notion of a 'welfare monarchy'. In one of the most important interpretive studies of the development of the modern British monarchy, Frank Prochaska has examined how the royal family sought to bolster its legitimacy by associating its members with voluntary service and philanthropy.[49] This strategy also served as an ideological buttress against the challenge from socialism in the twentieth century. Female members of the royal family played an important part in constructing this role. There was a tendency to regard a voluntarist approach to welfare—with its echoes of the nurturing functions of the family—as essentially 'feminine' in contrast to the 'masculine' character of an impersonal welfare state. Prochaska is keen not to push this argument too far, noting that the loss of political power by the monarchy has made the adoption of voluntary causes an attractive rationale for members of the royal family, be they male or female.[50] Yet Elizabeth II's reign has certainly served to reinforce this tendency. At the same time, the Commonwealth has provided a fertile area for voluntary work. Writing in the 1990s, Prochaska estimated that, of the 3,500 organizations to which royal patronage extended, about 500 were foreign or Commonwealth-based.[51]

A common feature of the recollections of those closest to the Queen is the suggestion that her ability to serve as an effective figurehead for the Commonwealth owes something to the fact that she is a woman, and that she is perceived in terms of female archetypes. As Martin Charteris later recalled (perhaps revealing more about the psychology of the Queen's male courtiers than of Commonwealth leaders),

> Singapore [in 1971] was the one Commonwealth Conference that was really sour and bad tempered and that was because she couldn't attend. If she's there, you see, they behave. It's like nanny being there. Or perhaps it's Mummy.[52]

A later private secretary, Sir William Heseltine, reached for similar in describing the Queen's rapport with some of the longer-established Af of the Commonwealth: 'they grew up together and had a relationship v some cases, quite affectionate and certainly respectful. And I think they began to regard her as a mother figure in the Commonwealth.'[53]

As with Victoria, Elizabeth II was to some extent expected to conform to a subordinate role within the ideal family at the heart of the Commonwealth. During the royal visit of 1954 the Australian press were keen to present the Queen and the Duke of Edinburgh as adhering to the stereotypes of husband and wife. Readers of the *Australian Women's Weekly* were assured that 'the Duke has lost none of his masculine dignity for walking two paces behind and beside her. She sees to that.' The magazine speculated that

> [i]t must be a great relief for Her Majesty, who of necessity, often finds herself in factories and establishments, the mechanics of which hold little of feminine interest, to know that the sharp, masculine mind of the Duke will soon be involved to the enormous delight of the person showing them through, in the examination of some complicated process.[54]

More significantly, gender stereotypes arguably served to increase the fragility of the Queen's role as the embodiment of national dignity. She was constructed in British official discourse as being almost infinitely susceptible to 'embarrassment'; and 'embarrassment' carried with it the threat that British prestige might be undermined. While similar concerns would certainly have surrounded a male head of state, the examination below of the deployment of members of the House of Windsor to represent the Queen at independence ceremonies suggests that such concerns were heightened when female members of the royal family were involved.

MONARCHY AND THE POLITICS OF DECOLONIZATION

The genesis of this book lay in a puzzle which emerged while the author was editing the Central Africa volume of the *British Documents on the End of Empire* project (BDEEP). It became clear that from around 1962, instead of encouraging its soon-to-be former colonies in Africa to retain the Queen as Head of State as a means of cementing relations with the UK, the British government was actively encouraging them to become republics at independence. Looking through the existing secondary works there were only scattered clues as to why that should have been the case. The general approach of much of the literature on the Crown and the Commonwealth has been to stress the positive aspects of the relationship, in particular the success with which the institution of the monarchy adapted to Britain's changing international role, and the personal devotion of the current Queen to the Commonwealth.[55] Yet none of this adequately explains why British officials and ministers in the early 1960s were not only reconciled to the spread of republicanism in Anglophone Africa, but positively encouraged it.

The position of the monarchy relates to the broader issue of the UK's relations with its former colonies. It is difficult to escape the impression that the process of British withdrawal from empire was geared more towards minimizing short-term risks than maximizing long-term influence. This impression becomes more pronounced when one compares Britain's relations with tropical Africa over the previous fifty years with the far closer ones enjoyed by France. As David Fieldhouse notes, the French embraced the task of associating their former African colonies with France and the European Economic Community 'without embarrassment' and with remarkable success.[56] The greater concentration by the French on their relations with Africa clearly owes much to the very different means by which Britain and France adjusted to the loss of great-power status after 1945. The British saw their relationship with the United States as the key to their continued influence in the post-war world, and were prepared to accept the loss of empire as, to some extent, a price worth paying for continued American cooperation.[57] By contrast, France's more distant relations with the Americans lent greater weight to imperial and post-imperial bonds.

Yet beside these diplomatic considerations, there was surely also, as Tony Chafer has argued, a cultural dimension.[58] The inheritance of the French Revolution was an ideology of liberty, equality, and fraternity which could claim to be universal in its application. It lent an element of 'messianism' to French imperialism, and enabled post-war French leaders to place an emancipatory gloss on the imperial connection. By contrast, except in areas of significant white settlement, the British were cautious about the feasibility or indeed the desirability of exporting their culture, or their political institutions. At the heart of 'indirect rule' was the assumption that, even under the colonial state, the moral and political framework of most people would continue to be based almost entirely on 'traditional' indigenous structures. An important element of the public defence of late colonial rule was, of course, that it was geared to preparing colonial peoples for self-government through the development of representative institutions. Yet, in private, British officials were far from convinced that their own institutions would provide suitable models. In so far as they eventually found themselves exporting the trappings of their parliamentary system to Africa and other parts of the world, this was due largely to local demand. In March 1960 a civil servant at the CRO complained that attempts to devise political systems better suited for 'these backward and immature territories' had been frustrated by the fact that 'Africans like the "made in England" mark on their constitutions'.[59]

Against this background, it was possible to see British policy towards the Crown during the decolonization of Africa in terms of an interplay of some of the elements described earlier. For all the attempts in official rhetoric to construct the royal family as the object of veneration of peoples across the Commonwealth, there was a widespread assumption among British policy-makers after 1945 that loyalty to the Crown was strongest amongst those of 'British stock'; and that this emerged not so much from an abstract identification with British values, as from a more concrete sense of racial-national identity.[60] Officials and ministers feared that, in involving the Crown in the politics of post-colonial Africa, they might be exposing the Queen to potential 'embarrassment' in a way that would damage national prestige and undermine her capacity to serve as the focus of a specifically *British* national identity. This threat of 'embarrassment' was enhanced both by the gender politics surrounding the Queen and by quasi-religious status the royal family had acquired in British national life.

It was from this basic insight that the present book gradually emerged. The broader relationship of the monarchy to the post-war Commonwealth and deco-lonization is potentially such a vast and multifaceted subject that no single work can hope to do it justice. The current study uses as its focus the attitude of the British government to this relationship, and is based primarily on British official sources. While this inevitably excludes important aspects of the subject in favour of a single perspective, it does allow a fairly coherent picture to emerge. Essentially, the British government recognized that the monarchy could provide a valuable tool in forging Imperial unity and subsequently in easing the transition from Empire to Common-wealth. Yet that latter process created a series of bewilderingly complex constitu-tional arrangements which sometimes appeared to Whitehall to be impediments to the pursuit of UK national interests. Disillusionment with the Commonwealth at an official and ministerial level led to tensions with the Palace, which had embraced the institution with enthusiasm. Furthermore, a belief in Whitehall that loyalty to the Crown in the Commonwealth realms was likely to diminish over time led to fears that the process of transition to republican status might be accompanied by campaigns of a distinctly anti-British character. How Whitehall and the Palace negotiated these challenges is the essential subject of what follows.

2

'The Pivot of Empire': Monarchy and the Commonwealth, 1918–1945

On 23 November 1918 King George V, accompanied by other members of the royal family, rode to Hyde Park to review 35,000 ex-servicemen.[1] Although it initially gave a warm welcome to the royal party, the crowd took the opportunity to express its grievances about a variety of issues, including housing, unemployment, and pensions. The mood of the gathering became increasingly hostile and the police eventually had to intervene. On his return to Buckingham Palace, the King commented that the ex-servicemen had been 'in a funny temper'. It was by no means unimaginable at the end of 1918 that this mood of discontent might deepen and spread to the extent that it could threaten the very survival of the House of Windsor. In continental Europe the war and its immediate aftermath drove from their thrones the Habsburg, Hohenzollern, and Romanov dynasties and caused massive social and economic dislocation, creating fertile ground for revolutionary politics. Many within British ruling circles feared that the Bolshevik seizure of power in Russia might be the prelude to an insurrectionary movement that would eventually undermine the established order at home. The Representation of the People Act of February 1918, which conceded universal manhood suffrage, heightened this sense of insecurity. The war had also placed strains on the fragile mechanisms that enabled Whitehall to govern not only the colonial Empire but the British Isles themselves. Indeed, a dangerous sign of what was to come occurred perilously close to home when in 1916 the British faced a revolt in the streets of Dublin. In the elections that followed the war the republicans of Sinn Fein won 73 seats. They refused to take up their places in Westminster, establishing an assembly of their own, which was not recognized by the British government. In 1920 Ireland was effectively partitioned by the Government of Ireland Act. In the South attempts at repression ultimately failed, and in 1921 London granted Southern Ireland a form of Dominion status. The British government now had on its doorstep, in the form of the Irish Free State, a nation forged in rebellion and prepared to stretch the definitions of Dominion status to breaking point.

In this uncertain political climate, an enhanced emphasis on the Imperial role of the Crown appeared to many to be a vital means of both enhancing the prestige of the monarchy at home and maintaining British power overseas. Just days before the First World War ended the leading courtier and Liberal politician Lord Esher warned the King's private secretary that the 'Monarchy and its cost will have to be justified in the future in the eyes of a war-worn and hungry proletariat, endowed with a huge preponderance of voting power. I see a great future for the King in connection with the consolidation of "Imperial" control of our public affairs; but imagination and boldness will be required, necessitating the abandonment of many old theories of Constitutional Kingship.'[2] Both the Palace and the British government proved responsive to this line of argument, enhancing the role of the Crown in Imperial affairs while making it more protean. Yet the interwar period also demonstrated that if the Empire could be a means of strengthening and legitimizing the monarchy, it could also be invoked as a pretext to unseat kings.

THE RULES OF THE GAME: THE 1926 BALFOUR REPORT

The constitutional framework within which the Crown operated in a Commonwealth sense for the rest of the century was, to a very significant extent, defined at the Imperial Conference that took place in London in October and November 1926. The broader background of the conference was the need to arrive at a definition of the constitutional status of the Dominions in relation to the UK which would be acceptable to a group of governments with very different notions of what that status should be. Two specific factors lent urgency to the process. The first was the demand by General Hertzog, who had become prime minister of South Africa in 1924, for formal recognition of his country's independence.[3] The second was the constitutional crisis that had been sparked earlier in the year when the Governor General of Canada, Lord Byng, refused a request by his prime minister, Mackenzie King, for a dissolution of parliament. Mackenzie King arrived at the 1926 conference determined that the Governor General should cease to be the representative of the UK government.[4]

In the course of the 1926 Conference the central constitutional issues were dealt with by a special 'Inter-Imperial Relations Committee' made up of prime ministers and heads of delegation and chaired by the former British prime minister Arthur Balfour. The report of this committee provided the basis for the Statute of Westminster of 1931, which sought to lend legal status to the decisions of the 1926 Imperial Conference.

The Balfour Report of 1926 strenuously avoided the term 'independence', which would have struck at the roots of the notion of Imperial unity. Instead, it spoke of the Dominions as

> autonomous Communities within the British Empire, equal in status, in no way subordinate one to another in any aspect of their domestic or external affairs, though united by a common allegiance to the Crown, and freely associated as members of the British Commonwealth of Nations.[5]

The notions of autonomy and equality had an important corollary in terms of the right of the British government to advise the Crown on matters relating to the Dominions. The Balfour Report stated that apart from provisions embodied in constitutions or in specific statutes expressly providing for reservation, it is recognised that it is the right of the Government of each Dominion to advise the Crown in all matters relating to its own affairs. Consequently, it would not be in accordance with constitutional practice for advice to be tendered to His Majesty by His Majesty's Government in Great Britain in any matter appertaining to the affairs of a Dominion against the views of the Government of that Dominion.[6]

In Australia this created an anomaly. To allow either Commonwealth or state ministers to advise the Crown on matters of reservation, disallowance, or the appointment of governors in relation to the Australian states would have disrupted the fine balance of powers within the federal system. As a consequence, the Crown continued to act in these matters on the advice of British ministers. In effect, as Anne Twomey notes, the Australian states 'remained colonial dependencies of the British Crown, even though they were constituent parts of an independent sovereign nation'.[7]

The doctrine of the equality of members of the Commonwealth also had repercussions for the position of Governors General. The Balfour Report asserted that the Governor General of a Dominion was 'the representative of the Crown holding in all essential respects the same position in relation to the administration of public affairs in the Dominion as is held by His Majesty the King in Great Britain', and that he was *not* 'the representative or agent of His Majesty's Government in Great Britain or of any Department of that Government'.[8]

This doctrine had implications for the system of Commonwealth high commissions, which had been developing since 1880 when Canada had appointed its first high commissioner to London to promote its interests in the UK. New Zealand had followed in 1905, with the Commonwealth of Australia doing so in 1910, the Union of South Africa in 1911, Newfoundland in 1918, and the Irish Free State in 1922.[9] So long as Governors General were effectively agents of the British government the UK felt no need to reciprocate. With the new doctrine set out in the Balfour Report, however, this changed. In 1928 Britain duly appointed its first high commissioner to Canada. It was not until 1935, however, that a British high commissioner was appointed to Australia. The New Zealand government, which was concerned that the constitutional innovations that had followed the Balfour Report would undermine Imperial unity, only agreed to the appointment of a British high commissioner in 1939 (and it was two years later before one was actually in place).[10] In the case of the Irish Free State its high commissioner in London, John Dulanty, discouraged the British from making a reciprocal appointment in Dublin, fearing that it would undermine his own role as intermediary between the two governments. This restricted Britain's ability to gather political information on the Free State. In line with Eamon de Valera's efforts to sever the remaining constitutional ties with the UK, when a British counterpart to Dulanty was finally appointed to Dublin in 1939 he was recognized by the Free State government merely as a 'representative' rather than high commissioner.

British ministers had effectively surrendered the right to advise the Crown on most matters relating to the domestic affairs of a Dominion. Yet if the Crown was expected to act in these matters on the advice of the ministers of the Dominion concerned, should it also do so over the appointment of the Dominion's Governor General? Both the Australian and South African governments maintained that it should. Matters came to a head in 1930 when the Australian Labor government of J. H. Scullin informed London that it intended to advise George V that the Australian-born Sir Isaac Isaacs should be appointed as Australian Governor General. The King told Lord Passfield, the Secretary of State for the Dominions and Colonies, that he did not accept the Australian government's right to advise him on this issue. He maintained that the terms of the Balfour Report left him free to act on his own initiative in the appointment of Governors General.[11] Passfield, understandably, regarded this as a dangerous doctrine that might draw the Crown into political controversy. The King's private secretary, Lord Stamfordham, shared Passfield's concern that the King would potentially be exposed to criticism if he did not have the protection of constitutional advice when appointing Governors General.[12]

The matter was discussed at the Imperial Conference in early November and a compromise was reached: a Governor General should be appointed on the advice of the Dominion government concerned and the British government should have no say in the matter. The Dominion government should, however, informally consult with the King before any advice was tendered to enable him to express his own views. In the light of this decision, and fearful of inflaming opinion in Australia, the King felt obliged to accept Scullin's advice, despite not having been consulted in advance. In audience with the Australian prime minister, however, he made clear that he did so with great reluctance and he continued to press his objections to Isaacs, not least because he believed that his representative in a Dominion should be personally known to him. He also felt that Isaacs was too old and that as an Australian he would not have the necessary degree of detachment from local politics. When Scullin somewhat unwisely raised the precedent of the Irish Free State, which in 1922 had insisted on the appointment as Governor General of Tim Healy, a veteran Irish nationalist (although an anti-republican), the King was not impressed. According to the record of the audience made by Stamfordham,

the King in effect said that Ireland was a spoilt child and, after making a Treaty with the Free State, she had to be humoured. But does Australia, with her traditional loyalty to the Throne, wish to be compared with Ireland, where, alas! a considerable element of disloyalty exists?[13]

On this occasion, the King had backed down rather than risk becoming the target of criticism from, as Stamfordham put it, 'an ill-disposed minority' in Australia consisting of 'Trades Unions, Communists and Irish, not of the highest class'. Yet the King continued to maintain that he would have been 'well within his right' to reject Scullin's advice.[14]

The compromise reached in 1930 did not mean that the British government completely withdrew from any involvement in the appointment of Governors General. Shortly after the 1930 Imperial Conference, when consultations took place about the appointment of a new Canadian Governor General the Secretary of State for the Dominions in Britain's Labour government, J. H. Thomas, felt entitled to raise objections to one of the names suggested by the Canadian government: ironically, that of the Duke of York, the future King George VI. Clive Wigram, George V's assistant private secretary, told Stamfordham that Thomas 'was not very keen about the Duke of York and I asked him for the reason; he said that they did not want royalty in Canada as it was too close to the USA and the Canadians pride themselves on being as democratic as the Americans. I cannot believe that is true—however there it is!'[15] This intervention from a British minister points to two elements which will recur at fairly regular intervals over the course of this book: the way in which the particularly close relationship between the Palace and the British government has tended to undercut the modern notion of the divisibility of the Crown; and the fact that private scepticism within the British government about the attachment of the Dominions to the Crown was sometimes at odds with public pronouncements on the subject.

From the point of view of the British government, the 1930 compromise largely removed the danger that the monarch might be exposed to political controversy by acting unilaterally over the appointment or dismissal of Governors General. Yet many questions remained, including whether the King was bound to accept the advice of Dominions prime ministers in those circumstances. As the King himself had suggested to Scullin, the notion that monarchs should simply follow such advice in all circumstances raised the possibility that they would be obliged to accede to partisan demands for a new Governor General following a change in government. It had the additional consequence that Governors General could well feel constrained in the exercise of their reserve powers by the fear that the prime minister would simply request their dismissal if they refused to accept ministerial advice.[16]

Characteristically, it was the Irish Free State which first presented the Palace with a concrete example of this dilemma. In 1932, only months after assuming office, the Irish prime minister Eamon de Valera advised George V to dismiss the Governor General, James McNeill, and replace him with a Fianna Fáil party loyalist, Donal Buckley.[17] A potentially more serious constitutional crisis arose in the winter of 1934–5, when the leader of the Canadian Opposition, William Mackenzie King, indicated that he would not accept any Governor General put in place on the recommendation of the prime minister, R. B. Bennett, ahead of an impending general election; and that were he returned to power he would reopen the issue. The Palace let it be known that if Mackenzie King sought to dismiss the new Governor General following an election the King could ignore his advice.[18] There was therefore huge relief at the Palace when it emerged that Mackenzie King and Bennett were both enthusiastic about the prospect of John Buchan becoming Governor General. Their only reservation was that Buchan was a commoner. Again, this drew in the British government. After an approach from the Palace, the British prime minister Ramsay MacDonald readily agreed to recommend Buchan for a peerage.

Despite these early complications, over subsequent decades monarchs have not been inclined to reject the advice of Commonwealth prime ministers over the appointment of Governors General. As we shall see, however, there have been some occasions when that advice has generated resentment in the Palace. That outright clashes have proved so rare has partly been owing to the deference of most Commonwealth premiers towards the monarch. Certainly in the case of Australia, the principles outlined at the 1930 Imperial Conference for the appointment of Governors General were honoured well into the post-war decades. Sir William Heseltine, who served from 1955 to 1959 as private secretary to Australia's longest serving prime minister, Sir Robert Menzies, later claimed that there was 'no question of confronting the Sovereign with formal constitutional advice with a capital "A". There was a genuine exchange of views and agreement between the two before the formal processes were put in train.'[19]

The situation also seems to have been eased by the fact that, well into the middle of the twentieth century, Commonwealth prime ministers often preferred prominent figures from the UK to their own compatriots in the post of Governor General. It was only in 1967 that the first New Zealand-born Governor General took up his commission in Wellington.[20] As well as stressing the link with the 'mother country', Governors General from Britain were regarded as having the advantage of lacking direct links with local political parties, enabling them to play their non-partisan role with greater credibility.

Constitutional innovations of the interwar period brought a subtle change in the relationship between the monarch and Commonwealth prime ministers. In the process of shuffling off Imperial control, statesmen like Mackenzie King effectively ensured that the Governor General would, in the future, be little more than a rubber stamp. In that respect, although the Governors General were the monarch's representative, exercising prerogative powers on his or her behalf at key moments in the political cycle, there was little sense that they were active participants in daily political life. This was also the case in New Zealand, where in 1949 the incoming prime minister was told that the Governor General was 'not informed of Cabinet proceedings'.[21] In marked contrast to the three rights which in the 1860s Walter Bagehot believed that a constitutional monarch could claim in relation to the British government—to be consulted, to encourage, and to warn—Governors General could often expect to exert no comparable personal influence over their prime ministers. George V, however, had insisted on those three rights in relation to the appointment of Governors General, in effect assuming in his Commonwealth realms something of the personal role he already played in the UK. As Mallory says of the interwar Dominions prime ministers, 'Rid of the Governor General, they did not bargain for the acquisition of a king'.[22] This raised important questions about the role of both the monarch and the Governors General which would remain resonant in the reign of Elizabeth II.

An issue that might have appeared of little relevance to policy-makers in the early 1930s, but that would actually confront them within a generation, was whether the potentially unlimited powers that were available to the executive via the prerogative powers of the Crown would create problems in the case of newly independent regimes unused to operating the Westminster system. It belatedly occurred to British policy-makers as India and Pakistan approached independence in 1947 that the monarchical system offered the potential for 'a regime of autocratic rule by the Governor-General dissimilar to that in other parts of the British Commonwealth'.[23] Such fears would not be realized in the case of India, where in its brief period of a monarchy from 1947 to 1950, the leader of the ruling Indian National Congress,

Jawaharlal Nehru, was happy to occupy the office of prime minister and confine the Governor General to the role of (an admittedly highly influential) figurehead. A more troubling precedent was set in Pakistan, where the leader of the ruling Muslim League, Muhammad Ali Jinnah, assumed the post of Governor General, and clearly expected his prime minister to play a subordinate role.

With the dissolution of formal controls over the Dominions, the role of the Crown as a unifying force certainly gave the monarchy—and more specifically what R. F. Holland calls 'the critical idea of the single Kingship'—a renewed significance.[24] Yet the very notion of a 'single Kingship' embracing the whole Empire was already contentious and became increasingly difficult to defend. Given that the Dominions had been recognized as fully sovereign states in all practical respects, should they, then, have the right to conduct their relations with *their* monarch without reference to any other members of the Commonwealth? This was the argument of an article by the constitutional expert and author of *The Governance of England*, Sir Sidney Low, published in the *Sunday Times* in November 1926 in the wake of the Balfour Report. It suggested that the notion of the equality of the UK and the Dominions precluded the British Cabinet from being the conduit of advice from Dominion governments to the King. The direct transmission of that advice, however, implied the existence of separate 'Kingdoms'.[25] The Dominions Secretary, Leo Amery, denounced this as a 'fatal heresy'.[26] He argued that the Empire consisted of a series of local jurisdictions within a single indivisible kingdom, with each parliament owing a common allegiance to the throne.[27] Defending his position in private correspondence with Amery, however, Low noted that he had simply repeated what was a widespread interpretation of the implications of the Balfour Report shared, among others, by General Hertzog of South Africa, who had spoken of a 'free alliance of England and the six Dominions'.[28] Indeed, South Africa under Hertzog maintained the position that the Commonwealth consisted of a series of quite distinct kingships vested in the same individual, just as, in the eighteenth century, Britain and Hanover, although having the same person as their king, were entirely separate entities, with different laws and rules of succession.[29] While the British continued to insist upon the indivisibility of the Crown until well into the post-war era, one constitutional expert noted in 1953 that this doctrine had proved 'the chief victim of the reluctance of political facts to conform to the requirements of the legal purist'.[30] Indeed, as we shall see, by the end of the 1930s political developments had powerfully undermined the notion of a single kingship.

PROJECTING AN IMPERIAL MONARCHY

It is something of a commonplace to suggest that an effort was made between the wars to combat these centrifugal tendencies by promoting the King as the 'father' of a global Imperial family, making particular use of new forms of technology to accomplish the task. Yet then, as subsequently, this project was impeded by the extreme conservatism of the Palace and by the characters of Britain's interwar monarchs. Perhaps the most significant innovation in this period which linked the King to his subjects around the globe was his Christmas Day message. This was inaugurated in 1932 by George V, broadcasting from Sandringham.[31] The metaphor of the Imperial family played a prominent part in these messages. In 1933, the King began by expressing his 'pleasure and privilege to speak directly to all the members of our world-wide family'.[32] The following year he told listeners:

> This day with its hallowed memories is the Festival of the Family. I would like to think that you who are listening to me now in whatever part of the world you may be, and all the Peoples of the Realm and Empire, are bound to me and to one another by the Spirit of one great Family.[33]

Indeed, his message was preceded by a programme called *The Great Family*, which the BBC had devised in conjunction with the broadcasting authorities in Australia, New Zealand, Africa, Canada, India, and Palestine.[34]

The initiative for the Christmas messages had come from John Reith, who had been appointed general manager of the newly created British Broadcasting Company in 1922. He clearly saw a royal broadcast as a means of enhancing the profile and prestige of the new medium, and first suggested the idea of a Christmas Day message to the Palace in October 1923. His approach was rebuffed, although he was able to gain permission to broadcast the speeches of the King and the Prince of Wales at the Wembley Empire Exhibition the following year.[35] Further attempts to persuade the Palace to agree to a Christmas Broadcast in 1927 or a royal broadcast on Armistice Day 1928 also failed, leading Reith to complain in his diary 'it is extraordinary how conservative they are'.[36]

Having finally been persuaded to make the 1932 broadcast, the King was impressed by its impact and established it as a 'tradition' over the remaining Christmases of his reign. Yet George VI, who notoriously struggled with a serious stammer and lacked his father's natural facility in front of a microphone, found such broadcasts a trial. He failed to make a broadcast in either 1936 or 1938. He began his brief Christmas Day message in 1937, the year of his coronation, in a strikingly sombre and self-deprecating manner, telling his listeners:

> Many of you will remember the Christmas broadcasts of former years, when my father spoke to his peoples at home and overseas as the revered head of a great family . . . I cannot aspire to take his place—nor do I think you would wish me to carry on, unvaried, a tradition so personal to him.[37]

It was only the outbreak of the Second World War in 1939 that convinced George VI of the need to revive the tradition.

George's older brother, who reigned for a matter of months in 1936 and whose abdication brought George to the throne, was an experienced and fluent broadcaster who would have adapted easily to this new aspect of the monarch's duties. In most other respects, however, Edward VIII was an unlikely and uncomfortable Imperial figurehead. His abdication represented the greatest threat to the British monarchy in the twentieth century, and it was also a crisis for the Imperial Crown. As Prince of Wales he had played a significant role within the Empire, one that had been fashioned for him by Prime Minister David Lloyd George. With the conclusion of the First World War, in which Edward had served as an army officer, there was the problem of reintegrating the young heir to the throne into royal duties at home. This was made all the more difficult by his lack of patience with the stuffy protocols of the court and his potentially scandalous infatuation with a married woman, Freda Dudley Ward. Meanwhile the war itself had placed enormous strains on the rickety structures that bound the Empire together. Dispatching Edward on a series of tours across the Empire seemed to address both sets of problems. In terms of shoring up British rule and Imperial unity, Lloyd George expressed the hope that '[t]he appearance of the popular Prince of Wales might do more to calm the discord than half a dozen solemn Imperial Conferences'.[38] Meanwhile, putting him on display in the Dominions would separate him from his mistress and, it was hoped, oblige him to conform to an exacting set of moral standards. George V's private secretary, Lord Stamfordham, warned Edward, 'Your visit to the Dominions will be made or marred according as you do and *say* the right thing [*sic*]'. He impressed on Edward that the Prince's behaviour had profound implications for the fate of the Empire as a whole, telling him '[t]he Throne is the pivot upon which the Empire will more than ever hinge. Its strength and stability will depend entirely on its occupant.'[39]

Edward's highly successful tour of Canada in 1919, the first of a series of such engagements, seemed to suggest that the twin pursuits of promoting Imperial unity and keeping the heir to the throne on a tight rein could be successfully combined. Yet the impression was not to last. During a visit to Canada in 1927 in the company of British prime minister Stanley Baldwin, Edward's erratic behaviour shocked his own assistant private secretary, Alan Lascelles. Lascelles confided in Baldwin that 'the Heir Apparent, in his unbridled pursuit of wine and women, and whatever selfish whim occupied him at the moment, was rapidly going to the devil, and unless he mended his ways, would soon become no fit wearer of the British Crown'. When Lascelles confessed that he sometimes thought the best thing would be for Edward to break his neck in a point-to-point race, Baldwin apparently replied, 'God forgive me, I have often thought the same'.[40] If the Canadian visit proved a strain to Lascelles, Edward's trip to East Africa in 1928 finally prompted his resignation. The notoriously louche company of Kenya's 'Happy Valley' settler community inevitably brought out the worst in the Prince of Wales, providing ample opportunities for the pursuit of 'wine and women'. It was, however, Edward's dismissive response to the news that reached him in Dodoma in Tanganyika that his father was dangerously ill that finally exhausted Lascelles' patience. In a rare outburst, Lascelles told Edward, 'the King of England is dying; if that means nothing to you, it means a great deal to me'. At this, Lascelles later recorded, Edward 'looked at me, went out without a word, and spent the remainder of the evening in the successful seduction of a Mrs Barnes, wife of the local commissioner. He told me so himself, next morning.'[41] Following their return to England, Lascelles resigned. At around the same time, Edward's private secretary, Godfrey Thomas, recorded his concerns about the impact the Prince of Wales's behaviour might have on Imperial relations:

> Overseas there is a deplorable decline in HRH's stock. One of the most serious aspects of the whole affair is the accepted fact that the Dominions are all held together by their

common loyalty to the Crown. What will happen if they find their sole link is in the person of a sovereign for whom they have little respect?[42]

THE ABDICATION CRISIS

Concerns over the reactions of the Dominions were to play an important role in the extraordinary drama that unfolded following the death of George V. In 1934 Wallis Simpson became the latest married woman to attract the attentions of the Prince of Wales. Having already been divorced once, the American-born Mrs Simpson shared with Edward a love of fashion and contempt for the manners and morality of George V's court. That the heir to the throne should have a mistress was hardly a novelty. What made this liaison particularly dangerous, however, was that Edward was increasingly indiscreet and that, from a relatively early stage, he appears to have been determined to marry Mrs Simpson.

For British policy-makers the manner in which the Crown had been configured, as the linchpin of the Imperial settlement formalized in the Statute of Westminster, invested this private affair with potentially disastrous implications. Speaking during the celebrations of George V's Jubilee in 1935, Prime Minister Stanley Baldwin claimed, 'If in any cataclysm the Crown vanished, the Empire would vanish with it'.[43] With the death of George V in January 1936, the potential scandal surrounding Edward's private life took on a new significance. Even before Edward's relationship with Mrs Simpson had become an international political issue, the manner of his accession had signalled the fragility of the ties that bound the Commonwealth together. In 1928, as part of a general review of measures to give effect to the definition of Dominion status agreed at the 1926 Imperial Conference, the Dominions Office had decided that on the King's death Commonwealth high commissioners in London should attend the Council held to proclaim the accession of the new monarch.[44] Yet, in the event, this gesture, which was intended to demonstrate Imperial unity, merely highlighted the extent to which the relationship with the Crown was a matter of contention.

The government of the Irish Free State took the opportunity to keep its representative away from the ceremony in January 1936. At one level, this could simply be seen as a further assertion of the divisibility of the Crown, and it was a stand with which the South African government also clearly had some sympathy. Yet it was also indicative of a more profound change that had been going on since de Valera's government had taken power under which a conscious effort had been made to construct a political culture that had no place for a British monarch. Even the major religious gathering in the Free State during that period, the 1932 Eucharistic Congress, suggested an attempt to replace royal ceremony with that of the Roman Catholic Church. Banners proclaimed 'God Bless Christ the King', and the reception of the Papal Legate at Dún Laoghaire was reminiscent of a royal visit.[45] It was a sign of a society which, as de Valera would later explain to a British official, was determined to draw its legitimacy from the Holy Trinity and the people rather than from the Crown. Three years later de Valera pointedly refused to allow representatives of the Free State to be associated with the celebrations of George V's jubilee in London, explaining to the Dominions Secretary that Ireland had been 'incorporated in the Commonwealth by force'.[46]

Dublin's refusal to allow its high commissioner, John Dulanty, to participate in the Accession Council in 1936 was just a further stage in that process. Dulanty gave every indication of being highly embarrassed by the role assigned to him by his government. He was adamant, however, that instructions from Dublin expressly prevented him from either attending the Council or signing the Accession Proclamation. He was warned by the British that if he were not present when the new King greeted the other high commissioners 'this might well be considered as something very near to rudeness'.[47] Dulanty undertook to ask his political masters at least to allow him to attend the Council. Yet Dublin did not relent. Indeed, in its subsequent account of the affair, the Dominions Office could not resist adding for the sake of 'completeness' that 'Mr Dulanty was not allowed by the Irish Free State Government to *watch* the Proclamation of the King from the roof of St. James's Palace on 22nd January'.

The South African high commissioner, Charles te Water, also raised difficulties. He was prepared to attend the Accession Council but was unsure as to whether his government would agree to him signing the Proclamation. There was even some discussion among British civil servants as to whether, if both Dulanty and te Water refused to sign, it would be better for none of the high commissioners to do so. In the event, te Water was invited to sign, and again expressed some qualms about this. He eventually did so, although 'with all due reserve', explaining that 'it must be understood that it would be open to himself or to the Union Government' to question this procedure in the future.

Turning to the abdication crisis itself, the attitude of Dominion premiers may merely have provided British prime minister Stanley Baldwin with a pretext to remove a monarch whom he regarded as dangerously erratic and untrustworthy.[48] As we shall see, Baldwin was in fact less than candid with Edward in the way in which he presented the King with the reactions of his fellow prime ministers. Nevertheless, however much he might have manipulated this evidence to support a course on which he was already determined, he had good reason to worry about what the crisis might do to Britain's already fragile Commonwealth relationships. His concerns had been strengthened by a conversation in the middle of November with Stanley Bruce, the Australian high commissioner. Bruce, who had already spoken to the King's private secretary, Sir Alexander Hardinge, expressed his grave concerns about the affair. In notes he made for Baldwin to be used in his conversations with the King, Bruce warned that, if Edward married Mrs Simpson, '[t]he people of this country and the Dominions would never accept her as Queen, quite possibly the House of Commons would cancel the Civil List, the throne would be imperilled, the Empire would be endangered'.[49]

In an attempt to find some way out of this dangerous confrontation, Esmond Harmsworth, the chairman of the Newspaper Proprietors Association, suggested to Mrs Simpson that the King might make a morganatic marriage with her, under which she would remain a private citizen. She would therefore not become Queen and any children they might have would not be in line to the throne. This formed the basis of a proposal which Edward put to Baldwin on 25 November. Baldwin expressed the private opinion that Parliament would never pass a bill to allow a morganatic marriage, but that if the King wanted a formal response it would be necessary to consult the prime ministers of the Dominions. This was in line with the preamble to the Statute of Westminster. Edward agreed, but almost immediately realized that 'with that simple request I had gone a long way towards sealing my own fate'.[50]

The constitutional propriety of Baldwin's actions in 'collecting' Commonwealth opinions was subsequently questioned. Strictly speaking, Commonwealth countries had the right of direct access to the King and the King himself should have been allowed to consult directly with his Commonwealth prime ministers. The practical justification for Baldwin's actions was that the King might have been placed in an invidious position had he been faced with conflicting advice. Intergovernmental consultations were therefore desirable in order to ensure that the King was presented with unanimous advice.[51] Nevertheless, the King had provided Baldwin with a powerful bargaining tool, not only in being able to offer collective advice on the matter on behalf of Britain and the Dominions, but also of being able to shape the terms of the question in order to arrive at the required answer.

On 28 November Baldwin sent telegrams to the prime ministers of Australia, New Zealand, Canada, and South Africa. It was decided that the acting permanent undersecretary at the Dominions Office, Sir Henry Batterbee, would personally hand a message to de Valera. The premiers were informed that three options were under discussion: a marriage under which Mrs Simpson would become Queen; a morganatic marriage; and abdication. They were asked in strict secrecy to give their personal opinions. Baldwin offered an unmistakable 'steer' to the Dominion premiers by suggesting that the British parliament and the majority of the public would not be prepared to accept a marriage, whether or not it was morganatic. When on 2 December Baldwin reported back on their reactions he claimed that, although the process of consultation had not been completed, it suggested that there was no support for a morganatic marriage. As Susan Williams has demonstrated, this was a serious misrepresentation of the responses Baldwin had received. Although the Australian, South African, and Canadian prime ministers certainly took this line (albeit with the Canadian premier, MacKenzie King, insisting that abdication should be voluntary and not forced on the King), the prime minister of New Zealand, M. J. Savage, while acknowledging that there might be insuperable obstacles attached to a morganatic marriage, suggested that 'if some solution along these lines were found to be practicable it would no doubt be acceptable to the majority of the people of New Zealand'.[52] Furthermore, perhaps already relishing the opportunity to fish in troubled waters, de Valera told Batterbee that his personal inclination would be to favour a morganatic marriage. Although Catholic countries (like his own) did not recognize divorce—and hence the right of divorcees to remarry—Edward was head of a Protestant country and many young people might, de Valera suggested, 'be attracted by the idea of a young King ready to give up all for love'.[53] Only after Batterbee had, by his own account, provided de Valera with 'some information as to Mrs Simpson's antecedents and the divorce proceedings' and warned him that British public opinion 'would not tolerate the King marrying a woman of the nature of Mrs Simpson' did de Valera concede that abdication might be the only option.[54] Batterbee also tried to appeal to de Valera's broader political sympathies by arguing that, whatever Ireland's attitude to the Crown, 'there could be no doubt that in the present dangerous and crumbling international situation the British monarchy was a pillar of stability against the forces of Bolshevism, and that, from this point of view, it was important to avoid anything which would impair its integrity'.

Batterbee's discussions with de Valera provided an early indication that the Statute of Westminster of 1931 would not provide a neat mechanism for ensuring Commonwealth unity over this issue. The preamble to the Statute had asserted that

> it would be in accord with the established constitutional position of all the members of the Commonwealth in relation to one another that any alteration in the law touching the Succession to the Throne or the Royal Style and Titles shall hereafter require the assent as well of the Parliaments of all the Dominions as of the Parliament of the United Kingdom.

From the British government's perspective, the preferred means of granting that 'assent' was signalled in Article 4 of the Statute, which stated that no act of the UK Parliament would extend to a Dominion 'unless it is expressly declared in that Act that that Dominion has requested, and consented to, the enactment thereof'. Batterbee put it to de Valera that Article 4 provided the best way for the Dominions to deal with the situation, and suggested that 'the minimum of discussion and debate was most strongly to be desired in the circumstances'. De Valera responded, however, that he 'could not consent to the UK Parliament legislating "off their own bat" without exposing himself to the charge that he had not preserved for the Irish Free State the position of complete equality in constitutional matters which had been attained under the Statute of Westminster'.

An insight into de Valera's thinking on the matter may be provided by a memorandum on the crisis from the Irish Free State's Department of External Affairs. This suggested:

> Just as the British have used political divisions here for their political advantage we are entitled and are bound to turn their present difficulty to our own account. If the proposed marriage takes place, whether by special legislation or otherwise, it will undoubtedly—(a) weaken the British Monarchy as an institution and (b) weaken the Constitutional position in Great Britain of the British Cabinet. It will strengthen the Constitutional position of those Dominion Cabinets which are slow or reluctant to follow the British Cabinet's lead in the present crisis. For all these reasons we should be slow to impede the proposed marriage, and in my view should give the impression that a morganatic arrangement should suffice to meet the British Cabinet's point of view.[55]

If the Irish government saw strategic advantages in supporting Edward's marriage, Baldwin moved quickly to remove this option. Keen to deter press comment that might strengthen the King's hand, he announced in the Commons on 4 December that the British government would not legislate for a morganatic marriage, and he informed Dominion prime ministers that he had presented Edward with an ultimatum: to choose between giving up Mrs Simpson or abdication. De Valera telegraphed Baldwin warning him that 'legislation in our Parliament would be necessary in order to regularise the situation about public declaration. Such legislation at this moment would cause grave difficulty.'[56] When Baldwin pressed ahead, de Valera himself moved swiftly to take advantage of Britain's 'present difficulty'.

This contributed to a remarkably untidy end to Edward's reign across the Commonwealth. He signed the Instrument of Abdication on 10 December. The following day, the UK parliament passed the Act of Abdication. Following the terms of the Statute of Westminster, the Canadian parliament 'requested and consented to' the UK Act. Furthermore, although neither country had actually ratified the Statute, both the Australian and New Zealand parliaments also assented to the Act. The South Africans, however, keen to give expression to the notion of the divisibility of the Crown, claimed that under Roman-Dutch law, the Instrument of Abdication had effectively produced a 'Demise of the Crown'. According to this interpretation, George VI had automatically become King of South Africa on 10 December, not on the 11th when the UK act was passed with the assent of Canada, Australia, and New Zealand.[57] An even more radical position was taken by the Irish Free State, in the form of two bills introduced by de Valera's government. On 11 December the Dáil passed the Constitutional Amendment Bill, which removed the executive powers of the Crown from the internal affairs of the Irish Free State, making it virtually a *de facto* republic. The Irish government correctly calculated that, with the British political system in turmoil, they could take this momentous step with the minimum of resistance from London. The broader implications of this step will be considered in the next chapter. The following day the Dáil passed the External Relations Act, which recognized that the King retained a role in certain aspects of the international affairs of the Free State, such as diplomatic accreditation. The Act also gave effect to the Abdication, meaning that Edward's reign over the Free State officially ended on 12 December. There were, therefore, three separate dates for the Abdication across the Commonwealth.[58]

As the crisis reached its culmination, the British government took soundings on the impact of the affair on opinion within the Dominions. The British high commission in South Africa relayed to the Dominions Office the reaction of the South African press, which had deployed some of the more sanctimonious themes of British rhetoric about the Crown as a means to berate Edward VIII. The *Volksblad* argued that, as the chief symbolic link of the Empire, the King must be above reproach since any weakening of kingship would weaken the empire.[59] *The Natal Mercury* echoed these sentiments, speaking of the Crown as the only real link holding the Empire together and warning that the issue of the King's marriage might precipitate a grave Imperial crisis.[60] The *Rand Daily Mail* claimed that in recent years the King had come to be regarded not merely as a ruler but as a model of behaviour, with a consequent blurring between the private and the public. It warned that marriage would be unacceptable to the people of South Africa.[61]

Perhaps the most telling post mortem came from the British high commissioner in Canada, F. L. C. Floud, in a despatch to the Secretary of State for the Dominions, Malcolm MacDonald. Floud suggested that—at least in the short term—far from weakening the ties of Empire, the affair had actually strengthened them.[62] Baldwin's insistence that the Dominions had the same right as the UK to arbitrate on the matter had tended to 'flatter the self-conscious Canadian', demonstrating the significance of Dominion status and bolstering pride 'in the stability and prestige of the British race'. Yet Floud also pointed to the possibility of more damaging consequences. He told MacDonald:

> There will, I suggest, be many in Canada to whom the Crown will have been found to have lost much of its sacredness, there may be bitterness and there will be ridicule, or at least a weakened resistance to ridicule deriving from United States sources. And there will be those who suggest that the Crown is no longer a necessary link between the peoples of the Commonwealth, that as it is now primarily a decoration of the United Kingdom it will shortly cease to have any significance outside.

Floud warned that, although the image of the Crown had survived the recent crisis, it was clear 'that for a long time to come it will be impossible without disaster to face another such shock'.

THE COMING OF WAR

Floud had suggested that a royal visit to Canada might serve to repair some of the damage that had been done to the image of the monarchy. When George VI did indeed finally visit the country in 1939 his tour occurred in the shadow of impending war. In the circumstances, the Palace and UK representatives were highly sensitive to any signs that the Canadian government might be using the tour to emphasize the divisibility of the Crown. Recording his impressions of the visit towards the end of June 1939 Floud's successor, Sir Gerald Campbell, noted with satisfaction that there had been an 'apparent absence of any unwarrantable stress during the Royal tour on the concept of His Majesty as King of Canada *per se*'.[63] He had earlier expressed concerns 'that undue encouragement was being given albeit in all innocence, to the development of a theory which tended elsewhere towards disunity rather than the reverse'. An early sign of this had come in March when Canadian prime minister Mackenzie King had insisted that the British Commander-in-Chief of the American and West Indian Station should not be present in his flagship on the arrival of the royal party in Quebec. He was keen that the Royal Canadian Navy should have the honour of accompanying the King up the St Lawrence to Quebec and claimed that 'it would only emphasise its smallness if the Royal Navy were to send ships which would dwarf it'.[64] In more general terms, Mackenzie King had insisted to Campbell on 'the desirability, nay necessity, for the visit to be Canadian in every possible way without anything "Imperial" mixed up with it'. The Palace itself appears to have had little sympathy for this approach, the King's private secretary, Sir Alexander Hardinge, describing it to the Dominions Office as 'very petty'.[65]

Yet the very process by which war on Germany was declared in September 1939 undermined the notion of a unified Crown. Of the Dominions, only the Australian prime minister, Robert Menzies, adopted the view that George VI's declaration of war on 3 September committed all his Imperial subjects to the conflict.[66] The Governor General of New Zealand declared war only a few hours later, but not before the country's prime minister, M. J. Savage, had discussed the matter with his Cabinet. In Canada, Mackenzie King went through the process of consulting Parliament about the decision to go to war. As a consequence, Canada formally remained neutral for a further week and George VI only signed a declaration of war in his capacity as King of Canada on 10 September. At least in the case of Canada, the Parliamentary vote was something of a formality. In South Africa, where the prime minister, Hertzog, favoured neutrality, his deputy, Smuts, only narrowly won the division in Parliament, which brought the country into the war. The Irish Free State, meanwhile, shattered the illusion of Imperial unity by remaining neutral.

From that point on, US support in the war became the great prize for Britain. The King and Queen's visit to the United States in June 1939 was judged to have been a success in terms of cultivating pro-British sentiment.[67] Yet US suspicion of British imperialism remained. In his wartime broadcasts George VI felt the need to address this issue. In his message on Empire Day 1940 he challenged the way in which Britain's enemies invoked Empire as a means of attacking the UK:

> By it *they* mean the spirit of domination and lust for conquest. We free peoples of the Empire cast the word back in their teeth. It is *they* who have these evil aspirations. *Our* one object has been peace: peace in which our institutions may be developed, the condition of our peoples improved and the problems of government solved in a spirit of good will.[68]

Yet the very autonomy that characterized the Dominions' relationship with the UK, combined with wartime prime minister Winston Churchill's sometimes insensitive attitude towards their desire for a genuine say in the conduct of the war, placed strains upon the Commonwealth alliance. George VI noted these strains with concern. Perhaps the most striking public manifestation of this tension was the statement by the Australian prime minister, John Curtin, in December 1941 following Japan's entry into the war 'that Australia looks to America, free of any pangs about our traditional links of kinship with Britain'.[69] Australian resentment focused in part on Churchill's reluctance to allow Australia and the other Dominions permanent representation on the War Cabinet in London. Curtin's statement was followed on 14 January 1942 by a vote in the South African parliament on a motion calling for the creation of a republic and the secession of South Africa from the Commonwealth. Although the motion was defeated, the vote of 90 to 48 indicated a worrying level of hostility towards the Commonwealth. The King was moved to urge Churchill to reconsider his position on ministerial representation for the Dominions. On 17 January Sir Alexander Hardinge told Churchill:

> His Majesty is genuinely alarmed at the feeling which appears to be growing in Australia and may well be aggravated by further reverses in the Far East. He very

much hopes, therefore, that it may be possible to adopt as soon as possible some procedure which will succeed in arresting these dangerous developments without impairing the efficiency of the existing machinery.[70]

Churchill's attitude towards the Dominions remained a matter of concern to the Palace. In October 1943 Alan Lascelles, who had taken over from Hardinge as the King's private secretary earlier in the year, recorded in his diary that Lord Cranborne, the Secretary of State for the Dominions, was 'disturbed by Winston's persistent refusal to let the Dominions know our plans for future foreign policy etc. Winston is incurably colonial-minded.' In a note which he added to this entry in 1967, Lascelles wrote, 'By this I meant that Winston tended to think of the self-governing Dominions as Victorian colonies. I don't think he had ever absorbed the 1931 Statute of Westminster.'[71]

The war also posed problems about what to do with the King's brother, the Duke of Windsor. In its early months he was attached to the British Military Mission in France. With the fall of France he was evacuated to Spain, and from there to Portugal, where he became the focus of German intrigue.[72] Widely regarded as being sympathetic to Nazi Germany, the Duke appears to have made little attempt to disguise his opposition to the war. A post in one of the more remote corners of the Empire seemed an obvious way of keeping him safely out of view. Since there was a marked lack of enthusiasm among the governments of the Dominions for the prospect of accommodating their former King, Churchill approached the Colonial Office for suggestions as to a territory of which the Duke could be governor. The Colonial Secretary, Lord Lloyd, initially suggested the Bahamas as a small colony where the Duke could do little harm, although he quickly changed his mind and opposed the appointment.[73] Nevertheless, the Duke was offered the Bahamas and grudgingly accepted. Like many members of the royal family who subsequently undertook visits to the colonies, he was vividly impressed by the extreme poverty of the Bahamas. He wrote, 'I have personally rarely seen such slums and squalor as exist in most of the native settlements and many of the Out Islands have no doctor at all.'[74] In his efforts to ameliorate this poverty, the Duke proved a relatively diligent governor. His record was, however, tarnished by his mishandling of the investigation of the brutal murder of a leading local businessman, Sir Harry Oakes, an incident that has generated much rumour and speculation about the Duke's motives.[75]

As the war neared its end, the question arose as to what to do next with the Duke. The attitude of the Palace to this problem was conveyed in a striking simile by the King's private secretary, Alan Lascelles. Recording a candid private conversation with the Duke in October 1945, Lascelles wrote in his diary:

> The British Empire was like the clock on the mantelpiece; it had to be kept ticking away, but its machinery was delicate and was getting more so with the passage of time. We had, so to speak, taken that clock to pieces a hundred times and tried to fit it together again with the inclusion of an extra wheel—the wheel of an ex-King. We had never found a way of doing this without damaging the works.[76]

The Duke had objected that 'the wheel had fitted all right in the Bahamas'. Lascelles replied that, while the Duke had proved a good governor, his appointment 'had been an emergency solution of the problem of what to do with him during the war (and, incidentally—though I did not say this—of how to keep him and the Duchess out of this country); the experiment had worked once, but it couldn't safely be repeated'.[77]

Meanwhile, developments in India were causing particular concern for the Duke's brother, George VI. Following the fall of Singapore in 1942 Churchill, who had led the opposition to constitutional reform in the 1930s, was faced with the prospect of having to promise to grant India full Dominion status when hostilities ended in an effort to sustain Indian support for the war effort. If Churchill was uncomfortable with this the King was even more so, particularly with the suggestion that this offer should include the right to secede from the Commonwealth should the Indian government so desire. The King recorded in his diary, 'Why mention secession as it is what Congress has always wanted to do. Many Provinces won't want to join it, or the Indian Princes either. Many Indians still want to owe allegiance to me as King Emperor.'[78] When, in April 1942, a mission to India by Sir Stafford Cripps failed to persuade leaders of Congress to accept a deal along these lines Hardinge told the Viceroy, Lord Linlithgow, that the King 'never had much confidence that the declaration would commend itself to the party leaders in India'. The King noted in his diary that the Cripps mission had, however, 'cleared up many ambiguities for the rest of the world, especially America, as to our rule in India and what it has done for the Indian peoples'.[79]

The following year, the King intervened directly to influence the choice of Linlithgow's successor as Viceroy. Both Churchill and the Secretary of State for India, Leo Amery, favoured the appointment of the Foreign Secretary, Anthony Eden. The King, however, wrote directly to Churchill to express his concerns about the choice of Eden, largely on the grounds of the undesirability of moving him from his current post. Eden was temporarily dropped from consideration and Churchill eventually chose Lord Wavell to replace Linlithgow, although not before having attempted and failed to persuade the King of the virtues of allowing Eden to be both Viceroy and a member of the War Cabinet.[80] As Rhodes James notes, the negotiations over the selection of the Viceroy were complex, the King attempting to keep an open mind over the choice of Eden (unlike Hardinge who was resolutely opposed), and it would be untrue to say that the King vetoed Eden's appointment.[81] Nevertheless, the incident points to the extent to which the King was involved in and able to influence key decisions by the British government. For all the King's devotion to it, however, Britain's Indian Empire was entering its final days. Its demise would present both the Commonwealth and the Palace with a fresh set of challenges.

3

'A Common Act of Will': The Making of the New Commonwealth, 1945–1952

As the Raj entered its final days it was far from clear that King George VI had reconciled himself to the inevitability of British withdrawal. Recording a conversation with Churchill in July 1942, he noted in his diary that the prime minister had

> amazed me by saying that his colleagues & both, or all 3, parties in Parliament were quite prepared to give up India to the Indians after the war. He felt they had already been talked into giving up India. Cripps, the Press & U.S. public opinion have all contributed to make their minds up that our rule in India is wrong & has always been wrong for India. I disagree & have always said India has got to be governed, & this will have to be our policy.[1]

With the ending of the War it became ever more apparent in London that Britain could not hope to retain India. Yet at some level it seems that the King himself never fully abandoned the belief that Britain had a duty to remain in India and maintain order. Even in December 1946 when approving the appointment as Viceroy of Lord Mountbatten, who was to preside over the formal liquidation of the Raj, the King stipulated that he should have 'concrete orders as to what he is to do. Is he to lead the retreat out of India or is he to work for the reconciliation of Hindus and Muslims?'[2] The King clearly hoped the latter would be possible. Yet Mountbatten was to accelerate further the pace of withdrawal, leading to a transfer of power to the independent governments of India and Pakistan in August 1947. It was a matter of regret to the King that as Emperor of India he had never managed to visit the subcontinent. In 1944 he had proposed doing so, but had been dissuaded by Churchill.[3] One minor but symbolic consequence of Indian independence was that the King ceased to sign himself G.R.I. (Georgius Rex Imperator), as he was no longer Emperor of India, and instead used 'George R'. Receiving a letter from him on 18 August 1947, three days after the granting of independence to India, his mother, Queen Mary, wrote on the back of the envelope, 'The first time Bertie wrote me a letter with the I for Emperor of India left out, very sad'.[4]

THE 'IMPERIAL FAMILY' AND THE ROYAL VISIT TO SOUTHERN AFRICA

The use of members of the royal family as Imperial plenipotentiaries had a long pedigree. As Cannadine has noted, Queen Victoria's son the Duke of Connaught served as Governor General of Canada from 1911 to 1916; his son, Prince Arthur, was Governor General of South Africa from 1920 to 1924. The Duke of Windsor was governor of the Bahamas during the Second World War and in 1945 his younger brother, the Duke of Gloucester, was made Governor General of Australia. A number of similar schemes were canvassed but failed to come to fruition. One, dating from between the wars, was for George V's four sons to be simultaneously appointed Governors General of the Dominions.[5] Equally imaginative was the 'private project' Churchill mentioned to his private secretary in April 1952, just two months after the death of George VI, to have Queen Elizabeth the Queen Mother appointed as the next Governor General of Australia.[6] Again, this ultimately came to nothing. Speculation about the possibility of a member of the royal family being appointed as Governor General of New Zealand continued well into the post-war era although, when the idea was discussed in 1966, officials in London suspected that the enthusiasm of ministers there would be 'sensibly diminished' once they appreciated the additional expense that would be entailed by accommodating a member of the royal family.[7]

Perhaps the most radical suggestion to use the Windsors to promote Imperial unity came from Shuldman Redfern, secretary to the Governor General of Canada from 1939 to 1945, who had been involved in organizing the royal tour of 1939. Redfern argued for a peripatetic monarch who would migrate over the course of the year between his or her various realms, an idea he floated publicly in *The Spectator* in 1946.[8] Discussing this idea with him, Alan Lascelles, the King's principal private secretary, was not impressed. He recorded in his diary that this was 'all very fine in theory; but in practice, I reminded him, any such activities must be quadrupled, for what the Sovereign does for one Dominion he must do for all'.[9] As for Redfern's assertion that air travel made the arrangement feasible, Lascelles objected that 'even flying to and from Canada is a physical strain, and for many years to come there will be an element of danger in long distance flights that could not be ignored'. The Palace was, however, prepared to contemplate a less physically demanding way of symbolizing the Commonwealth-wide character of the monarchy. As the British Cabinet Secretary, Sir Norman Brook, told the New Zealand prime minister, Peter Fraser, in August 1948, Britain

> might also have a Governor-General, who would act when the King was out of the United Kingdom. The United Kingdom would have no objection to establishing such an office, and in fact the King himself thought it would be a good idea in that it would remind people of the United Kingdom that he was King of places beside the United Kingdom.[10]

Again, this never came to fruition (although the idea was periodically revived). In the absence of a peripatetic monarchy, the other realms of the Commonwealth would have to make do with occasional visits from their sovereign. By far the most significant of these in the second half of the 1940s was the royal family's visit to southern Africa in 1947. The visit would embrace South Africa, the High Commission territories, and the Rhodesias. Lascelles had envisaged the visit to southern Africa partly as an opportunity to allow the King to enjoy something of a holiday after the pressures of the war years. South African Prime Minister Jan Smuts, however, proved increasingly keen to choreograph the visit to the political advantage of his United Party, clearly hoping it would encourage popular enthusiasm for Empire and embarrass his opponents in the Afrikaner-dominated National Party.[11] When plans for the visit were announced in March 1946, the Nationalist press focused upon this point, accusing Smuts of having proposed the visit as a political move intended to influence the outcome of the next general election.[12]

The South African government also wished to stress the divisibility of the Crown, emphasizing George VI's position as 'King of South Africa'.[13] The Palace itself, at Lascelles' suggestion, sought to give tangible expression to the Statute of Westminster by telling the Dominions that, instead of Imperial affairs being dealt with by a Council of State in the UK, the King would deal directly with them in South Africa.[14] Although Counsellors of State were appointed to act for the King in his capacity as the British monarch, they were not empowered to act for the Dominions. *The Times* reported that the Canadian government had sent the names of candidates for diplomatic appointments to the King in South Africa for his approval, commenting 'Cape Town thus temporarily supersedes London as the capital of the Commonwealth'.[15]

The nature of the tour was shaped by a number of other agendas. The British government, which was keen to promote an image of national power and resurgence, transported the royal party to South Africa on board the Royal Navy's most powerful battleship, HMS *Vanguard*.[16] It also sought to promote the notion of 'multiracialism', based on the premise that the gradual social, economic, and political 'development' of the indigenous majority in southern Africa could help to reconcile its interests with those of the European settler communities and other minority groups. One means of doing this was by stressing the contribution in the Second World War of ex-servicemen, both black and white. During the South African leg of the tour, however, this message of multiracialism proved conspicuously at odds with the insistence of the authorities that events be strictly racially segregated and that there should be no physical contact between the King and the African ex-servicemen to whom he presented medals.[17] For its part, the European settler-dominated government of Southern Rhodesia was anxious to affirm the loyalty of its territory to the Crown in contrast to what it regarded as the disloyalty of large sections of the Afrikaner community in South Africa.

Meetings with Africans during the course of the tour were organized principally in the form of chiefly *indabas*, which sought to convey the message that the mass of indigenous people identified primarily with their 'tribal leaders' rather than with radical nationalists and that 'tribal' peoples had an innate respect for traditional structures of authority, with King George VI at their apex.[18] Equally carefully staged meetings were arranged in urban settings, intended to portray Africans as the beneficiaries of the modernizing impact of European rule. Yet Africans and members of other ethnic communities were far from passive actors in this royal pageant: they had agendas and strategies of their own. The size of some of the crowds that gathered at the *indabas* and their enthusiastic reception of the royal party indicated a genuine interest in and affection for the King.[19] Among the more radical elements of the Indian and African communities in South Africa opinion was divided as to how opponents of the government should react to the tour. One approach was articulated by *Inkundla*, the newspaper closest to the African National Congress (ANC) Youth League, which argued that the visit was 'a cause of great rejoicing among many Africans who still view the British sovereign as their ultimate protector'.[20] The young Nelson Mandela, a descendent of the Thembu royal family, was among those arguing that the British monarchy should be received respectfully.[21] The opposing view was embodied in a resolution passed by the ANC at its Bloemfontein conference late in 1946 which called for the tour to be boycotted 'as a protest against the barbarous policy of the Union Government of denying the elementary rights to Africans, and in view of the fact that these injustices are perpetrated and maintained in the name of His Majesty, King George VI'.[22] As a consequence of these divisions, although protest was significant it was a sporadic feature of the tour and it took the form not only of boycotts but also of calls on the King as the protector of his people to redress their grievances. Meanwhile, sections of the Afrikaner nationalist press either ignored the tour or were openly critical of it.[23]

Far from providing an opportunity for the royal family to relax, the schedule which Smuts helped to devise for them on the South African stage of the tour was exhausting. Beginning at the Cape, it would take them through the Orange Free State, Basutoland, Natal, and the Transvaal aboard the infelicitously titled 'white train'.[24] This, in turn, made it difficult for Whitehall to insist to the other governments involved that their own itineraries should not place too much strain on the King and his family. In June 1946 the Dominions Office wrote to the governor of Southern Rhodesia, Sir Campbell Tait, noting that the emphasis should be on 'rest and relaxation'. The Southern Rhodesian prime minister, Sir Godfrey Huggins, who was shown the telegram by Tait, took exception to this phrase and expressed the hope that it did not mean having to cut 'the meagre programme' his country had proposed. Tait explained, with regard to the programme for the South African leg of the visit, that '[w]hat moves [Huggins] and will move every Rhodesian as soon as they read it, is the number of towns and drops in the Union known to be disaffected and disloyal through which the Royal party are to be dragged ... Now if the proposed [Southern Rhodesian] programme is cut because of the probable exhaustion caused by the Union tour, the Cabinet will certainly have something to say, not in public certainly, but around the table.'[25]

The arch-exponent of British Shintoism Dermot Morrah was at hand to provide a suitably reverential account of the visit. This was published as *The Royal Family in Africa*.[26] Its tone was set in a Foreword by Smuts himself, who claimed that the royal party's 'journey through the Union was to be more of a sustained triumphal progress than the sort of visit we had originally planned'.[27] In fact, the visit was problematic from the very start. As the royal family left London for Cape Town at the beginning of February the UK was in the grips of economic crisis, a fuel shortage, and one of the worst winters on record. During the journey to South Africa the King and Queen received disturbing reports that their absence from the UK at such a testing time had attracted criticism. The King was sufficiently worried by this to consult the British prime minister, Clement Attlee, about whether the visit should be curtailed. Attlee emphatically advised against, concerned that any such move 'would magnify unduly the extent of the difficulties we are facing and surmounting at home, especially in the eyes of foreign observers'.[28] Overcrowding aboard HMS *Vanguard*, due in part to the size of the royal retinue, was to lead to a virtual mutiny among the crew (although not while the royal family were on board).[29] The King's sense that he should have remained at home added to the strains of a rough sea crossing and a strenuous programme of engagements once the royal party had embarked in South Africa. His notoriously short temper frequently snapped. The suspicion that he and his family were being deployed as political pawns, the overbearing South African police presence, and the sense of barely concealed hostility on the part of the Afrikaner community all took their toll on the King's never entirely placid temper.[30]

Despite all these setbacks, there was a sense of relief on the part of the organizers of the tour that, in the words of Evelyn Baring, Britain's high commissioner in South Africa, there had been 'a complete absence of unfortunate incidents'. This was combined with a belief that physical exposure to the royal family did, ultimately, serve to strengthen Imperial sentiment. Baring claimed that one of the achievements of the tour was the opportunity it had afforded for 'the typical farmer, usually an Afrikaner, to speak with the King and Queen and, especially when conversation turned on country topics, to realise how false is the Nationalist picture of a family of proud people remote from the cares of ordinary life and lacking all interest in the affairs of rural South Africa'.[31] Baring correctly predicted that the tour would make little difference to the electoral arithmetic in South Africa. More optimistically, however, he suggested that there were grounds to hope 'that either Nationalism will become less uncompromisingly bitter or that if that does not happen then the appeal of the Nationalist Party will be weakened', although he thought this would be a gradual process. He also confidently predicted that English-speaking South Africans would have been 'confirmed in their loyalty to the Crown and their adherence to the British connection'.

The Palace also pulled off a major public relations coup in the form of the broadcast Princess Elizabeth made on her twenty-first birthday, which fell at the end of the South African tour. Her speech, which was written by Lascelles, in many ways defined her subsequent relationship with the Commonwealth. She told her listeners,

> I declare before you all that my whole life, whether it be long or short, shall be devoted to your service and the service of our great Imperial family to which we all belong, but I shall not have the strength to carry out that resolution alone unless you join in it with me, as I now invite you to do.[32]

Yet one of the problems faced by those within the British government seeking to deploy the monarchy as a means of binding together this 'Imperial family' was that the Palace itself was not always a particularly cooperative partner. In June 1948 K. W. Blackburne, director of information at the Colonial Office, argued that greater use should be made of the monarchy as a means of cementing links with the

Commonwealth. He began from the assumption that 'it is difficult to argue that Britain is still a leading power in the world and that the Colonies derive great economic and strategic advantage from association with us'.[33] If colonies were to be persuaded to remain within the Commonwealth on independence, therefore, it was important 'to pay attention to the other more intangible factors which have hitherto helped to maintain the unity of the Commonwealth—the ties of tradition and of friendship'. The former were, Blackburne argued, 'most clearly shown in the loyalty and respect of all the colonial peoples for the Royal Family', even those with strong nationalist leanings.

Blackburne urged that greater use should be made of this resource. He recognized that the King and Queen themselves were unlikely to be able to make regular visits to the colonies. He suggested, however, that there were other means by which colonial peoples could be brought into contact with the royal family. A greater effort might, for example, be made to provide invitations for royal occasions to colonial peoples and representatives of the colonial press (as opposed to British officials posted in the colonies). There was, he suggested, a particular need to supply colonial peoples, who were denied direct experience of the King and Queen, with images of their monarch and he strongly implied that staff at the Palace had not been sufficiently cooperative in this respect. Finally, Blackburne suggested that leading figures might be granted audiences with the King during visits to the UK and that Princess Elizabeth and her husband might be encouraged to undertake tours of the colonies. Blackburne's complaints about the lack of cooperation from the Palace were echoed by one of his colleagues who noted that the failure to arrange suitable photographic sittings for the King and Queen 'allied to the difficulties encountered on various occasions to achieve Royal recognition of the local importance of visiting Colonials, is a cause of considerable concern to those endeavouring to project Britain and the British way of life to members of our Colonial Empire'.[34]

Evidence that the Palace did not share Blackburne's aspirations came shortly after this exchange, when the permanent undersecretary at the Colonial Office, Sir Thomas Lloyd, proposed that the King should receive delegates attending a major conference in London on British colonial Africa which was due to begin at the end of September 1948.[35] Problems arose when the Colonial Office sought to arrange with the Palace's notoriously recalcitrant press secretary, Commander Richard Colville, for photographs to be taken of the audience. Colville replied that this would be contrary to all precedent and he did not think the King would be prepared to be photographed with the delegates either before or after the formal audience.[36] Blackburne, who was convinced of the importance of being able to distribute photographs of the event across the African colonies, complained that 'if the King can be photographed with the Australian Cricketers at Balmoral, surely he can be photographed with the leaders of African political life in London'.[37] Lloyd was forced to appeal over the head of Colville directly to the King's private secretary, Sir Alan Lascelles. He stressed the value of the photographs, claiming that 'a really immense amount of good will be done by their distribution in the Colonies from which the delegates have come'.[38] The Palace relented, and Lloyd was later able to claim that the audience and the resulting photographs had 'aroused in the Colonies considerable fervour and loyalty'.[39]

The Palace proved similarly reluctant to accommodate requests from the Colonial Office for royal tours of the colonies, no doubt because of the King's failing health. In April 1948, the newspaper *West Africa*, commenting on the recent royal visit to South Africa and the visit planned for 1949 to Australia and New Zealand, asked, 'When will be the turn of West Africa?'[40] Five months later, the governor of the Gold Coast, Sir Alan Burns, put the suggestion to London of a royal visit to the colonies. Lloyd replied that the Colonial Office had had similar requests from the West Indies and Far Eastern territories, if only for brief stopovers by the royal family on their way to the Dominions.[41] According to Lloyd, however, Lascelles had insisted that 'if once the King were to depart from the general principle that this visit is to the two Dominions only the time and distance of the tour would be increased to a quite impracticable length'. It would not be until the following reign that frequent royal tours became an important means by which the monarch gave substance to a title created in 1949: that of Head of the Commonwealth.

THE HEADSHIP OF THE COMMONWEALTH

The determination of newly independent India to move rapidly towards republican status posed a major constitutional challenge, one that drew the Attlee administration and other Commonwealth governments into a complex debate about the nature of Commonwealth membership. It was broadly accepted at the beginning of 1949 that this had three essential elements: the equality of its members, their free association, and their common allegiance to the Crown. It was the final element that had raised problems in Ireland, and now posed them in the case of India. As W. David McIntyre notes, as early as his talks with the British government in November 1921, the Irish nationalist leader Eamon de Valera had seized upon the notion of symbolism to suggest that Ireland could be associated with the British Commonwealth by recognizing the Crown 'as the symbol and accepted head of the Association' rather than owing it direct allegiance.[42] The Balfour Report of 1926 described the King as 'the symbol of the special relationship between the different parts of the Empire'.[43] Likewise, the preamble to the Statute of Westminster described the Crown as 'the symbol of the free association of the members of the British Commonwealth of Nations'. Yet both documents were premised on the fact that those nations were also 'united by a common allegiance to the Crown'. De Valera's very different conception of the role of the Crown found constitutional expression fifteen years after 1921 in the External Relations Act, passed in the wake of the abdication crisis, which recognized the Crown purely for the purposes of diplomatic accreditation and international agreements. In the Act the de Valera government expressed the Irish Free State's willingness to follow Commonwealth states in recognizing the King 'as the symbol of their cooperation', but found no place for the concept of allegiance. The idea that the former without the latter could form a sufficient basis for Commonwealth membership would ultimately be embodied in the London Declaration of April 1949, and there was a direct line of descent from de Valera's 1921 proposals.

The Irish model had been very much in the minds of British policy-makers when in 1947 they discussed Burma's desire to become a republic on independence. The governor of Burma, Sir Hubert Rance, had told London of his hope that the country would be accommodated within the Commonwealth as a republic, arguing that 'the time seems ripe for a new conception of association within the Commonwealth not necessarily owing allegiance to the Crown especially for those countries which have no ties of blood culture or religion'.[44] Malcolm MacDonald, who was then Governor General of Malaya, expressed support for Rance's plea, drawing on his earlier experience as Secretary of State for the Dominions at the time of the passing of the External Relations Act. In late June 1947 he reminded London that he had advised the Cabinet that Éire's new constitution should not be regarded as placing it outside the Commonwealth. MacDonald explained that one reason he had done so

> was that it seemed likely that when the time came for India, Burma and other non-white countries in the Empire to attain dominion status, some, at least, of them would adopt a similar attitude to the Southern Irish towards the British Crown. It seemed wise to accept a compromise in Eire which might, in due course, open the way to a similar compromise enabling India and other Empire countries to stay as full partners in the Commonwealth.[45]

Yet ministers were reluctant to make concessions to Burma on this issue, fearing that this would make it more difficult to persuade India to remain in the Commonwealth on the basis of something like conventional Dominion status.[46] The assassination of the Burmese leader Aung San on 17 July 1947, whether or not it represented a turning point in the country's attitude towards the Commonwealth, was certainly not conducive to Britain pursuing the issue of trying to accommodate a republican Burma. When Burma achieved full independence at the beginning of January 1948, it did so outside the Commonwealth.

Yet the notion that something like the Irish model might be applicable to India remained current. At a lecture in November 1947 attended by a number of Cabinet ministers the Professor of Commonwealth Relations at Chatham House, Nicholas Mansergh, specifically suggested that de Valera's approach might provide a way forward for the Commonwealth. This prompted a paper by Percy Stent, a former Indian Civil Service official then working for the Foreign Office, which, along with Mansergh's lecture, was considered by the Cabinet's Commonwealth Relations Committee. Stent commended the Irish model and the purely voluntary basis of association this implied and suggested that republics should be accommodated within the Commonwealth, with the King being recognized as 'titular head of the Union or Commonwealth for purposes of common action'.[47]

The idea that something like the Irish model of 'external association' (with the Crown being recognized for diplomatic purposes) might be applicable to India appeared to have considerable support within the Commonwealth. This was, however, dealt a powerful blow when in September 1948 John A. Costello announced Éire's intention to quit the Commonwealth. It was in many respects the logical outcome of the path pursued by de Valera, but arose from the defeat of his government in 1948 and its replacement by a coalition of Costello's Fine Gael and Clann na Poblachta led by Seán MacBride. MacBride, a resolutely anti-British republican whose father had been executed in the wake of the Easter Rising of 1916, was appointed Minister for External Affairs. In July 1948 MacBride declared that Éire was not a member of the Commonwealth, a claim that was repeated shortly afterwards by the Taoiseach, Costello. Yet the suddenness of Costello's announcement in October 1948 while at a Commonwealth Conference in Canada that Éire was to be a fully fledged republic seemed to take everyone by surprise.[48] Speculation began to circulate that it might have been occasioned by some sort of snub to Costello and his wife by the Governor General of Canada, Lord Alexander. Whatever the cause, George VI seems to have taken the matter remarkably personally, more so than the independence of India. He pointedly asked the Irish representative in London, 'Why leave the family?' The King even asked if he personally had done anything to provoke the move. Dulanty recorded that George 'was distressed by the whole business. He had been glad to see relations with Éire improving; he had looked forward to the day when he would visit Dublin; now it was impossible.'[49] Southern Ireland formally became an independent republic on Easter Monday 1949.

The move was to add a further level of sensitivity to the question of relations between Northern and Southern Ireland. The Ireland Act of 1949, under which the UK recognized the independence of the new republic, also enshrined the principle that there could be no change in the constitutional status of Northern Ireland without the consent of its parliament. Éire's repudiation of the King and the Commonwealth made the British government all the more determined to uphold the principle of consent. Although the Costello government was keen to press the UK on the future of partition, Sir Gilbert Laithwaite, the British representative in Dublin, argued in December 1950 that it would be

> impossible politically for any Government in the United Kingdom to urge any part of the Commonwealth to secede from the Commonwealth against its will and to join a State which does not recognise The King, and which, though it has close economic and racial ties with the United Kingdom, save in name, is completely foreign.[50]

This would become a familiar theme of subsequent Anglo-Irish discussions on the issue of partition. In October 1952 when the British Secretary of State for Commonwealth Relations, Lord Salisbury, met the Irish Minister for External Affairs, Frank Aiken, the former claimed that Éire's return to the Commonwealth 'would make the unification of the country much easier'.[51] Perhaps surprisingly for the arch-Imperial 'diehard' of the Churchill and Eden governments, Salisbury claimed to have responded to Aiken's assertion that partition was bound to end eventually by suggesting that this 'might well be so, but surely it would be better to allow that result to come about by the action of natural forces rather than to try and hurry it up unduly'.

When, during his third period as Taoiseach from 1957 to 1959, de Valera proposed a compromise under which a united Ireland would re-join the Commonwealth and, while not owing allegiance to the Queen, would recognize her as head of the Commonwealth, the idea did not find favour with the British government. Lord Home, the Commonwealth Secretary, doubted whether public opinion in Southern Ireland would allow for such an arrangement and suggested that the UK 'could not be expected to go to Northern Ireland and suggest that its people should be less loyal than they wished to be'. Even assuming that a solution along those lines could be achieved, British ministers were not enthusiastic about the prospect. They remembered the Free State as a disruptive influence within the Commonwealth before 1949 and Prime Minster Harold Macmillan wrote, 'I do not think that a united Ireland—with de Valera as a sort of Irish Nehru—would do us much good. Let us stand by our friends.'[52]

To return to 1948, in the wake of Costello's announcement that Éire would leave the Commonwealth, Patrick Gordon Walker, the parliamentary undersecretary at the Commonwealth Relations Office, fixed on an even more radical solution to India's status. By that stage he had come to the conclusion that it would be difficult to reach agreement with India about a form of Commonwealth link through the Crown that would be acceptable to Britain and other Commonwealth members.[53] In an extremely important paper written at the very end of the year Gordon Walker suggested, instead, returning to the essential principle that 'India wants to be in the Commonwealth and all its other members want to accept her into membership. Could we not base ourselves on a Commonwealth relationship resting upon the will and intent of all its members?' This would entail nothing less than 'the deliberate and friendly snapping of the Crown-link by mutual consent and the simultaneous absorption of a completely non-monarchical Dominion into the Commonwealth, but a Dominion that genuinely and sincerely wishes to remain in the Commonwealth.' It might be done, Gordon Walker suggested, by the permanent delegation of the King's functions to the Indian president. The advantages of this clean break might include, Gordon Walker suggested, the possibility of the Irish Republic and Burma returning to the Commonwealth. Describing in his diary the meeting of the Cabinet's Commonwealth Affairs Committee on 7 January 1949 at which he presented his paper, Gordon Walker summarized it in the following terms:

> The Crown link is out. Let's fit in India as a Republic, based on the reality of a common act of will. Then let's add embellishments, which could become valuable: though they are dangerous if we try to *constitute* the link out of them.[54]

One of a number of possible 'embellishments' to which Gordon Walker referred in his paper was the notion that the King might become 'Head of the Commonwealth'. Yet he remained highly sceptical about the value or appropriateness of this term. He expressed doubts about the suggestion 'that the King would for certain purposes act as Head of the Commonwealth—for instance, for the summoning of Prime Ministers' meetings or for the conferment of honours' on the basis that 'no direct link between India and the Crown would be created; nor would the King have any Indian Ministers to advise him'.[55] Gordon Walker returned to this issue in February 1949, complaining that the term 'Head of the Commonwealth' was unsuitable 'for there is no Commonwealth of such a sort that can have a "Head"'.[56] Gordon Walker thought that the term 'President', although in some ways better, had 'too precise and too republican a connotation'. In his quest for 'a unique and special word' he suggested that 'Protector' or even 'Lord Protector' had good English precedent and would derive some meaning from, and give some meaning to, the concept of a 'Commonwealth citizen'. While that may have been true, these terms would no doubt have carried with them darkly Cromwellian overtones for ardent monarchists.

The attempt to accommodate India within the Commonwealth took place within the context of deepening Cold War tensions and Britain's efforts to re-establish itself as a global power. As the inevitability of a transfer of power in India became ever more apparent, British policy-makers continued to hope that its vast supply of military manpower would provide a vital prop in a Commonwealth-wide system of defence which would, in turn, continue to underwrite Britain's great-power status. Indeed, these hopes survived the transfer of power.[57] It was this issue which finally swayed Britain's Foreign Secretary Ernest Bevin, who had in the discussions in early 1949 been highly sceptical of the idea of the Commonwealth link being watered down to accommodate India, even suggesting that it would be better for the Commonwealth to be dissolved.[58] By the time of the London conference in April, however, the Foreign Office had swung round to the view that the hostility that might be generated by India's ejection from the Common-wealth would be more dangerous than allowing a looser form of association. Attlee set out the Cold War logic behind this in a letter to the King in February. He suggested,

> If India against her will, is obliged to leave the Commonwealth, it would encourage Russia in her efforts to disrupt South East Asia, while India, as the most important national state in the area, would tend to become the leader of an anti-European Asiatic movement. On the other hand, if she remains in the Commonwealth, there is a great possibility of building up in South East Asia something analogous to [*sic*] Western Union.[59]

Having consulted the Conservative Opposition on the matter, Attlee obtained the Cabinet's approval for the principle of seeking to devise a link that would enable a republican India to remain in the Cabinet. In a neat reversal of Britain's traditional position that allegiance to the Crown was the lynchpin of the Commonwealth, this was justified to the Cabinet on the grounds that 'it would be a disservice to the Crown if Commonwealth Ministers allowed a position to develop in which the Crown was made to appear a stumbling block' to Commonwealth cohesion.[60] A common thread implicit in much of the discussions of India's future member-ship, and which Gordon Walker had made explicit in his paper, was that the key element of Commonwealth cohesion was the *will* of its members to maintain an association with one another.

As the meeting of Commonwealth prime ministers approached, Gordon Walker's position underwent a significant change. This was prompted in part by a series of consultations with Commonwealth governments in March which revealed serious reservations about a republican India remaining in the Commonwealth, particularly on the part of Pakistan, Ceylon, and South Africa.[61] Conversely, it was also inspired by Gordon Walker's own talks with Nehru towards the end of March, which suggested that the Indian prime minister's position on the Crown might be softening. In the course of these discussions, Nehru himself had independently raised the possibility of India recognizing the King 'as head or symbol of unity of the Commonwealth as a whole'.[62] On 6 April, Gordon Walker wrote that he was 'personally more doubtful' than he had previously been able on the desirability of simply cutting the relationship with the Crown. He was correspondingly more receptive, as he told the Cabinet, to 'some mention of India's acceptance of the King, not as territorial King of any country of the Commonwealth but as being in some way personally pre-eminent in the Commonwealth and the symbol of its unity'.[63] Indeed, four days earlier, Norman Brook had noted that the Indian high commissioner, Krishna Menon, had also raised the possibility of the King being recognized as King of the Commonwealth but not King of India.[64] Yet Gordon Walker's specific description of the formula in terms of the King being 'personally pre-eminent' and a 'symbol' of Commonwealth unity had, as we shall see, important implications for the nature of this new role.

When the prime ministers' meeting opened on 22 April, the representatives largely took the positions which Gordon Walker had predicted, with the prime ministers of Australia and New Zealand rejecting any change in their own countries' relationships with the Crown, and those of Pakistan and Ceylon both registering concerns at the implications for the Commonwealth of India shedding its allegiance. The one leader whose comments caused surprise was the prime minister of South Africa, D. F. Malan. Malan urged flexibility in accommodating India's desire to become a republic, noting that, while the Crown was a unifying element in countries 'with a more or less uniform population of British descent', in those with 'a mixed population' unity was not likely to be achieved 'by emphasising an external constitutional connection, which was apt to become a bone of contention between various sections of the population'.[65] Malan's apparent willingness to help lay the foundations of a multiracial Commonwealth should not distract from the fact that he was following a familiar South African Afrikaner nationalist line of stressing the autonomy of Commonwealth members. Nevertheless, the speech Malan made to the opening session was a powerful statement of a number of the principles that ultimately underlay the new dispensation. He argued that India's desire to remain in the Commonwealth, and even Éire's wish not to be regarded as a foreign nation, demonstrated that common allegiance to the Crown was not the only 'and not even the strongest link, which binds the Commonwealth together'.[66] Indeed, in certain cases the issue of allegiance could actually be an obstacle to unity. More potent factors promoting unity were tradition, common outlook, and interests, but above all 'the Commonwealth's adaptiveness to changing circumstances, and her respect for freedom and liberty'.

Malan's key intervention came in the final stages of the conference when it seemed that agreement was likely over India's continued membership on the basis that it recognized the King as head of the Commonwealth. He objected that this might imply that the Commonwealth itself was a constitutional entity, a notion that South Africa would find it difficult to accept. Malan's reservations were addressed in two ways. First, the words 'as such' were inserted into the final Declaration so that it spoke of India's 'acceptance of the King as the symbol of the free association of its independent member nations and *as such* Head of the Commonwealth'. This was, in itself, a significant weakening of the concept of the headship, although one that partly met Gordon Walker's own earlier objections. Secondly it was agreed it should specifically be put on record that the new title did not imply that the King discharged any constitutional function by virtue of the headship.[67]

The formula secured what was in some cases the grudging agreement of the Commonwealth prime ministers. The Australian prime minister J. B. Chifley, for example, was prepared to agree to the compromise, despite strong opposition on the part of his foreign minister, H. V. Evatt, to any settlement under which there was no recognition by India of the King's prerogatives. That Evatt, a hero of the Australian Left, should have adopted such an uncompromising position is, as Frank Bongiorno has noted, a sign of the extent to which there remained in the 1940s a sense that Australia was a 'British nation' and that the monarchy was a vital element in this ethnic, racial, and national identity.[68] New Zealand's prime minister took a stronger line than the Australians, making plain his compatriots' strong allegiance to the monarchy and his own consternation at the prospect of this allegiance no longer being the basis of Commonwealth membership.[69]

One significant question which the London Declaration left unanswered was whether the title of Head of the Commonwealth is hereditary. W. David McIntyre dissents from the standard line of constitutional experts (and indeed, recently, the Commonwealth Secretariat itself) in maintaining that—at least in terms of the intentions behind the Declaration—it is. He notes that the Declaration refers to 'the King' and not George VI in person. On that basis, he suggests that 'Elizabeth II succeeded to the title as she did the Crown. She is, surely, Head of the Commonwealth by virtue of being Queen of Britain and her other realms and is recognized by all member countries as the symbol of their free association.'[70]

There is a further argument that might be made in favour of this position: at a time when the divisibility of the Crown was still a significant point of contention, it is difficult to imagine how the Declaration could have specified the hereditary nature of the headship without being unacceptable to most of the representatives at the London conference. Had the final Declaration spoken of India's 'acceptance of the British monarch as the symbol of the free association of its independent member nations', it would have clearly signaled that the post was hereditary. Yet any such description of their own sovereign would almost certainly have drawn objections from the other Dominions' prime ministers. 'The King' was very much a shorthand term for the emerging notion of a monarch who was equally and separately sovereign of all his realms. In so far as these realms had legislative independence, they were at least morally bound by the agreement in the preamble to the Statute of Westminster of 1931 'that any alteration in the law touching the Succession to the Throne or the Royal Style and Titles shall hereafter require the assent as well of the Parliaments of all the Dominions as of the Parliament of the United Kingdom'. In that respect, the identity of the Head of the Commonwealth could be said to be a hereditary monarch, with the laws of succession to their throne being governed by those states that owned them allegiance.

In fact, the issue of whether it was hereditary seems hardly to have entered into the discussions of the headship either in Whitehall or among Commonwealth prime ministers. A rare comment on the matter came from John Rowlatt, a parliamentary counsel to the Treasury, who noted, in effect, that the title could not be hereditary in any formal legal sense as this would require a law covering the Commonwealth as a whole and there was 'no body capable of passing a Commonwealth law, but only a number of bodies capable of passing laws for part of the Commonwealth'.[71] This is cited by Vernon Bogdanor as evidence that the headship 'was not conferred as a hereditary title'.[72] As we shall see, however, the assumption within the British government well into the current reign was both that the title was, in practice, hereditary and that this was in the UK's broad interests. The way in which they sought to square this with the lack of any legal mechanism governing the succession will be examined in Chapter 6.

Once the title 'Head of the Commonwealth' had been agreed by the April meeting, the task commenced of translating it into Latin so that it could be inserted, seamlessly, into the list of the monarch's other titles. A group of senior civil servants, including the Cabinet Secretary Sir Norman Brook, met to discuss the matter at the beginning of June. It was reported that the Home Office had explored the problem with a great number of classicists 'both in London and at the Universities' and the prime minister himself 'had discussed the matter in the Senior Common Room at Oriel during a recent visit'.[73] The distinguished gathering considered various renderings of 'Commonwealth', rejecting outright the use of 'republica' on the grounds that 'the word could have only one connotation— and that the wrong one—to the man in the street'. A note on the meeting by C. G. L. Sayers went on to record:

> The body of officials did not like [the] suggestion for 'Head of the Commonwealth'— which was 'civitatis gentium supremum caput'; we all hated 'supremum caput' and none of us liked 'civitatis'. Our objection to 'civitatis' was partly that the first meaning of the word was 'citizenship' and the secondary meaning 'state', partly that it did not seem to us to mean an amalgam of states, which is what we denote by the word 'Commonwealth'. I made the point... that scholars in Canada and South Africa would almost certainly object to 'civitatis' on the ground that it suggested a super-state, which is <u>not</u> their conception of the Commonwealth.

The meeting finally agreed on a translation for the King's new title, in which 'Head of the Commonwealth' was rendered 'Consortionis Gentium Princeps'. The Whitehall mandarins then submitted their text to Colin Hardie, a classicist at Magdalen College, Oxford, rather like nervous schoolboys handing in their Latin homework. Sayers recorded, 'Mr Hardie said that there was nothing wrong with the grammar of our translation (which was gratifying to a number of officials who in the dim past did not do too badly in Honour Mods)'.[74] Hardie did have some reservations about the text, a couple of which related to the title of Head of the Commonwealth. According to Sayers, 'Mr Hardie cordially accepted "consortionis" which is a relief… But he disliked "gentium" which he said connoted not "nations" but "races". He therefore recommended "populorum"'. The mandarins meekly accepted this. They were not, however, prepared to accept Hardie's suggestion that 'princeps' be changed to 'caput'. As Sayers noted, 'It may be that "princeps" has, to the trained Latinist, odd associations, but I do not myself feel that "caput" is a very honorific title for His Majesty the King.' While further discussion on this matter was temporarily shelved on the advice of the prime minister, the Latin rendering of Head of the Commonwealth which was ultimately agreed was indeed 'Consortionis Populorum Princeps'.

The changes within the Commonwealth that had necessitated the invention of the title 'Head of the Commonwealth' would also require alterations to her other titles when a new monarch ascended to the throne in 1952. This process, the Coronation itself, and the subsequent royal tour of the Commonwealth were to point to tensions not far beneath the facade of Imperial unity.

4

'A Personal and Living Bond': Accession, Coronation, and Commonwealth Tour, 1952–1954

During his final years the fragile health of George VI prevented him from visiting his overseas realms. A tour of Australia and New Zealand planned for 1949 had to be postponed owing to illness. By the time the King's condition had improved, it was too late to reschedule the visit in 1950 and the celebrations of the Festival of Britain in 1951 meant it would not be feasible that year.[1] Tentative plans were therefore made for it to happen early in 1952, taking in Ceylon on the way. The King was concerned that the Labour government's slender majority following the 1950 General Election might lead Attlee to request a fresh election at around the time of the visit, necessitating its postponement or his premature return. He wrote to Attlee at the beginning of September 1951, warning that 'the people of those countries which I have promised to visit would never understand the reason for such a postponement or interruption—and would never forgive it'.[2] He was extremely relieved when Attlee, partly out of a desire to avoid any political crises while the King was out of the country, indicated that he had decided to request a dissolution of Parliament in the first week of October. Yet within days of this exchange, the King's failing health necessitated a further change of plan. It was decided that Princess Elizabeth and her husband, the Duke of Edinburgh, would make the trip in his place, travelling via East Africa. All the same, the King still harboured hopes of being able to make a private visit to South Africa in March 1952, where the country's prime minister, Dr Malan, had placed a house at his disposal.[3]

In the early hours of 6 February 1952, George VI died in his sleep of a coronary thrombosis. Princess Elizabeth was in Kenya on the first stage of her Commonwealth tour when she learned that she had become Queen. In his broadcast on the King's death, the British prime minister, Winston Churchill, described the Crown as 'the magic link . . . which unites our loosely bound but strongly interwoven Commonwealth of nations'.[4] Yet if the monarchy was still viewed by the British government as a means of promoting Imperial unity, the events of 1952–4 would underline its increasing tendency to become a symbolic battleground on which Commonwealth countries and rival communities within them would seek to assert their own particular political claims. Even expressions of extreme loyalty to the Crown could convey complex and sometimes uncomfortable signals to the Queen's ministers in London.

THE ROYAL TITLE

George VI's steadily failing health had given the British government time to make discreet preparations for his death. It was keen that the arrangements for the proclamation of his successor should not provide the occasion for a protest by one or more members of the Commonwealth, as had occurred in 1936. This entailed opening up consultations with other Commonwealth nations on the subject of the royal title. The title agreed by the Royal Style and Title Act of 1927 was 'George V, by the grace of God, of Great Britain, Ireland and the British Dominions beyond the Seas King, Defender of the Faith, Emperor of India'. This form of words was used to proclaim the accessions of Edward VIII and George VI. The Indian Independence Act had already deleted the words 'Emperor of India' from the monarch's title, a move that had been endorsed by the parliaments of Canada, Australia, New Zealand, and South Africa.[5] Yet even before the London Declaration of April 1949 by which India accepted George VI as 'head of the Commonwealth', it was clear that further changes in the title would also be necessary. The prospect of the Republic of Ireland Act coming into force meant that it would no longer be appropriate to include the term 'Ireland' in the title, and instead it was proposed to refer to 'Northern Ireland'. When, however, in January 1949 Britain sought Commonwealth approval for the substitution of 'Northern Ireland' for 'Ireland', the Canadian government replied that it could not refer this change to its parliament unless other anomalies were addressed.[6] The Canadians were unhappy with the reference to 'British Dominions beyond the Seas', which did not differentiate between colonies and self-governing members of the Commonwealth. In a further sign of the problems that could be caused by the Latin rendering of royal titles, they particularly disliked the use of the phrase 'terrarum quea in *ditione* sunt Britannica' [author's italics], implying that Canada was under British authority.

In September 1951, following the announcement that the King was to undergo an operation, the high Commissions of India, Pakistan, Ceylon, and South Africa were reminded of the 'custom' whereby on the death of the monarch an accession council was held, to which high commissioners were invited.[7] The Indian high commissioner, Krishna Menon, appears to have been pressed on whether he would feel able to sign the Accession Proclamation, given India's status as a republic. He suggested that if the phrase 'Head of the Commonwealth' was inserted into the proclamation, it would be possible for him to sign. In the process, India almost casually resolved what could have been a highly divisive issue, guaranteeing that the title 'Head of the Commonwealth' would pass to the King's successor.

The following month, an interdepartmental committee under the chairmanship of the Cabinet Secretary, Norman Brook, was convened to discuss the wording of the proclamation. The committee not only considered Menon's suggestion and the Canadian objection to the expression 'British Dominions beyond the Seas', but also went in search of any terms in the existing proclamation that could possibly generate friction. Attention turned to the passage in the proclamation which asserted that 'the Imperial Crown of Great Britain, Ireland, and all other His former Majesty's dominions' had rightfully passed to the new monarch. Objections to the phrase 'Imperial Crown' had been raised during the Dominions Office's earlier review in 1928, but at that stage it had been decided that the term should be retained.[8] By the early 1950s, however, the presence in the Commonwealth of republican India heightened concerns that the phrase might be open to 'misunderstanding'.

Brook's committee devised a new form of words for the Accession Proclamation. Armed with this document, Whitehall was able to act remarkably quickly when the time came. Only hours after the death of George VI on 6 February 1952, the Cabinet met and approved a paper by Brook setting down the new terms of the proclamation. Among other changes, it was agreed that the term 'Imperial Crown' should be dropped on the grounds that it was 'likely to be associated with the Indian Empire'.[9] The consequence was that the 1952 accession proclamation used the title 'Queen Elizabeth the Second, by the Grace of God Queen of this Realm and of all Her other Realms and Territories, Head of the Commonwealth, Defender of the Faith'. Furthermore, in place of the phrase 'Imperial Crown of Great Britain, Ireland, and all other His former Majesty's dominions' was the simple term 'the Crown'.

A speedy decision on the text had been essential. Opponents of these innovations had little choice, therefore, but to bite their tongues. Nevertheless, Churchill in particular resented having to tamper with the Proclamation.[10] Writing to him three days later, Brook urged Churchill not to press the matter. The government could not, he argued, 'restore the Empire of the nineteenth century by talking as though it still existed. But we can consolidate the Commonwealth of the twentieth century by moulding the old constitutional forms to fit the new facts.'[11] Yet the principle at stake mattered sufficiently to Churchill that on 14 February he circulated to his Cabinet colleagues a brief historical note on the emergence of the term 'Imperial Crown'. The phrase 'Imperial' had, the prime minister explained, first appeared in documents from the reign of Henry VIII. Moreover:

> The use of the expression 'Imperial Crown of this realm' in the Accession Proclamation certainly dates from the reign of Edward VI, the earliest proclamation of which there is a complete text.[12]

In short, the term 'Imperial Crown' had no connection whatsoever with the Indian Empire. Churchill's paper was never actually debated in Cabinet. Yet in taking a stand on this apparently arcane issue, Churchill was pointing to a question which was to have a broader resonance: how far should specifically British traditions and institutions be amended in order to avoid offending the sensibilities of Commonwealth states?

The efforts of Brook's committee did not, in any case, manage to achieve the desired display of unity. Although Ireland had by then left the Commonwealth, problems again arose from South Africa when the Accession Council met on the afternoon of 6 February. In the light of the events of January 1936, British officials had anticipated that there might be difficulties from that quarter, although they were clearly taken aback when the South Africans chose this solemn occasion to make their stand. All other Commonwealth representatives agreed to sign. Yet acting on instructions he had received from his government earlier that afternoon, Dr Geyer, the South African high commissioner, refused to do so. He claimed that the Proclamation was a purely United Kingdom ceremony and that it would therefore be inappropriate for him to participate. Geyer was pressed by British officials on the 'deplorable effect if comment arose from the fact that South Africa's representative was the only one who did not sign on an occasion of deep signifi-cance for the Commonwealth'.[13] Churchill sent a personal message to the Union's prime minister, Dr Malan, asking him to reconsider the decision. Nevertheless, the South Africans refused to budge.

Notwithstanding South Africa's actions, the British government was able to incorporate a form of wording into Elizabeth II's accession proclamation which was broadly acceptable to Commonwealth governments. Nevertheless, formal consultations had not been properly concluded by the time of George VI's death, and the new form of words still had to be incorporated into law. During consulta-tions in the early months of the new Queen's reign, the Churchill administration recognized that there were likely to be local variations across the Commonwealth realms. The term 'Defender of the Faith', for example, would be inappropriate in many cases. Yet the British government wished there to be, so far as possible, a generic title adopted throughout the Commonwealth with only minor modifica-tions. The formula Britain proposed was extremely close to the form of words used at the Accession Council on George VI's death.[14] It was hoped that each Com-monwealth country would adopt the title: 'Queen Elizabeth, by the Grace of God, Queen of [their own name], and of Her other Realms and Territories, Head of the Commonwealth [and where appropriate] Defender of the Faith'. In the case of the UK, this would specify 'of the United Kingdom and Northern Ireland and of Her other Realms and Territories'. Representations from de Valera's government that the term 'Northern Ireland' was divisive and should therefore be dropped received short shrift from Whitehall.[15] Canada, New Zealand, and South Africa were initially happy to adopt this formula, with South Africa deleting 'Defender of the Faith'. Australia, however, was keen to include in the title the names of all those independent Commonwealth countries of which Elizabeth was Queen.[16] Alterna-tively, Australia was prepared to accept 'of the United Kingdom of Great Britain and Northern Ireland, Australia and all other Her Realms and Territories Queen'. In either case, Australian Prime Minister Robert Menzies was keen to stress the link with the United Kingdom and the shared laws relating to the succession.[17] The British government was unhappy with both Australian formulations. The longer version would, it was suggested, have required legislation to be passed by all member states, amending the royal title with every addition to the list of indepen-dent Commonwealth monarchies. It would also have served to draw attention to India's status as the only independent member of the Commonwealth that did not owe allegiance to the Crown. Indeed, Britain feared that any explicit mention of the United Kingdom in the royal title would be unacceptable to South Africa as well as to other Commonwealth members.[18] Menzies, however, lobbied St Laurent of Canada during a visit to Ottawa and persuaded him that it would be wrong to drop the reference to the United Kingdom. New Zealand also proved susceptible to this argument. As such, the final form of words for Australia, Canada, and New Zealand, incorporated in the 1953 Act, read, 'Elizabeth II, by the Grace of God of the United Kingdom [Canada/Australia/New Zealand] and her other Realms and Territories Queen, Head of the Commonwealth, Defender of the Faith'. Given South Africa's long history of insisting on the divisibility of the Crown, it is hardly surprising that it could not support this formula. Instead—along with Ceylon—it adopted the shorter form, 'Elizabeth II, Queen of [South Africa/Ceylon] and of her other Realms and Territories, Head of the Commonwealth'. Pakistan, which still owed allegiance to the Crown, but was currently debating its constitutional future, did not even feel able to assent to a form of words which explicitly acknowledged Elizabeth II as its own Queen. Instead, it adopted the form 'Elizabeth II, Queen of the United Kingdom and of her other Realms and Territories, Head of the Commonwealth'.[19]

The Royal Style and Titles Bill of 1953, which incorporated these changes into law, thus allowed for significant differences in the royal title across the Commonwealth. When it was debated in the Commons in March 1953 it was hailed by Patrick Gordon Walker, speaking from the Opposition benches, as the first occasion on which the idea of the divisibility of the Crown had been completely accepted in a formal document.[20] The Churchill government, which had struggled to find a common form of words acceptable to all Commonwealth countries, was less enthusiastic about explicitly conceding the principle of the divisibility of the Crown. Conservative ministers were therefore clearly irritated when one of their own backbenchers rose in the debate in March 1953 to attack the bill. This was to be the first of many powerful interventions by J. Enoch Powell, questioning what he regarded as the constitutional fictions which had attached themselves to the Commonwealth. Powell accused the government of 'formally and deliberately' surrendering the unity of the Crown and replacing it with 'a fortuitous aggregation of a number of separate entities'.[21] He suggested that this had been the logical conclusion of the 1948 British Nationality Act, which had 'removed the status of "subject of the King" as the basis of British nationality, and substituted for allegiance to the Crown the concept of a number—I think it was nine—separate citizenships combined together by statute'.[22] He reserved particular scorn for the title of 'Head of the Commonwealth', suggesting that it was the product of developments—specifically India's deliberate decision to 'cast off allegiance' to the Crown—that had robbed the Commonwealth of the essential guarantee of unity in any polity: that the individual parts would sacrifice themselves in the interests of the whole. As such, in Powell's view, 'this formula "Head of the Commonwealth" and the declaration in which it is inscribed, are essentially a sham. They are essentially something which we have invented to blind ourselves to the reality of the position.'[23]

The irritable response of the Home Secretary, Sir David Maxwell-Fyfe, was that 'it is easy to make difficulties, especially verbal difficulties', a rebuke the *New Statesman* described as being of the sort 'usually uttered only by Emperors to those who draw attention to their absence of clothes'.[24]

THE CORONATION

Preparations for the coronation of Elizabeth II in June 1953 represented a huge bureaucratic undertaking. Gathering together leaders and representatives from around the world, marshalling the large crowds, and choreographing the ceremony itself posed major challenges. Westminster Abbey was closed to visitors for almost a year before the ceremony to allow temporary alterations to take place, including the construction of galleries in the north and south transepts which enabled the Abbey's usual seating capacity of 2,000 to be increased to 8,000.[25] Yet what made the event accessible to a mass audience was not the extra rows of seats vertiginously close to the Abbey's ceiling, but the presence of BBC television cameras broadcasting live to millions of viewers. The ceremony gave a major boost to television ownership in the UK, with the number of licenses doubling to three million in the preceding months.[26] It is hardly surprising then that a recent account of the coronation in the context of English national identity should have stressed the extent to which the themes of 'national rejuvenation and modernity' were prominent in the way it was presented.[27] Indeed, Wendy Webster points out that they had already featured in the then Princess Elizabeth's famous broadcast from Cape Town on her twenty-first birthday in 1947. On that occasion the Princess had spoken of the fact that 'through the inventions of science' she could do what was not possible for any of her ancestors, namely to make her 'solemn act of dedication with the whole Empire listening'. Six years later it was television which was the new symbol of modernity. The announcement the day of the coronation that Edmund Hillary, a New Zealander, had climbed Mount Everest, fuelled talk of a 'new Elizabethan age' which linked the Commonwealth and technological achievement with the buccaneering spirit of an idealized past.[28]

Yet it is easy to forget how much resistance there was to some of the key elements of 'modernization' that characterized the coronation, not least the presence of television cameras. When government records from the time were released in the 1980s it became clear that the Queen herself had (at least initially) opposed the broadcast of the ceremony on television. She was supported in this by the Coronation Joint Executive, chaired by the Duke of Edinburgh. She was also supported by the Archbishop of Canterbury, by Churchill, and ultimately by the Cabinet, which was mindful of 'the importance of avoiding unnecessary strain for Her Majesty and upholding the sanctity of the ceremony'.[29] Only after a public outcry was the decision to exclude the cameras reversed.

Concerns to preserve the 'sanctity' of this 'ancient' ceremony proved a powerful barrier to attempts to introduce any other elements of novelty. This was the challenge that faced those who argued the modern Commonwealth should be properly represented at the coronation. The September 1952 edition of *The Round Table* contained an article entitled 'The Coronation and the Commonwealth'.[30] As with all articles in the journal until 1966, it was anonymous, although the author seems likely to have been Dermot Morrah, the editor of *Round Table*.[31] The article rejected the idea that Britain faced a choice between maintaining the established elements of monarchical ritual and adapting them to accommodate the needs of the 'New Commonwealth'. Indeed, the solution to the dilemma of how to involve the Commonwealth more fully in the coronation, the article suggested, was to revive one of its more ancient traditions, last witnessed in the 'Gothick' corona- tion of George IV, namely the enthronement in Westminster Hall. If the members of the British peerage could play their role in the coronation through this ritual, descended from 'the custom of the Teutonic warbands of the Anglo-Saxon inva- sion', they might be prepared to relinquish their right to sit in the Abbey, thus creating space for representatives of the Commonwealth. The piece suggested a number of ways in which some of these representatives might actively be involved in the ceremony at the Abbey, including carrying the four ceremonial swords used in the investiture, and helping to place the Imperial state crown on the Queen's head.[32] It was also suggested that representatives from every part of the Empire and Commonwealth should perform a common act of allegiance.

Whitehall, however, remained largely unmoved. The matter had already been discussed by a meeting of officials at the Cabinet Office in July chaired by Norman Brook and the idea of making substantive changes to the ceremony to increase the role of the Commonwealth was rejected, just as it had been in 1937.[33] This was due not least to the fear that changes would reawaken controversy about the divisibility of the Crown, leading to the 'serious risk that some Members of the Common- wealth might take the line that they could not participate in the ceremony in London at all' and should instead hold separate ceremonies in their own coun- tries.[34] The Canadian high commissioner had already expressed private objections to any change in the service.

When a delegation from the Conservative backbench Imperial Affairs Committee approached the Secretary of State for Commonwealth Relations, Lord Salisbury, in October about the matter, Salisbury reiterated the point that any enhanced Com- monwealth role in the ceremony was likely to meet objections from 'some of the Members, especially the Union of South Africa, having regard to their views on the divisibility of the Crown'.[35] He also suggested that any such change would exclude India and serve to draw attention to its republican status. Salisbury suggested that an enthronement ceremony in Westminster Hall 'would place an intolerable burden on the Queen to attend both the Enthronement and the Coronation on the same day'.

If Commonwealth governments had resisted incorporation in the coronation ceremony, the Commonwealth itself was represented in some of the visual imagery of the event. Queen Elizabeth's coronation dress, designed by Norman Hartnell, was decorated with the floral emblems of eleven Commonwealth countries.[36] Following the ceremony, an exhibition containing the dress and other coronation robes and regalia toured Canada, Australia, and New Zealand. A pamphlet, *Most Excellent Majesty*, produced by the British Central Office of Information in 1953, was chosen to accompany the exhibition. It was written, appropriately enough, by Dermot Morrah.

As a concession to those calling for a greater Imperial presence in the coronation, it was decided that a number of colonial representatives should be given seats in the Abbey near enough to the throne to allow them to play an active part in the acclamation of the Queen. At the insistence of the Commonwealth Relations

Office (CRO), however, it was stipulated that the colonial and Commonwealth representatives should be kept separate in the Abbey, and that the former should not be given superior places to the latter.[37]

The desire of the British government to make clear distinctions between the levels of constitutional progress achieved by individual colonies created some intricate problems of protocol. In particular, Maltese reaction to the arrangements for the coronation came close to sparking a crisis. In line with the precedent of the previous coronation of 1937, the Maltese government, in common with that of the other colonial territories, did not initially receive a formal invitation. Instead, the governor was invited to nominate two representatives of the Maltese community as a whole to attend the ceremony.[38] It was to be left up to the prime minister of Malta, Dr Borg Olivier, whether he wished one or both of the representatives to be members of his government. Nor was it originally intended that representatives of the Maltese nobility should be invited. Again, this followed the precedent of 1937 when the Malta nobility had been excluded, even though they had been represented at the two previous coronations. The governor of Malta, Sir Gerald Creasy, urged London to change its mind on both points. He was particularly anxious that an invitation to the coronation should be sent to Olivier and his wife, predicting that if one was not forthcoming, 'the Prime Minister may do very little as regards our local celebrations and, in particular, may ask the assembly to vote a quite inadequate sum for them'.[39] He pointed out that since 1937 Malta had achieved self-governing status and that the Maltese prime minister and his wife had received a special invitation to the Queen's wedding in 1947.

The issue of the Maltese nobility was settled by the Queen herself, who had lived in Malta for periods between 1949 and 1951 when her husband had been stationed there as a naval officer. Members of the nobility had lobbied the Duke of Edinburgh on the matter when he visited the island in 1952, and he undertook to raise it with the Queen. She decided that she wished to revert to the pre-1937 arrangements, and two seats were duly made available for representatives of the nobility.[40] In order to address Maltese sensitivities on the other matters of concern, a compromise was recommended by the Coronation Joint Committee and approved by the Queen. As a result, Olivier was informed in December that the Queen would welcome his presence at the Coronation. He and his wife would be treated as 'Distinguished Guests' and provided with seats in the Abbey. They would, however, come to London on their own account and at their own expense.[41] This did not, however, settle matters. When further details of the ceremony were released in late March 1953, Olivier questioned why he had not been included in the procession of Commonwealth prime ministers to and from the Abbey, and why he was to be seated among colonial representatives. He was not satisfied with the explanation that this was because Malta was not a full member of the Commonwealth and demanded that he be treated on a par with the prime minister of Southern Rhodesia. The formidable Maltese politician Mabel Strickland made explicit the implicit racial element in Olivier's objections, telling the acting governor that the Maltese resented being 'lumped in with the African colonies'.[42]

Olivier also identified an even more esoteric source of grievance: the arrangements for flying the flag of Malta at the ceremony. Olivier had demanded that only one flag be flown to represent Malta, namely, the 'national' Maltese flag of red and white emblazoned with a George Cross. This had, however, never formally been recognized by the Crown as the flag of Malta and it was usual on ceremonial occasions to represent Malta by a blue ensign bearing the Maltese crest. Olivier was not satisfied by the British government's response that both flags would be flown at the coronation. On 11 May, he wrote to the acting governor, announcing his intention to boycott the coronation and cancelling the nomination of Malta's two other representatives at the ceremony. On the same day, he informed the Maltese legislative assembly of the action he was taking, and won a vote of support.[43]

The issue was discussed by the British Cabinet on 19 May, and a compromise was agreed and put to Olivier by Churchill over the telephone: only the Maltese 'national' flag would be flown, and Olivier would be seated with the Commonwealth prime ministers in the abbey and invited along with them to Commonwealth functions in London. This was justified on the basis not of Malta's constitutional status, but on her wartime record, which had been recognized with the award of the George Cross.[44] Accommodating Olivier in his new position in the abbey next to the prime minister of Southern Rhodesia meant, according to John Colville, reorganizing 'nearly the whole seating in the choir'.[45] Nevertheless, the package proved sufficient to persuade Olivier to lift his boycott of the ceremony.[46] When, however, upon his arrival in Britain, Olivier continued to raise objections about matters of protocol, Churchill's patience finally snapped. He told the Colonial Secretary, Oliver Lyttelton, 'If after all the trouble we have taken he threatens to go back to Malta, we should help him in every way. I do not wish to be troubled with this matter again and leave it for you to decide. On no account let the Queen be burdened with any aspects of it.'[47]

A similar set of problems was raised by the question of the Gold Coast's representation at the coronation, although the far more emollient reaction of the territory's leader, Kwame Nkrumah, served to avert any crisis. Since March 1952, as part of a package of constitutional reforms agreed the previous month, Nkrumah had been formally acknowledged as the prime minister of the Gold Coast. Yet since the Gold Coast was not yet a fully independent member of the Commonwealth, he was not entitled to attend Commonwealth prime ministers' meetings. A Commonwealth prime ministers' meeting had been arranged to coincide with the coronation and it was feared that it would be awkward if Nkrumah were to attend the coronation celebrations and yet be excluded from this political gathering. The difficulty was compounded by the fact that Southern Rhodesia, although formally a Crown colony, had traditionally been granted a seat at Commonwealth prime ministers' meetings. For the Southern Rhodesian prime minister, Sir Godfrey Huggins, to be allowed to attend this meeting in 1953, while Nkrumah was excluded would, it was feared, encourage criticism in the press and in parliament that the distinction was being made on racial grounds. As such, the Colonial Office had originally attempted to dissuade Nkrumah from coming to London for the coronation.[48]

Reviewing this position, however, the Colonial Office decided that the dangers of trying to keep Nkrumah away from the coronation probably outweighed the threat of embarrassment if he did attend. It was noted that the Gold Coast, although a major contributor to the sterling area, was being denied ministerial representation at a forthcoming Commonwealth economic conference. Were Nkrumah also to be denied an invitation to the coronation, this might, it was feared, 'leave in his mind the feeling that he was Prime Minister on sufferance and only in the Commonwealth on sufferance, which might seriously affect our relations with the Gold Coast at a later stage when the Gold Coast is closer to full independence'.[49] Ironically, Olivier's insistence on attending the coronation made Nkrumah's attendance less problematical. As the Colonial Office noted, it would be easier to defend Nkrumah's exclusion from the Commonwealth prime ministers' meeting if this prohibition also applied to another prime minister (and a white one at that—although it was not felt necessary to spell this point out).[50] In the event, after some prevarication, Nkrumah decided not to go to London on the grounds that, according to the governor of the Gold Coast, Sir Charles Arden-Clarke, although he understood the reason for his exclusion from the Commonwealth prime ministers' meeting, he wished to avoid 'any situation that might call public attention to the inferior status of his Premiership'.[51]

The question of Kenyan representation at the ceremony was complicated by the severe racial tensions arising from—and indeed predating—the declaration of the emergency the previous year in response to the Mau Mau insurgency. Kenya was originally allocated four representatives. The governor, Sir Evelyn Baring, asked, however, for a fifth so that separate representation could be granted to the territory's 'five different communities': European, Asian Muslim, Asian non-Muslim, Arab, and African.[52] The Colonial Office was reluctant to increase the number of official representatives, for fear of disrupting the arrangements already made with other territories. It was agreed, however, that a fifth Kenyan should be allowed a seat in the abbey on non-official terms, and Baring put forward Sheihk Mbarak Ali. The Colonial Office was therefore somewhat perturbed to learn that of the four other representatives nominated by the governor, two were European, one an Indian Muslim, and the fourth an African. The need to privilege the Europeans clearly overrode the objective of 'equal' representation for Kenya's different communities. In February 1953 Baring requested that a place be made available for a second African. Paradoxically, however, this turned out to be a further move to appease Kenya's European settlers. The governor explained to London that there had been considerable European criticism when it was announced that Muchohi Gikonyo would be the African representative at the coronation. This was on the grounds that 'he is a Kikuyu Member of the Legislative Council who has never spoken strongly in support of the fight against Mau Mau'.[53] Baring was reluctant to exclude Gikonyo, since his government was about to arrest Walter Odede, the moderate Luo acting president of the Kenya African Union (KAU), and he did not want to be seen to be pursuing a vendetta against African political leaders. He therefore proposed adding to the Kenya representatives 'a prominent Luo such as Paul [sic] Mboya'. This would, Baring explained, be 'a friendly gesture to the Luo at a time when they will probably be upset by Odede's detention'. As with the governor's previous request, the Colonial Office agreed, on the basis that the additional representative be included on non-official terms.[54]

One of the more bizarre controversies that arose from the seating plans at the abbey related to Pitcairn Island in the Pacific. The coronation supplement to the *Sydney Morning Herald* boasted that one of the most 'glamorous' colonial guests lending 'Oriental and exotic spendour' to the ceremony would be a Miss Jan Christian, the self-styled 'Princess of Pitcairn Island'. This report provoked an indignant letter from John Christian, chief magistrate on Pitcairn Island to the governor of Fiji, complaining that—as a resident of Tahiti who had never set foot on Pitcairn—Miss Christian had no right to the title, and that if there were to be a Princess of Pitcairn 'there are many girls on the island who are more entitled to the honour'.[55] Forwarding the letter to the Colonial Office, the governor of Fiji explained that, although Miss Christian was indeed a descendent of Fletcher Christian, her branch of the family had been resident in Tahiti for over 100 years. The resentment of the Picairners had been compounded by the fact that, whereas the 'Princess' had been allotted a seat in the abbey, the chief magistrate had only been offered a seat in the stands on the route of the procession.[56]

The complexities and sensitivities generated by the Commonwealth at the time of the coronation also proved perplexing for those seeking to celebrate the event in more modest ways. The BBC planned to mark Empire Day on 24 May 1953 with a children's radio broadcast originally to be entitled 'The Queen's Dominions'. This was intended to illustrate, through dialogue and music, the ways in which children across the Commonwealth would celebrate the coronation, and to look forward to the Queen's forthcoming tour. The producer, Gwen Pain, sought advice from the Overseas Liaison Officer at Bush House about a number of issues. While she was keen to secure contributions from Canada, Australia, and New Zealand, she wondered about whether India, Pakistan, and Ceylon should be involved, explaining, 'I don't want to upset anyone's constitutional rights to be included under the title of "The Queen's Dominions"'.[57] In the case of the South African contribution, she was uncertain 'whether we should risk asking for Afrikaans [*sic*] and other European children to have a Coronation get-together in one programme or whether we should ask for British emigrant children to do a piece from there'. The question of whether the newer Commonwealth members should be included was resolved by changing the title of the programme from 'The Queen's Dominions' to 'The Queen's Commonwealth'. In the case of South Africa, a judicious ethnic balance was achieved through the inclusion of music by Elgar, two songs in Afrikaans, and a musical tribute by 'an old Zulu gentleman'.[58]

Pain's reaction to the programme revealed both a rather condescending attitude towards the Commonwealth contributions and faint amusement at their effusive expressions of loyalty to the Queen. In the Canadian case, Pain felt that the standard of singing was 'pretty low' and commented that the 'Coronation Pledge' recited by the young participants (which included a promise to 'follow the leadership of Canada's beloved Queen towards a new and better world of peace and brotherhood') was 'embarrassing to English ears but acceptable as a Canadian contribution'.[59] Ceylon provided 'not at all an exciting contribution'. From Malta, the choral standard was 'not high but perfectly acceptable'. Australia provided a 'very appropriate song not particularly well sung'. In the midst of this,

India received some rather grudging praise tinged, one might suspect, with a hint of latent republicanism:

> A very curious contribution—a group of children singing albeit rather beautifully, a song from the Ramayana . . . At first sight this contribution seemed to be quite outside the run of the programme and to bear no relation to what we wanted, but when I came to fit it into the total programme I found it after all a rather charming exception to the general run of extreme loyalty to the Queen. To anyone familiar with India's position in the Commonwealth it was quite understandable.[60]

Yet for all the well-choreographed expressions of loyalty that accompanied the coronation, as Commonwealth leaders gathered in London it was clear that the trend towards republicanism was growing. A keen and extremely well-informed observer of this process was the Irish ambassador in London, F. H. Boland. Although obviously not present at the official sessions of the 1953 Commonwealth prime ministers' meeting itself, Boland was able to use the gathering to have private meetings with an impressive number of Commonwealth leaders. He reported back to Dublin that it was now certain Pakistan would become a republic. In Boland's talks with the Pakistani prime minister, Mohammad Ali Bogra, the latter was apparently evasive about what this would mean for Pakistan's relationship with the Commonwealth. Boland recorded that the Pakistani prime minister 'asked me questions about our association with the Commonwealth prior to the repeal of the External Relations Act—although, indeed, he seemed to have a pretty competent knowledge of this subject himself'.[61] The notion that some of the existing Commonwealth realms might be looking to Ireland as a model for a republican or quasi-republican form of association with the Commonwealth seemed to be confirmed by Boland's discussions with the South African finance minister, Nicolaas Havenga. According to Boland, Havenga talked about 'the policies adopted by the Taoiseach in the past and the Taoiseach's views about the Republic of Ireland Act, 1948. He displayed a close and accurate knowledge of the latter.'

THE ROYAL TOUR OF THE COMMONWEALTH, 1953–4

The royal tour of the Commonwealth undertaken by the Queen and the Duke of Edinburgh in 1953–4 in the wake of the coronation provided an opportunity to reaffirm the durability of the British Empire and give substance to the relatively new title of Head of the Commonwealth. It represented what turned out to be a brief period of Imperial self-confidence between the crisis years of 1947–8—which witnessed the loss of India, the abandonment of the Palestine Mandate, and the departure of Ireland from the Commonwealth—and the Suez Crisis of 1956.[62] The tour lasted six months and covered 40,000 miles. It took in Bermuda, the Bahamas, Jamaica, Belize, Fiji, Tonga, New Zealand, Australia, Ceylon, Aden, Uganda, Malta, and Gibraltar.[63]

As with the coronation itself, the royal tour served a number of different political purposes and varied in its character according to the interest groups and territories involved. As Anne Spry Rush has noted, the visit to Jamaica in November 1953 saw elaborate displays of loyalty on the part of the territory's political elite for the Queen. Given that the Queen's British administration had only weeks before ousted the elected prime minister of one of Jamaica's neighbours—British Guiana, which earlier in the year had voted into office the radical People's Progressive Party led by Cheddi Jagan—this could be regarded as a placatory act of obeisance to the Imperial power. Yet the territory's leaders were also, Rush suggests, acknowledging the genuine affection with which the Queen was regarded by the Jamaican people, an affection that was to endure long after independence.[64] At the same time, they were keen to place their own particular political 'spin' on that popular enthusiasm. *Public Opinion*, the Jamaican newspaper that supported Norman Manley's left-wing People's National Party, suggested in the wake of the visit that the monarchy's popularity in the UK emerged from its position at the head of a democratic system and that, in Jamaica, any deviation from democratic ideals could 'only harm the very traditions which the visit of Queen Elizabeth II is intended to symbolize and entrench'.[65]

The Queen's visit to New Zealand provided an opportunity to stress the concrete role of the Crown within the country's constitution. She held a meeting of the Privy Council in Government House in Wellington with the New Zealand prime minister performing the role of 'acting Lord President' of the council. She also opened the New Zealand parliament in its centennial year.[66] The symbolism of all this was not lost on the British high commissioner, Sir Geoffrey Scoones, who commended the visit for its reaffirmation of the Crown as a symbol of Imperial unity (at least among those countries that were 'fundamentally of British stock'). He reported to London that the physical presence of the Queen 'in regal splendour and dignity' had 'put the United Kingdom in its proper constitutional perspective as only one of (even if still pre-eminent among) several kingdoms owing allegiance to the Crown'.[67]

In a highly symbolic move, the Queen made her 1953 Christmas Day broadcast from Auckland in New Zealand. This provided an opportunity to reaffirm not just the unity but also, in a sense, the 'Britishness' of the Commonwealth. She began by noting that although she had 'travelled some thousands of miles', she found herself 'completely and most happily at home'.[68] It was, she noted, the first time a Queen of England had travelled around the world. But the purpose of the tour was a more serious one: 'to show that the Crown is not merely an abstract symbol of our unity but a personal and living bond between you and me'. Here was another sense in which—like the Christmas Day message itself—modern technology was supposedly helping to enhance the familial links of the Commonwealth, with the monarchy as its focus. Yet there was also a pointed, almost defensive, denial of the association between the Commonwealth and Imperialism, which echoed her father's wartime broadcast on Empire Day 1940. The Commonwealth, she claimed,

> bears no resemblance to the Empires of the past. It is an entirely new conception— built on the highest qualities of the spirit of man; friendship, loyalty, and the desire for freedom and peace. To that new conception of an equal partnership of nations and races I shall give my heart and soul every day of my life.

The royal party arrived in Australia on 3 February 1954. As the self-proclaimed republican historian Jane Connors has noted, the Queen's tour of Australia is something of a disappointment for scholars searching for a hidden history of anti-monarchist dissent.[69] Nor can it be easily written off as a case of conservative manipulation of public opinion. The astonishing statistics presented at the time have stood up well to more recent scrutiny. As such, it seems reasonable to suggest that between 6 and 7 million Australians in 1954 out of a total of 9 million, or around 75 per cent of the population, turned out to see the royal couple at least once. During an eight-week stay, they made 207 car journeys and 33 air flights, keeping up to 5 engagements a day.[70] Instances of genuine protest at the royal tour are extremely difficult to identify. Even the Australian Communist Party failed to mount a con-certed challenge to the prevailing loyalist mood—although this may have owed something to an ultimately unsuccessful prosecution of three party members for an article critical of the coronation which had appeared in the *Communist Review* the previous year.[71]

Echoing the comments of Scoones in New Zealand, the British high commis-sioner in Australia, Sir Stephen Holmes, stressed the value of the physical presence of the monarch in providing ordinary Australians with a personal sense of the significance of the Commonwealth relationship. His despatches dwelt on the importance of the royal visit in shaping a sense of Australian national identity, particularly among children and immigrants. A regular feature of post-war reports from British High Commissions in the older Commonwealth realms was a concern that non-British immigration to these countries might loosen bonds of loyalty to the monarchy. In the case of the 1954 royal visit to Australia, Holmes confidently predicted that recent immigrants 'will have been immensely impressed and stirred by the evidence of what the Crown means to us in the British Commonwealth; from whatever country they come they will, I believe, now feel that Australia "has something" and something for them, which they did not realise before'.[72]

This optimism about the development of a form of Australian national identity with the monarchy at its core was of particular significance given Australia's strategic value to the UK and British concerns about the creeping 'Americaniza-tion' of the country. The Queen's tour had been preceded by a series of visits by British ministers, including the Commonwealth Secretary, Lord Swinton, and Churchill's scientific guru, Lord Cherwell. One reason for this renewed interest in Australia was its role in the development of UK atomic weapons technology. During the visit by Swinton and Cherwell two atomic bombs had been tested.[73] In the course of the tour, the Duke of Edinburgh pointedly visited the Woomera rocket range, an engagement that the Australian press duly described as 'emphasis-ing the interdependence of British peoples' and South Australia's 'unique role in Imperial defence'.[74] On the issue of Americanization, Holmes took some comfort from the fact that Australia's prime minister, Robert Menzies, claimed to dislike the huge memorial to the Americans who had died in the defence of Australia during the Second World War which the Queen opened in the course of her visit.[75]

A practical question arising from the divisibility of the Crown surfaced during the Queen's tour of Australia, one that would periodically raise its head again in subsequent years: what rights did the British government have to advise the Queen on matters relating to her safety when she was visiting another realm? The dilemma arose because of an outbreak of poliomyelitis in Western Australia, which the royal party was due to visit on 26 March. The Commonwealth Secretary, Lord Swinton, told the Cabinet that the expert advice he had received indicated that the risk to the Queen was 'very small'. Nevertheless, he reported that he had sent a private telegram to the governor of Western Australia asking for further information and had copied this to the British high commissioner in Canberra.[76] Both Swinton and Lord Salisbury noted that this was essentially a matter for the Menzies government and the Cabinet clearly felt that they had no right to advise the Queen not to go to Western Australia. Salisbury suggested instead that Churchill should write to Menzies promising his support if the Australian government decided to cancel the visit. The Cabinet adopted this proposal.

The route home, taking in Ceylon, Uganda, and Gibraltar, raised potentially more serious political problems. In September 1953 Dudley Senanayake, the prime minister of Ceylon (known from 1972 as Sri Lanka), warned Lord Swinton that Communist-inspired unrest in his country and probable criticism of its likely cost might make it necessary for him to advise that the Queen's visit be cancelled.[77] Swinton urged him to allow the visit to go ahead, suggesting that its cancellation would play into the hands of the Communists.[78] Nevertheless, Senanayake retained his doubts, claiming that it might allow his opponents to whip up unrest and hence undermine his efforts to keep Ceylon in the Commonwealth.[79] The CRO suggested to the Palace that if the visit was cancelled it would be best to explain this in terms of financial stringency, just as the cancellation of a planned coronation Durbar in India in 1938 had been justified on the grounds that the King 'would not be justified in imposing any additional burden on the existing revenues of India at a time when calls on them ... are already heavy'.[80] Britain continued to press Senanayake over the matter, who wavered sufficiently for the British government to assume that the visit would go ahead after all.[81] Senanayake finally resigned from office in October and his successor, Sir John Kotelawala, swiftly confirmed that he wished the visit to go ahead.[82]

Shortly after Kotelawala's government confirmed that the visit would take place, however, the new prime minister became embroiled in what appeared to be a bad-tempered row with the Governor General, Lord Soulbury. Towards the end of October, Kotelawala's cabinet decided that, although the British national anthem would be played when the Queen was visiting Ceylon, on other official occasions when the Governor General was representing the Queen the Ceylon national anthem would be used and the Union flag would not be flown.[83] Soulbury appears to have queried this decision. The press in Ceylon and the UK carried what purported to be the contents of Kotelawala's response to the Governor General. In his note, the prime minister claimed that the people of Ceylon were not able to understand why, since they lived in an independent country, they should have 'a foreign Governor General', 'an English flag' and 'an English national anthem'.[84] Kotalawala subsequently denied the accuracy of the press reports, which had resulted in headlines in the UK suggesting that Soulbury and Britain more generally had been snubbed.[85]

In the event, the royal visit to Ceylon was generally regarded as one of the highlights of the royal tour. Notwithstanding the problems that preceded the Queen's arrival, in the years immediately following independence Ceylon made a particular point of stressing its loyalty to Britain and to the Crown. Part of this, as Kumarasingham suggests, may have been owing to a desire on the part of the country's Anglophile ruling elite to construct a counterweight to their potentially over-mighty neighbour, India. The choreography of the Queen's visit in 1954 was intended to stress these bonds of loyalty. She opened both houses of parliament in a ceremony that sought consciously to echo the state opening of the Westminster parliament and, at the insistence of Kotalawala's cabinet, she did so wearing her heavy coronation robes.[86] Given the way in which Ceylon sought to position itself in relation to the UK, it is perhaps telling that issues of protocol around the royal visit were still capable of generating tensions.

The visit to Uganda also had the potential to create political difficulties. In 1953, the governor, Sir Andrew Cohen, had deposed and exiled the Kabaka of Buganda, the traditional ruler of the largest of Uganda's kingdoms inhabited by its most populous ethnic group. The Kabaka's offence had been to demand the secession of Buganda from the Protectorate. A case testing the legality of the governor's actions was before the Ugandan high court, making it impossible to appoint a new kabaka before the Queen's arrival in the territory at the end of April. She was due to spend the first day of her visit in the capital, Entebbe, and the second in Kampala. Both were in Buganda. In January 1954 Buganda's traditional parliament, the Lukiko, had passed a resolution asking for the Queen's visit to be postponed on the grounds that their people would not be able to give her a suitable welcome in the absence of a kabaka. The following month, the Secretary of State for the Colonies, Oliver Lyttelton, told the Cabinet it was Cohen's view that the Queen's visit to Uganda should go ahead and that there would be no implications for her security. He was also confident that 'there is no likelihood of embarrassing demonstrations during the visit or other embarrassment to Her Majesty'.[87] He felt that the visit was 'just what the Protectorate now needs' and that its cancellation would have 'a very adverse effect on the political situation'. The Cabinet agreed the Queen should be advised to go ahead with the trip.

The Queen's visit to Gibraltar of 1954 was opposed by the government of General Franco in Spain. It raised the issue in September 1953 and the following January the Spanish ambassador called on the British Foreign Secretary, Anthony Eden, and reportedly demanded that the visit be cancelled.[88] This request was firmly dismissed by the British government. It has been suggested that the Franco government's bellicosity was encouraged by a defence pact between Spain and the USA signed in September 1953 which allowed the Americans to construct a series of bases on Spanish territory. In abandoning their neutrality they may have hoped, among other things, for US support for their claims over Gibraltar.[89] Previous visits by Edward VII in 1903 and George V in 1911 had passed without incident, and planned visits by George VI in 1943 and 1951 had not been accompanied by significant protests. In the months preceding the Queen's visit in 1954, however, there was an appreciable ratcheting up of anti-British rhetoric in the Spanish press reiterating Spain's claim to Gibraltar. At the end of January 1954 it was announced that a planned visit to Spanish ports by the British navy had been cancelled in the light of deteriorating relations.[90] The Spanish Ministry of Information pointedly noted that territories including British Guiana and Cyprus had been omitted from the Queen's itinerary because of their political sensitivity and suggested that similar considerations should have excluded Gibraltar from the route of the tour.[91]

In the light of this growing agitation the governor of Gibraltar, Sir Gordon MacMillan, committed a major *faux pas* when, without clearing it first with the Cabinet or the Palace, he issued a statement claiming that although the circumstances did not allow him officially to invite 'any of our Spanish friends', he nevertheless wished 'to extend a warm welcome to any Spaniards ... who wish to see the Queen and for that reason I do not propose to close the frontier'.[92] The suggestion that the border with Spain would be open at the time of the Queen's visit concerned the Colonial Office, which felt that the implications of this action should have been properly explored before any statement was made. The governor was recalled to London to explain himself. Churchill seems to have been particularly upset by his statement, especially his welcome to Spanish visitors. According to the Cabinet Secretary's notebooks, Churchill complained that the Spanish were 'v[ery] excitable people' and that the governor had been guilty of 'Bravado at [the] Queen's expense'.[93] These concerns were no doubt reinforced in March when the leaders of the British Liberal and Labour parties received letters threatening the Queen's life if she set foot in Gibraltar.[94] In the event, as the Queen's visit in May approached, security precautions on the border were stricter than they had been during the Second World War, with the 12,000 Spanish workers who passed daily into Gibraltar being subjected to intensive checks, leading to long queues.[95] Spain closed its consulate in Gibraltar at the beginning of May and closed the border for the two days of the Queen's visit.

Given the perceived threat from Spain, the people of Gibraltar were keen to use the occasion as a chance to display their loyalty to the Crown. This was, incidentally, an opportunity denied to the Falkland islanders the following decade, when their territory was excluded from the itinerary of the royal tour of South America in 1968 for fear of offending Argentina.[96] Yet the symbolism of the visit lay not only in the Gibraltarians' reaffirmation of their desire to maintain the connection with Great Britain, but with Britain's own ability to preside over such an event in the face of threats of disruption. The very presence of Prince Charles and Princess Anne in Gibraltar to greet their parents took on a particular significance in this context. *The Daily Express* noted, 'So much for the efforts of the hotheads to scare the Queen away from the Rock of Gibraltar. She not only came ashore herself today but she allowed the children to come too.'[97]

As has already been suggested, for all the intricate matters of protocol which had to be negotiated as a consequence of constitutional changes across the Commonwealth, the coronation and the Royal Tour of 1953–4 represented in many ways the zenith of the UK's post-war Imperial self-confidence. Winds of change were, however, about to alter the character of the Commonwealth out of all recognition, creating new challenges for the monarchy.

5

Winds of Change and the Royal Family

SUEZ

On 24 October 1956 an extraordinary document was signed by the Israeli prime minister, David Ben-Gurion, the French foreign minister, Christian Pineau, and a senior official at the British Foreign Office, Patrick Dean, who was standing in for his secretary of state, Selwyn Lloyd. It summarized the result of secret talks that had been taking place between British, French, and Israeli representatives in the Parisian suburb of Sèvres over the previous three days. The so-called Sèvres Protocol contained the following key elements: on 29 October Israel would attack Egypt with the objective of reaching the Suez Canal. The following day, Britain and France would call on both sides to cease hostilities and demand that Israel withdraw its troops ten miles to the east of the canal and that Egypt accept the temporary occupation of key positions on the canal by Anglo-French forces. If either side refused, Anglo-French forces would intervene. In the event of an Egyptian refusal, intervention would take place on the morning of 31 October. The terms of this agreement would be kept secret by all parties.

Britain had been planning for an attack on Egypt since its leader, Abdel Nasser, had announced the nationalization of the Suez Canal in July 1956. The prospect of the use of force against Nasser had already proved a deeply divisive one among senior British ministers, officials, and military chiefs. The additional element of collusion with the Israelis as a means of justifying the operation to international opinion, which became a key part of British plans from the middle of October, added a sinister and scandalous dimension to the invasion. British prime minister Anthony Eden, one of the architects of the Sèvres Protocol, would subsequently attempt to conceal it from many of his ministerial colleagues and senior officials, would lie about it to Parliament, and display an almost pathological determination to deny its existence for the rest of his life. The invasion itself, which duly followed the Israeli attack, was brought to an ignominious halt by pressure from the Eisenhower administration, furious that Britain had embarked upon such a reckless act during an American election campaign. Eden would rapidly resign, citing ill health, and be replaced as prime minister by Harold Macmillan. The shabby subterfuge surrounding Suez, as much as its shambolic aftermath, has made it a symbol of the collapse of British global power in the post-war era. The role of the Palace in the affair remains obscure, but it seems unlikely that the Queen and her senior courtiers would have been unaffected by the shock Suez delivered to the UK's sense of Imperial self-confidence.

In terms of the Queen's knowledge of and reaction to the Suez operation, certain points can be stated with some confidence. Her immediate circle was divided over the issue. Her private secretary, Sir Michael Adeane, supported the invasion while her deputy and assistant private secretaries, Martin Charteris and Edward Ford, opposed it. Both Charteris, an ex-head of military intelligence in Palestine, and Ford, a former tutor to Prince Farouk of Egypt, brought to the issue a keen awareness of the damage that might be done to Britain's relations with the Arab world.[1] More significantly still, Prince Philip's uncle, Lord Louis Mountbatten, as First Sea Lord was privy to the developing plans for the invasion of Egypt. Mountbatten found himself increasingly uncomfortable with Eden's policy and in August 1956 drafted but did not send a letter of resignation to the prime minister.[2] Eden's biographer was critical of Mountbatten for not making his objections known within the Egypt Committee, which was coordinating the planning process.[3] It would have been extremely surprising, however, had he not impressed them upon the Queen, with whom he had regular contact. Indeed, Martin Charteris later recalled:

> Dickie [Mountbatten] was talking to her . . . He wanted her to know what he thought about it—he was saying something like, 'I think they are being absolutely lunatic'. He was typically devious. He didn't mean it as a message to be conveyed directly to Eden, but hoped she would pass it on to him as her own thoughts.[4]

Hugh Thomas's account of the Suez affair suggests that, specifically, just as British ground forces were about to go into action 'Mountbatten became angry and spoke to the Queen who apparently then presented Eden with the suggestion that, before he committed the nation to this extension of the battle, he should consult [the leader of the Opposition Hugh] Gaitskell.'[5]

The Queen had other sources of information on the build-up to the Suez invasion. As Charteris reminded Ben Pimlott, she received 'all the Foreign Office telegrams and papers', and in that respect was probably better informed than some members of the Cabinet. She was, therefore, as Ford recalled, able to gain a sense of the unease felt within the Foreign Office about Eden's policy, especially from British representatives in the Middle East.[6] She also had direct access to the views of the prime ministers of her Commonwealth realms. In September 1956 Robert Menzies, the Australian prime minister, briefed her in person on his talks with Nasser. Menzies himself was broadly supportive of the British position, but the issue of Suez was a major source of division within the Commonwealth, with most other governments adopting a highly critical stance. In September 1956 Eden's Secretary of State for Defence, Sir Walter Monckton, recorded his own severe reservations about the use of force, mentioning the risk that India and Ceylon might leave the Commonwealth.[7] This in itself is likely to have been a major source of concern to the Queen. It certainly placed her in a highly sensitive and potentially embarrassing position in terms of how far she should disclose to any of her prime ministers information she had received from other sources. In the wake of the invasion, she was also clearly aware of the damage that had been done to Anglo-American relations. Churchill forwarded to her a letter he had received from

President Eisenhower which was highly critical of the operation. In response, she expressed the hope to Churchill that 'the present feeling that this country and America are not seeing eye-to-eye will soon be speedily replaced by even stronger ties between us'.[8]

The question remains as to both what was the Queen's personal view about Suez and how candid was Eden with her about the full extent of the collusion with France and Israel. Mountbatten appears to have been one of two sources behind an article published by Robert Lacey in the *Sunday Times* in 1976 which implied that the Queen had been strongly opposed to the Suez invasion but was unable to prevent it.[9] In his subsequent biography of the Queen Lacey claimed, on the basis of information from 'at least one of [Eden's] close colleagues' (again appearing to point to Mountbatten), that the Queen had not been given a full account of the events leading up to the Sèvres agreement.[10] In his vigilant attempts to police the history of the Suez operation Eden, by then Lord Avon, tackled Sir Martin Charteris about the matter (perhaps suspecting that he was another source) and dismissed Mountbatten as 'ga-ga [and] a congenital liar'.[11] Nevertheless, Piers Brendon and Philip Whitehead claim that a letter from the Queen to Mountbatten in her handwriting 'confirms his story but has been kept out of the public domain'.[12] One of Pimlott's anonymous sources suggested that the Queen 'believed Eden was mad'. Charteris, who was prepared to speak on the record, did not go as far as this but did claim in a British television documentary broadcast in 1994 that she was 'personally worried' about Suez and that the 'basic dishonesty of the whole thing' was part of the trouble.[13] He also speculated that the Queen might have said to Eden 'are you sure you are being wise?'[14] Eden himself rejected any suggestion that the Queen was opposed to the operation but did, tellingly, admit 'nor would I claim that she was pro-Suez'.[15] He also claimed that she had been properly briefed, saying she 'understood what we were doing very well'. On this latter point she would certainly have been aware of the planning for a possible military operation that had been going on since the nationalization of the Suez Canal in July 1956. Furthermore, when the operation began the Palace was supplied with detailed intelligence material from MI6 and GCHQ on its progress and international reactions to it. This included attempts to gauge whether the Soviet Union would respond militarily. On 22 November, Adeane passed the Queen's thanks to those who had produced the intelligence bulletins 'for the trouble taken during the last two anxious weeks to keep her supplied with up to date information'.[16]

A more intriguing and still largely unanswerable question is how detailed a picture she received of plans for secretly coordinated action between the UK, France, and Israel. Eden had discussed the outlines of possible collusion in a meeting with French representatives on 14 October. Two days later he provided an informal briefing on the plan to an inner circle of ministers.[17] Over the weekend of 20–21 October, just before the Foreign Secretary was dispatched to Paris to agree terms with the French and Israelis at Sèvres, Eden again consulted this inner ministerial group and the Cabinet Secretary, Norman Brook.[18] It would be surprising had Eden or Brook not taken steps to keep the Palace informed of these vital developments (if only informally). How explicit that information was is another matter. Notoriously, when the full Cabinet met on the morning of 25 October it does not appear to have been informed of the secret deal that had just been agreed at Sèvres.[19] Equally notoriously, Eden attempted, unsuccessfully, to have all copies of the Sèvres protocol destroyed.[20] Downing Street also insisted on the suppression of copies of Foreign Office telegrams that provided hints that collusion had taken place.[21] In short then, we cannot be at all confident that Eden would have been absolutely candid with the Palace about the level of collusion. Nor is it clear, despite the large quantity of documents to which the Queen potentially had access, that they would have revealed the full extent of the conspiracy. If and when more extensive records are made available to historians about Suez and the Palace, it will be important to see *precisely* what the Queen was actually told. In the meantime, the balance of anecdotal evidence suggests strongly that she was not a supporter of the invasion of Egypt and may well have had very serious reservations about it. This may, in turn, have shaped her attitude to the 'wind of change' which forced the pace of British decolonization in the early 1960s. There were certainly signs that she was more willing than her father to accept the need to reach an accommodation with the forces of colonial nationalism.

THE QUEEN AND THE WIND OF CHANGE

Speaking to the South African Parliament in Cape Town on 3 February 1960, Harold Macmillan famously remarked that the 'wind of change is blowing through this continent and whether we like it or not, this growth of national consciousness is a political fact. We must all accept it as a fact, and our national policies must take account of it.' It is surely significant that the Queen took the unusual step of indicating her personal approval of Macmillan's words. Philip de Zulueta, one of Macmillan's principal advisers in Downing Street, cabled the prime minister's party in South Africa with the message, 'Michael Adeane has asked me to let you know that the Queen was very interested and much impressed by the Prime Minister's speech on February 3rd'.[22]

Macmillan's words have often been interpreted as signalling a determination on the part of his government to undertake a rapid withdrawal from Africa. This interpretation is all the more plausible given that within four years of the speech the process of decolonization in East, West, and Central Africa was largely complete, stalling only in Southern Rhodesia. In fact, far from intending to fire the starting pistol on rapid withdrawal from Africa, at the time of the Cape Town speech Macmillan was still seeking some new dispensation that could balance the forces of African nationalism on the one hand and white settler nationalism on the other. The bitter controversies over the massacre of prisoners at the Hola Detention Camp in Kenya and the declaration of a state of emergency in Nyasaland, both of which occurred early in March 1959, strongly suggested that the status quo was no longer viable. Yet in charting a new course that would avoid the recurrence of such scandals, Macmillan also wanted to avoid giving the impression, as he put it so tellingly in his diary in the summer of 1959, that the Africans had got 'the white man on the run'.[23] In the British public imagination, the forces of African nationalism found personification in the figure of Kwame Nkrumah. Nkrumah had been elected prime minister in 1951 of what was then the Gold Coast and six years later had led his country to freedom as Ghana, the first of Britain's tropical African colonies to achieve its independence. Meanwhile, intransigent Afrikaner nationalism found its embodiment in the South African prime minister, Dr Henrik Verwoerd, a fervent advocate of the policy of apartheid. The British settler communities in Eastern and Central Africa found a figurehead in the perhaps unlikely guise of the prime minister of the Central African Federation, Sir Roy Welensky. The Federation had been established in 1953 to bring together the British territories of Northern and Southern Rhodesia and Nyasaland and was firmly under the political control of the region's European minority. A trades union leader turned politician, Welensky famously described himself as half-Jewish, half-Afrikaner, and 'a hundred per cent British'. He had forged strong links with the British Conservative Party and utilized these links in his efforts to resist the spread of African nationalism and the break-up of the Federation. It was fairly late in the day before Macmillan gave up hope of being able to find a place for all three—Nkrumah, Verwoerd, and Welensky—in an expanding Commonwealth.

Royal patronage and royal visits offered important instruments in Macmillan's efforts to achieve this balance in the crucial years 1959–61. In terms of the Queen's Commonwealth tours, plans had to be significantly revised owing to the period of pregnancy leading to the birth of her second son, Andrew, in February 1960. Macmillan had first learned of the Queen's condition at an audience on 15 June 1959. Rather typically, his first thought seems to have been for the electoral prospects of the Conservative Party. The Queen was about to embark on a tour of Canada and America and Macmillan recorded his concern that if the government allowed it to take place and anything were to go wrong 'we sh[oul]d not be forgiven'.[24] It is, incidentally, a mark of the way in which the complex royal itinerary entailed by the Queen's Commonwealth responsibilities continued to shape British domestic politics that her planned tour of Canada was one of the factors that decided Macmillan against holding a snap general election in June. In August, when Macmillan actually did request a dissolution of Parliament, he recorded that '[o]f course [the Queen] expects this, and was really grateful to me for not advising it in June'.[25]

The Queen's pregnancy had implications for two other overseas engagements: a visit to Ghana in October–November 1959 and one to the Central African Federation pencilled in for May 1960. Both provided fertile ground for controversy. The planned visit to Ghana aroused hostility on the right wing of the Conservative Party. When the idea was originally mooted in 1958, Lord Salisbury, the doyen of the Tory Party's Imperial right wing and subsequently one of the leading critics of the government's African policy, wrote to Macmillan suggesting that, in the light of Nkrumah's 'crude, barbaric nationalism', the visit should be postponed indefinitely.[26] A factor that added further potential for embarrassment was that Nkrumah seemed determined to institute a republic in Ghana. British officials suspected that this would occur on 21 September 1960, Nkrumah's birthday, which was celebrated as 'Founder's Day'.[27] Yet, despite his republican instincts, Nkrumah had a deep personal affection for the Queen and he worried about the impact of the move to a republic on Ghana's relations with the rest of the Commonwealth. Referring to the Queen, he apparently told his private secretary, Erica Powell, 'It would be too bad for that young girl if we left the Common-wealth'.[28] As such, Nkrumah placed great importance on the Queen's visit going ahead. One means by which the republican issue could be squared with the Queen's presence in Ghana was raised by the British Governor General, probably at Nkrumah's suggestion: namely, that during her visit the Queen should make some reference to the decision to become a republic, perhaps along the lines that if such a move went ahead the country would have her very best wishes, and that she was glad Ghana wished to remain within the Commonwealth.[29]

This suggestion found little favour within Whitehall, where there was already apprehension that a switch to republican status coming too soon after the royal visit would appear as a snub to the Queen. The idea that she should refer to the planned constitutional change in a conciliatory manner raised all sorts of problems. It was feared that such a statement might encourage republicanism in Nigeria (which was due to become independent in October 1960) and even in South Africa.[30] Ghana had yet, formally, to announce its intention to become a republic or to seek continued membership of the Commonwealth. As such, the suggested statement might be misinterpreted, not merely as inviting Ghana to sever its current links with the Crown, but as committing those Commonwealth countries of which the Queen was Head of State to a decision on Ghana's future membership. There was, however, lurking behind these fine constitutional points a deeper concern about public reaction in Britain. As one official noted,

> I can see many people thinking that there is really something indecent about the government of Ghana (with or without the connivance of the Government of the UK) putting into the Queen's mouth, e.g. in a speech from the Throne, what could be interpreted as meaning that She understood that the Government of Ghana wanted to get rid of her as Queen. Personally, I feel that this public relations aspect of the matter is more important that the constitutional niceties.[31]

The Commonwealth Secretary, Lord Home, accepted these arguments as did the Queen's private secretary, Michael Adeane, and the idea of a statement was rejected.

In the circumstances, and particularly given Nkrumah's personal commitment to it, the postponement of the Queen's visit to Ghana was a matter of some sensitivity. Her assistant private secretary, Martin Charteris, was dispatched to Ghana at the end of June to explain to Nkrumah that the pregnancy (which would not be announced until August) would necessitate a postponement. Charteris later recalled that his instructions from the Queen for his conversation with Nkrumah were to 'explain the situation and tell him to keep his mouth shut'.[32] As Macmillan had anticipated, Nkrumah was indeed deeply disappointed. Charteris recalled him saying, 'Had you told me my mother had just died you could not have given me a greater shock.' To soften the blow, the Queen took the unusual step of inviting Nkrumah to visit her at Balmoral, a privilege that had not, hitherto, been extended to any other Commonwealth leader.[33] He would make his visit shortly after the Queen's return from Canada.

The Queen's pregnancy also necessitated the cancellation of her planned visit to Central Africa to open the Kariba Dam—the showpiece engineering project of the Central African Federation. In October 1958 Welensky had written to Home suggesting that the Queen might perform the opening.[34] After consultations with the Palace, including a conversation between Welensky and the Queen, it was tentatively decided that the visit should take place in May 1960 and should last for up to three weeks, allowing for visits to all the Federal territories. Yet as unrest swept through the Federation in the early months of 1959 and all three territorial governments acted to suppress their local African nationalist movements, the Macmillan government began to have second thoughts. Ministers feared that the visit—the plans for which had already leaked into the public domain—might involve the Queen in political controversy. Writing to Macmillan at the end of May 1959, Home told him,

> I have had a letter from Mr Stonehouse, [the Labour] MP, suggesting that the Queen should not go to the Federation on the grounds that the Federal and Southern Rhodesian governments are behaving so badly. It is just possible that others in the Labour Party might take this up and you may feel it right privately to consult Mr Gaitskell, although it is tricky as we can't risk anything like a veto by him and his friends.[35]

The Queen's condition finally ruled out the possibility of the trip going ahead. Yet while Nkrumah's disappointment at the postponement of the visit to Ghana had been assuaged by the offer of a special visit to the UK (and ultimately by the award of a privy councillorship), Welensky's frustration at the cancellation of the Queen's trip to the Federation was not. On 11 August, only four days after the announcement of the cancellation of the Queen's public engagements, Macmillan telegraphed Welensky to warn him that he would read in the follow day's papers of the award of a privy councillorship to Nkrumah. He explained that the award was timely because of the 'great disappointment' caused to the government and people of Ghana by the fact that the Queen's visit there would not now go ahead. He added that 'they have a genuine affection for The Queen which is, I think, in our general interest to sustain, whether they remain in direct allegiance to the Crown or, like India and Pakistan, become a Republic, recognizing The Queen as Head of the Commonwealth'.[36] Yet Macmillan made no suggestion that Welensky might also, in due course, receive a privy councillorship.

Welensky's reply to this message was predictably resentful. He complained bitterly that the fact that he had not been made a privy councillor 'has not escaped public attention here and Nkrumah's appointment will aggravate the position'. As to Macmillan's comment on the need to keep Ghana in the Commonwealth, while endorsing this sentiment he suggested 'there doesn't seem to be much of a premium on loyalty'.[37] On the issue of the Queen's cancelled visit, Welensky suggested that another member of the royal family be asked to perform the opening of the Kariba Dam and expressed a preference for the Queen Mother or the Duke of Edinburgh. In the event, it was the Queen Mother who presided over the official opening of the Dam. Unrest in Northern Rhodesia early in May 1960 led the European mineworkers union to send a telegram to Iain Macleod questioning the wisdom of the visit.[38] As Macmillan recorded in his diary, the preparations for the Queen Mother's trip to Central Africa, in which she visited all three of the Federal territories, caused the British government 'a good deal of anxiety', but they allowed it to go ahead.[39] In fact, it passed off without serious incident. Indeed, the atmosphere of the visit was something of a throwback to earlier years with the stress in the Queen Mother's speech at the opening of Kariba on multiracial cooperation and understanding, her encounter with 'traditional' Africa in the form of the Paramount Chief of Barotseland, and her inspection of members of the British South Africa Police.[40] One more concrete outcome of her visit to the Federation, however, may have been to hasten the release of the Nyasaland nationalist leader, Hastings Banda. While the Nyasaland government had been keen to keep Banda in detention until June, it had been impressed on them that it would be a source of embarrassment if he was still behind bars at the time of the Queen Mother's visit in May.[41] In the event, he was released from detention early in April.

The fact that the Queen herself would not visit Africa in 1960 served to give greater prominence and significance to Macmillan's own tour of the continent early that year. In retrospect, one of the most remarkable features of Macmillan's famous address to the South African Parliament in Cape Town on 3 February 1960—his 'Wind of Change' speech—was that it made no direct mention of a significant issue affecting Anglo-South African relations: the Verwoerd government's determination to achieve republican status. In discussions with Macmillan only a month before the Africa trip Sir John Maud, the British high commissioner to South Africa, had suggested that because of its political sensitivity the republican issue would 'never' be made the subject of a referendum and that Verwoerd might delay before taking any steps in that direction.[42] Nevertheless, he had warned that Verwoerd was determined to create a republic one day and might make it the issue of a snap general election. Having achieved that goal, the South African government might then say that they did not want to recognize the Queen as Head of the Commonwealth, something that would be 'very awkward'.

In fact, to Maud's surprise, Verwoerd took the opportunity of a no-confidence debate on 20 January to announce that there would be a referendum among the white electorate on the issue of a republic. Maud had believed Verwoerd would at least avoid raising the issue until events marking the Union's fiftieth anniversary had been completed. In fact, he announced that the referendum would take place after 31 May, when the celebrations had finished. By this stage, the initial planning for the Cape Town speech had been made and Macmillan had already commenced his Africa tour. Maud and other British officials suspected that, in making the announcement of a referendum in advance of Macmillan's arrival in South Africa, Verwoerd hoped to obtain some benefit from the visit for his campaign for a republic. In the first instance, in treating the British prime minister as an honoured guest he might reassure English-speaking voters that the move to a republic would not damage relations with the UK.[43] Secondly, he perhaps hoped that Macmillan might be persuaded to say something along the lines that this was a matter for South Africa itself and that Britain would welcome a republican South Africa into the Commonwealth.[44] Well aware of this elephant trap, Macmillan and his advisers were careful to avoid explicit reference to the looming referendum in his Cape Town speech (although his words commending 'the flexibility of our Commonwealth institutions' were taken by some sections of the press in South Africa as a veiled suggestion that a republican South Africa would still be welcome within the Commonwealth).

The day after delivering his 'Wind of Change' speech, Macmillan had a long discussion with Verwoerd on the question of South Africa becoming a republic. Despite his briefing from Sir John Maud in December, Macmillan claimed to have been dismayed when Verwoerd suggested 'there was still a strong feeling in South Africa against recognizing The Queen as head of the Commonwealth'.[45] This promised to complicate the task of ensuring that South Africa remained in the Commonwealth. There was no formal requirement for members seeking continued membership of the Commonwealth to recognize the Queen as its head. Nevertheless, as Macmillan told the Queen in January 1960, reporting on the first stage of his African tour, Nkrumah's attitude suggested that Ghana would continue to recognize her as Head of the Commonwealth once it had become a republic.[46] At the Commonwealth prime ministers' meeting in May 1960, at which memories of the Sharpeville massacre were fresh in the minds of those present, Macmillan managed to forestall any attempts to force South Africa out of the Commonwealth. Meanwhile, the meeting endorsed Ghana's request to remain a member of the Commonwealth on becoming a republic. Yet the referendum on a republic in South Africa, which went ahead in October 1960, effectively forced the issue of South Africa's membership of the Commonwealth. The vote went in favour of republican status, with the consequence that South Africa was required to make a formal request for its membership to continue. Yet at the Commonwealth prime ministers' conference in March 1961 South Africa could count on the unqualified support of only Australia. Meanwhile, Julius Nyerere, the chief minister of Tanganyika, which was only months away from independence, had indicated publicly that a decision to allow apartheid South Africa to remain a member of the Commonwealth would make it impossible for his own country to join.[47] The Canadian prime minister, John Diefenbaker, was—like Macmillan—reluctant to force South Africa out, but was fearful that an attempt to accommodate Verwoerd's regime would lead to the disintegration of the Commonwealth, which remained a cornerstone of his country's foreign policy.[48] As such, he sought to persuade the South Africans to make some concessions to international opinion. Verwoerd, however, remained intractable. With no movement from the South Africans and opinion across most of the other Commonwealth states hardening against Pretoria, Verwoerd was ultimately obliged to withdraw his country's application for continued membership.

South Africa's departure from the Commonwealth at the end of May 1961 with the introduction of the republican constitution was a decisive watershed in the history of the organization. Combined with the consequences of rapid decolonization, it meant that the Commonwealth no longer retained even the residual character of a 'white men's club'. Instead, it would increasingly champion the interests of the developing world. Furthermore, the process by which South Africa had been excluded from membership brought into question the long-standing principle of non-interference in the internal affairs of member states. If it was still difficult to speak of the Commonwealth as an organization united by 'common values', the policy of racial discrimination practised in South Africa had certainly proved inimical to the new spirit of this rapidly expanding association.

Other events of 1961, in which the Queen played a direct part, served to emphasize the changing character of the Commonwealth and her own personal accommodation with this new dispensation. Her visits to India and Pakistan in February–March 1961 were of particular significance. They played a large part in setting the ground rules for royal tours of Commonwealth republics. As the British high commissioner, Paul Gore-Booth, pointed out, the visit to India set two important precedents. First, the Queen was invited in her capacity as Queen of the United Kingdom rather than as Head of the Commonwealth, since the latter might have implied 'the existence in some degree of authority residing in Her Majesty over the Republic of India'.[49] Secondly, Malcolm MacDonald, Gore-Booth's predecessor, agreed a formula with the other Commonwealth high commissioners in Delhi that while the Queen would be visiting India in her capacity as Queen of the United Kingdom, she was also Queen of her other realms, and head of the Commonwealth. As such, her programme had been drawn up by the Indian authorities 'in agreement with other Commonwealth Governments concerned in order to allow recognition of that fact where appropriate'.

Yet as a memorandum from October 1961 by the CRO's constitutional expert, C. W. Dixon noted, this did not entirely settle the broader constitutional question of whether all royal visits to Commonwealth republics should be conducted on that basis.[50] In the case of the visits to India and Pakistan, the Canadian government had felt that these should be presented as being made by the Queen as sovereign of all her realms. The British government resisted this idea on the pragmatic grounds that the visits had been made on the advice of British ministers 'and that both the Indian and Pakistan Governments attached some importance to the visit being regarded as paid Her Majesty's capacity as Queen of the United Kingdom and not as Head of the Commonwealth, since it was feared that the latter might give the misleading impression that, as Head of the Commonwealth, She exercised some constitutional functions in relation to India and Pakistan'.[51]

The decision in 1961 to go ahead with the Queen's postponed visit to Ghana raised even more serious political and constitutional issues. What appeared to be the deteriorating political situation in the country only heightened the sorts of concerns that had originally surfaced in 1958–9. As early as December 1960, Adeane had told Harold Macmillan's private secretary that secret reports about

Nkrumah's regime from the British high commissioner in Accra did not fill him 'with either enthusiasm or confidence' (although he denied that either the Queen or Prince Philip had expressed any concerns).[52] In September 1961, Nkrumah made an extensive tour of Eastern Europe and China, which was peppered with speeches denouncing Western imperialism. This raised fears that Nkrumah might be preparing to align Ghana more closely with the Eastern bloc. The following month, on his return to Ghana, Nkrumah had arrested fifty of his political opponents, including leading figures such as J. B. Danquah and Joe Appiah.[53] This clampdown came against a background of disturbing reports from a variety of official and unofficial sources about the security situation in Ghana. The attention of the Commonwealth Secretary, Duncan Sandys, was caught in particular by a secret minute by Tom Stacy of the *Sunday Times*, who had been persuaded to record his impressions of Ghana by one of Sandys's officials. Stacy warned that 'there is a danger of an attempt by disaffected individuals to take the life of Nkrumah', and that 'they would be given an ideal opportunity to do this during the visit of the Queen'.[54]

The dilemma posed to Harold Macmillan as to whether to advise the Queen to go ahead with her visit, scheduled for November 1961, was acute.[55] On the one hand, Macmillan faced accusations from some within his own party—particularly those who opposed the rapid pace of constitutional reform in Africa—that he was placing the Queen's life in jeopardy. On the other hand, were the visit to be cancelled, there was a danger that Nkrumah might withdraw Ghana from the Commonwealth. This latter prospect was not one that disturbed some critics of the visit. In October 1961, following a meeting with Anthony Eden (recently ennobled as the Earl of Avon), Winston Churchill wrote to Macmillan to express their shared concerns. These focused both on the Queen's safety and on fears that she might be seen to be endorsing Nkrumah's 'thoroughly authoritarian' regime.[56] Racial and gender stereotypes undoubtedly served to exacerbate the outcry from within the Conservative party over the issue of 'the Queen in danger'. As Simon Ball notes, 'She was so beloved, so delicate, the flower of English womanhood, they declared, how could the government think of placing her safety in the hands of the vile Nkrumah?'[57]

Nkrumah attached particular importance to the Queen's visit being made in her capacity as Head of the Commonwealth. In the light of this, and of the significant security concerns that surrounded the visit, the question arose as to whether ministers in other Commonwealth countries had the right to advise the Queen on the matter. The Australian high commissioner in Accra clearly felt they did. The British government, however, resisted this idea. After discussing the matter with the Secretary of State for Commonwealth Relations and the Palace, the British representative in Ghana, Sir Arthur Snelling, told his fellow high commissioners that 'The Queen enjoyed the Title [*sic*] of Head of the Commonwealth wherever she was, but that this did not denote a capacity in which advice in the Constitutional sense could be given or received'.[58] In suggesting that the Queen should act solely on British ministerial advice, the UK government focused on the simple fact that it was the one actually responsible for getting the Queen out to Accra and back. The Palace supported this practical and pragmatic approach. The Queen's private secretary, Michael Adeane, was keen to avoid 'constitutional altercations' which were 'unprofitable in themselves and do not interest many of the people in the countries concerned'. He suggested that visits to Commonwealth republics

> should be carried out on the advice and responsibility of the British Government very much in the same way as foreign visits. I do not think it would be wise or beneficial to The Queen or the Commonwealth to consult beforehand with the other monarchical members, but I think that they, and the others, should be informed at the earliest possible moment <u>after</u> a decision has been taken and if possible before an announcement.[59]

He pointed out in passing that the British government had a special formal veto over the Queen's movements possessed by no other Commonwealth government: it could prevent her leaving the UK 'by the simple expedient of declining to advise her to appoint Counsellors of State to act in her absence'. In private, however, the CRO's constitutional expert admitted that '[f]rom a strictly constitutional point of view, it might be said that a visit to a Commonwealth country, of which Her Majesty is not Queen, is a matter on which all Commonwealth governments, or at any rate those of countries of which She is Queen, are entitled to advise Her'.[60]

For the Tory party's Imperial right wing, insisting on Commonwealth consultation was a means of seeking to ensure that the visit did not take place. Lord Colyton, one of Lord Salisbury's allies on colonial affairs in the House of Lords, raised the matter in private talks at the CRO.[61] From Macmillan's perspective it therefore became of paramount importance, in terms of the reaction both of the Commonwealth and of his own parliamentary party, to demonstrate his government's concern for the Queen's safety without actually cancelling the visit. The Macmillan government managed this through a dramatic intervention by the Commonwealth Secretary, Duncan Sandys. Sandys, who had visited Ghana only a month before for talks with Nkrumah, made a return visit from 5 to 7 November following reports of bomb explosions in the capital. In a very public affirmation of his faith in Nkrumah's security arrangements, Sandys took part in a rehearsal for the Queen's visit, driving through the streets of Accra at the Ghanaian president's side in front of the world's press.[62] The suggestion that they drive t   along the Queen's proposed route appears to have been Sandys's own, an   that won admiration for his courage from members of Nkrumah's i   Sandys returned to London unscathed and Macmillan announced   would go ahead.

The Queen's own position over this seems to have been unequivocal. On 18 November, Macmillan's press secretary, Harold Evans, recorded in his diary a conversation with the prime minister about the controversy. 'What a splendid girl she is,' Macmillan had apparently exclaimed. He told Evans that the Queen had been indignant at the idea of the trip being called off: 'The House of Commons, she thought, should not show lack of moral fibre in this way. She took very seriously her Commonwealth responsibilities, said the P.M., and rightly so for the responsibilities of the U.K. monarchy had so shrunk that if you left it at that you might as well have a film star.'[64] This was in many respects a pivotal moment in the Queen's relationship with the 'new' Commonwealth. Anticipating that the visit might be cancelled, Michael Cummings prepared a cartoon for the *Daily Express* showing a beleaguered Nkrumah seeking refuge from an angry crowd inside a giant Crown, but being barred from entry (see Illustration 3). This version never appeared in print. Instead, perhaps the defining image of the visit was one that would have offered far less comfort to *Express* readers: Ian Berry's charming photograph of a relaxed and delighted Queen dancing with the Ghanaian president (see Illustration 2).

Two interesting counter factual questions arise from the Queen's role in the 'Wind of Change'. First, if her visit to Ghana had gone ahead as planned in the autumn of 1959 would Macmillan have undertaken his Africa trip when he did, or would he have considered that it was too close to the royal visit? After all, Macmillan's visit to South Africa was only finally confirmed on 11 November 1959 when Verwoerd telegrammed him welcoming the idea (to Macmillan's considerable surprise).[65] Second, if the royal visit to Ghana had gone ahead in 1959 might it have assumed something of the symbolic importance of Macmillan's Cape Town speech as a sign that the British establishment was bowing to the inevitability of an Africa run by Africans rather than Europeans? Might the Queen, rather than Macmillan, have been the harbinger of the 'Wind of Change'?

REPORTING BACK: VISITS BY OTHER MEMBERS OF THE ROYAL FAMILY

Visits by members of the royal family were seen as an important means of promoting cohesion at a time of rapid change across the Commonwealth. Yet the process of coordinating these tours sometimes involved officials from Whitehall and the Palace in a process of choreography as complex as that practised by air traffic controllers. As early as 1954 an attempt had been made to regulate the number of royal visits to Commonwealth countries. In May 1954 Michael Adeane produced a memorandum for royal private secretaries and ladies-in-waiting which sought to ensure that the Queen knew of and had approved in advance overseas visits by members of the royal family.[66] The document had been produced in response to a glut of royal visits to Canada in 1954.[67] The British high commissioner in Canada, Sir Archibald Nye, who had already complained to London that royal visits were 'getting out of hand', felt that Adeane's memorandum did not go far enough in coordinating those visits. He told the CRO:

> This year for example in Canada we are having Prince Philip, The Duchess of Kent and the Queen Mother and we very nearly had The Princess Royal. It seems fair to assume that the next year or two will perhaps be more bleak and, whilst obviously the initiative for invitations must rest with the individual countries, I would have thought that some encouragement might be given to them to try and distribute the visits over the years.[68]

The situation appears not to have improved significantly over the next few years and in 1959 there was a further complaint that royal visits were 'getting a little out of hand', this time from Prime Minister Harold Macmillan. Macmillan suggested to the Palace that some form of committee needed to be convened to coordinate them. Adeane, who felt that he himself had shouldered much of the burden of this in the past, was enthusiastic about the idea and proposed that the Cabinet Secretary, Sir Norman Brook, should chair the committee. He pointed out, however, that the committee would not be competent to deal with invitations from 'full members of the Overseas Commonwealth' who had the right of direct access to the Queen and 'would soon take offence if they thought that they were being filtered in Whitehall'.[69] The Cabinet committee on 'Royal Visits Overseas and Visits by Foreign Heads of State' met for the first time in July 1959, and included representatives from the Foreign Office, the Colonial Office, the Commonwealth Relations Office, the Treasury, and the Palace.[70] The committee may, however, have taken a little time to bed down, as in October 1959 Adeane complained that Sir Hilton Poynton of the Colonial Office still regarded him 'as a clearing office for invitations to Members of the Royal Family other than the Queen'.[71] He suggested that the role of the Committee should be to try to 'weed out from among the various proposals those that should not be entertained at all', to identify those suitable for the Queen, and to place the others in order of priority. It would thereafter be up to the government departments concerned to consult with the private secretaries of the other royal households about filling this latter class of engagement. If willing members of the royal family were found, the Queen's permission would then be sought before formal invitations were dispatched.

Among the most striking features of royal visits around the Commonwealth were the often candid reports members of the royal family and their staff sent back to the UK. They were sometimes shocked by the poverty they witnessed in colonial territories and by the inadequacy of the British response. Following a visit to Ethiopia and the Somaliland Protectorate by the Duke and Duchess of Gloucester in January 1959, the Duke's equerry, Maj or Michael Hawkins, wrote to the colonial secretary, Alan Lennox-Boyd, to record his recollections. Of Somaliland, he noted, 'The first and last impression is the extreme poverty and how little has been done in the past by the British Government. . . . And indicative of the neglect by the home Government for years were the offices of the Secretariat in Hargeisa, where you would not house a servant in this country.'[72] He blamed hostile coverage of the royal visit on Radio Cairo for the fact that 'the majority of the Sultans and Elders did <u>not</u> bow to Their Royal highnesses on presentation', and expressed surprise that the station had not been jammed. He also complained that the British ambassador in Addis Ababa and the governor of Somaliland had spoken openly of their mutual hostility in front of the Duke of Gloucester and members of his staff. The governor, although a charming host, was, Hawkins claimed, 'completely inept politically' and 'would have been happier as a D[istrict] C[ommissioner]'.

The Duke of Edinburgh's reports back to Whitehall on his visits to dependent territories sometimes had the proprietorial air of a landowner complaining to his staff about the condition of his estate. In November 1964, following a tour of the Caribbean, he forwarded some characteristically trenchant notes to Downing Street. He recorded having found the 'general outlook' of Dr Eric Williams, the prime minister of Trinidad and Tobago, 'depressing and his equivocation rather frightening. He is unfortunately impressed by his African opposite numbers and I think he would be very happy to have a single-party state in Trinidad.'[73]

He expressed regret that the Wilson government had reinstated the post of colonial secretary, suggesting that there were 'several other territories such as the Pacific islands which cannot look forward to a viable independence and would be quite happy with a degree of dependence on Britain but would obviously prefer to be members of the Commonwealth rather than explicitly British Colonies'. He was also highly critical of the system of grant-in-aid, which was 'unpopular and frustrating with both ministers and officials'.

Many of these complaints were repeated following a visit by the Queen and the Duke to the West Indies in 1966. The visit was judged by the Colonial Office to have been a success, despite an incident in St Lucia when a pageant float nearly fell on the Queen. The royal couple had a particularly warm reception in Barbados, which, as the Colonial Office noted, was 'generally referred to in the West Indies as "Little England" '.[74] The Duke's general impression of conditions in the region's British dependencies was not, however, particularly favourable. Writing to the colonial secretary, Lord Longford, towards the end of the visit he complained that on the whole the islands were 'not in a very good state, largely, I suspect, because both for administrative talent and material resources they have been at the bottom of the Colonial Office priority list'.[75] Basic services and infrastructure were in a poor condition. Although the standard of the police, judiciary, and civil service was 'remarkably high', that of local politicians and trades unionists was 'remarkably low'. In his diagnosis of these problems, the Duke seemed determined to open up a number of debates about colonial administration that had long ago appeared to have been resolved. In seeking to explain the poor quality of local politicians and trades unionists, he commented on their lack of political education, adding that 'the almost complete absence of any form of local government in any part of the British Colonial Empire might be taken as a reason for the political weakness of so many of the recently independent countries'. The notion of using reformed structures of local government to provide a relatively prolonged political apprenticeship for aspiring leaders had been popular in the Colonial Office in the late 1940s, but had already lost ground by the 1950s as the pace of decolonization accelerated.[76] At the same time, the Duke also appeared to be advocating a more *dirigiste*—some might say authoritarian—style of government for the islands. Complaining that the Queen's representatives tended to be relatively junior appointments, and therefore at a disadvantage in their relations with their chief ministers, he suggested that 'the appointment of senior experienced Governors to these islands at least for a period of five to ten years would do them a great deal of good'. Finally, he complained that:

> The offer of so-called constitutional advance is merely the cheapest and easiest way of trying to restrict general dissatisfaction in the islands. It is not the constitutional position which worries the inhabitants, it is the efficient administration and their economic future.

The Queen's personal secretary, Michael Adeane, also sent ministers pointed impressions on the royal tours in which he participated. In February 1963 he briefed Macmillan on the latest stage of the royal tour of Australasia and the Pacific. He took the opportunity to stress the utility of the royal yacht *Britannia*: its convenience ('no packing and unpacking... and a reasonable number of early nights'), the impression it made when arriving and leaving, and the ability it gave the Queen to entertain large numbers of people.[77] *Britannia*'s most recent stop had been in New Zealand, which the Queen had last visited as part of her Common-wealth tour of 1953–4. Adeane claimed to have detected significant changes in the New Zealanders themselves during the intervening period: 'In 1954 they appeared to be stodgy, chiefly because of their isolation from the rest of the world, and almost paralysed by their peculiar version of the Welfare State.' Now, however, Adeane's impression was that they were 'a great deal less stodgy and more conscious of being part of the world outside. Also I suspect they are doing more work.'

BRINGING DOWN THE FLAG: THE ROYAL FAMILY AND INDEPENDENCE CEREMONIES

Members of the royal family are perhaps most closely associated with decoloniza-tion in the public mind in terms of their role as representatives of the monarch at independence ceremonies. The Queen herself never witnessed the lowering of the Union Jack. It was, as Sir Hilton Poynton noted in May 1966, 'a well-established Palace rule' that neither the Queen nor the Queen Mother presided over indepen-dence celebrations.[78] Indeed, when the question of royal representation at Gha-naian independence in 1957 was considered, it was decided by the Colonial and Commonwealth Relations offices that neither 'the Queen herself nor Prince Philip nor the Queen Mother nor Princess Margaret should be asked to undertake this sort of ceremony'. The reason given was that the task 'would be a recurring one—though not in quick succession'.[79] Hence, when Malaya's independence leader asked if Princess Margaret could represent the Queen at Malaya's independence ceremony which followed a few months after Ghana's, he was told this would not be possible.

The prohibition on Princess Margaret's use as the Queen's representative was quickly dropped. She was scheduled to attend the Nigerian independence celebra-tions in 1960, but withdrew a few months beforehand in favour of Princess Alexandra of Kent. This, it was explained by the Palace, was to allow her some months of privacy following her marriage to Antony Armstrong Jones in May.[80] She did, however, represent the Queen at Jamaica's independence celebrations in 1962.

Until the middle of 1961, officials at the Colonial Office continued to be uncomfortable with the idea of Prince Philip attending independence celebrations. They feared that his presence at such an event might create 'jealousies' in other newly independent countries not similarly favoured.[81] Iain Macleod, the Colonial Secretary, was, however, extremely keen that the Prince should represent the

Queen at Tanganyika's independence ceremony at the end of the year. Once he had done so, he became the prize catch for any independence celebration. In July 1966, the Colonial Office told the Palace of the preferred 'batting order' of Barbados Ministers for their country's independence day: 'first Prince Philip; second, the Prince of Wales; third the Duke of Kent, with Princess Alexandra in reserve if she was able to undertake public engagements again'.[82] At that time, however, the Palace judged the Prince of Wales to be too young to undertake such engagements, and it was not until 1970 that he came on stream, representing the Queen at Fiji's independence celebrations.

While the government was prepared to relax its initial prohibition on Prince Philip and Princess Margaret attending independence celebrations, it remained adamant that the Queen and the Queen Mother did not involve themselves in transfers of power. This did not, however, prevent colonial governments from inviting the Queen to their ceremonies. In August 1963, for example, the governor of Kenya, Malcolm MacDonald, told Duncan Sandys that 'the Kenyan Cabinet have unanimously decided that Her Majesty the Queen should be invited to preside at the Independence Day Celebrations in Kenya on December 12th'.[83] Although MacDonald was sympathetic, Sandys minuted, 'There can be no question of advising the Queen to go to the Independence celebrations'.[84]

Slightly less prestigious representatives of the Queen than Prince Philip and Princess Margaret but perfectly respectable ones were the stalwarts of independence ceremonies, the Gloucesters and the Kents. The Duke of Gloucester, a younger brother of George VI, presided over the independence days of Ceylon in 1948 and Malaya in 1957. Princess Marina, the widow of another of George VI's brothers, George, Duke of Kent, represented the Queen at Ghana's independence in 1957. Her daughter, Princess Alexandra, did so in Nigeria three years later. But it was Marina's son, Edward Duke of Kent, who perhaps the most prolific royal participant in independence celebrations. He acted as the Queen's representative in Sierra Leone, Uganda, the Gambia, and British Guiana. At times, the Kents seemed to pick up these engagements in the way that other families would select package holidays. In January 1966, Hilton Poynton noted,

> I understand that it has been virtually decided that the Duke of Kent should do British Guiana and that Princess Marina should do Basutoland and Bechuanaland. We had originally thought the other way round; but Princess Marina has apparently said that she is particularly keen to do the African ones and the Duke of Kent, who has never been to the Western hemisphere, would like to do British Guiana.[85]

Further down the royal hierarchy came the more distant royal relations, and there was some anxiety about deploying them lest this would create the impression that the territory in question was not highly regarded by Britain. In January 1966 the Colonial Office told the Palace that the Governor of British Guiana had proved unenthusiastic about the proposal that Lord Mountbatten should represent the Queen at the territory's independence celebrations. He claimed that there would be real disappointment if a 'Royal proper' could not do it. One official at the Colonial Office sympathized with this view. He suggested that, since Barbados, which was likely to get its independence shortly after British Guiana, was likely to ask for a bona fide member of the royal family, 'it would not help British Guiana to feel any less slighted than they already showed signs of being, if they were to get Lord Mountbatten instead of a Royal'.[86]

There was considerable anxiety in Whitehall that members of the royal family should be accorded proper respect and not be overshadowed by the independence ceremonies themselves. It was initially suggested by the Colonial and Commonwealth Relations secretaries that Princess Marina of Kent should make a visit to the Gold Coast to coincide with the independence celebrations, and that she should formally open the first session of the new legislature. They recommended, however, that the Princess should not be present on independence day, as '[t]here would be a real risk that the significance of her presence would be overlooked in the excitement of the celebrations'.[87] The acting governor of the Gold Coast, however, insisted that it was important that the Princess should be present on independence day, and insisted that her 'significance' would not be overlooked. With the messy aftermath of the Suez Crisis dominating the agenda in Whitehall, Nkrumah was prevailed upon to provide a 'categorical assurance' that neither Nasser nor any other official representative of Egypt would be invited to the celebrations. On the basis of these assurances, the government overturned its earlier decision and approached the Queen with the suggestion that the Duchess open the Ghanaian parliament on 6 March—independence day itself. British anxieties, however, continued to focus on the way in which the Princess would be perceived, and the prospect of her opening the Ghanaian parliament led one official to complain that 'such politically unsophisticated people as the Gold Coasters would all too easily identify the royal representative with one political party, and this would be most undesirable at a time when we are striving to promote unity'.[88]

In the case of Malaya the problem, in the eyes of the Colonial Office, arose from the fact that the Queen would not be the head of state upon independence. Instead, one of the Malay Sultans would be installed as Yang di-Pertuan Besar, the representative of the collective sovereignty of the rulers. The Colonial Office worried that ceremonies involving the new Malayan head of state might raise 'awkward questions' regarding 'the precedence of the member of the Royal Family representing the Queen, in relation to the Yang di-Pertuan Besar', particularly given the probable desire of the Malays 'to surround their own head of state with the maximum pomp and circumstance'.[89] The Colonial Office suggested to the British high commissioner in Malaya that it might be better if the Queen were represented not by a member of the British royal family but by 'one of the high officers of state' such as the Lord Chamberlain or Lord Steward. The Malayan prime minister, however, was extremely keen that a member of the royal family should attend, and the authorities in Malaya assured London that 'the ceremonies could and would, be so arranged that all possible courtesies would be paid and that no embarrassment to the royal personage could possibly result'.[90] Like Nkrumah, the Tunku was also obliged to promise that no official representative of the Egyptian government would be invited. On the basis of these undertakings, the government recommended that the Queen choose the Duke of Gloucester as her representative.[91]

These sorts of concerns did not entirely disappear as independence days became more regular events. In July 1963, when it was decided that the Duke of Edinburgh should represent the Queen at Kenya's independence celebrations, the question arose over whether he should also stay on to attend the inauguration of the East African Federation, which had been expected to occur a few days later. The Colonial Secretary, Duncan Sandys, had his doubts about this—and again the Egyptians were a factor. As one of Sandys's officials explained, 'At the Kenya Celebrations, the Duke of Edinburgh would naturally take pride of place. There is, however, some possibility that at the East African Federal Celebrations he might be simply "lumped in" with various dignitaries. It may even be that the occasion will be used for Pan-African gestures, e.g., by President Nasser, though this seems unlikely.'[92]

The concern to preserve royal dignity derived not merely from a desire to maintain British national prestige, but from a perception that the former colonies themselves expected the Queen's representative to have all the proper trappings of office. At times, this consideration came into conflict with the desire for economy. In advance of her visit to Jamaica in 1962 for the country's independence celebrations, a question was raised about whether Princess Margaret should travel there on a specially chartered flight, or whether she should take the considerably cheaper option of a scheduled flight. As a Downing Street official noted, Margaret was anxious 'not to expose herself to any charge of extravagance'.[93] Adeane, however, expressed concerns about the use of a scheduled flight, helpfully explaining that 'he was not concerned with Princess Margaret's comfort or convenience but with the fact that she would be The Queen's representative on this occasion and that the Jamaicans might make unfavourable comparisons between what was done for them and what had been done for other Commonwealth countries'.[94] In the event, the Ministry of Aviation persuaded Macmillan to charter a BOAC plane for Margaret, on the basis that they were 'the national flag carriers'.[95]

Sometimes official anxieties focused on rather more serious concerns. On one occasion—that of Mauritius in 1968—a royal visit to an independence celebration had to be cancelled altogether because of security concerns. Again, however, the anxieties of those responsible for organizing the visit related not merely to the possibility that physical harm might come to the royal representatives, but that their dignity might in some way be undermined. In this respect, it was significant that the intended royal visitor was a woman—Princess Alexandra. In March 1968, with a state of emergency in place aimed at containing communal violence, Lord Shepherd, the governor of Mauritius, advised that the visit should be cancelled. While admitting that the likelihood of any direct personal attack was remote, Shepherd noted that 'a degree of risk of embarrassment, marginal though it might be in the eyes of the security experts, does exist'.[96] It was clearly assumed that a man would be less susceptible to embarrassment and less of a concern for the security experts, and both the Cabinet of Mauritius and officials in London were keen to explore the possibilities of deploying a male member of the royal family in

Princess Alexandra's place. In the end, however, the security situation was judged to be such that no royal should be sent.

An instructive parallel can be drawn with the situation in Sierra Leone in 1961. In this case, the prospective royal representative at the independence celebrations was a man—the Duke of Kent. With independence day approaching, the governor proposed declaring a state of emergency, principally aimed at opposition from Siaka Stevens' All People's Congress. He told London that once some of the instigators of unrest were detained 'everything should be perfectly quiet for H.R.H's visit'.[97] The Queen was consulted about the matter and she appears to have agreed with the Colonial Secretary's view that, unless the situation deteriorated, the royal visit should go ahead.[98] In the case of Sierra Leone the threat of violence seems to have been considerably less than it was in Mauritius seven years later. Yet the discourse of 'embarrassment' which attached itself so firmly to discussions about the safety of a female member of the royal family was notably absent from the correspondence relating to the Duke of Kent's visit in 1961. Indeed, it was even suggested that the Duke should send a personal letter to the governor of Sierra Leone, expressing his regret at the unrest but saying that he was still looking forward to his visit.[99]

Efforts were made to coordinate the dates of independence to facilitate royal visits. For example, the Colonial Office had originally hoped that the transfers of power in Jamaica, Trinidad, and British Guiana could be synchronized so that a member of the royal family could represent the Queen at all three independence celebrations in the course of a single visit.[100] In the case of Tanganyika, the date of independence was actually brought forward slightly to allow Prince Philip to attend the independence celebrations. It was originally set for 28 December 1961, but Nyerere had objected that a date so close to Christmas might make it difficult for foreign dignitaries to travel to the country. It was therefore proposed to change the date to 20 December. Before an announcement of the change was made, however, Nyerere and his Cabinet requested that the Queen be represented at the celebrations by the Duke of Edinburgh. The Colonial Office learned from Michael Adeane that this might be possible. Since the Duke was due to end a tour of West Africa on 6 December, however, the date of independence would have to be brought forward still further to fit into his programme.[101] Officials at the Colonial Office were, as has already been mentioned, initially sceptical about this idea.[102] The Colonial Secretary, Iain Macleod, however, appears to have overruled these objections. His enthusiasm for the Duke's visit to go ahead was due at least in part to the fact that the Tanganyikan government had been contemplating adopting a republican constitution. He hoped that 'to meet their request for the presence of the Duke of Edinburgh at their independence celebrations might avert this'.[103] Macleod also felt that the earlier date would be easier to defend at the UN as it might appear to have been chosen to allow Tanganyika's admission to the General Assembly before it went into recess. Hence, on 4 July 1961, Macleod announced that Tanganyika's independence was to be brought forward to 9 December, although he neglected to explain that the new date had been chosen to fit into the royal schedule.

In the case of the Gilbert Islands, the scheduling of a royal visit helped oblige the government of Margaret Thatcher to honour the decision to grant independence in July 1979, when it might otherwise have been inclined to postpone it. The date had been agreed at a constitutional conference in December 1978.[104] The following month the chief minister of the Gilbert Islands was informed that the Queen had chosen Princess Anne as her representative at the independence celebrations. In order to fit in with Anne's schedule, London suggested to the chief minister either 9 or 10 July as the date for independence (so as not to clash with the 7 July anniversary of the independence of the Solomon Islands).[105] After further discussions, it was fixed as 12 July. Anne arranged a tour of South Asia and Australia around the visit to the Gilbert Islands. A bill (the 'Kiribati Bill') providing for the independence of the Gilbert Islands began its progress, but fell in April when Parliament was dissolved to make way for a general election.

Following the Conservative victory in the election early in May, the future of the Kiribati Bill became a pressing issue and the schedule was extremely tight. To meet the 12 July date for independence it would be necessary for the Kiribati Bill to have passed its second reading by the time of the Whitsun recess on 25 May, allowing for royal assent by mid-June and for the Privy Council to approve the necessary Order in Council. The problem for the newly elected Conservative government was that the Kiribati Bill was potentially divisive, and the party leadership was not enthusiastic about having it as one of their first pieces of legislation. In accordance with the outcome of the constitutional conference in December, it provided that Banaba (Ocean Island), which had been administered as part of the Gilbert Islands since 1900, should remain part of the newly independent state. During the wartime occupation of this small, mineral-rich island by the Japanese, its population had been expelled. The Banabans, who had settled on the Fijian island of Rabi, had lobbied unsuccessfully for the separation of their island from the Gilbert Islands before independence, and they retained influential friends within both Houses of Parliament, particularly on the Conservative benches.[106] The Conservative chief whip, Michael Jopling, was worried that the independence bill might split the party.[107] The Foreign Office, however, advised that any delay or alteration in the granting of independence would cause severe damage to relations with the Gilbertese.[108] In the event, the Foreign Office view prevailed and, despite the active opposition from some on the government backbenches, the bill was carried on its second reading in the Commons on 24 May and completed its remaining stages in time for the agreed date of independence.

Protecting the royal visitors at independence celebrations presented complex logistical problems for the authorities in London. While this process remains shrouded in some secrecy, one gets a rare glimpse of what was involved from a Metropolitan Police file on the arrangements for the Bahamas in July 1973. It illustrates the exhausting schedule that was sometimes imposed on the royal representative, and the close interest the Queen herself took in the arrangements. In the case of the Bahamas, Prince Charles was selected to represent the monarch. At the personal request of the Queen her own detective, Commander Albert Perkins, was sent to the Bahamas about a month ahead of the visit on a reconnaissance mission.[109] Perkins liaised with the governor, Sir John Paul, the commissioner of police, the assistant commissioner in charge of Special Branch, and Kit Bird, the MI5 security liaison officer in the Caribbean. Perkins judged that two Metropolitan Police royal protection officers, supported by two specially seconded local officers would be sufficient to ensure Prince Charles's safety. While he judged that any threat to Charles was remote, he insisted on altering the Prince's demanding schedule for independence day. He noted that the day was a very long one, ending with three state balls. The Prince was 'then expected to view the "Junkanoo Parade" at 4.50 a.m. from the balcony of the Prince George Hotel overlooking Bay Street'.[110] Perkins expressed concerns about the logistics of getting Charles into the hotel and onto the balcony. Once it was established that Charles's absence from the Junkanoo Parade would not cause offence, this final item on his itinerary was dropped. While this was done on security grounds, it is clear that there were other considerations at play. Perkins was a long-standing member of the royal household and was clearly well-attuned to the Queen's wishes. As the deputy commissioner of the Metropolitan Police recorded,

> I know from talking to Perkins that he had 'orders' before he left that if the Prince were to go to all the events it would make it too long a day especially as he was to leave at 10 am in the morning and the Lady concerned felt that Perkins could use his influence on the grounds of security to curtail what would have been an unnecessarily trying time for HRH who himself was trying to find an excuse to get out of attending the 'Junkanoo'.[111]

This was not to be the final occasion when Prince Charles found himself representing his mother at the lowering of the Union Jack. In 1997 he attended the ceremony which marked the 'handing back' of Hong Kong to China. Eight years later, in November 2005, the British press published extracts from a private diary kept by Prince Charles on this occasion. Like some of his father's reports back from his overseas visits they were both vivid and candid. They attracted particular attention for the Prince's highly critical remarks about the Chinese regime, describing its officials as 'appalling old waxworks' and bemoaning the 'awful Soviet-style display' which attended the transfer of sovereignty. Yet one of the Prince's most striking comments related not to the former colony's new rulers, but to his own treatment on the flight from Britain to Hong Kong. He recorded that he and his staff were seated 'on the top deck in what is normally club class. It took me some time to realise that this was not first class although it puzzled me as to why the seat seemed so uncomfortable'. He then discovered that a party of other British dignitaries, including former Prime Minister Edward Heath, had been placed in first class. 'Such is the end of Empire', the Prince lamented.[112]

6

'A poor sort of courtesy to Her Majesty': Republics, Realms, and Rebels, 1960–1970

By 1960, when Kwame Nkrumah declared Ghana a republic and Cyprus achieved independence within the Commonwealth under a republican constitution, a gradual loosening of links to the Crown was a less alarming prospect in Whitehall than would have been the case in earlier decades. The London Declaration had provided a suitably deferential formula for the move to republican status, one that had been followed in the case of Pakistan, when Commonwealth prime ministers, meeting in February 1955, unanimously supported the country's wish to become a republic and yet remain in the Commonwealth.[1] The Commonwealth was even flexible enough to accommodate the highly idiosyncratic case of Malaya, which achieved its independence in 1957 under a constitution which allowed for the position of sovereign to rotate among the Malay Rulers. This was very much the logical conclusion of the fact that the Malayan Federation had been governed by the British as a series of protectorates, with the Malay Rulers enjoying considerable autonomy. Nevertheless, it was complicated by the fact that Malacca and Penang, which were also to make up the independent state of Malaya, had been crown colonies where the Queen was sovereign.[2]

Nigeria became an independent monarchy in 1960. Yet, as the CRO had already anticipated, that was not the end of the matter. In May 1961 the UK high commissioner in the Federation of Nigeria, Antony Head, warned of growing indications that Nigerian leaders wished to move towards a republican constitution. He noted:

> As a Monarchy within the Commonwealth in Africa Nigeria is almost unique. Until Sierra Leone became independent on 27th April, Ceylon was the only other new Commonwealth country in Asia and Africa which had not ceased to recognise the Crown as Head of State; and Ceylon has expressed her intentions of becoming a republic eventually. It is almost old-fashioned to have a Governor-General. The trend in Asia and Africa has been towards Republican constitutions and many Nigerians feel that they must inevitably follow the trend.[3]

Head was broadly sympathetic towards this trend. He recognized that Nigeria's status as a monarchy tended to detract somewhat from the dignity of its prime minister. While his fellow African leaders were accorded full honours at international gatherings, Nigeria's prime minister, Abubakar Tafawa Balewa, was not. More importantly, however, Head argued that, unlike in the white Commonwealth:

The Crown is not thought of as part of Nigeria's life but almost as a last remaining relic of colonial rule. Understandably, the ordinary Nigerian does not feel the same personal affection and allegiance for the Crown as does a New Zealander, Australian or Canadian who is of British stock.

The CRO recognized that the strict constitutional position was less important than the way in which the role of the Crown was perceived. And, by 1961, there was concern that misconceptions were not restricted to the inhabitants of former colonial territories. In response to Head's despatch, one official at the CRO minuted:

My experience in Ghana indicated that it is not only the 'natives' who do not understand the constitutional position of the Queen: the 'British' also are liable to take exception to things they dislike being done in the Queen's name.[4]

Indeed, this tendency was in evidence within the CRO itself. Another official minuted that 'if there were any possibility of Nigerian policy developing on lines which we should dislike, there is a good deal to be said for the Queen not being the Head of State'.[5]

The idea that the Crown might be tarnished by association with African politics was also in the minds of officials at the Colonial Office. Permanent undersecretary of state Hilton Poynton noted that 'the prospect of Kenyatta as the Governor-General of an independent Kenya is considerably more distressing for a Kenya European to contemplate than that of Kenyatta as the President of a Republic.'[6]

In short, there was by 1961 a growing sense within Whitehall—and particularly within the CRO—that the practice of African states retaining monarchical status on independence might be a political liability for all parties concerned. Indeed, the suggestion that African nations should be *discouraged* from having the Queen as their head of state was beginning to be articulated in some quarters. Yet this was by no means the dominant view. Ministers remained keen that Nigeria should retain the Crown. During a visit to Nigeria early in May 1961, the Commonwealth Relations Secretary, Duncan Sandys, warned of 'the dampening effect which recent talk of a Republican constitution for Nigeria has had on the excellent disposition of the people of the United Kingdom towards Nigeria'.[7] Two months later, during a visit to Britain by the Nigerian Governor General, Dr Azikiwe, Sandys reiterated the hope 'that Nigeria would continue to owe direct allegiance to the Queen'.[8]

Meanwhile, in March 1961, the Colonial Secretary, Iain Macleod, had narrowly managed to persuade the leader of another African state—Julius Nyerere of Tanganyika—to drop his demand for a republic during the last major round of talks before independence. Macleod cited fears that this would undermine confidence among expatriates in the Tanganyika government service.[9] A more immediate concern of Macleod, however, seems to have been to reassure his own backbenchers, some of whom were already expressing concern about the pace of decolonization in Africa.[10] He apparently urged Nyerere to 'agree to have a Governor-General for at least a couple of years or so'. Nyerere objected that it 'seemed a poor sort of courtesy to Her Majesty' to enter into such an arrangement when the pressures to move to a republic were so strong. Nevertheless, he agreed to this, apparently out of a desire to spare Macleod any embarrassment.[11]

In the event, Nyerere reopened the republican issue only a few weeks after independence. In a White Paper on the issue, reportedly drafted by Nyerere himself, the government of Tanganyika stressed that, as a former League of Nations mandate and subsequently a UN trusteeship territory, Tanganyika had never been part of the British monarch's dominions. The monarch had simply been the Head of State of the country charged with administering it. As such, the British monarchy had always been 'a foreign institution'.[12] In setting out the form of republic it intended to adopt, the White Paper rejected a non-executive presidency, claiming that this too would be 'foreign to our tradition'. It argued that the 'honour and respect accorded to a Chief, or a King, or, under a republic, to a President, are forces indistinguishable from the power that he wields'.

The principal lesson that both the Colonial and Commonwealth Relations Offices drew was that if there was any uncertainty about whether a territory wished to retain the Queen as Head of State, then it was better for it to become a republic on independence. Beyond that, however, there remained a discernible difference in emphasis among some of Whitehall's leading policy-makers. Writing in December 1962, the month in which Tanganyika formally became a republic, Hilton Poynton commented that, although 'current thinking' favoured immediate republican status for waverers, it was 'what the territory itself wants that matters, and it is unthinkable that we should press all territories which may become independent in the future to adopt a republican form of constitution even in cases where the territory itself clearly wishes to remain a monarchy'.[13] The reaction of Duncan Sandys to the events of 1962 was, however, considerably more robust. In October he told an official at the Colonial Office that 'he was not going to agree to anything which might permit a repetition of Tanganyika's action'.[14]

In March 1962 a separate Central Africa Office (CAO) was established. This brought together the Central African departments of the Colonial and Commonwealth Relations Offices.[15] Its senior civil servant was Sir Mark Tennant, who, despite having served on the Monckton Commission on the Central African Federation, had spent most of his career in the Ministry of Labour. Ministerial responsibility for the CAO was given to the Home Secretary, R. A. Butler, who, like Tennant, had no previous connection with either the Colonial Office or the CRO.[16] Meanwhile, in July 1962, Sandys became Secretary of State for the Colonies, while retaining his responsibility for Commonwealth Relations. Understandably, given its hybrid nature, the CAO did not have a well-defined approach to the future of the monarchy. Butler himself took a fairly independent line on this issue.[17] What one can identify, however, is a growing determination on the part of the CRO that African nations should be discouraged from keeping the Queen as their Head of State on independence. And, whatever compromises he subsequently had to make in his role as Colonial Secretary, Sandys's sympathies remained essentially with the CRO on this issue.

These divisions within Whitehall came to the surface as plans were being made for the transfers of power in Nyasaland, Kenya, and Northern Rhodesia. Despite the fact that Northern Rhodesia and Nyasaland were the responsibility of the CAO, and Kenya that of the Colonial Office, the CRO continued to pay close attention to the terms under which these territories would achieve independence and it consistently argued that they should do so as republics. Yet for a variety of reasons its views on this matter did not prevail.

Both Hastings Banda in Nyasaland and Jomo Kenyatta in Kenya performed something of a U-turn. In July 1963 Banda told Butler that he wished Nyasaland to become a republic on independence.[18] Butler, however, was instinctively cautious about this. He was concerned about Nyasaland's political and financial stability and was reluctant to surrender any potential sources of British influence. He sought the advice of the governor of Nyasaland, Sir Glyn Jones. Jones shared Butler's caution, noting, 'we feel that on balance and particularly from the financial point of view we should try to obtain a period of independence under a Governor-General'.[19] He told London that 'The Queen's representative as Head of State will have a sentimental influence and independence under the Crown could have advantageous effects on British businessmen and investors.'[20] Alongside these objective considerations, Jones may have welcomed the chance to remain there for a little longer in the less onerous post of Governor General.[21] At the same time, Jones made it clear to London that this transitional role was likely to be short-lived. He noted, 'it seems quite certain that Banda would not agree to a period of independence under a Governor General lasting longer than a year and possibly six months would be the maximum he would feel able to agree to'.[22]

Indications that Jones and Butler might be attempting to dissuade Banda from moving immediately to republican status on independence were not well received in the CRO. One of its officials, John Chadwick, was dismissive of Jones's suggestion that expatriate officers and businessmen would be reassured if Nyasaland retained the Queen as its Head of State. In August 1963, he told the CAO:

> You will know, I think, of my own Secretary of State's anxiety that from now on we should avoid the tiresome and troublesome dual procedure under which a new Commonwealth country begins life as a monarchy and shortly thereafter switches over to a Republican constitution. In Africa we have already lived through this with Ghana and Tanganyika, and are faced with two other cases in the shape of Nigeria (1st October next) and Uganda (9 days thereafter). Mr Sandys has, I believe, made it clear to Kenya Leaders that in his view Kenya should start her independent existence as a Republic. The reasons are fairly obvious. In the first place, there are Parliamentary problems in the shape of consequential legislation which we have to deal with when a change of this kind occurs after Independence. Secondly, there are difficulties with appeals to the Judicial Committee of the Privy Council. But third, and most important, these changes so soon after Independence have an undercurrent of personal insult to the Sovereign herself.[23]

Sandys strongly endorsed this position, arguing that 'to use the monarchy as a stop-gap arrangement' was 'derogatory to the Queen', and that subsequent moves towards republican status tended to be justified by political arguments which, by their nature, had an 'anti-British flavour'.[24] In the case of Nyasaland, however, he was forced to back down.[25] Once Banda had indicated that he wished Jones to remain as Governor General after independence, it was difficult for Sandys to prevent this from happening without appearing actively to conspire in the removal of the Queen as Head of State. Jones became Governor General of Malawi on independence in 1964 and remained in that post until the declaration of a republic in July 1966.

In the case of Kenya, the question of the territory becoming a republic on independence was discussed in the Colonial Policy Committee as early as February 1962.[26] The following month, Saville Garner of the CRO told his counterpart at the Colonial Office that 'there would certainly seem to be much advantage in the country becoming a republic straight away'.[27] This also seemed to be the desire of Kenyatta and his colleagues. Towards the end of June 1963 the CRO told the Palace that the Kenya Government wished their country to achieve independence as a republic.[28] A complicating factor was provided, however, by plans to create an East African Federation of Kenya, Tanganyika, and Uganda. Federation could not come about until Kenya was independent. Kenyatta and his colleagues were therefore pressed by the governments of Uganda and Tanganyika to call for independence by the end of 1963. Kenya's governor, Malcolm MacDonald, urged London to accommodate this desire, arguing that the British government must not appear to be impeding the laudable policy of federation.[29] The Cabinet accepted this argument and in June 1963 it agreed in principle that the transfer of power should occur in December.[30] It was expected that Kenya would join the federation very soon afterwards. Since Tanganyika was already a republic and Uganda was shortly to become one, it would have been anomalous had the Queen been sovereign of one part of the East African Federation but not of the others. Hence, from the points of view of both British and Kenyan ministers, there was a strong case for Kenya becoming a republic on independence.

By August, however, the situation had changed significantly. The prospect of the federation being established by the end of the year was receding, yet the date of Kenya's independence had already been set. Kenyan ministers feared that the process of defining the powers of their own president might complicate the already delicate negotiations surrounding the federation. There were also disputes with the opposition about the nature of the presidency, which potentially threatened the all-important goal of achieving independence in December.[31] In the circumstances, Kenyan ministers decided that it would be more convenient to remain a monarchy at independence. Officials at the CRO expressed predictable concern at this news. They reiterated their fears that the subsequent adoption of a republic might 'appear as a slight on the Queen', and noted the undesirability of the monarchy being seen 'as an expedient being made use of for the sake of avoiding local, and often personal differences'.[32] The fact that former Colonial Secretary Iain Macleod had made precisely this use of the monarchy in the Tanganyikan independence negotiations was conveniently overlooked.

MacDonald put these concerns directly to Kenyatta. He reported back to London that the Kenyan prime minister had 'looked slightly embarrassed' and had promised to reconsider the question.[33] When they discussed the matter again MacDonald reiterated the view that a monarchical constitution would only be welcomed by Britain if it was likely to continue 'for a considerable time'; 'otherwise it would not be properly respectful of the Queen and the Monarchy'.[34] Yet Kenyatta made no promises about the length of time such a constitution was likely to survive. He explained that one of the main problems was the term, 'The Queen's Dominions': while Kenyans respected the Queen, they would find it embarrassing 'to be regarded as part of her property'. According to MacDonald, Kenyatta added

> that many African V.I.Ps. would attend the Independence Celebrations. Perhaps some of them would accuse him on this particular point. They might say 'What the Hell! We thought Kenya is to be Independent but you are still to be part of Her British majesty's dominions.' He would be able to answer that and contest it; but if an agitation supported by such people was raised against Kenya, he did not know how long he and his colleagues would be able to maintain the Monarchy.[35]

In the circumstances, the British government had little option but to accept Kenyatta's position. Hence, in November 1963, just a month before independence, the Colonial Office informed the Palace of their Secretary of State's advice that Kenyatta's proposal be accepted.[36] As Kenyatta had predicted, his country's monarchical status did not last long. Kenya became a republic in December 1964, only a year after independence.

Northern Rhodesia was, from the British perspective, probably the least problematic of the three cases under discussion. In February 1964 Kenneth Kaunda, leader of Northern Rhodesia's ruling United National Independence Party (UNIP), announced that he wished his country to become a republic on independence. Perhaps surprisingly, the question of whether to retain a Governor General for a period after the formal transfer of power was not a matter about which the British administration in Northern Rhodesia appears to have given much thought. In March the deputy governor approached the CAO to seek its advice on the matter. He admitted, 'We are rather ignorant of the arguments for or against such a move; nor do we know what the Secretary of State's views are.'[37] It seems clear that, despite his declared aims, Kaunda was prepared to give ground on the issue. According to the deputy governor, Kaunda had assured him that 'he would not be a party to anything which in his own words could be described as "unfriendly or dishonourable" '. In line with what they regarded as the 'current philosophy' on this issue, namely 'to encourage territories to go straight to Republican status', the CAO decided that the governor and his deputy should not seek to dissuade Kaunda and his colleagues from their stated course of action.[38] In October 1964 Zambia became a republic with Kaunda as its president.

THE CARIBBEAN

The former British colonies of the Caribbean provide a striking contrast to the African case in terms of the general sequence of decolonization and the specific issue of the monarchy. The granting of full independence extended over a much longer period owing to factors that included the repercussions of the break-up of the Federation of the West Indies and fears of the establishment of a Marxist government in Guyana (formerly British Guiana). On the collapse of the Federation in 1962, both Jamaica and Trinidad and Tobago were granted full independence. There were, however, protracted talks about federating the remaining dependent territories in the region, which delayed the granting of independence to the Federation's other former members. At the same time, the UK came under considerable pressure from the United States government not to grant full independence to British Guiana. This pressure intensified after elections there in October 1961, which were comfortably won by the People's Progressive Party (PPP) under its Marxist leader, Cheddi Jagan. The USA feared the creation of another Communist regime in the region in the mould of Fidel Castro's Cuba, and was keen to secure British cooperation for a campaign of covert action to bring down the Jagan government. The British Security Service, MI5, which operated in the Commonwealth and colonial territories, was apparently cautious about this, believing that it would be counterproductive.[39] British ministers, meanwhile, were indignant that US enthusiasm for decolonization appeared to stop at its own doorstep. Nevertheless, with at least tacit British consent the CIA launched a concerted campaign of 'special political action', encouraging and funding a general strike and diverting money to Jagan's political opponents. The PPP lost the December 1964 general election and was replaced in power by a coalition of the People's National Congress, led by Forbes Burnham, and the United Force, led by Peter D'Aguiar.

Guyana finally received its independence in 1966 on the basis of a constitution agreed by Burnham and D'Aguiar. Barbados also became independent in 1966. They were followed by The Bahamas (1973), Grenada (1974), Dominica (1978), Saint Lucia (1979), Saint Vincent and the Grenadines (1979), Antigua and Barbuda (1981), Belize (1981), and Saint Kitts and Nevis (1983). The survival of constitutional monarchies among the Commonwealth's Caribbean members has been a remarkable feature of their post-colonial history. Only Dominica achieved independence as a republic, and at the time of writing only Guyana and Trinidad and Tobago have made the transition to republican status, in 1970 and 1976 respectively. In Grenada, as we shall see, the monarchy even survived a Marxist coup in 1979.

Whitehall tended to explain this attachment to the monarchy in terms of the Caribbean's long association with British forms of administration. As the CRO noted in December 1962, 'The continuity of British institutions in Jamaica is still marked by vestigial traces of the 17th century in such venerable institutions as the Jamaican Privy Council, the Parish Custodes and the Broad Seal.' It also noted 'the deep constitutional entrenchment of the British monarchy, which appears to reflect the attitude of the great majority of Jamaicans, though there are pockets of republicanism especially among the young and the intelligentsia'.[40] In the case of Trinidad and Tobago, the position of the monarchy was entrenched in the constitution agreed at the 1962 Lancaster House conference. In a concession to the Democratic Labour Party (DLP) Opposition, the country's prime minister, Eric Williams, had agreed that any move to a republic would be among the constitutional changes which would require a three-quarters majority vote in the lower house and a two-thirds majority in the upper house.[41] Yet politicians in the West Indies were not oblivious to developments in Africa, and British officials rightly suspected that this would not be the end of the matter. In May 1963, for example, N. E. Costar, the British high commissioner in Port of Spain noted that Williams' interest in the issue had been revived by the announcement that Nigeria would shortly become a republic, and that the prime minister had suggested there would be a majority for a republic were a referendum to be held.[42] Costar doubted this claim, but thought it would not be an impossible outcome if Williams threw the weight of his party, the People's National Movement, behind a republican campaign. In the event, the constitutional impediments to any such move delayed concrete developments until the middle of the following decade.

Guyana represented an anomaly in the history of British decolonization. Although its independence constitution established the country as a Common-wealth realm, in an unprecedented move it also made provision for a change to a republican form of government at a future stage. Although the Colonial Office was clearly uncomfortable about this, it agreed to the innovation at least in part in order to hold the Burnham–D'Aguiar coalition together. The provision enabled a change to republican status to be made by the House of Assembly passing a resolution moved by the prime minister and supported by a majority of all members of the House. Notice of this motion could, however, only be given by the prime minister at least forty-two months after the date of independence, and three further months needed to elapse before the passing of the resolution.[43] The permanent under-secretary at the Colonial Office, Sir Hilton Poynton, confessed to feeling 'a certain distaste if not impertinence in advising my S[ecretary] of S[tate] to ask H[er] M[ajesty] to become Queen of Guyana on 42 months probation'.[44] Nevertheless, he recognized that a transitional period of monarchical rule could 'have a consider-able bearing on credit-worthiness and on the morale of expatriate businessmen and investors'.[45] Moreover, the provisions would at least allow Britain to influence the way in which any future constitutional change was made. Yet Poynton noted that 'the most powerful argument' for accepting the arrangement was that it represented a compromise between Burnham's republican instincts and D'Aguiar's desire to retain the monarchy. Without it, the future of the coalition government might be jeopardized and fresh elections rendered necessary. In the light of Guyana's recent past, this was clearly the very last thing Britain wanted. The Queen herself was unperturbed by the proposal. Her private secretary told Poynton, 'Her Majesty's comment was that if a country fully intended to become a Republic after Inde-pendence, there was something to be said for including provisions in the constitu-tion to regulate when this was to take place.'[46] Indeed, he later mentioned that the Queen 'had been rather attracted by the idea'.[47]

THE 'OLD DOMINIONS'

British officials increasingly made a clear distinction between those parts of the Empire settled by people of 'British stock', where affection for the Crown was assumed to be strong, and those whose peoples had no direct link to the UK, where the move towards republicanism seemed an almost inevitable by-product of in-dependence. As we have seen, they tended to regard the Caribbean as a special case in which, by reason of their long association with British institutions, the peoples had a particular affection for the monarchy. Yet by the mid-1960s, the experience of witnessing the rise of republicanism in Africa had clearly begun to shape British official attitudes towards the position of the Crown in some of the older members of the Commonwealth.

In June 1964 Britain's high commissioner in Canada, Sir Henry Lintott, recorded his personal impressions of Canadian attitudes to the Queen in a letter to the CRO. He noted having met 'hardly anyone who has any deep feelings about The Queen as Queen of Canada. People of the most various opinions and attitudes speak to me of Her Majesty as "your Queen".'[48] He warned that this situation created 'something of a vacuum in Canada, at a time when general devotion to a national head of state could be an invaluable element in the uneasy search for Canadian unity and identity'. Lintott expressed doubts about whether the current arrangement could survive without 'some radical transformation in the status and practice of the monarchy such that the monarch is seen to be as much a Canadian person as a British person'. He came close to endorsing Shuldman Redfern's idea of a peripatetic monarchy, suggesting that such a transformation 'would probably involve substantial periods of residence each year in Canada (and presumably, therefore, in Australia and New Zealand as well)'. At the very least, he suggested, the Queen needed to spend more time in Canada. He noted that prior to her visit planned for later that year she had made only two formal visits to Canada since coming to the throne. She should, he suggested, 'spend more of Her time, more often and more informally, in Canada, doing the sort of things that She does in Britain, rather than "paying a visit"'. In response to this latter point, Sir Saville Garner at the CRO raised the delicate question of money. He noted that the considerable cost of royal travel had 'normally been borne, willingly (but quite inappropriately), by the British Government, and Commonwealth Governments as a whole have shown some reluctance in assuming this burden'.[49]

The Queen's subsequent visit to Canada in October 1964 did nothing to undermine Lintott's warning about the lack of enthusiasm for the monarchy, although it did raise questions about the ameliorative effects of the royal presence. Threats from Quebec nationalist groups in advance of the trip raised serious fears in Whitehall about the Queen's safety. The trip itself was not a success, with the heavy-handed policing of the Queen's visit to Quebec City arousing particular criticism.[50] A CRO note on the affair played down some of the controversy, blaming the poor public turnout during her visit in part on the weather. Yet it admitted that there 'may have been a feeling that The Queen was a somewhat remote figure, and a tendency to think of Her as a British Queen rather than as Queen of Canada'.[51]

On 13 April 1966 Lintott provided London with another pessimistic assessment of the future of the monarchy in Canada. He suggested that the controversy surrounding the Queen's visit in 1964 had begun 'a tendency to air in public questions about the future of the Monarchy which were previously reserved for private discussions'. He noted, for example, that the *Toronto Star* had commented on the monarchy's 'increasing irrelevance to and remoteness from the realities of Canadian life'.[52] Lintott concluded that the number of convinced monarchists in Canada was steadily decreasing, with a corresponding rise in the proportion of those—particularly of the younger generation—who were indifferent or actively hostile. At the same time, however, he admitted that the difficulties raised by a move from the monarchical system made change in the near future unlikely. As to the desirability of such a change, Lintott hinted heavily that he personally felt the move to a republic would be no bad thing. He suggested that if the monarchy was abolished in Canada,

> Britain would not be blamed by implication for the alleged unsuitability of the Crown as part of the Canadian constitutional structure or embarrassed by suggestions that it is a vestige of British Colonial power. I feel, therefore, looking at the matter in a hard practical way, that it would not necessarily do damage to the relationship between Britain and Canada if Canada were to become a republic, and that it might indeed remove certain equivocal or confusing elements in that relationship.

Reading Lintott's despatch in the light of the CRO's recent experiences in Africa, J. B. Johnston warned against the dangers 'of engaging in a battle which in the nature of things we are bound to lose once it is fully joined'. He explained,

> A few years ago we did our utmost to persuade African States proceeding to independence to retain the Monarchy; experience showed that, because such retention was not rooted in the national life of the countries concerned, it did not last; and in the interim the position of the Queen in those countries was not respected and was in many ways resented ... Similar processes involving similar national self-consciousness and nationalist sensitivity, seem to be at work in Canada, and I think we have to accept them as we accepted them in Africa.[53]

This fatalism was shared by Johnston's colleague, G. B. Shannon, who placed the Canadian case in the context of the European trend of monarchies 'falling out of fashion', with 'difficulties in the last few years for the Crown in Belgium, Holland and Greece'.[54] With a boldly republican flourish, Shannon argued that pageantry was becoming less popular with 'a sophisticated public' and that the royal family 'fitted in well when a hereditary nobility led the nation but has become an anachronism in the different society of today'. Canada had, in any case, 'always been more democratic and less formal', and would 'no doubt become a Republic sooner or later'. What mattered more, from Shannon's point of view, was that this should not happen before British attitudes to the Commonwealth had 'evolved to a point at which we can take this in our stride'. Otherwise, 'it would deal another serious blow to the self-confidence of the country and to its faith in the Commonwealth'.

In March 1967 Lintott once again returned to his theme of the inexorable decline of Canadian identification with and sense of loyalty towards the monarchy. In a general despatch on the political situation in Canada, he again claimed that there was 'something of a vacuum in what Walter Bagehot called the "dignified" part of the Constitution', and that there was 'no person or institution at the centre of Canada that has the magic, for Canadians, of either the monarchy for the British or the President's office for the Americans'.[55]

The success of the Queen's visit to Canada in late June and early July might have been expected to stem these counsels of despair, and even Lintott himself was forced to admit that the trip had been a personal triumph for the monarch.[56] Only four months later, however, Lintott dropped a constitutional bombshell. In the middle of November he told the CRO of a recent discussion with Lester Pearson which made it clear that the Canadian prime minister 'now believes that the days of the monarchy in Canada are numbered, and that Canada should have her own head of state sooner rather than later'.[57] Lintott claimed that this view had also been expressed in recent weeks by three or four of Pearson's Cabinet colleagues and 'may well represent a consensus in the Government'.

Lintott's letter caused predictable alarm in Whitehall. Garner described it as 'staggering' and claimed that it suggested 'an astonishing change in atmosphere' since his own days as high commissioner. On the other hand, he recognized that the problem of Quebec demanded some solution 'and it is becoming increasingly recognised that the Monarchy is an obstacle to such a solution'.[58] Garner obtained approval to warn Adeane informally about the substance of Lintott's letter and the British prime minister, Harold Wilson, was also briefed on the matter. Wilson discussed it with Pearson in February, at which point the Canadian prime minister had already announced his intention to resign and preparations were under way for his Liberal Party to elect a new leader. Lintott produced a minute of this meeting in which Pearson was recorded as saying that 'it would be necessary to deal with [the issue of the monarchy] at some stage, perhaps within the next five years or so', possibly by making the Governor General a purely Canadian head of state, selected by an electoral college.[59]

When the minute was shown to Adeane, he expressed the view that Lintott had 'a bee in his bonnet' about the monarchy in Canada and asked whether Wilson had approved it as an accurate record of his discussion with Pearson.[60] Wilson claimed that although the note was accurate 'it failed to represent the balance of the discussion', with much of the conversation devoted to the contest for the Liberal leadership and other more mundane constitutional matters. The reference to the monarchy had arisen 'quite incidentally' in the course of these discussions.[61] Support for Adeane's assessment came in the form of Lintott's own record of his valedictory meeting with Pearson's successor, Pierre Trudeau, in June 1968. According to this, when Lintott asked the prime minister whether the future of the monarchy was likely to arise in forthcoming constitutional talks, Trudeau replied that he 'thought it unlikely and that it would be quite a long time before the monarchy faded out in Canada—"perhaps not before it disappears in Britain".'[62]

Whether or not Lintott did indeed have a 'bee on his bonnet', his departure from Canada did not lead to any immediate alteration in the tone of the reports on the monarchy that London received from its high commission in Ottawa. In February 1970 his successor, Sir Colin Crowe, told the Foreign Secretary that 'as a matter of (unstated) policy the Trudeau Government are steadily chipping away at such manifestations of the traditional royal connection as can be dispensed with quietly'.[63] What had altered, however, was the assumption that change in a republican direction might be imminent. Due in part to the lack of enthusiasm for the likely alternatives, Crowe suggested that the possibility could not be excluded 'that the Monarchy may survive for a long time in Canada yet'. The Duke of Edinburgh had made a characteristically robust contribution to the debate at a press conference during a visit to Ottawa in October 1969. The Duke said:

> The monarchy exists in Canada for historical reasons and it exists in the sense that it is of benefit, to the country or to the nation. If at any stage any nation decides that the system is unacceptable then it's up to them to change it. I think it's a complete misconception to imagine that the Monarchy exists in the interests of the Monarch—it doesn't. It exists in the interests of the people: in a sense—we don't come here for our health, so to speak. We can think of other ways of enjoying ourselves and, judging by some of the programmes we are required to do here and considering how little we get out of it, really you can assume that this is done in the interests of Canada and the Canadian people and not in our interest. I think that the important thing about it is that if, at any stage, people feel that it has no further part to play, then for goodness sake let's end the thing on amicable terms without having a row about it.[64]

British official reports from Australia during this period contained echoes of the Canadian experience, while taking a slightly more optimistic view of the future of the monarchy. Writing in January 1967, Britain's high commissioner in Canberra, C. H. Johnston, sketched out the historical reasons why—in his view—the links to the Crown had weakened and were likely to weaken further. These included the rise of a specifically Australian nationalism, Britain's apparent retreat from the Commonwealth with the implementation of the Commonwealth Immigrants Act and moves to join the Common Market, and conversely Australia's ever closer ties with the United States culminating in the 'political love-affair' between President Lyndon Johnson and Australia's prime minister, Harold Holt.[65] Additionally, migration to Australia by non-British Europeans since the war had weakened the ties of loyalty to the UK and the monarchy. Nevertheless, Johnston claimed, republicanism remained largely confined to a small group of intellectuals and academics, with the Crown continuing to be seen as a guarantor of the powers of the states against those of the federal government. As in Canada, the alternatives to a monarchy had limited appeal. Hence, even if the Crown was regarded with a diminishing amount of affection, it was unlikely to be dispensed with in the immediate future.

Returning to the subject in May 1970, Johnston was able to report a significant shift in Australian public opinion in favour of the monarchy. This, he claimed, had a number of causes. One was a growing disillusionment with the United States. Another was the success of royal visits by Prince Charles, Princess Anne, and most recently by the Queen herself. He suggested that 'the fact that the Sovereign and the Royal Family can circulate in crowded cities virtually unprotected' had contrasted sharply with 'President Johnson's trotting Secret-Servicemen, and the bull-horn voice from the armoured limousine'.[66]

This sparked a debate within the Foreign Office as to why Canada and Australia should be on such apparently different trajectories. One official cited a number of differences between the two that might provide part of an explanation, including the influence of the Quebec French ('Australia has not had to deal with a sizeable population of non-British origin with an inherited chip on its shoulder about defeat in battle') and of the proximity of Canada to the United States. Canada's 'at times nauseatingly high-minded' attitude to racial questions was cited as another factor. 'The Canadian winter', it was suggested, made 'for isolation, introspection and inward-lookingness' as did Canada's relative security in terms of defence.[67]

The rumblings of incipient republicanism that British representatives in Canada and Australia identified in the 1960s would, as we shall see, grow in intensity the following decade. In the process, the notion that Australia was in some sense less susceptible to republicanism would be neatly inverted.

RHODESIA

So far we have considered the question of how the British government regarded the rise of republicanism in the Commonwealth. In the case of Southern Rhodesia (more commonly referred to from the time of Northern Rhodesia's independence as Zambia in 1964 simply as 'Rhodesia') the UK faced a very different problem—how to deal with a country determined to defy the will of the Commonwealth while claiming to remain loyal to the Crown.

The possibility of the Queen becoming 'caught in the crossfire' in any break-down of relations between Rhodesia and the UK was apparent well before Ian Smith made his illegal unilateral declaration of independence (UDI) in November 1965. The threat seemed particularly acute given the assumption that Rhodesia's white minority population remained 'loyal' to the Crown, whatever hostility they felt towards the British government. In February 1964 the British prime minister's private secretary, Tim Bligh, warned the CRO of the difficulties that would be involved in the event of UDI if the Queen were to be advised that she should cease to be Rhodesia's Head of State:

> This would have the effect of putting the Crown in an intolerable position. The Queen would be seen to be confronted by the alternative of rejecting the advice of her UK ministers or of refusing the loyalty of 250,000 people of British stock.[68]

The problem for the Palace was compounded after the October 1964 general election by British domestic politics. The narrow victory of Harold Wilson's Labour Party with a bare majority made a resolution of the Rhodesian problem more difficult. Wilson was under pressure from the Commonwealth and from the left wing of his own party not to concede independence to Rhodesia while power still rested in the hands of the territory's white settlers. Yet he lacked effective levers to bring about significant constitutional reform in Southern Rhodesia, which had effectively been self-governing since the 1920s; and, like his Conservative prede-cessors, he was unwilling to use military force to assert British authority.[69]

Meanwhile, the Conservative Opposition was split on the issue, with a significant section of its 'right wing' displaying a marked sympathy for the Rhodesian settlers. Smith had little incentive to accept any deal offered by Wilson's Labour government while there remained the possibility of fresh elections producing a Conservative administration more likely to offer concessions.

Against this background, and with few other instruments available to him, Wilson was keen to exploit the Rhodesian settlers' supposed loyalty to the Crown as a means, first of seeking to avert UDI, and then of undermining the Smith regime. The Palace, however, was cautious. Early in October 1965 Wilson's private secretary, Derek Mitchell, discussed the possibility of a personal intervention by the Queen with Michael Adeane and Martin Charteris. Both were concerned that since the issue had become the focus of party political argument in the UK, there might be constitutional objections to her appearing to side with the policy of the government.[70] On the other hand, they accepted that there could be no valid objection to the Queen simply urging Smith to act constitutionally. In advance of a visit by Wilson to Rhodesia in a last-minute attempt to avert UDI, Mitchell and Adeane drafted a letter to Smith from the Queen which the prime minister was to deliver personally.[71] In it, the Queen expressed the hope that a resolution to the crisis could be found, and pointedly asked for her good wishes to be conveyed to 'all' her peoples in Rhodesia.[72] Yet the tone was so emollient that Smith was able to turn the gesture around, reading it aloud at a banquet held for Wilson and describing it as 'a wonderful message from this gracious lady'.[73] This was the beginning of a process in which both Smith and Wilson sought to marshal the Crown behind their respective causes. When Smith made his illegal declaration of independence on 11 November the governor, Sir Humphrey Gibbs, dismissed the Rhodesian Cabinet. Smith responded with a new constitution under which Gibbs was to be replaced by an officer administering the government. Gibbs, for his part, refused a request from Smith for him to resign and remained in Government House, where he was joined in an apparent gesture of solidarity by the Rhodesian Chief Justice, Sir Hugh Beadle.[74]

Perhaps the most extraordinary example of Wilson's attempts to deploy the Crown as a diplomatic resource in the Rhodesian crisis was his attempt to persuade Lord Mountbatten to make a personal intervention.[75] At an audience with the Queen in October Wilson had won her approval in principle for the idea that Mountbatten might replace Gibbs as governor.[76] Mountbatten himself, however, found the prospect unappealing and declined the offer, believing he was too old to revive the glory days of his time as Viceroy of India and that he could do nothing that Gibbs had not already tried.[77] Instead, Wilson suggested a more limited operation to the Queen at an audience on 16 November. He received a sufficiently enthusiastic response to allow him to discuss the idea with Mountbatten himself at a meeting in the House of Commons the following day. Wilson told Mountbatten that he had been considering asking him to visit Salisbury as an emissary of the Queen in order to make contact with the governor 'and possibly to hand to him a message from The Queen'.[78] He might even confer an honour on Gibbs.

Perhaps understandably, Mountbatten's reaction was, according to Downing Street's account of the meeting, one of 'hesitation'. He noted that any such visit would require 'very careful and detailed planning'. Yet the scheme clearly appealed to his sense of adventure, as two days later he wrote to Wilson to say that he was 'convinced' the visit should go ahead, and to express the view that there might be 'disastrous' consequences for Britain's relations with the Afro-Asian bloc if active steps were not taken to deal with the Rhodesian crisis. It was, however, already clear that the Palace was beginning to have doubts about the scheme. Adeane insisted that if Wilson was determined to pursue the proposal, the Queen would want 'very definite advice, in terms, in writing and preferably publishable. Moreover, since this was a matter in which She was involved personally, it must be recognised by the Prime Minister that a negative answer might be returned.'[79] He added, 'The Queen had stressed that there would have to be nothing slapdash about the mission since there would be a very considerable risk to the person of Lord Mountbatten' and that she was not prepared to let any of her personal household go to Salisbury. Adeane also stressed that he was opposed to Mountbatten taking a written message from the Queen, as any failure to deliver this would be 'a personal rebuff' to her. They were adamant that Mountbatten would have to be sent—and seen to be sent—on his mission by the British government itself.

Mountbatten remained enthusiastic about the proposal and promised Downing Street that he would use a weekend party with the Queen 'to overcome any inhibitions She might have at present'.[80] By this stage, however, Downing Street was developing inhibitions of its own. Wilson accepted that Mountbatten's mission could only proceed on the basis of advice to the Queen for which his government would have to take 'full collective responsibility'.[81] Yet this would have undermined the object of the exercise, which was to suggest that the Queen personally was hostile to the actions of the Rhodesian Front government.[82] An impending visit to Salisbury by Gibbs' brother (who was expected to offer a boost to the governor's morale as well as acting as a conduit for any advice from Gibbs to London) was used by Downing Street as an opportunity to postpone the visit. It was never revived.

As efforts to resolve the Rhodesian dispute continued, Gibbs remained in Government House, an uncomfortable reminder of Smith's breach with London. Meanwhile, the Rhodesian Front regime continued to profess loyalty to the Queen and to go through the charade of offering her 'advice' on ministerial appointments.[83] This loyalty was felt particularly keenly within the Rhodesian armed forces, whose members took an oath of allegiance to the Queen and who valued their links with their British counterparts. According to the Rhodesian intelligence chief, Ken Flower, as late as 1968 the prospect of a move to republican status elicited protests not merely from the commanders of the armed forces, but from his own Central Intelligence Organisation (CIO).[84] Despite the abandonment of plans for a visit by Mountbatten, other ideas circulated in London as to how this supposed affection for the royal family might be turned to Britain's advantage. Perhaps the most bizarre came from the prime minister of Northern Ireland, Terence O'Neill, early in October 1966. During a visit by the governor's wife,

Lady Gibbs, O'Neill put to her the idea of 'smuggling the Queen Mother out to Government House'. In a handwritten note to Harold Wilson delivered in person by his close political ally, Ken Bloomfield, O'Neill set out how this might be done:

> A plane could leave England after dark carrying officials. It would be known that Lady Gibbs was on board—perhaps even a female Gibbs relative could be said to be in the party. At Salisbury Airport the secret would emerge, but the Q[ueen] M[other]'s fantastic natural charm would win the day. Vast crowds would gather outside Government House to express their loyalty. Smithy would be 'on the spot'. If he tried to expel the Queen Mother the Regime would risk offending the strong latent pro-British sentiment, which I gather still exists in Rhodesia today. As you know the Q[ueen] M[other] is a strange amalgam. By nature she is a die-hard Tory—yet this is allied to a wonderful & instinctive sympathy. Even my odious 2nd cousin Montrose might wilt in her presence. All those in the Regime of British stock would fall over themselves to meet her at Government House. She just might bring this off.[85]

The Commonwealth Office was understandably less than enthusiastic about the idea, concluding that, though it was an attractive one, 'we hardly think it stands up to a moment's thought'.[86] Indeed, the logic behind the plan arguably said more about the mindset of the Ulster Unionists than that of the Rhodesian settlers. Wilson politely declined to proceed with the idea.[87]

Talks between Wilson and Smith aboard HMS *Tiger* in December 1966 failed to return Rhodesia to legality. Meanwhile, the Rhodesian Front government was keen to maintain the fiction that their rebellion was against the British government rather than the Crown. One by-product of this was that the regime sought to avoid possible conflicts with the Privy Council, which retained ultimate legal authority over the carrying out of death sentences. As such, no executions were carried out for over two years after UDI. It was therefore a major and highly emotive challenge to the Queen's authority when the Rhodesian government announced in 1967 that it would carry out the death sentence on three Africans convicted of murder. The regime's right to do so was challenged in the Rhodesian courts; however, in January 1968 four of the five judges, including Chief Justice Hugh Beadle, ruled in its favour on the grounds that it was the *de facto* government of Rhodesia.[88] In March the Queen commuted the death sentences, but Beadle dismissed this on the grounds that her intervention had been unconstitutional and, in the face of an international outcry, the executions went ahead. Although it was to be another two years until a republic was formally instituted, from this point on the myth of the Rhodesian Front's loyalty to the Crown became increasingly difficult to maintain.

As fresh talks between the Rhodesian and UK governments approached in October 1968, it occurred to British officials that their successful outcome might place the Crown in a highly invidious position. The Wilson government was prepared to consider a solution that would entail the granting of independence on the basis of a constitution which, while falling short of African majority rule, would allow 'unimpeded progress' towards that goal over a number of years. Any such settlement was unlikely to be acceptable to the majority of Commonwealth members, who wished to hold Wilson to a pledge that there would be no independence before majority rule. This opened the possibility that an independent country with the Queen as its Head of State would not be a member of the Commonwealth. As one official noted, while there were by this time plenty of cases of republican states within the Commonwealth, there was no precedent for a country outside it which retained the Queen as their Head of State.[89] There might be no legal implications in terms of the doctrine of the divisibility of the Crown, but there could be political ones. It was feared that

> there might be a general feeling in some Commonwealth countries that The Queen's position as Head of the Commonwealth was not compatible with her being Head of State of a country outside the Commonwealth. And quite apart from such considerations, countries such as Jamaica, Trinidad and Sierra Leone might well feel that they themselves could not continue to 'share' The Queen with Rhodesia. For these and other reasons, The Queen herself might feel that she was being put in an intolerable position.[90]

The question then arose as to 'whether it would be competent to United Kingdom Ministers [*sic*] to tender binding advice to Her Majesty on whether she should be monarch of another independent State'. Officials recalled that there had been reluctance on the part of ministers about the Queen continuing to be Head of State in Kenya and Nyasaland after independence, but that they had not pressed the matter and the Queen herself had raised no objections. While it was suggested that UK ministers might well be competent to advise the Queen not to accept the crown of an independent Rhodesia, it was recognized that 'it would clearly be very undesirable to get into a situation where the Rhodesians insisted on inviting Her Majesty to be their Queen and we had to say that we would advise Her Majesty to refuse'. It was therefore suggested that, in any future negotiations, British representatives should try to persuade the Rhodesians to 'abandon any notion of Rhodesia remaining part of Her Majesty's dominions after independence'. For its part, however, as her private secretary later made clear to the Foreign and Commonwealth Office (FCO), the Palace appears to have assumed that the Queen would be subject to the advice of British ministers on the question of whether she remained Rhodesia's sovereign.[91]

The talks, which took place on board HMS *Fearless* in October 1968, again failed to resolve the constitutional future of Rhodesia and the British negotiators proved reluctant to raise the issue of the Crown. At subsequent talks in Salisbury in November, however, Smith himself claimed that he and his colleagues had concluded that if independence was to be achieved on roughly similar terms as those on offer in the *Fearless* talks, Rhodesia would not be accepted as a member of the Commonwealth and would have to become a republic.[92] In fact, the latter did not automatically follow from the former.

In a minute to Wilson on 8 November, the attorney general endorsed the previous advice of the Foreign Office that there would be severe political difficulties if the Queen were to remain as Head of State of an independent Rhodesia which was outside the Commonwealth. But he noted that the legal obstacles to such a situation were not insuperable.[93] It was therefore with notable equanimity that British officials received the news in April 1969 that Smith intended to hold a referendum on the issue of a republic. Nevertheless, they were keen that British representatives should avoid giving the impression that 'the [Smith] regime was doing us a service by declaring a republic and thereby avoiding embarrassment to Her Majesty The Queen' or that they were 'pleased at the opportunity to wash our hands of the regime's present theoretical allegiance to the Queen'.[94]

The principal practical question to be addressed was how the Palace should respond should the referendum result in Rhodesia opting to become a republic. The connection with the Crown was marked in a number of different ways: the term 'Royal' in the titles of the Royal Rhodesia Regiment and the Royal Rhodesian Air Force; the royal charters of a number of Rhodesian organizations; the Rhodesian coat of arms granted by royal warrant in 1924; the Queen's status as Honorary Colonel-in-Chief of the Royal Rhodesia Regiment; and the Queen Mother's role as Chancellor of University College, Salisbury, and Honorary commissioner of the British South Africa Police (BSAP). The question was to what extent and in what ways should these marks of royal favour be withdrawn. The Foreign Office assumed that the Smith regime would play its own role in resolving some of these issues by removing the royal titles from the Royal Rhodesia Regiment and Royal Rhodesian Air Force, lest they served as suggestions that the move to republican status was not a permanent one.[95]

Any sweeping action at Britain's instigation to remove marks of royal favour faced a number of problems. First, those organizations which wished to retain their royal title might actually want to do so as a mark of defiance against the Smith regime. Second, University College was regarded as a special case as it was not under direct control of the Rhodesian government and had established itself as a relatively liberal enclave within the country. There was, of course, a more general objection that, in initiating actions of its own, the Palace and the British government would be recognizing the right of the illegal regime in Salisbury to declare a republic and be undermining the doctrine that the Crown remained sovereign over Rhodesia. For that reason, Wilson suggested that titles, connections, and marks of royal favour should merely be regarded as having gone into abeyance rather than having been withdrawn.[96] A further problem was the Queen Mother herself. Her 'die-hard Tory' views to which O'Neill referred were pronounced in the case of Rhodesia. She would reputedly urge British ministers 'not to be nasty to Smithy'.[97] The Queen Mother was clearly critical of the Wilson government's approach to Rhodesia and was unhappy about any suggestion that she should sever her own links with the country. George Thomson, then Minister without Portfolio, who had been closely involved in earlier negotiations over Rhodesia, learned from her private secretary, Martin Gilliat, that the Queen Mother was 'attached' to her links with University College and the BSAP and 'would be sad to give them up'.[98] The government's response was that the Queen Mother would be risking embarrassment either by continuing her association with Rhodesia or, conversely, by leaving herself open to being dismissed by the Smith regime or the College.[99]

The Smith government finally declared Rhodesia a republic in March 1970. Following advice from the British government, the Palace responded by announcing that the Queen had approved the suspension of the grant of the title 'Royal' to the Royal Rhodesia Regiment and Royal Rhodesian Air Force, and the suspension of her own appointment as Colonel-in-Chief of the Royal Rhodesia Regiment and of the Queen Mother's appointment as Honorary commissioner of the BSAP. The Queen Mother was also persuaded to relinquish the chancellorship of University College.

The cause of seeking to move both Rhodesia and South Africa to black majority rule was taken up with rigour by the Commonwealth. As this issue gained prominence and the character of the Commonwealth changed, the cause began to lose friends among many of its erstwhile supporters in the UK. This would create potential problems for the Queen as she sought to augment her role as Head of the Commonwealth.

7

'A Fragile Flower': Britain and the Headship of the Commonwealth

THE 'NEW' COMMONWEALTH

The genesis of the 'modern' Commonwealth is often dated back to the London Declaration of 1949. Arguably, however, an even more decisive turning point came in 1960, when Cyprus joined as an independent republic. This represented a decisive move away from a notion of the Commonwealth as an association of major states that would serve to bolster Britain's economic and strategic position. Instead, it would increasingly be an organization of mainly small states which would look to the Commonwealth for aid and assistance. The British government had made considerable efforts to resist this development by drafting elaborate plans for a multi-tier Commonwealth.[1] Yet as in the case of Cyprus—which was initially offered a form of associate membership—these schemes invariably came to nothing, due largely to the reluctance of newly independent states to accept 'second-class' status.

Cyprus was a state that had far stronger cultural links to Greece and Turkey than to the UK. The negotiations over its entry into the Commonwealth came at the end of a bloody campaign of terror and counter terror in which the Greek Cypriot leader, Archbishop Makarios, had been heavily implicated. None of this escaped the attention of the Cabinet Secretary, Norman Brook, who in December 1959 questioned whether it was really in Britain's interests for Cyprus to be admitted, suggesting that it would be 'much more of a liability than an asset to the Commonwealth'.[2] For the British governing elite, the Commonwealth was becoming a less comfortable organization and its benefits to Britain increasingly more obscure. In April 1962 Brook summed up Whitehall's dilemma in terms of the following three questions:

> What is the significance and purpose of the Commonwealth in the years ahead? What function and value will this new Commonwealth have in the modern world? What are the links that bind its members together?[3]

The answers to these questions were far from clear. As we have seen, common allegiance to the Crown no longer bound the Commonwealth together. It had ceased to be a military bloc in any meaningful sense.[4] Rapid decolonization led to a rapid increase in the number of states within the organization that lacked a clear commitment to the Western position in the Cold War. Britain's decision in 1961 to apply for membership of the EEC appeared to signal a realignment of UK trade away from the Commonwealth. Likewise, the Commonwealth Immigrants Act of 1962 stripped the notion of Commonwealth citizenship of much of its practical significance within the context of the UK, and reflected a growing sense among policy-makers that popular hostility to Commonwealth immigration was becoming a potent political force.

Despite all of this, the shock of General de Gaulle's decision in 1963 to veto the UK's first application to join the EEC led to a brief revival of interest in the Commonwealth as a potential means of promoting British influence and prosperity.[5] Over the next couple of years there was a highly creative period of institution-building which witnessed the creation of the Commonwealth Secretariat and Foundation (initiatives which came largely from the 'new' Commonwealth but to which British ministers and officials acquiesced with varying degrees of enthusiasm).[6] This atmosphere of optimism about the Commonwealth appeared to gain further momentum from the election in 1964 of a Labour government under the premiership of Harold Wilson, which initially seemed more in tune than its predecessor with the values of many Commonwealth members from the developing world.

This atmosphere of optimism on the side of Britain was fatally undermined by the issue of Rhodesia. British representatives came under fierce attack at Commonwealth meetings over the UK's refusal to use force to end UDI, and began to see such gatherings as an ordeal to be endured rather than an opportunity to advance UK interests.[7] Meanwhile, on the right wing of the British Conservative party there developed an explicit strain of hostility to the Commonwealth which cohered around the twin poles of support for the white minorities of Rhodesia and South Africa and opposition to immigration from the developing world.[8]

An early warning of the difficulties this growing alienation from the Commonwealth might present to the Queen appeared in April 1964. In the second of three anonymous articles in *The Times* under the pseudonym 'A Conservative', Enoch Powell denounced the Commonwealth as 'a gigantic farce'.[9] He sought to strip bare what he regarded as the delusions surrounding the Commonwealth, not least of which was the role of the Crown. Powell complained:

> If the monarchy is a precious and irreplaceable heritage of the people of Britain—and most Conservatives believe that it is—it is dangerous to prostitute to the service of a transparent fiction the subtle emotions of loyalty and affection on which that heritage depends. A great and growing number of people of these islands do not like to see the Sovereign whom they regard as their own by every claim of history and sentiment playing an alien part as one of the characters in the Commonwealth charade.

The article caused predictable indignation among officials at the CRO.[10] Yet, in a sign that Powell's comments might reflect a broader shift in opinion within the Conservative Party, the Commonwealth Secretary himself, Duncan Sandys, was notably reluctant to condemn them. His verdict on the article was 'I do not like it; but it contains much that is unfortunately true.'[11]

The Labour government that took power in October 1964 professed a strong commitment to the Commonwealth. Yet a relatively obscure episode involving

Lord Mountbatten and Prince Philip suggests that members of both the Wilson administration and the royal family shared some of these concerns about the way the Commonwealth was developing. The rather bizarre story of the short-lived plan to establish a Commonwealth conference on the lines of the Bilderberg Group is told at greater length elsewhere.[12] Certain points are, however, worth repeating here. The Bilderberg Group takes its name from the hotel near Arnhem where its first conference took place in May 1954. It still meets in secret annually, in a different location each year, and brings together high-level politicians, industrialists, financiers, trades unionists, and academics from Europe and the United States. Its purpose is to allow them to discuss matters of global significance informally and off the record. In its early years it had strong links to the Anglo-American intelligence community and counted among its most active members leading figures within the two major parties in the UK, including Denis Healey, who would serve in a series of Cabinet posts in the Labour governments of the 1960s and 1970s.

The initiative for a Bilderberg-style Commonwealth conference came not long after the general election from Harold Wilson himself and from Healey, his Secretary of State for Defence. They raised the matter in a discussion with Prince Philip's uncle, the First Lord of the Admiralty, Lord Mountbatten.[13] The following month Wilson mentioned the idea of 'establishing a Commonwealth movement analogous to the Bilderberg Foundation' to the Canadian prime minister, Lester Pearson (who was himself a Bilderberg veteran).[14] In January 1965, the plans were discussed further by Wilson, Mountbatten, and Prince Philip.[15] In a further preliminary attempt to canvas Commonwealth opinion, Mountbatten raised the issue during talks with the Australian prime minister, Sir Robert Menzies, in early March.[16]

Hints as to why Labour ministers and members of the royal family had been so keen to promote the Commonwealth Bilderberg scheme can be gleaned from a briefing paper which was quickly drawn up in May by Mountbatten's personal assistant, Ronald Brockman, in consultation with Mountbatten himself.[17] Perhaps owing to the speed of its production, the document (entitled 'A New Type of Commonwealth Conference') is neither particularly lucid, nor indeed grammatical. Explaining the need for the new body, the paper asserted that:

> Political decisions of the magnitude which have taken place in the Commonwealth in recent years are rarely understood by the public. It is, therefore, not surprising that the policies of many emerging Commonwealth countries have been misunderstood by elements in other Commonwealth countries. Others, while not denying the necessity and desirability of the continuation of the British Commonwealth of Nations, doubted whether the proper means of collaboration were being applied in the changing circumstances. Objections based on nationalistic and isolationistic sentiments have been voiced and at times there has been a feeling of uneasiness among some Commonwealth countries.[18]

It is difficult not to conclude from it that there was 'a feeling of uneasiness' in the minds of Mountbatten and Brockman themselves at the way in which rapid decolonization had disrupted the comfortable structures of the pre-war Commonwealth and handed power to colonial agitators. The sense that the Commonwealth prime ministers' meeting had now become a forum in which British representatives would be ritually harangued is apparent from the paper's justification for the private and unofficial nature of the Bilderberg-style conference:

> The same confidential surroundings remove any incentive to make personal propaganda; the danger of interminable speeches for the sake of publicity would not exist in Commonwealth meetings of this type.

Both of the passages quoted above were removed from the much-revised version of 'A New Type of Commonwealth Conference', which was subsequently given wider distribution among Commonwealth leaders, perhaps because they pointed rather too blatantly to the motivations of the scheme's British sponsors.[19] Consultations with Commonwealth leaders revealed distinctly lukewarm levels of enthusiasm. What essentially led to it being abandoned, however, was Rhodesian UDI in November 1965: British ministers and officials were reluctant to create another forum in which they could be criticized over their policy towards the Smith regime. The Bilderberg plan has largely gone unnoticed in histories of the modern Commonwealth. Yet it provides further evidence for the way in which the Commonwealth was increasingly coming to be regarded as something alien and hostile within British elite circles. It is all the more ironic, then, that against this background the Palace sought to build a major role for the Queen around the nebulous concept of the headship of the Commonwealth. It was a project that was almost bound to lead to tensions with British politicians. It also, arguably, shackled the British government to an organization in which it was increasingly losing faith.

THE HEADSHIP OF THE COMMONWEALTH:
QUESTIONS AND DILEMMAS

The Queen's dedication to the Commonwealth can be traced back to her pledge on her twenty-first birthday to dedicate her life to Britain's 'Imperial family'. Yet the headship of the Commonwealth was a rather fragile vessel to bear the weight of this commitment. Its creation in 1949 was essentially a means to allow India to remain in the Commonwealth by creating a tenuous link to the Crown to which even a republic could subscribe. It is hardly surprising, then, that little thought was given to some fundamental questions about its nature: what did it entail; did all new members have to recognize the incumbent as Head of the Commonwealth; and was it hereditary or might it pass to someone outside the royal family and even from another state?

A briefing paper produced by the CRO shortly before the Queen's coronation noted that no attempt had yet been made 'to define the practical significance of the conception thus accepted by India' in 1949, and admitted that there was much force in Enoch Powell's comment during the debate on the Royal Style and Titles Bill that '[the] status of India resulting from these changes and declarations is an ungraspable one in law and in fact'.[20] It also admitted that, as matters stood, India's relationship to the Crown could be defined only in negative terms: the Queen was not India's head of state, India owed no allegiance to her, and all the constitutional functions performed by her in other Commonwealth countries were in India's case performed by its president. The CRO noted, however, that there had been some low-key attempts to give tangible form to 'the special relationship of the Queen to India resulting from her position as Head of the Commonwealth'. India had, for example, signed the Queen's accession proclamation; the 'letters of commission' accrediting Indian and British high commissioners to each other's countries were significantly different from the 'letters of credence' accrediting foreign ambassadors; and the invitation to the coronation sent to the Indian prime minister was also different from that sent to foreign representatives. Nevertheless, Indian leaders had proved 'extremely nervous of domestic criticism' of this continued link to the Crown.

By the end of the 1960s Whitehall could still only define the headship in terms of what it was not. When seeking to supply a definition of the Queen's position as Head of the Commonwealth for his colleagues in autumn 1969, G. A. Duggan of the FCO's Commonwealth Co-ordination Department, admitted that this could only be done 'in the negative. It involves no constitutional duties, no ties of allegiance by individuals, no obligation to visit and does not find any expression in a formal international context.'[21]

The Palace itself was, at least in the 1950s, adamant that the Queen's position as Head of the Commonwealth was an entirely symbolic one. As Adeane noted in September 1959, 'No constitutional function was attached to it [at the time of the London declaration] and none can belong to it now because no Head of the Commonwealth could act in a commonwealth [*sic*] sense without constitutional advisers and no such commonwealth advisers exist.'[22]

Commonwealth governments were keen to police this minimalist conception of the headship. In the summer of 1956 leaders attending a Commonwealth prime ministers' conference were consulted by the British government over a proposal to confer the title of 'Prince of the Commonwealth' on the Duke of Edinburgh. The Canadian prime minister, St Laurent, among others, claimed that the title was inappropriate since the Commonwealth had no government of its own, and hence there could be no titles attached to it.[23] The plan was withdrawn and instead it was recommended to the Queen that she confer upon Philip 'the Style and Dignity of a Prince of the United Kingdom of Great Britain and Northern Ireland'.

The following year, as Adeane recalled:

> It was tentatively suggested . . . that when The Queen addressed the United Nations in New York she might do so as head of the Commonwealth and speak from a text approved or acquiesced in by the various Commonwealth Prime Ministers. The Union Government lost no time in dissociating itself from this suggestion and made it clear that exception would be taken to its being adopted by other Governments. It was dropped.

As Adeane commented in November 1959, 'The idea of "The Head of the Commonwealth" is quite a fragile flower of which the life can be endangered just as easily by too much watering as by too little.'[24] Whilst he did not rule out the possibility of the Head of the Commonwealth becoming 'a constitutional personality' at some time in the future, he believed this could only come about through the combined actions of Commonwealth members.[25]

On the question of whether new member states were required formally to recognize the Queen as Head of the Commonwealth, there was also a considerable amount of doubt and ambiguity. The London Declaration of 1949, under which India recognized the King as Head of the Commonwealth, set a precedent which was subsequently applied to Pakistan. Commonwealth prime ministers, meeting in February 1955, accepted Churchill's proposal that they unanimously advise the Queen that they accepted Pakistan's wish to become a republic but to remain a full member of the Commonwealth, 'recognising Your Majesty as the symbol of the free association of its independent member nations, and as such Head of the Commonwealth'.[26] In associating itself with this decision, India established a further important precedent: that the leader of a republican member state had the right to offer advice to the Queen in her capacity as Head of the Commonwealth on a matter affecting the Commonwealth as a whole.

From the British point of view, the act of recognizing the Queen as Head of the Commonwealth served a number of practical purposes. As the Colonial Office explained to the governor of Cyprus in December 1959, shortly before the territory achieved independence as a republic:

> [The] Principal reason for [the] recognition of [the] Queen as 'head of the Commonwealth'... is that this is [the] practice of other republics in the Commonwealth. We and other Commonwealth members attach importance to it. Further reasons are that such recognition makes it easier for us to justify in [the] eyes of foreign countries [the] grant of Commonwealth preference. It would also make much more acceptable to [the] UK and foreign opinion arrangements whereby Cypriots would continue to enjoy Commonwealth citizenship. This is only enjoyed at present by citizens of countries who recognise [the] Queen as head of [the] Commonwealth.[27]

Yet there was no formal requirement as such that states wishing to join the Commonwealth should make an explicit statement of recognition. As we shall see, Whitehall was periodically to return to this issue before it was finally resolved at the 2007 Heads of Government Meeting. As early as the mid-1960s, however, many of the considerations that had made the UK so keen that Cyprus should recognize the Queen as Head of the Commonwealth on independence had become less pressing as the tangible benefits offered by Britain to its Commonwealth partners diminished. In an influential minute on the future of the Commonwealth produced at the beginning of July 1965, the deputy Cabinet Secretary, Philip Rogers, questioned the significance of the monarchy for the Commonwealth. He suggested,

> I cannot for the moment think that the concept of The Queen as head of the Commonwealth has any real meaning (which is a very different thing from saying that the pageantry, and frankly the snobbery, attached to attending functions at the Palace may not be extremely valuable. I have always thought of snobbery in this context as being a most useful force!)[28]

Another residual benefit of the headship to Britain suggested by officials was that it made it easier to negotiate the complex constitutional relationship between the Queen and the other Commonwealth realms. As a civil servant at the CRO noted in November 1966:

> Whilst a Commonwealth exists, it is possible to justify its Head residing in the senior Member: if the Commonwealth ceased to exist it is most likely that the monarchical countries would expect the Queen to reside with them for some part of the year; would expect to have a greater say in the advising of the Queen. The present working relationship is only possible because of the Commonwealth.[29]

On the question of whether the headship was a hereditary title, as we have seen in Chapter 3 very little thought appears to have been given to this matter at the time of the London Declaration of 1949. It would probably be true to say, however, that the parties to the Declaration simply assumed that in due course it would pass to George VI's successor as monarch. In the event, the question was decided on a bilateral basis between London and the other Commonwealth states at the time of the final illness and death of George VI, without any decision being made on the broader principle. Yet the lack of controversy around the issue suggests a general assumption in London and other Commonwealth capitals that the headship was hereditary. Much turned—as it had in 1949—on the fact that India was prepared to be accommodating. As we have seen, during George VI's final illness the Indian High Commissioner, Krishna Menon, suggested that if the phrase 'Head of the Commonwealth' was inserted into the accession proclamation, it would be possible for him to sign it. On the King's death, Nehru wrote to Queen Elizabeth II welcoming her as the 'new Head of the Commonwealth'.[30]

Within the British government, one detects from the documentary record a broad assumption that the Queen's successor as sovereign of the United Kingdom would automatically inherit the title of Head of the Commonwealth. There was certainly little attempt to adopt a strict terminology that would have suggested otherwise. In September 1959, when informing British high commissions around the world of the terms on which Cyprus could be allowed 'internal association' with the Commonwealth, the CRO stated that it would be required to 'recognise the Sovereign as Head of the Commonwealth'.[31] The assumption that Prince Charles would inherit the title of Head of the Commonwealth as a matter of course was also reflected in the planning for his investiture as Prince of Wales at Caernarvon Castle in July 1969. The ceremony was a quintessential piece of 'invented tradition', the only modern precedent being the equally contrived investiture of the future Edward VIII in 1911. The CRO took a close interest in the question of whether there was to be any Commonwealth representation at the investiture. In a brief for the Welsh Office in July 1967, it noted that '[s]trictly speaking, the Investiture has no constitutional significance for the Commonwealth. Nevertheless, it marks an important step in the upbringing of the Heir to the Throne, who in the normal course of events will become Head of the Commonwealth on his accession. The opportunity should therefore be taken to emphasize the Commonwealth link.'[32] When informing the prime minister of the arrangements for the ceremony, the

Secretary of State for Wales, Cledwyn Hughes, explained that it was 'one which involves the future Head of the Commonwealth'.[33]

There was, of course, the complicating fact that there was no law of succession for the headship, since there was no legislative body capable of making such a law for the Commonwealth as a whole. Whitehall addressed this problem by taking regular discreet soundings among Commonwealth countries—both monarchies and republics—to establish whether, on the Queen's death, they would be prepared to send their high commissioners to attend the Accession Council in London.[34] As in 1952, the accession proclamation was expected to include among the titles of the Queen's successor 'Head of the Commonwealth'. So long as it was clear that Commonwealth governments were prepared to send a representative to the accession council, the question of the succession to the headship was not in doubt.

The figure who in the early 1960s presided over this planning process was the CRO's constitutional adviser, Sir Charles Dixon. At times, Dixon almost seemed to regard the turbulent politics of the Commonwealth solely in terms of the attainment of that magic moment when all its members would be prepared in principle to attend the council. His crowning moment came in the spring of 1961 when the Ghanaian government indicated that it had no objection to its representative in London being present. Against this background, the recent departure of South Africa from the Commonwealth, which appeared to some as a tragic breach in Commonwealth unity, was seen by Dixon as the providential falling into place of the final piece of this jigsaw puzzle. He minuted:

> The effect [of Ghana's decision] is that, unless the Indian authorities have changed their minds since 1952 or the Cyprus authorities feel any scruples, it will be possible for all the High Commissioners in London to attend and sign the Proclamation if the event should unhappily occur in the near future . . . South Africa's departure from the Commonwealth disposes of one anomaly which occurred in 1952 . . . since there is no question of inviting representatives of foreign states.[35]

From the small amount of documentary evidence currently available on plans for the demise of the crown after the 1960s, it is unclear how long officials continued to assume that the term 'Head of the Commonwealth' should automatically be included in the title of the new monarch in the Accession Proclamation.[36] What is clear, however, as we shall see in Chapter 11, is that this assumption no longer applies.

Before the 1970s, very little thought seems to have been given to a more radical solution to the future of the headship: that it might pass from the House of Windsor and rotate among representatives of other Commonwealth nations. A figure who played a major part in raising this issue was the British journalist Derek Ingram, Managing Director of the Gemini News Service. Speaking to the Royal Commonwealth Society in March 1972 after a tour of India and the Far East, Ingram claimed that he had encountered bewilderment as to why the Queen should permanently occupy the role of Head of the Commonwealth. He predicted there would be growing pressure to allow it to pass to candidates from elsewhere in the Commonwealth. The reaction of the Foreign Office was that any change would be difficult to execute for a number of reasons. These would subsequently be rehearsed at regular intervals: first, if the role of Head of the Commonwealth was essentially symbolic, it was 'difficult to see how a succession of different people' could fill it without the nature of that role changing.[37] Second, if not the Queen, then who was to fill the role? If the position was to rotate among heads of government, then this would create its own problems. If the leader of each Commonwealth government was to occupy the post for as little as a year, this would mean some countries having to wait decades for their turn. And what would be the order of rotation? There was a risk that weaker candidates would be given precedence, as they were less likely to overshadow their fellow heads of government. Conversely, were the Commonwealth's more notoriously autocratic leaders to be given a turn? Third, there was likely to be an adverse reaction within the 'Old Dominions' to the Queen relinquishing the role of Head of the Commonwealth; and, fourth, the British public might also react adversely towards the Common-wealth, feeling that their monarch had been slighted.

This question was raised again by the FCO in November 1973 in response to 'some talk in academic circles and among journalists, at home and abroad' (of whom Ingram was presumably one) of the role of Head of the Commonwealth rotating. Martin Reith of the Commonwealth Coordination Department produced a short paper on the issue. Again, it was feared that some heads of government might wish to give the role of Head of the Commonwealth something more than a purely symbolic character. Overall, Reith expressed the feeling that, however marginal the benefits to Britain might be of the Queen's role of Head of the Commonwealth, it would be wrong voluntarily to relinquish these in her lifetime: 'Since we already have possession, there can only be disadvantage in having any debate about the entitlement to it.'[38] He noted that it might be thought advanta-geous on the Queen's death 'to drop the title altogether on the basis that it is functionless, useless but potentially troublesome'. There were, however, two ser-ious objections to this: first, that the title was incorporated in the Royal Style and Title of all the Queen's realms, and there would therefore need to be considerable Commonwealth consultation beforehand. Second, Reith suggested, 'although the title is functionless in our hands and useless to us, it would not be so in others' hands and could then be much more troublesome. If the new King sought to abandon the title it would only leave the field free for others to pick it up.'

Reith's paper mentioned a separate but related issue: whether Commonwealth countries should continue to have to seek the agreement of their fellow members to remain in the Commonwealth on becoming republics. This had been raised by Emeka Anyaoku, then assistant director of international affairs at the Common-wealth Secretariat, in a discussion with L. E. T. Storar of the Commonwealth Coordination Department in May the previous year. Anyaoku had asked whether this requirement 'should not quietly be dropped since it seemed rather an irrelevant exercise in the modern Commonwealth'.[39] Storar had told him that she 'personally had some sympathy for this view', but that she thought any change would require broader consultation with Commonwealth heads of government. Neither Anyaoku nor Storar had any appetite for such consultations, fearing that they would open up a range of potentially embarrassing issues. Storar told her colleagues that 'for the sake of letting sleeping dogs lie' the current practice was probably best left unchanged.

Nevertheless, when in the mid-1970s first Malta and then Trinidad and Tobago moved to republican status, the principle of letting 'sleeping dogs lie' seems to have led the Commonwealth Secretariat to change its own procedures.[40] In March 1976 the British High Commission in Port of Spain was informed that the same process would be applied in the case of Trinidad and Tobago as had been followed when Malta became a republic in December 1974: the Secretariat would inform other Commonwealth members of the country's intention to become a republic and its wish to remain within the organization. Rather than asking for their acquiescence in its continuing membership, however, this would simply be assumed unless anyone objected.[41] Nor would there be any mention of Trinidad and Tobago continuing to recognize the Queen as Head of the Commonwealth. The Foreign Office explained to the High Commission that 'in the contemporary Commonwealth climate we do not wish to give the more racially-minded Commonwealth members any opportunity to question the Queen's present role.'[42] As we shall see, it would not be until the 1990s (ironically during Emeka Anyaoku's term as Secretary-General) that the Commonwealth was prepared to address this issue in a more forthright and positive manner.

GIVING SUBSTANCE TO THE HEADSHIP: COMMONWEALTH VISITS

The reason that a debate about a rotating headship only really gained momentum in the 1970s may have been that the notion of the headship as a ceremonial role had taken so long to emerge. As we have seen, there was initially a great deal of resistance to the idea that it was anything but a purely symbolic position. That it became something more substantial was very much owing to the Queen's own efforts to make it so. The rest of this chapter will consider a number of ways in which she has given meaning to the headship.

One of the most conspicuous ways in which the Queen has given substance to her role as Head of the Commonwealth is through her impressive record of overseas visits. To date she has visited all but two of the Commonwealth's member states (Cameroon and Rwanda). Yet Commonwealth visits have raised significant logistical and constitutional problems for the British government. As the example of the Queen's visit to Ghana in 1961 has already demonstrated, the key constitutional dilemma was whether the prime ministers of the Queen's other realms had the right to offer her advice on Commonwealth visits (outside the realms), particularly in cases where her safety might be in jeopardy. As we have seen, the British government was characteristically reluctant to offer any firm ruling on the question of principle, preferring to rely on the practical argument that, since it essentially paid for these visits, it should have the ultimate say.

The British government periodically returned to this point when seeking to navigate some of the constitutional uncertainties surrounding the Headship. In 1971, faced with the prospect of a Parliamentary Select Committee review of the civil list, officials at the Foreign Office were asked to consider the additional expense imposed by the Queen's increasing Commonwealth responsibilities, and to comment on the value to Britain of her role as Head of the Commonwealth. Officials were keen to stress the benefits to Britain of Commonwealth tours. One suggested,

> I think we should bear in mind... that the Queen was created head of the Commonwealth with the full backing of the British Government in order to foster the new Commonwealth relationship. This was an act of Government policy and She acts in support of Government policy when She carries out her functions as head of the Commonwealth.[43]

Although both historically questionable and wildly at odds with the spirit of the 'new' Commonwealth, this nicely encapsulated the rationale for Britain underwriting the cost of the Queen's Commonwealth engagements and, by extension, those of other members of the royal family. At some level, however, the UK was prepared to bear a disproportionate amount of the cost of the Queen's 'Commonwealth' duties, not so much because she was acting as an instrument of British policy, but because this avoided opening up more difficult constitutional issues about her relationship to the Commonwealth. This was clear from discussions surrounding her attendance at the 1973 Commonwealth Heads of Government Meeting (CHOGM). As we shall see in the next chapter, she came at the invitation of the Canadian prime minister and with—at best—only the grudging assent of the British government. As such, the Foreign Office questioned whether the responsibility for the cost of the visit should properly rest with the Canadian government. Yet it was reluctant to press the issue. Officials were concerned that the Canadians might suggest that other Commonwealth governments should also contribute, on the grounds that the Queen was attending the meeting in Ottawa as Head of the Commonwealth. As one of them noted:

> We might even prefer to pay up ourselves on the basis that such a claim on other Commonwealth Governments could only open up the question of whether the Queen alone should be the head of the Commonwealth or whether it should rotate among other Commonwealth Heads of State. This would be a development to be avoided at all costs.[44]

THE MULTI-FAITH OBSERVANCE

Another way in which the Queen gave substance to her role as Head of the Commonwealth was through her regular attendance at the Commonwealth Day 'Multi-Faith Observance'. This too was not without controversy. It was decided in 1965, with the approval of the Queen, that Commonwealth Day should be moved to coincide with her official birthday on the second Saturday in June. It had hitherto been on 24 May, Queen Victoria's birthday, which had been chosen as the date for Empire Day when this was first introduced in Canada at the end of the nineteenth century. It was felt in the CRO that the historical connotations of 24 May were 'outmoded', and the date had the additional disadvantage of falling on a different day of the week each year.[45] The change took effect in the United Kingdom in 1966. No attempt was made to coordinate this date across the Commonwealth, although Commonwealth countries and the remaining colonies were informed of the change in advance in case they wished to follow suit.

In 1975 the Canadian government proposed that Commonwealth Day should be harmonized across the Commonwealth. Following a proposal first raised in 1973 by the Canadian National Council of the Royal Commonwealth Society (RCS), the Canadian government suggested that the second Monday in March would be a suitable date as children from across the Commonwealth would be in school, allowing them to participate in special celebrations.[46] At a meeting of senior officials in Canberra in May 1976, the Commonwealth agreed to the Canadian proposal. The decision, which would see Commonwealth Day move in the UK from the Queen's official birthday, was denounced by the William Hickey column in the *Daily Express* as 'another kick in the teeth' to tradition. The column asked, rhetorically, whether this was '[a]nother snub to the Queen from Commonwealth "militants"?'[47]

In a further innovation, Commonwealth Day in June 1966 was marked by a multifaith service, held at St Martin-in-the-Fields Church in London. This had been proposed by the executive secretary of the RCS, and was based on a ceremony held the previous year during the Commonwealth Arts Festival.[48] It did not, however, meet the approval of either the Bishop of London or the Archbishop of Canterbury. The latter had, Downing Street learned, expressed the view 'that it really makes nonsense of the whole concept of Anglicanism if Hindus and Muslims are invited to take part in an Anglican religious ceremony'.[49] Difficulties in finding a secular building for the ceremony meant that it did not take place in 1967. It was, however, revived in 1968 as an 'act of witness' in the Guildhall, where it was held for four years. Apparently on the initiative of the Queen, it was moved in 1972 to Westminster Abbey, which, as a 'Royal Peculiar', was the formal responsibility of neither the Bishop of London nor the Archbishop of Canterbury, but of the Queen herself.[50]

While the Queen attended the first service to be held in the Guildhall in 1968, she was understood to be unwilling to attend further services in person until it was again held in a church.[51] Since 1972, however, she has made a point of signalling her support for the service by being present except when she was prevented from doing so by overseas visits (and it was therefore a newsworthy development when it was announced that she would not attend the 2013 Observance owing to illness). Given the sensitivities surrounding the event, great thought was devoted to the choice of hymns and prayers. At a meeting of the Joint Commonwealth Societies Council in 1978, for example, which discussed the form that the following year's service would take, some concern was expressed at the choice of the hymn 'City of God, How Broad and Far' on the grounds that it contained the line 'how grandly hath thine Empire grown'.[52]

Nevertheless, the nature of the Commonwealth Day service continued to attract some criticism, particularly from the evangelical wing of the Church of England.[53] In more recent years, habitués of the event have complained that the genuinely multifaith elements of the observance have been marginalized and that greater emphasis has been given to Christian prayers and hymns. John Hall, who became Dean of Westminster in 2006, has recently confirmed that he had some doubts about aspects of the ceremony and believed the Abbey 'could take some steps to dress and fashion the event as a service, introduce more clearly familiar elements of Christian worship, and allow the other faiths to represent more clearly their own tradition'.[54]

Despite these controversies, the Queen herself has remained a stalwart of the observance. Her commitment to the ceremony no doubt owes something to a sense that it reflects the multicultural nature of Britain itself. This sense has manifested itself in recent debates about the form the next coronation might take. In a distinct echo of the debate which *The Round Table* attempted to ignite in 1952–3, the idea that Westminster Hall might be incorporated into the ceremony has been revived in recent years. Again, the intention behind this is to allow a proper representation of the Commonwealth. Yet in a sign of the way the UK itself has changed since the early 1950s, the aim would be to represent and celebrate multifaith Britain. Prince Charles has famously suggested that he might be styled 'Defender of Faith' rather than 'Defender of the Faith', to reflect that diversity.[55] The historian Roy Strong and the former Dean of Westminster, Dr Wesley Carr, have both suggested that, while the ceremony in the Abbey should remain a largely Christian affair, a separate ceremony in Westminster Hall could be used to allow leaders of other faiths to perform some act of recognition of the new monarch.[56] In the revised edition of his book *God Save the Queen: The Spiritual Heart of the Monarchy*, issued to coincide with the 2012 Diamond Jubilee, the historian and theologian Ian Bradley has endorsed this idea.[57] Indeed, in the wake of the Bradford riots in 2001, Bradley even suggested that there might be a separate ceremony of 'enthronement and homage' in the city 'reflecting the themes of the Commonwealth, the monarch as Defender of Faith and guardian of the British tradition of tolerance and openness, and the affirmation of loyalty to the Crown by representatives of diverse ethnic and faith communities'.[58]

THE COMMONWEALTH GAMES

In terms of its public visibility, the Commonwealth may be best known for the international sporting festival it hosts every four years. This is another context in which the headship has attained a ceremonial character. In 1954, when the Duke of Edinburgh assumed the presidency of what was then known as the British Empire and Commonwealth Games Federation, an important function of the Games from the royal family's perspective was clearly to raise the Duke's profile and add to his list of 'meaningful' activities. The title of the event was changed to British Commonwealth Games in 1970 and Commonwealth Games in 1978. The

Duke appears to have been instrumental in the latter change of title, which was agreed at the Christchurch games in 1974. The suggestion to drop the word 'British', which was supported by the Commonwealth Secretary-General, Arnold Smith, met fierce resistance from representatives from Canada, Australia, and New Zealand. According to Smith, Prince Philip discreetly sided with those advocating change and managed to win round some of the more conservative members of the Federation.[59] The Prince acted again as a moderating influence during the disastrous Commonwealth Games in Edinburgh in 1986. Already beset by financial problems, the Games faced a major boycott by Commonwealth nations over the issue of sporting links with South Africa. In the end, thirty-two nations withdrew their athletes, leaving only twenty-six teams actually competing.[60] Some members of the Federation clearly wished to take action against boycotting nations, either imposing financial penalties or excluding them from future tournaments. Yet this might have prompted threats to leave the Commonwealth on the part of a number of African and Caribbean nations. When, following a meeting of the Federation, no such measures were announced, journalists covering the Games strongly suspected that Philip had used his influence to avert a crisis.[61]

As president from 1954 to 1990, the Duke opened most of the early games of the Queen's reign. The Queen herself, however, opened the games for the first time in 1978, and made a point of attending all the games from 1970 to 2006. The Games have provided fertile ground for invented traditions around the headship. In the 'Queen's Relay', first introduced in 1958, the Queen hands a baton to a medallist from the previous games containing an address by the Head of the Commonwealth, which is conveyed by relay runners to the venue of the next games, where it is read by the Queen or her representative at the opening ceremony. The baton for the Commonwealth games in Delhi in October 2010 was dispatched by the Queen in October 2009. Its high-tech features reportedly included a text messaging capability to enable people to send messages of congratulations and encouragement to the baton bearers. The Palace's website described the Queen's Relay as 'a powerful symbol of the unity and diversity of the Commonwealth of Nations'.[62]

As in some of its other aspects, the construction of a role for the Head of the Commonwealth around the Games raised the issue of the extent to which the Queen was subject to ministerial advice. Ahead of the 1970 Commonwealth Games in Edinburgh, the Queen's private secretary, Michael Adeane, sounded out the permanent undersecretary at the Foreign Office, Denis Greenhill, on the possibility of the Queen inviting one or two Commonwealth heads of government to stay with her at Holyrood House while the Games were taking place. Two possible candidates who were mentioned in subsequent discussions were Pierre Trudeau and the Ghanaian prime minister, Kofi Busia.[63] This, however raised the issue of how the list of guests was to be justified. It was suggested by one official in the Commonwealth Co-ordination Department of the FCO that, ultimately, on Commonwealth occasions like this, it was 'open to The Queen to invite whom She wished'.[64] This doctrine did not find favour with Sir John Johnston, deputy secretary of state at the FCO. He argued,

I do not think ... we can suggest that The Queen should in her personal capacity (or in her indeterminate capacity as "Head of the Commonwealth") arbitrarily select and invite two of the 28 Commonwealth Prime Ministers for this mark of favour leaving it to the Palace to defend the selection if it is criticised either by the press here or by other Commonwealth Prime Ministers who may later decide to come to the Games.[65]

A more recent Commonwealth Games has demonstrated the sensitivities that can be aroused by the Queen's role and the danger that, if the Palace does not coordinate its actions carefully with the British government, it has the potential to undermine the foreign policy of the UK. The announcement from the Palace in May 2010 that the Queen would not attend the games in Delhi later that year and would be represented, instead, by Prince Charles provoked accusations from the Indian Press of a 'royal snub'.[66] There subsequently developed a bizarre diplomatic tussle as to who should open the Games, which came to a head in the week before they were to commence. While conceding that the Indian president would have a prominent role in the opening ceremony, Prince Charles's staff at Clarence House told the press that, as the Queen's representative, he would 'read out the Queen's baton message, ending by declaring the games open'.[67] The suggestion that the act of reading out the Queen's message itself marked the formal opening of the Games was reinforced by a passage from the Palace's own website dealing with the Queen's Relay. This read, 'as the final relay runner hands the baton back to Her Majesty, or her representative, and the message is read aloud. At that moment the relay ends and the Games begin.'[68]

Meanwhile, however, Indian officials apparently insisted that, in terms of protocol, the honour of opening the Games should go to their president.[69] A curious and rather mind-bending compromise was finally arrived at. As the British high commissioner in India, Sir Richard Stagg, told the press: '[Prince Charles] will read out the Queen's message and receive the Queen's Baton [and declare] the Games open. After that, President Patil, on behalf of Delhi, will declare the Games open.'[70] Nevertheless, the controversy came close to undermining the efforts of British Prime Minster David Cameron to use the Games as an opportunity to foster good relations with India and, in particular, to promote British trade.

CHRISTMAS DAY MESSAGES

From the beginning of her reign the Queen had followed the tradition established by her grandfather in 1932 of broadcasting a Christmas Day message to the Commonwealth. Before the 1960s this had only been broken on two occasions: in 1936 and 1938. In 1957, for the first time, the message took the form of a television broadcast, and between then and Christmas 1968 the messages continued to be televised with the exceptions of 1959 and 1963 when pre-recorded sound broadcasts were used, presumably because on both occasions the Queen was pregnant.[71]

It is part of Commonwealth orthodoxy that the Queen does not take advice from her ministers on the content of either her Christmas or Commonwealth Day messages. In practice, the situation was rather more complex than this. The standard doctrine was indeed, as Edward Heath's private secretary noted in December 1972 following talks with the Queen's private secretary, Martin Charteris, that 'the broadcast is to the whole of the Commonwealth, not just to the Queen's subjects in this country and that the text of the broadcast is not therefore a matter on which the Queen expects to receive formal advice from the Prime Minister'.[72] This placed the British government in a somewhat invidious position, for in 1957 Charteris, the Queen's then assistant private secretary, had ruled that it was, nevertheless, responsible for anything the Queen might say in the Christmas broadcast.[73]

Given the dilemma this posed to the UK government, the Palace recognized that the Christmas Day message should, at the very least, not take the British prime minister by surprise. When the Foreign Office probed into this issue in 1971, it was told by the press secretary at Buckingham Palace 'that no formal Ministerial advice is asked or tendered in respect of the Queen's Christmas Broadcast, though as a courtesy, it is shown to the (British) Prime Minister before publication'. No mention was made of Commonwealth governments and the FCO official who investigated the matter was left with the impression 'that the Press Secretary regards this as very much his own prerogative'.[74]

In fact, the Palace proved willing to go beyond simply providing the British prime minister with a text of the message in advance as a courtesy. As Charteris put it in 1972, when 'the text contains matters of substance which are the concern of the United Kingdom Government, it is proper that the Prime Minister should be given full opportunity to see the text and give advice as he sees fit'.[75] The question remained as to what matters could legitimately be included in this category. In the broadcast of 1972 the Queen proposed to mention the situation in Northern Ireland and the impact of Britain's forthcoming entry into the EEC on its relations with the Commonwealth. Both matters were considered by the Palace to be ones on which the British government could legitimately give advice. Indeed, Heath appears to have regarded himself as being in a position to 'approve' what the Queen said on these matters, and made a number of suggestions.[76]

In early December 1968 Adeane told Downing Street that, whereas 'the practice usually followed is for someone outside the household staff to be asked to draft the message', that year the Queen and Prince Philip had done so themselves. Adeane suspected that the idea for the main theme of the message, 'the brotherhood of man', was Prince Philip's. Although the speech was largely concerned in very general terms with the Commonwealth, Michael Halls, Wilson's private secretary, suggested that not only should Wilson look at it 'from the point of view of any political overtones, but the FCO should also see it'.[77] The text was sent to the permanent undersecretary at the FCO, Paul Gore-Booth, who confessed to finding himself 'in a very difficult position' given the authorship. He clearly disliked some of the ways in which the message was phrased and suggested that ideally 'considerable changes' might be made. Yet recognizing that this was probably beyond his brief, he confined himself to advising that he 'could find nothing in the draft which should upset opinion in the Commonwealth'.[78]

In October 1969, the Palace announced that the Christmas Day message would not be broadcast on either radio or television. Instead, it would be issued in written form on Christmas Eve. It explained that 1969 had witnessed the investiture of Prince Charles as Prince of Wales and the broadcast of the groundbreaking television documentary 'The Royal Family'. The BBC was due to televise the Christmas morning service from St George's Chapel Windsor and to repeat 'The Royal Family' later in the day. The clear implication of this statement was that the Queen was in danger of media 'overexposure'.

In deciding that no broadcast should be made, not only did the Palace not consult the prime minister, Harold Wilson, but it told the BBC of its decision before it told Downing Street. As Wilson's private secretary noted, this put the prime minister in a very difficult position. The decision would be controversial, and however Wilson responded he was likely to be damaged politically. If the Queen changed her mind as a result of his advice, the BBC would know that Downing Street had intervened and might publicize the matter. If he did nothing, Wilson might well be accused, as his private secretary told him, of 'intervening . . . to keep Her off the television so that you can hog it'.[79]

Within the Foreign Office, there was also concern at the way in which this announcement had been handled. The FCO itself does not appear to have been consulted or even informed prior to the announcement. Downing Street had been informed just a few days before the announcement that it was the Queen's personal decision not to make the broadcast, but did not pass this news on to the FCO. The Governors General of Canada, Australia, and New Zealand had also been informed by telegram, but other Commonwealth governments had not.[80] B. G. Smallman of the FCO's Commonwealth Co-ordination Department suggested that this final aspect of the arrangements seemed to reveal 'an old-style concept of Commonwealth among the Palace advisers and could be misinterpreted, if it became known, as a reflection of the Queen's own view of Her position as Head of the Commonwealth'.[81] In regretting that neither Downing Street nor the FCO were consulted by the Palace about the Commonwealth implications of its announcement, he noted that, while 'the UK have in theory a 1 in 28 standing in what The Queen does as Head of the Commonwealth . . . in practice we are closely concerned because any weakening of Her position as Head of the Commonwealth is likely to come because people see Her as Queen of Britain first.'

Writing in *The Observer*, Ivan Yates was among a number of journalists who made a connection between the announcement about the Christmas broadcast and the Duke of Edinburgh's 'outburst' in Canada about the future of the Crown. Yates suggested that they pointed to uncertainty about the value of constitutional monarchy in both Britain and the Commonwealth.[82] René MacColl in the *Daily Express* also made a link between the two developments, suggesting that they reflected an anxiety about public reactions to the standard, repetitious protocol-bound royal engagements—'the danger that it may all become a great, big, thunderous bore'.[83]

THE COMMONWEALTH SECRETARIAT, THE SECRETARY-GENERAL, AND THE HIGH COMMISSIONS

The royal connection with the Commonwealth Secretariat in some respects actually preceded its creation. The Queen's commitment to the 'new' Commonwealth found concrete expression in the announcement in February 1959 that she was making the royal palace of Marlborough House available to the British government for a variety of Commonwealth purposes. At a Commonwealth Trade and Economic Conference in Montreal in September 1958 there had been, in the words of the Commonwealth Secretary, Lord Home, 'almost embarrassing enthusiasm' for a British proposal for a 'Commonwealth House' in London to provide the base for a variety of organizations and activities.[84] At a chance meeting between the Chancellor of the Exchequer, Derick-Heathcote Amory, and the Duke of Edinburgh, the latter had suggested that the Queen might be willing to make Marlborough House available for this purpose. The prime minister, Harold Macmillan, raised this with her in December, suggesting that the building's association with the royal family and the Duke of Marlborough would be regarded favourably even by republican members of the Commonwealth.[85]

The fact that the house had traditionally been the home of either the Queen Mother or the heir to the throne involved some sensitive negotiations with British political leaders. Although receptive to the idea that Marlborough House should be used as a Commonwealth centre, the Queen had expressed the hope that the British government would be able to make some other building available when the time came for the Prince of Wales to have a home of his own.[86] Such an undertaking would only be meaningful, however, if it commanded cross-party support, and Macmillan therefore had to raise the matter with Hugh Gaitskell and Jo Grimond, the leaders, respectively, of the Labour and Liberal parties. Macmillan reported back on this meeting to the Queen on 3 February. He noted that Gaitskell and Grimond had been 'rather stuffy' about giving any undertakings regarding the Prince of Wales, but they were ready to support a statement along the lines that another Parliament would 'think it right when the time comes to make suitable provision for the Heir to the Throne'. Macmillan suggested that although they were not hostile to the throne, they were 'very unwilling to open any flanks' and hence were keen to avoid anything with the appearance of a formal obligation. He added that he had also thought it better to avoid reference to building or buying a home for the heir to the throne: 'These notions shock the Left very much. It could after all be provided by seizing it from some other unhappy owner. I explained all this to the Queen who was very much amused and not put out about it.'[87]

The royal household, for its part, was keen that Marlborough House should continue to be recognized as a Palace. As the Queen's private secretary told the Cabinet Secretary, it was felt to be 'in the Queen's interest if this could be arranged because it would show the Commonwealth users that they are working in one of Her Majesty's own houses and it may also act, in years to come, as a reminder that Marlborough House still belongs to the Queen though it is on loan for this especial Commonwealth purpose'.[88] Correspondingly, the Queen took a close interest in the work of converting Marlborough House to accommodate its new role. For example, she vetoed plans to remove the gallery from the central salon to make room for a new corridor.[89] The costs of the refurbishment were to be met in their entirety by the British government. While there was some discussion of inviting Commonwealth governments to make a contribution to the upkeep of Marlborough House, British officials were keen not to give them any pretext for interfering in the management of the building.[90] Above all, they were horrified by the idea that Commonwealth governments might make any contributions in kind to furnishing it. The Cabinet Secretary, Sir Norman Brook, noted, 'We certainly do not want to see the house cluttered up with statuary from India or Ghana, or even with modern furniture from Canada or Australia.'[91]

As the 1960s progressed, various suggestions were made for something resembling a secretariat to coordinate Commonwealth activities. The Commonwealth prime ministers' meeting of 1964 represented a turning point. Although the UK preferred to concentrate on a series of initiatives geared towards development in the Commonwealth, an influential group of leaders from the 'new' Commonwealth led by Kwame Nkrumah of Ghana proposed the idea of a secretariat. Once momentum had gathered behind the idea, the efforts of the British government were geared, as the Cabinet Secretary put it in January 1965, to making it work 'while keeping its activities within prescribed limits, and preventing it from becoming a political pressure group'.[92] The report of the committee of officials which developed concrete plans for the secretariat reflected this concern that the new body should not be able to establish a power-base of its own and that it should operate 'on a modest footing'.[93]

This nervousness about the role of the secretariat inevitably led to tensions when the organization began work in Marlborough House later in 1965. The first Secretary-General of the Commonwealth, the Canadian Arnold Smith, makes it clear in his memoirs that this tension extended to questions about the relationship between the secretariat and the Crown. Smith notes that during his first weeks as Secretary-General, 'members of the Royal Family made what was clearly a concerted effort to give us a welcome and to impress upon Whitehall that I was to be considered one of the Queen's advisers'. Yet 'a few Whitehall officials needed some Royal prodding before they accepted the Commonwealth Secretary-General's position in the way the Queen saw it'.[94]

Indeed, the relationship between the monarch and the Commonwealth Secretary-General remained poorly defined. When considering the issue in 1969, the Foreign Office seems to have had no explicit guidance about it, and it was forced to seek the advice of the Commonwealth secretariat itself.[95] The secretariat noted that the Secretary-General had never had a formal audience with the Queen and that his only personal contact with her was at dinners for Commonwealth prime ministers and other diplomatic gatherings.[96] His access to her was through her private secretary. Via this channel, the Queen would use the Secretary-General to convey messages to and from Commonwealth governments. He would also send her notice of Commonwealth prime ministers' meetings and, subsequently, the minutes of these meetings.

This latter function was clearly something Smith had lobbied the Palace to be allowed to undertake. When the matter was considered in 1966, the preference of the British government was that it should continue to pass these minutes to the Queen or, if that was not acceptable to the Commonwealth Secretary-General, that the host country should do so. Smith, however, managed to persuade Sir Michael Adeane that the Secretary-General should personally pass a copy to the Palace.[97] British officials learned that Smith had insisted that 'as a servant of the Prime Ministers of the multilateral Commonwealth, of which the Queen is the Head, he had a perfect right to send the copy direct to her Majesty on behalf of the Commonwealth Prime Ministers'. This interpretation of Smith's role was disputed in Whitehall, and fears were expressed that, once he had established a channel of communication with the Palace for this purpose, 'there is no telling where it will lead'.[98] Smith, however, prevailed.

The Palace appears to have given further informal support for a strengthening of its relationship with the Commonwealth secretariat. In May 1972, a couple of weeks before the Queen made a highly publicized visit to the secretariat's head-quarters at Marlborough House, the Deputy Secretary-General, Hunter Wade, discussed the matter with his old friend Philip Moore, the Queen's deputy private secretary. Wade suggested that there ought to be 'more or less regular arrangements for the Secretary-General to brief the Queen on significant developments within the Commonwealth'.[99] Moore expressed his private agreement with this idea. He estimated that 95 per cent of the despatches and papers that crossed the Queen's desk were from British government sources, and suggested that this was hardly in keeping with the Queen's role of Head of State of a number of Commonwealth countries and of Head of the Commonwealth. Moore feared that there might be resentment among ministers that their prerogative of giving advice to the sovereign was being undermined if it was announced that the Secretary-General was advising her on Commonwealth affairs. He therefore suggested that any meetings for this purpose should be informal and kept off the Court Circular. It is not clear how frequent were the subsequent briefings of the Queen by the Secretary-General. They did, however, discuss Commonwealth affairs on 24 July 1973, ahead of the CHOGM in Ottawa.[100]

As Lorna Lloyd has noted, the Queen has also been keen to stress her own and Britain's Commonwealth role by affording special treatment to Commonwealth high commissioners in London.[101] At royal receptions with the diplomatic corps, for example, they (and the Irish ambassador) are given precedence over other overseas representatives. When visiting other Commonwealth countries she has insisted on receiving high commissioners separately. More recently, at the service of thanksgiving at St Paul's Cathedral in June 2006 to mark the Queen's eightieth birthday, the high commissioners of Pakistan, Nigeria, Papua New Guinea, and Barbados were chosen to deliver prayers.[102] In 1968, when the CRO (which from 1925 had provided Commonwealth countries with a uniquely sympathetic although not especially powerful advocate within Whitehall) was merged with the Foreign Office to create the Foreign and Commonwealth Office, the Queen pointedly expressed the hope that this 'would not in any way diminish the special arrange-ments made for Commonwealth representatives'.[103]

One final way in which the Queen has given substance to the headship of the Commonwealth is through her presence at CHOGMs. In the 1990s this dedica-tion resulted in her being given a formal role in these gatherings—a further augmentation of the status of the headship. Yet, as the following chapter will demonstrate, this aspect of her Commonwealth role was, above all others, to bring her into conflict with British prime ministers and cause major concerns in Whitehall.

8

A Royal 'Duty': Commonwealth Heads of Government Meetings in the 1970s

The turbulent Commonwealth Heads of Government Meetings (CHOGMs) of the 1970s in many ways confirmed the Queen as a champion of the 'new' Commonwealth. It is no secret that they created tensions with her British ministers. Yet the growing assertiveness of the Palace within this arena also caused some concerns within the secretariat about the signals that a close association with the monarchy might send about the nature of the modern Commonwealth.

In May 1970 the Cabinet Secretary, Burke Trend, raised with British prime minister Harold Wilson the possibility of a visit by the Queen to Singapore the following January to coincide with the meeting there of the Commonwealth Prime Ministers' conference. This would be the first such gathering (with the exception of the 'emergency' meeting in Lagos in 1966) to be held outside the UK. Trend noted that in principle it was 'highly desirable that the Queen should be in a position to act, in her capacity of Head of the Commonwealth, as host wherever the Meeting of Commonwealth Prime Ministers may be held', and that Singapore would be convenient, since it would allow her to entertain on the royal yacht *Britannia*.[1] On the other hand, Trend was keen not to encourage the expectation that the Queen would be present at all future meetings since 'one can conceive of circumstances— for example, if it were decided to hold a Meeting . . . in certain inland African countries—in which it might be difficult or even impossible for her to act as host except in circumstances which might entail some embarrassment.' There was also the danger, Trend warned, of the impression being given that a visit by the Queen was 'an attempt on our part to assert British paramountcy in the Commonwealth to offset the fact that the meeting was being held in Singapore rather than in London'. Problems also arose, he suggested, from the fact that the Queen's 'functions and capacities' as Head of the Commonwealth had never been defined. In the light of all this, Trend suggested that a visit to Singapore by the Queen was only feasible if it could be presented as part of a more extensive tour of the region. Wilson, however, seemed to be more relaxed about the prospect of the Queen visiting the conference. He minuted on Trend's note, 'She might avoid creating a precedent by saying this was first P[rime] M[inister]s' <u>normal</u> m[ee]t[in]g outside London and she wanted to mark it.'

The Conservative victory in the June 1970 general election led to an appreciable hardening of the government's attitude. One of the Heath administration's first announcements was that it would resume arms sales to South Africa.[2] It was feared in Downing Street, not unreasonably, that this issue could create 'a somewhat explosive' Commonwealth conference, and that embarrassment could be caused to the Queen were she to be there.[3] Heath raised some of these concerns with the Queen during a visit to Balmoral in September. The Queen, however, expressed the view that 'it would not be understood' if she were to undertake a tour of South East Asia in 1971 and not attend the Singapore conference.[4] Edward Heath's principal private secretary, Robert Armstrong, had suggested to the prime minister that 'the first idea of the visit to Singapore came from the Duke of Edinburgh, who may well still be hankering after it'.[5] The Queen, however, was keen to make clear to Downing Street

> that her suggestion of attending this particular Conference did not arise from any particular personal wish to go to Singapore but because she thought that it ought to be understood that it was as appropriate for the Head of the Commonwealth to be present when the Prime Ministers were meeting formally outside Britain as when they met in London.[6]

She wanted this general principle to be acknowledged, whatever the government's specific advice on Singapore might be.

The Foreign Secretary, Sir Alec Douglas-Home, was prepared to accept that 'in normal circumstances, it is desirable that, as Head of the Commonwealth, The Queen should attend all such meetings'.[7] He was adamant, however, that 'we are not now planning in normal circumstances' and warned that the issue of arms for South Africa could lead to a 'walk-out or a rump meeting'. On this basis, he recommended that Heath advise the Queen not to attend the conference.

The omens for the Singapore conference worsened on 11 October when the president of Tanzania, Julius Nyerere, threatened to withdraw his country from the Commonwealth over the issue of arms for South Africa.[8] Four days later, Heath wrote to the Queen in the terms recommended by Douglas-Home, claiming that while in 'normal circumstances' it was desirable that she should attend such meetings, the danger of trouble over South Africa meant that, with 'considerable personal regret', he was bound to advise her not to go to the Singapore conference.[9] He added that it would be necessary to approach other Commonwealth governments about the Queen's visit and that this might 'run the risk of misrepresentation as well as of rebuff':

> We should be liable to be criticised by the "Old Commonwealth" Countries for putting The Queen in an embarrassing position, and by the newer members of the Commonwealth for seeking to use The Queen politically in an attempt to soften their position on our policies. I am afraid that the risks of criticism and embarrassment in these circumstances would not be confined to Your Majesty's Ministers but might extend to Your Majesty.

This suggestion that extensive Commonwealth consultations would be necessary, incidentally, ran contrary to the long-standing view of Adeane that the British government had the ultimate responsibility for advising the Queen on such visits.[10]

The Queen's reply, articulated by Adeane, accepted Heath's decision. Yet it seized on Heath's suggestion that the Queen should normally be present at Commonwealth meetings, welcoming this admission, and noting that it was 'The Queen's considered opinion that when there is a meeting of this nature it is desirable *and, indeed, it is her duty* as Head of the Commonwealth to be present' [author's italics].[11] The idea that the headship had specific duties attached to it was not something that would have been recognized by the Commonwealth prime ministers who agreed the title in April 1949. It is another sign of the Queen's own determination to augment the role and make it more tangible.

In the event, the Singapore CHOGM in January 1971 was as acrimonious as had been feared. From the perspective of the Palace, if Heath's advice to the Queen had been intended to spare her 'embarrassment', her very absence may, as Martin Charteris suggested, have added to the atmosphere of hostility by removing her restraining influence.[12] As the Foreign Office subsequently noted, during the Singapore conference the issue of South Africa 'came fairly close to wrecking the Commonwealth'. For Heath personally it was a trying experience—'nine days in the dock', as Douglas Hurd described it—facing denunciations of British policy not just from African leaders but from Trudeau of Canada.[13]

Difficulties with the Commonwealth came against the background of highly sensitive negotiations over the terms of Britain's entry into the European Common Market, an objective which divided both major parties in the UK but to which Heath was personally highly committed. The prime minister was clearly irritated when, during a key stage of those talks in Luxembourg in June 1971, Prince Philip made a speech to the Royal Agricultural Society which was seen by some as hostile to the Common Market. It led to a group of anti-European Conservative back-benchers signing a Commons motion 'warmly congratulating' the Prince on a speech that, they claimed, expressed the concerns of 'millions of British people who feel the deepest apprehension about casting away our Commonwealth agricultural policies'.[14] Philip wrote a suitably contrite letter to Heath expressing regret that 'some very casual remarks at a small conference in Edinburgh should have caused such a fuss'.[15] The Palace issued a statement claiming that the Prince's words had been misunderstood and that he had always been careful not to express any opinions about the Common Market. Heath's less than gracious response suggests he may have been somewhat sceptical about this. He told Philip, 'I must confess that the headlines that day in the middle of the Luxembourg Meetings, gave me a bad moment or two. But I hope and think that, thanks to the statement which your office put out, it all proved to be a storm in a teacup and the record is now straight again.'[16]

The scars from the Singapore CHOGM were still apparent when Heath set down his views on future heads of government meetings in October 1972. He claimed to see little point in holding them except to discuss specific issues, and he noted that the practice of fixing them at regular intervals made it impossible to predict what would dominate the agenda.[17] He also felt that the meetings were scheduled over too long a period: 'if the nine Heads of Government can settle the course of the European Community for the rest of the decade in two days, there is

1. Commonwealth Prime Ministers meeting at the time of the Coronation in June 1953.

© Commonwealth Secretariat.

2. The Queen dancing with Kwame Nkrumah during her visit to Ghana in 1961.

© Ian Berry/Magnum Photos.

3. 'No Hiding Place'. A cartoon produced by Michael Cummings for publication in the *Daily Express* at a time when it seemed likely that the Queen's planned visit to Ghana in 1961 would be cancelled. In fact the visit went ahead and Cummings re-drafted the cartoon to show Nkrumah seeking refuge within the crown.

© Michael Cummings, *Daily Express*, 22 October 1959. Supplied by the British Cartoon Archive, University of Kent, <www.cartoons.ac.uk>.

4. The Wind of Change: Commonwealth Prime Ministers meeting in London in September 1962.

© Commonwealth Secretariat.

5. The Commonwealth's first Secretary-General, Arnold Smith, with Archbishop Makarios of Cyprus in 1970.

© Commonwealth Secretariat.

6. Prime Minister Lee Kuan Yew of Singapore with British Prime Minister Edward Heath at Singapore CHOGM in 1971.

7. Maltese Prime Minister Dom Mintoff.

8. Commonwealth heads of government photographed ahead of a banquet at Buckingham Palace for the 1977 CHOGM in London.

© Commonwealth Secretariat.

9. Margaret Thatcher at a press conference during the 1979 CHOGM in Lusaka.

10. Ballroom diplomacy: Margaret Thatcher dances with President Kenneth Kaunda of Zambia during the 1979 CHOGM in Lusaka.

© Commonwealth Secretariat.

11. A senior member of the Indian delegation with Australian Prime Minister Bob Hawke, British Prime Minister Margaret Thatcher, and Canadian Prime Minister Pierre Trudeau at the New Delhi CHOGM in 1983.

12. Smoke without fire?

Private Eye cover, issue 642, 25 July 1986: 'Royal Couple Souvenir Picture' reproduced by kind permission of *Private Eye* magazine, <www.private-eye.co.uk>

13. The Queen with Commonwealth leaders aboard the royal yacht *Britannia* during the 1989 CHOGM in Kuala Lumpur.

© Commonwealth Secretariat.

14. Gold and silversmith Gerald Benney pictured with his design of the gold Commonwealth Mace, commissioned by the Royal Anniversary Trust.

© Commonwealth Secretariat.

15. Nelson Mandela with Commonwealth Secretary-General Chief Emeka Anyaoku standing in front of Marlborough House during Mandela's visit to London in 1993.

© Commonwealth Secretariat.

16. 'Mandela Medal', 21 March 1995. *Guardian* cartoonist Steve Bell was not impressed by the Queen's gesture in 'honouring' Nelson Mandela with the Order of Merit during her visit to South Africa in March 1995.

Reproduced by kind permission of Steve Bell © belltoons.

17. The Queen speaking at the opening ceremony of the CHOGM in Coolum, Australia, in March 2002.

© Commonwealth Secretariat.

18. The Queen at Marlborough House in May 2006 with three Commonwealth Secretaries-General: (from left to right) Chief Emeka Anyaoku, Don McKinnon (the then current Secretary-General), and Sir Shridath Ramphal.

© Commonwealth Secretariat.

19. The Queen with Commonwealth Secretary-General Emeka Anyaoku, leaving Westminster Abbey, London, after the annual Commonwealth Day Multi-Faith observance.

20. Twelve-year-old John Samson from the Jacaranda Foundation, Malawi, presents the Royal Commonwealth Society's Jubilee Time Capsule to the Queen in November 2012.
© Capsool/Joe Gardner.

no justification whatever for this old-fashioned jamboree'. He insisted that they should last for no more than two or three days and asserted, 'I have no intention of taking part in anything else.' The Commonwealth Secretary-General, Arnold Smith, was subsequently told by Sir Denis Greenhill, the permanent undersecretary at the FCO, that the next CHOGM would be 'Not in 1973 or 1974, possibly 1975 at the earliest'.[18]

Charteris, however, confirms that the Queen 'regretted' Heath having prevented her from attending the 1971 CHOGM and was 'determined it was not going to happen again'.[19] According to Smith, Heath was trapped by a pincer movement involving the secretariat and the Palace. Aware of Heath's hostility to regular heads of government meetings and determined that there should be one in 1973, Smith decided that Heath would find it difficult to dismiss proposals for a meeting if the offer to host it came from the Canadians. He therefore approached Trudeau with the suggestion that the meeting be held in Ottawa in 1973.[20] Trudeau raised the matter with the Queen during a visit to London in December 1972, and the Queen expressed a desire to go. He followed this conversation with a formal invitation, which the Palace duly accepted without reference to Downing Street. The Foreign Office subsequently learned that 'the [British] Prime Minister was perturbed by the Queen's decision to accept, as The Queen of Canada'.[21] Nevertheless, since the invitation had been framed in those terms, Downing Street was not entitled to any say in the matter.[22] Yet the British government remained concerned at the prospect of the Queen's attendance at the Ottawa conference, in large part because of the likely presence of the Ugandan dictator, Idi Amin.

There was a nice irony about the way in which Amin's presence was to haunt Commonwealth meetings and add to British anxieties about the Queen's presence. Amin had come to power in January 1971, when as chief of staff of the Ugandan army he had overthrown the government of Milton Obote while Obote himself was attending the heads of government meeting in Singapore. British officials had initially regarded the coup with considerable satisfaction. Obote had been one of the most prominent critics of the Heath government's decision to resume arms sales to South Africa, and had threatened to withdraw Uganda from the Commonwealth if they went ahead. Furthermore, in May 1970 he had announced a programme of nationalization which endangered the interests of some leading British firms. Following his overthrow, Britain had been one of the first countries to recognize the Amin regime and had encouraged other governments to do likewise. Harold Smedley, the assistant undersecretary of state at the FCO, noted with optimism that 'At long last we have a chance of placing our relations with Uganda on a friendly footing.'[23] Nor did the early signs that Amin's regime was likely to be highly repressive seem to have caused undue concern in Whitehall. When in July 1971 (in the wake of mass arrests and beatings which had been reported by the UK high commission in Kampala) Amin requested a visit to London, the government arranged for him to be treated as an honoured guest. This included organizing meetings with Heath and the Queen.[24] Amin used the visit to secure a contract for military equipment from the UK, a move that was supported in an editorial in the *Daily Telegraph*, which described the Ugandan leader as 'a staunch friend of

Britain'.[25] Over subsequent months, as it emerged that Amin was murdering his political opponents on a scale that was difficult to ignore, British officials became increasingly embarrassed about the UK being publicly associated with his regime. Finally, in August 1972, Amin announced his decision to expel 80,000 Ugandan Asians. This effectively ended any hopes British ministers and officials might have had of reaching some sort of accommodation with Amin; and in their determination to distance themselves from a regime they had initially supported, they began to focus on the position of the Queen.

During Trudeau's visit to London in December 1972 the British Foreign Secretary, Alec Douglas-Home, told the Canadian high commissioner in London that 'he believed the domestic British reaction to The Queen's participation in a conference with General Amin would be highly critical, and Sir Alec doubted whether it would be feasible for The Queen to attend a function with a Commonwealth Head of Government known to be a murderer'.[26] The Queen, however, clearly had other ideas. A few days later, Douglas-Home warned Heath that 'according to advice from the Palace, the Queen does not regard her undertaking to Mr Trudeau to be present in Ottawa at the time of the Commonwealth meeting as subject to reservation on account of Uganda'.[27]

As the date of the conference approached, the British government remained concerned about the prospect of the Queen coming into contact with General Amin, who in March 1973 had confirmed his intention to attend the Ottawa conference.[28] A little more than a month before the conference was due to begin, one official at the Foreign Office suggested,

> Since the man in the street in Britain, and in many parts of the Commonwealth, finds it difficult to distinguish The Queen in Her various roles as British Head of State, Head of State of a number of other Commonwealth countries and Head of the Commonwealth—and indeed may only be aware of the first—the sight of The Queen receiving President Amin in private audience in Ottawa (as she seems bound to do) and entertaining him along with the other Heads of Government (with the inevitable group photograph) presents a delicate situation. . . . Unfortunately President Amin's flamboyant self-confidence and his loudly proclaimed devotion to the Royal Family are unlikely to lead him to behave with discretion and he is all too likely to make the most publicly of such meetings as he has with The Queen.[29]

The Foreign Office noted in an internal memorandum that the Queen's 'British Ministers would not have advised that she should go' to the 1973 CHOGM, given Amin's likely presence there.[30] According to Arnold Smith, the Queen herself 'placed a high priority' on attending the Ottawa meeting, and her 'firmness in showing that she at any rate would be in Canada' finally persuaded even a reluctant Heath to attend.[31] Her presence there, however, was explicitly on the advice of the Canadian prime minister.

The election of a Labour government in the UK in 1974 brought to power an administration that was unquestionably better disposed towards the Commonwealth than its predecessor had been. On becoming foreign secretary after the general election in March that year, James Callaghan had made a point of telling the

Queen's private secretary, Sir Martin Charteris, that he hoped to build stronger links with the Commonwealth. The response he received and the Queen's subsequent comments to him left Callaghan 'in no doubt of the keenness with which she followed Commonwealth affairs and of her genuine concern for its wellbeing'.[32] In marked contrast to Edward Heath, Callaghan clearly welcomed the Queen's commitment to the Commonwealth. He later recalled:

> Her very perceptive understanding comes not only from many years spent reading Foreign Office documents but also from her numerous meetings with successive Commonwealth leaders and her regular overseas tours. These have given her a knowledge of Commonwealth politicians and politics unequalled by any member of the Diplomatic Service or any British politician.[33]

The Queen's presence at the 1973 CHOGM established a working assumption that she would attend future meetings. Indeed, the dates of the 1975 CHOGM, held in Kingston, Jamaica, from 29 April to 6 May, were specifically chosen to allow her to attend. At the 1973 meeting, Uganda, Kenya, and Jamaica had all offered to host the next CHOGM. From the point of view of the British government, Uganda was clearly out of the question, and Jamaica was preferred over Kenya. This was on the grounds that whereas 'Mr Manley would make a reasonably good chairman', President Kenyatta was 'no longer up to chairing a full meeting'.[34] The British government also feared that if the meeting was held in Africa, 'the Africans for their own political reasons would probably wish African issues to predominate', raising the prospect of prolonged arguments over Rhodesia and South Africa. Without consulting the British, Arnold Smith had already suggested that the meeting should begin on 7 May 1975. It was pointed out by the British Cabinet Secretary, John Hunt, that the Queen, 'who would almost certainly be asked, and wish, to be in Jamaica for part of the period of the meeting' was already committed to a state visit to Japan on that date.[35] Hunt consulted both the Foreign Office and the Palace and established that a starting date of 29 April would be more convenient for the Queen.

The 1977 CHOGM was held in London. The idea of holding the meeting there appears to have been the Queen's own. At the 1975 meeting, Kenneth Kaunda, president of Zambia, had been keen to offer Lusaka as the venue for the next one. Harold Wilson confessed to Arnold Smith that he was in a difficult position: the Queen had asked him to invite heads to meet in London in 1977 to coincide with the celebrations of her Silver Jubilee. Wilson, however, was reluctant to put in a counterbid for fear of offending Kaunda. In the event, when Smith explained the situation to Kaunda, he magnanimously agreed to postpone the invitation to 1979.[36] The fact that this was the Queen's own idea clearly carried great weight. Yet there were obvious dangers in associating the Commonwealth so specifically and publicly with a royal celebration. As Smith himself notes, 'Closer to the time of [the 1977] Summit, one or two people were concerned that the occasion, merging with the Jubilee celebrations, might be seen like an old-style Durbar.'[37]

Indeed, the Palace added to these fears by pushing for the Queen to play a role in the opening ceremony of the 1977 CHOGM. She had never previously done so.

Instead, a message of greeting from the Queen had been read out at opening ceremonies, and heads of government had sent a reply. In July 1975, at a meeting of a Home Office subcommittee dealing with the Silver Jubilee celebrations, her deputy private secretary, Philip Moore, suggested that at the formal opening of the 1977 CHOGM she might offer this welcome in person. The initiative for this appears to have come not from the Queen, but from her private secretary, Martin Charteris.[38]

Smith's recently installed successor as Commonwealth Secretary-General, Sonny Ramphal, was unhappy with the idea. He was clearly concerned in more general terms about the CHOGM being regarded as just another element of the Jubilee celebrations. According to the Foreign Office, he explained that:

> The genuine warmth and affection with which the Royal Family were received throughout the Commonwealth tended to obscure for the Palace the real political delicacies which had to be watched in the Commonwealth relationship to-day. There would be much resentment among other Commonwealth Heads of State if the British gave the impression that their presence in London in 1977 was primarily seen as for attendance at Her Majesty's Jubilee celebrations.[39]

On the question of the Queen attending the opening ceremony, Ramphal made his objections clear:

> If it were seen as a special once-only affair connected with the Jubilee, it would have the undesirable connotations he had already spoken of. If it were proposed as a precedent to be followed at other HGM in other countries, he would see even greater political objections to it.

Ramphal's approach clearly derived not merely from a desire to avoid offending the dignity of some other Commonwealth leaders, but also from a concern that the Commonwealth should not be seen as an adjunct of Britain and its royal family. Perhaps understandably, Ramphal appears to have been reluctant to raise the matter directly with the Palace.[40] He was, however, keen that his views should reach the ears of Harold Wilson. On a visit to Downing Street in November 1975, the Jamaican prime minister, Michael Manley, apparently told Wilson:

> the Commonwealth Secretary-General had asked him to mention, in the lowest possible key, his hope that the Jubilee aspect of the Commonwealth meeting could be played down as far as possible. Mr Ramphal had told him that the Jubilee aspect was causing some embarrassment to the non-monarchies in the Commonwealth, and had therefore asked Mr Manley to mention this point 'in a whisper'.[41]

The head of the Commonwealth Co-ordination Department at the Foreign Office regarded Ramphal's objections as 'well-founded' and saw 'no grounds for dissenting' from them.[42] Downing Street also seems to have taken the point. In the event, it would not be until 1997 that the Queen would participate in the opening ceremony of a CHOGM.

More immediate problems for the organizers of the 1977 CHOGM were again posed by Idi Amin. Reports from Uganda that he was intending to come to London for the CHOGM placed the British government in an extremely difficult position.

Consultations with fifteen Commonwealth governments by the former minister of state at the Foreign Office, George Thomson, revealed that, while there would be widespread relief if Amin could be dissuaded from coming, virtually all thought he had the right to attend and some questioned the UK's right—as merely one of thirty-six member states—to prevent him from doing so.[43] It was feared in the Foreign Office that any indication Britain intended to take action against Amin might enable him to mobilize the support of other African states, with the Nigerian government (which remained unhappy at Britain's refusal to extradite its former president, General Gowon, who had been implicated in a coup attempt in 1976) likely to cause problems. Keen not to involve other Commonwealth member states, therefore, the British used an emissary from the Saudi government to convey a letter from Callaghan to Amin, dated 22 May. This warned Amin that a visit by him would be harmful to Anglo-Ugandan relations and that the British government would be obliged to prevent him from entering the UK. It promised, however, that Britain would accept a Ugandan delegation which did not include Amin.[44] Should gentle persuasion prove ineffective, the British also drew up elaborate contingency plans ('Operation Bottle'), involving the anti-terrorist squad and police marksmen, to detain Amin on his arrival in the UK and to eject him from the country.[45] In the event—and to general relief—Amin failed to appear.

While it is not clear how much the Palace knew about these plans, it seems that the Queen remained concerned about the possibility Amin might somehow evade British security. Lord Mountbatten noted in his diary the Queen's apparent unease during the Jubilee Service of Thanksgiving at St Paul's Cathedral on 7 June. He noted,

> I asked her afterwards why she had looked rather cross and worried at one time and she laughed and said, 'I was just thinking how awful it would be if Amin . . . were to gate-crash the party and arrive after all.' I asked her what she had proposed to do and she said she had decided she would use the City's Pearl Sword which the Lord Mayor had placed in front of her to hit him hard over the head with.[46]

This was all somewhat at odds with the Queen's speech delivered at the Guildhall later that day on the enduring value of the Commonwealth, comparing it to an iceberg:

> The tip is represented by the occasional meetings of the heads of government and by the Commonwealth Secretariat, but nine tenths of Commonwealth activity takes place continuously beneath the surface and unseen. . . . And right at the base of the iceberg, the part that keeps the rest afloat, is friendship and communication largely in the English language between peoples who were originally brought together by the events of history and who now understand that they share a common humanity.[47]

In her concluding remarks, she reaffirmed the vow of service she had made in Cape Town at the age of twenty-one. Yet, whereas in her 1947 Cape Town broadcast she had promised that her life would be devoted 'to your service and the service of our great Imperial family to which we all belong', her Guildhall speech referred simply to having 'pledged my life to the service of our people'.[48]

The Silver Jubilee year of 1977 also witnessed Prince Charles making a series of public interventions on the Commonwealth. Charles had long-standing concerns about the low profile of the organization, as the record of a meeting he held with Commonwealth Secretary-General Arnold Smith in June 1970 reveals. The Prince of Wales mentioned that when he had been in Australia and New Zealand earlier in the year he had made a point of asking young people for their views on the Commonwealth, and had found that most of them 'had appeared pretty indifferent to it and advanced the view that there was not much to the association'.[49] He also worried that the Commonwealth did not receive a very good press in Britain and 'wondered whether this might be because African Commonwealth leaders tended to say rather harsh things about it on occasion'. He raised the questions of how the issues of immigration and entry into the EEC would influence Britain's Commonwealth relations. He also asked whether independence had come too soon for some Commonwealth nations (a concern which, as we have already seen, was shared by his father).

On 7 June 1977, on the eve of the CHOGM in London, Charles unveiled a portrait of his mother at Marlborough House by the Australian artist Paul Fitzgerald.[50] The painting was a gift to the Commonwealth secretariat by the Australian government. The following day, *The Times* published a special report on the Commonwealth to coincide with the start of the CHOGM. This carried an introduction by Charles in which he extolled the virtues of the organization's flexible character. While his comments were largely unremarkable, he came dangerously close to taking sides on one of the most contentious issues of the day when he suggested that much criticism of the Commonwealth arose from a 'rather selfish outlook', and compared this to 'the attitude of some towards the EEC that it is not what we can contribute but what we can get out of the organization that really matters'.[51] Coming just a couple of years after a referendum on Britain's membership of the EEC that had split both the major political parties, this was perhaps an unhappy analogy.

Prince Charles returned to this theme later that month in a major speech on 'The relevance of the Contemporary Commonwealth' delivered to the Royal Commonwealth Society. This represented a characteristically serious if rather tortuous attempt to tease out the significance of the organization. He referred to his mother's comparison in her Guildhall speech between the Commonwealth and an iceberg. Yet he was clearly not satisfied with the overwhelmingly positive picture she had painted of its enduring value. At one level, Charles noted, 'The Commonwealth exists because, quite simply, it is "there". Perhaps no-one quite knows why it is there, but since it is and because it has survived so many trials and tribulations . . . a considerable number of influential people must feel it has <u>some</u> relevance in the contemporary world.'[52] He added, however, 'I do not believe that interest and support will necessarily continue unless constant efforts are made to encourage the kind of activities and enterprise which inspire interest and support.' The press picked up on Charles's suggestion that the Commonwealth would not survive without renewed efforts to demonstrate its relevance.[53]

Charles had a further Commonwealth engagement the following month when he spoke at the opening of a conference in the UK organized by the Commonwealth Youth Exchange Council. His speech returned to the theme that if new enthusiasm was not injected into the Commonwealth 'it will just be a matter of time before the whole thing fades away from lack of interest'.[54] Yet he provided reporters with a headline quotation during questions when he claimed, 'I do not think it would be a disaster if Britain withdrew from the Commonwealth. I am sure it could survive without Britain.' This arresting pronouncement brought the President of the Royal Commonwealth Secretary, Malcolm MacDonald, running to his assistance with a letter to *The Times* in which he valiantly attempted to place a positive gloss on the remark. The Prince had 'in a rather dramatic way', MacDonald suggested, helped to dispel 'the persistent illusions about the Anglo-centricity of the Commonwealth', by drawing attention to the fact that Britain was just one nation among many in this 'free community of peoples'.[55]

This incident lends some credence to an anecdote by the entertainment impresario Harry M. Miller, which received considerable attention in the Australian and British press when it appeared in his memoirs in 2009. Prince Charles visited Australia in November 1977. Miller, who claimed to have been in close contact with Charles during the trip, recalled a conversation about the monarchy between the Prince of Wales and Michael Kirby during which the former confessed not to be able to understand 'why Australia bothered with us—we really are yesterday's news'.[56] Whatever the truth of this story, Charles's less than assured handling of the issue of the Commonwealth during the 1977 Jubilee year may have helped to plant the seeds of doubt in the minds of some about his suitability to head the organization.

RHODESIA AND THE LUSAKA CHOGM OF 1979

For the Wilson and Callaghan governments, the Commonwealth was of particular significance in their efforts to resolve the intractable problem of Rhodesia. It was in this area of policy that we have a rare glimpse of the Queen exerting a tangible influence over British foreign policy. By the early months of 1976, changes in the regional balance of power that would eventually help to bring about a solution in Rhodesia were threatening to escalate the conflict there. Mozambique, recently freed from Portuguese control, had switched from being an ally of the Smith regime to an enemy which provided a haven for those seeking its overthrow. London feared a significant escalation of the guerrilla war, perhaps involving Cuban forces, which might threaten to draw in the UK. The outbreak of a major regional conflict carried the further threat of an exodus of Rhodesians to the UK. It was noted in Cabinet that around 80,000 of them were UK citizens who had an absolute right of entry, and that around 75,000 could claim partial status, allowing them to settle in Britain.[57]

Against this background, in February 1976, the Foreign Secretary, James Callaghan, was told by his former colleague in the Labour parliamentary party, Lord

Robens, who had just returned from a visit to southern Africa, that a deal might be possible over Rhodesia.[58] Robens, who had met both Ian Smith and the South African prime minister, John Vorster, thought Smith might be amenable to talks about a relatively rapid transition to majority rule. It was decided to send the former permanent undersecretary at the Foreign Office, Lord Greenhill, on a secret mission to Salisbury. While Greenhill thought it possible that Smith could agree to a transfer to majority rule over, say, three years, his report was hardly encouraging, and Callaghan's advisers at the FCO suggested that Smith was probably just playing for time. At this point, Callaghan had a chance encounter with the Queen at a dinner hosted by the Italian ambassador in London. Callaghan explained to her that he was still undecided as to whether the British government should follow up Greenhill's visit. The following day, Callaghan received a letter from the Queen's private secretary, Martin Charteris. Charteris told him that the Queen 'recognises that any initiative you take may prove ineffective, but none the less believes it would be worthwhile to make an effort. Her Majesty sends you her best wishes for your efforts in dealing with this intractable problem.'[59]

According to Callaghan, 'the Queen's opinion was enough to tip the scales'. He agreed with his ministerial colleagues at the FCO that a message should be sent to Smith to the effect that if he was prepared to make a public commitment to majority rule and to hold elections within eighteen months to two years, the British government would help to facilitate talks between him and African leaders. This offer formed the basis of a statement Callaghan made in Parliament on 22 March.

As Callaghan's advisers had anticipated, Smith was not prepared to make such a bold move. Joshua Nkomo, the leader of the Zimbabwe African People's Union (ZAPU), also rejected the offer. The guerrilla war continued with Nkomo's forces fighting alongside those of Robert Mugabe's Zimbabwe African National Union (ZANU) in the uneasy alliance known as the Patriotic Front. Nevertheless, the British were gratified that Callaghan's statement received favourable reactions from such diverse sources as the South African government, President Nyerere of Tanzania, and US Secretary of State Henry Kissinger.[60] They were also confident that, despite Smith's intransigence, South African economic pressure on the regime would eventually force him to compromise. In an effort to improve South Africa's relations with its African neighbours, Vorster was determined to end the conflict in Rhodesia. A powerful weapon at his disposal was South Africa's ability to restrict Rhodesia's import of essential supplies by reducing the railway stock available to it. In March 1978 international pressure, particularly from South Africa and the United States, finally pushed Smith into reaching a deal with the more pliable elements of the African nationalist movement headed by Bishop Abel Muzorewa, leader of the ANC, and Ndabaningi Sithole, leader of the ZANU-Ndonga Party, which had broken with Mugabe's movement and renounced violence. The new constitution was, however, clearly designed to allow the white minority to retain a disproportionate hold on political power and, far from ending the civil war, the Patriotic Front intensified its offensive. Elections were scheduled for April 1979.

As Rhodesia's elections approached, so too did those in the UK. Although the Labour government had refused to recognize the 'internal settlement', the Conservative

Opposition signalled in their election manifesto that they would be prepared to do so, and lift sanctions, if the elections in Rhodesia demonstrated popular support for the new constitution. To that end, the leader of the Conservatives, Margaret Thatcher, sent a team of observers led by the former Colonial Secretary, Lord Boyd, to monitor the elections. By the time Boyd's commission presented its report to Mrs Thatcher in the middle of May 1979, the Conservatives had been returned to power in the British general election. For this reason, its findings had particular significance. Boyd and his colleagues concluded that the election had been conducted fairly, and that, although the conditions of civil war meant the vote could not be said to have been entirely free, any pressures on voters were not sufficient to invalidate the result.[61]

In the light of the Boyd report, the new administration in the UK came under considerable pressure from the right wing of the Conservative party to recognize the government that had been formed by Bishop Muzorewa following his victory in the elections, and to lift sanctions. Recently declassified documents suggest that in his first days in office Mrs Thatcher's Foreign Secretary, Lord Carrington, was broadly sympathetic towards this course of action.[62] As, however, his department took soundings of international opinion, his approach became far more cautious. He realized that a decision to recognize the government of the re-christened 'Zimbabwe Rhodesia' would do nothing to end the civil war and would leave the UK isolated from its Commonwealth and European partners.[63] This was also the predominant view within Whitehall. Yet, even before Boyd had presented her with his report, Mrs Thatcher herself was inclined to side with the right wing of her party. She shared with them a dismissive view of post-independence African governments, and a tendency to view southern Africa in Cold War terms. According to this mindset, armed opposition to white minority rule was the work of Marxist terrorists (a perspective she also applied to the South African ANC). Her views on assuming office are vividly demonstrated by her furious annotations on a memorandum by the Cabinet Secretary, John Hunt, which sought gently to guide her away from recognition. In this briefing document, written a day after the British general election, Hunt warned that the reaction to the establishment of the Muzorewa regime 'of the African governments most immediately concerned is violently negative and the rest of Africa and the Third World are likely to follow this lead'.[64] Beside this, Mrs Thatcher scribbled, 'Not if we give them a firm lead in the other direction.' To Hunt's expression of concern about whether the new Rhodesian constitution had conceded real power to the black majority, she responded, 'Tell me another country in Africa which has one person/one vote for 4 political parties.' To Hunt's warning that early recognition and the lifting of sanctions might lead to 'the blame being laid at our door for disruption of plans for the Queen's State Visit to Lusaka and for the Commonwealth Heads of Government Meeting immediately thereafter' she replied, 'They will do the disruption.' To Hunt's characteristically judicious conclusion that the issue needed to be handled with 'great care', her response was equally characteristic: 'I agree we need care but a little courage is necessary too'. With opinion at the highest levels of the British government divided on this issue, the heads of government meeting, which was due to take place in

Lusaka in August 1979, assumed an importance that few CHOGMs before or since could claim.

Mrs Thatcher was notoriously cautious about the prospect of the Queen visiting Lusaka for the 1979 heads of government meeting. The New Zealand prime minister, Robert Muldoon, publicly questioned whether she should go, and there were signs that Mrs Thatcher sympathized with his concerns. Zambia provided bases for the Patriotic Front and was subject to attacks from the Rhodesian security forces. There were suspicions, however, that, aside from any physical danger to the Queen, rather like Heath in the approach to the Singapore CHOGM, Mrs Thatcher simply did not want the Queen embroiled in a Commonwealth row.

Yet there is evidence that the British government's ostensible concerns about the Queen's safety had a strategic purpose. In a note of a discussion in June 1979 between Mrs Thatcher and Lord Harlech, who had recently returned from a mission to Southern Africa as an envoy of the British government, Bryan Cartledge, the prime minister's private secretary with responsibility for foreign affairs, recorded:

> The Prime Minister said that it was essential to make President Kaunda do something about the ground-to-air missiles in guerrilla hands in advance of the C.H.G.M. in Lusaka. If the missiles could once be taken away from the guerrillas, it might prove possible to ensure that they did not receive any more. The Queen's visit to Zambia, and the Conference in Lusaka, were strong cards which should be used to put pressure on President Kaunda.[65]

Nine days after this discussion, when Mrs Thatcher met with Lombe Chibesa-kunda, the Zambian high commissioner in London, she made a point of mentioning that the government 'was engaged in quiet enquiries relating to The Queen's security concerning, in particular, the possibility of an attack on The Queen's aircraft by ground-to-air missiles'.[66] She noted that Robert Muldoon had called on her four days earlier and had mentioned his concern about the Queen's safety both in private and subsequently to the press. This had led to questions in Parliament and suggestions that the conference should be moved to another location. Mrs Thatcher claimed that, whilst the British government was doing everything possible to reassure doubters, 'the final reassurance could only come from President Kaunda if he were to ensure that all missiles were removed from the guerrilla forces in Zambia and that no maverick fired one . . . The Queen's safety . . . had to be <u>seen</u> to be protected and the Prime Minister was answerable to Parliament for this.'

Nevertheless, concerns about the Queen's safety were genuine, and focused in part on the fear that Zambian forces might fire on her plane by mistake. The British high commissioner in Zambia, Sir Walter 'Len' Allinson, was recalled to London to advise Mrs Thatcher in person about this issue. Allinson's advice was that the visit by the Queen should go ahead, but that a military team should be sent out to review security with the Zambians.[67] This was duly dispatched, led by Air Vice Marshal Reed Purvis. According to Allinson, the Zambians were initially unco-operative. While the British military team was still in Zambia, however, the Rhodesians launched an audacious raid by helicopter on Joshua Nkomo's intelligence headquarters in a suburb of Lusaka. Zambian anti-aircraft guns failed to fire on the Rhodesian helicopters but did open up on their own fighter planes which appeared a few minutes after the Rhodesians had departed. The following morning the British team had a meeting with Kaunda, who was suddenly far more conciliatory, and a member of the British military mission was subsequently stationed at Lusaka airport with direct contact with Zambian anti-aircraft batteries to ensure that no similar errors occurred as the Queen's plane approached.

In addition to security concerns, two matters of protocol intervened to complicate the Queen's visit to Lusaka. The Zambians revealed that they wanted Nkomo to be included in the line-up to meet the Queen on her arrival at Lusaka. They initially backed down in the face of British objections, but the night before the Queen's arrival Allinson learned that Nkomo was indeed to be included in the line-up. He approached Mark Chona, Kaunda's political assistant, and warned that if plans went ahead for Nkomo's inclusion he would telegram the Queen's party in Botswana and ensure that she would not fly to Lusaka.[68] In the face of this threat, Kaunda again retreated, and Nkomo was not included in the line-up.

A second problem related to Kaunda's speech at the state banquet for the Queen. Allinson had seen a text of the speech and had warned that some of Kaunda's remarks would be unacceptable to the British. The Zambian president was, however, unwilling to compromise. Allinson briefed the royal party about the problem. This is an unusual case in which we have evidence of a direct and important intervention by the Queen. Her private secretary, Philip Moore, did not feel that Allinson's subsequent despatch on the visit properly recorded the significance of this incident. He told the Foreign Office:

> The Queen intervened personally with the President. When we arrived at Lusaka Len Allinson reported to me that while he had been able to persuade the President not to present Mr Nkomo on Her Majesty's arrival, he thought that the only way in which he could get the offending passages removed from Kaunda's speech was for The Queen to speak to him personally. This The Queen did in the motor car and later that evening. Mark Chona came to me to say that the President had agreed to make all the amendments for which we had asked.[69]

To the surprise of many, given the potential for an angry stand-off between Mrs Thatcher and her critics within the Commonwealth, the Lusaka summit succeeded in paving the way for a three-part settlement to the problem of Rhodesia, based on a constitutional conference in London in December 1979, a ceasefire by the Patriotic Front, and elections involving all parties in February 1980. Assessments varied as to the extent to which the Queen was personally responsible for establishing the conditions for this unlikely consensus.[70] As a relative newcomer to the field of international summitry, Mrs Thatcher was always likely to be swayed by her Foreign Secretary, and by the Australian prime minister, Malcolm Fraser, a trusted fellow-conservative who also urged compromise. Yet some participants were subsequently to go on the record with fulsome tributes to the Queen's role. Before arriving in Zambia, she had made a tour of neighbouring Commonwealth African countries, which had taken her to Tanzania, Malawi, and Botswana. She thus had a first-hand opportunity to gauge the strength of feeling over Rhodesia. She took with her to Lusaka not merely the insights gained from these consultations, but also her long experience of African and Commonwealth affairs. By contrast, Mrs Thatcher, who had never visited the continent before, was so alarmed at the novelty of landing in an African country that, according to Carrington, she wanted to wear dark glasses, fearing that acid might be thrown in her face.[71]

At the summit itself, as had become a tradition at heads of government meetings, the Queen hosted a banquet for all the leaders present. She made a point of remaining at the dinner until nearly midnight and speaking to as many national representatives as she could. Emeka Anyaoku, then a diplomat with the Commonwealth Secretariat, recalled, 'I am convinced that the intervention spurred the organisation—which was on the point of possibly splitting up—on to compromise.'[72] She also held individual audiences with Commonwealth leaders. Her skill, according to the then Commonwealth Secretary-General Sonny Ramphal, was in talking to them about everything except Rhodesia, drawing on her long association with many of them. She knew 'who had got what political scandal raging. She'd know the family side of things, if there were children or deaths in the family. She'd know about the economy, she'd know about elections coming up. They felt they were talking to a friend who cared about the country.'[73] While she might not have appealed directly to them to soften their rhetoric—as she did to President Kaunda—her interventions may have helped to encourage a more constructive debate, in the process, allowing Mrs Thatcher the space to make concessions. As we shall see in Chapter 10, however, the success of the Lusaka summit did not convert Mrs Thatcher to the value of the Commonwealth; and some of the latent tensions between Downing Street and the Palace which could be detected behind the scenes in the run-up to the 1979 CHOGM were to burst embarrassingly into the open as her term in office progressed.

9

'De-Dominionisation' in the 1970s

BRITAIN AND THE COMMONWEALTH REALMS IN THE 1970S

In early 1974, the strong possibility that Conservative prime minister Edward Heath might call a snap general election, necessitating the Queen's return from a Commonwealth tour, sparked a debate in Whitehall about the signals this would send for the Queen's relationship with her Commonwealth realms. On 10 January an editorial in *The Dominion* (a Wellington newspaper) complained of 'the prevailing assumption that the Queen is monarch of Britain first and of New Zealand and the other "equal" Commonwealth countries second'. It noted that the Queen's return from New Zealand was necessitated by the fact that she lacked a representative (analogous to a Governor General) to act for her in her absence. This, it claimed, 'still suggests second-best treatment for New Zealand. The evolving Commonwealth deserves a better formula.'[1] The idea that there was a potential role in the UK for its own version of a Governor General was not, as we have seen, a new one.

Although Downing Street itself was relatively dismissive of the broader significance of the Queen's possible recall from New Zealand, there was an acknowledgement within the Foreign Office that 'when an election in Britain is to take place, she is shown to be the Queen of Britain first and of other Commonwealth countries second'.[2] In the event, these concerns proved well-founded. When a dissolution of Parliament was granted to Heath on 8 February, the day the Queen left New Zealand, this was done *in absentia*.[3] Nevertheless, she was forced to return early from a tour of Australia to be present in London for the appointment of a new administration. It was announced in advance of her return that the Queen would resume her Pacific tour once a new government had been installed. The former Labour Cabinet minister Richard Crossman neatly underlined the point of the *Dominion* editorial when, in an article in *The Times*, he expressed astonishment that at a time of 'national crisis' the Queen was planning to leave the UK so hurriedly that she would miss the opening of Parliament.[4] He blamed this decision on the Queen's 'courtiers', claiming that they had 'misjudged public opinion'. The 'courtiers' offered a rather belated response in the form of a letter from Sir Edward Ford, which was published in *The Times* on 1 March, the day after the general election. Ford claimed that the Queen had a mind of her own on these matters. He also accused Crossman of having given 'no thought to the Queen's Australian subjects';

nor had he 'considered the resentment which they may feel at any further curtail-
ment of her long-planned engagements in their country'.[5]

The messy aftermath of the February 1974 general election did not, however,
lend itself to a swift resumption of the Queen's travels. Labour had gained margin-
ally more seats than the Conservatives but neither had a majority. With the results
in by Friday 1 March, negotiations dragged on over the weekend, with Heath
exploring the possibility of the Conservatives remaining in power with Liberal
support. It was not until the early evening of Monday 4 March that Heath tendered
his resignation to the Queen. The day before, with the issue still unresolved,
Charteris had told Sir Robert Armstrong that the Queen would have to decide
by the following morning whether to return to Australia on 6 March as she had
originally planned, or delay her departure. According to Armstrong's account, 'The
decision was one for The Queen to make without ministerial advice either from
British ministers or from Australian ministers, since only She was in a position to
balance the conflicting considerations. Sir Martin said that The Queen had
virtually made up her mind to delay her departure.'[6] Here was another instance
of the Palace claiming that the Queen was able to act, in a particular Commonwealth context, without ministerial advice.

The Palace was clearly also stung by suggestions that the Queen might have
been neglecting her domestic duties. On 8 March, *The Times* reported that the
Queen would not resume her tour of Australia. Instead, she would remain in the
UK for the opening of Parliament on 12 March and leave for a planned state visit
to Indonesia the following day. While it was her 'hope and intention' to visit
those areas of Australia that had been dropped from her itinerary—namely
Western Australia, South Australia, and the Northern Territory—she could
only promise to do so at some unspecified future date when it proved 'possible
and appropriate'.[7]

The Palace itself sometimes seemed less than perfectly attuned to the sensitivities
of the realms. In May 1976, following a successful visit to Finland by the Queen
and the Duke of Edinburgh, Charteris wrote to Sir Michael Palliser, the permanent
undersecretary at the FCO, about the potential value of state visits. Charteris
suggested that there was a danger of not making full use of such events. They
created, he argued, 'a short period of exceptional goodwill for Britain' in which
'diplomacy and commerce have a unique opportunity to flourish'.[8] Charteris
wondered whether the UK was taking sufficient advantage of these opportunities,
and he referred specifically to 'our efforts to cash in on State Visits'.

It was left to the FCO to point out the awkward implications this aggressively
business-focused approach might have for the Commonwealth realms. An FCO
paper on the value of state visits, drafted in response to Charteris's intervention,
noted that

> when the Queen combines in one journey a State Visit and a visit to one of Her
> Realms, as recently to the USA and Canada, local sensitivities in the Realm need to be
> carefully watched during the planning and execution of the journey. Too great a
> concentration on promoting UK exports during the State Visit to the States, for

instance, could produce an adverse reaction in Canada, where it could reasonably be claimed that the journey as a whole should not promote exclusively United Kingdom purposes.[9]

AUSTRALIA: THE WHITLAM AFFAIR, AND ITS AFTERMATH

As we have seen in Chapter 6, British representatives in Australia had been relatively optimistic about the position of the Crown (certainly in comparison to the situation in Canada). Events in the first half of the 1970s, culminating in the constitutional crisis of November 1975, were to change all that. Gough Whitlam's Labor government of 1972–5 was widely perceived as representing a move in the direction of republicanism, and the Opposition in Australia was certainly able to portray it as such. As Mark McKenna notes, there was plenty of evidence:

> Between 1972 and 1975 Whitlam gave Australia a new national anthem, a new honours system, abolished appeals from the High Court to the Privy Council, unsuccessfully tried to legislate for a new oath of citizenship which removed any reference to the Queen, and decided to appoint Australian Ambassadors without seeking the formal approval of the Queen.[10]

Whitlam himself claimed that he was simply seeking to put Australia's relationship with Britain on 'a more mature and contemporary basis'.[11] Yet it was striking that two months after his election a Morgan Gallup poll found support for a republic among the Australian population at 40 per cent, the highest recorded figure in any such poll between 1953 and 1991, and a higher figure than in December 1975, shortly after Whitlam's dismissal as prime minister. This may, as McKenna suggests, reflect the fact that republican sentiment tended to be higher at times of national self-confidence.[12] It was hardly surprising, however, that some contemporary observers saw Whitlam's reforms as the prelude to a more decisive constitutional break. Certainly, the British government kept a close eye on these developments and—despite the fact that they essentially represented a matter for the Queen and her Australian government—officials in London appear to have assumed that a broader UK interest was at stake.

Australia's 1973 Royal Style and Titles Act removed the references in the Queen's title both to the United Kingdom and to 'Defender of the Faith'. The British Foreign Office saw no particular objection to this, not least because most of the other Commonwealth realms used a similar shorter form of title.[13] The Palace was also apparently unconcerned. The Queen's private secretary, Martin Charteris, noted that as long ago as 1949 George VI had minuted in his own hand that he thought Commonwealth countries other than the UK should drop 'United Kingdom' and 'Defender of the Faith' from the royal title.[14] What did concern British officials was that Whitlam might seek the consent of other Commonwealth states for the change. Australia's 1953 Royal Style and Titles Act had referred back to the convention in the Preamble to the Statute of Westminster that any change in the

Royal Style and title in any Commonwealth state would require the assent of the Parliaments of the UK and all of the Dominions. Officials were sceptical that the Preamble could still be said to apply in this area of legislation. They were worried, however, about the possibility that Whitlam might seek to raise the matter at the 1973 CHOGM. These concerns centred not on the Queen's role within the Commonwealth realms but on her status as Head of the Commonwealth. As L. E. T. Storar of the FCO's Commonwealth Co-ordination Department put it:

> Once Commonwealth attention is focussed on the question of the Queen's Style and Titles, we run the risk that someone might then raise the point whether in the modern Commonwealth it is appropriate that the Queen should always be Head of the Commonwealth and whether some other practice would be preferable, e.g. permitting other distinguished Commonwealth citizens to occupy the position from time to time.[15]

Whitlam discussed a number of constitutional proposals with the Queen on a visit to Windsor in April 1973. Although this was notionally a matter between Whitlam and his sovereign, it is striking that Charteris provided the British Foreign Office with a candid account of the meeting, noting, 'As some of the above concerns matters which affect The Queen as Queen of Australia only [*sic*] I know you will treat this letter with great confidence.'[16] What is equally striking is that, according to Charteris's account, the Queen herself sought to shape Whitlam's policy, both in the way in which the visit was choreographed and in her forthright expression of her own preferences. Charteris claimed that Whitlam and his wife 'were far from unaffected by the atmosphere of Windsor and the charm of their hostess and her family which I have seldom seen so formidably deployed'. On matters of substance, she firmly dismissed some other changes to the royal title suggested by Whitlam, specifically the removal of the phrases 'The Second' (on the basis that Australia had never had Elizabeth I as its sovereign) and 'by the Grace of God'. Charteris explained that 'to drop "The Second" might have reactivated the row of 20 years ago with Scotland'.

The issue that had caused the greatest concern within the Palace in advance of Whitlam's visit was the suggestion that the Queen might cease to sign and receive diplomatic letters of credence.[17] Again, Charteris's account makes it clear that the Queen took a stand on this matter in her conversation with the Australian prime minister:

> The Queen made it plain that, as Head of State of Australia, she wished to continue signing Letters of Credence and having them addressed to her by Foreign Heads of State. Mr Whitlam accepted this and found it comparatively easy to do so because once the Style and Title is amended the heading of letters will appear totally Australian.

She did, however, concede that the approval of letters could be given on her behalf by the Governor General.

One area in which the Palace was not able to get its way, despite making an explicit attempt to influence the process, was over Whitlam's proposal to reform the honours system. Whitlam wished to introduce an Australian system, following the example of the Canadian government, which had already established the Order of Canada. The British government feared that this might bring Whitlam into conflict not merely with the Australian states but with the Palace.[18] In the event, the Palace proved conciliatory, but was keen to ensure that the process of reform took place gradually. Towards the end of December 1974 Charteris wrote to Geoffrey Yeend, Whitlam's Secretary of the Department of the Prime Minister and the Cabinet, setting out the Queen's views. Charteris claimed that the Queen considered the proposal for an Australian honours system 'a good one, in principle' and was ready to give her support. He noted concerns, however, that they were 'likely to be received with suspicion', and told Yeend that the Queen therefore considered 'every effort should be made to make the new Australian system of Honours as attractive and non-controversial as possible'.[19] She believed 'that its initial popularity might be enhanced if its introduction into use was made to coincide with the Jubilee of 1977', anticipating that the process of working out the practicalities of the new system 'could . . . well take the best part of two years'. While she noted Whitlam's desire that the new Australian system should eventually replace British honours in Australia, there were 'considerations which would make it unconstitutional for the Queen to give her support to this long term aim'. Aside from this, the Queen was sure 'that it would be a mistake to try to hurry this process, because doing so would be divisive and would thus defeat one of the main objects of the proposal' (namely to be a unifying force in Australia). Although there would be obvious problems involved in running two separate honours systems simultaneously, these need not, Charteris suggested, be insuperable, and there was greater chance of securing agreement to the termination of the British honours system once the new one had become established.

Despite having been made fully aware of the Queen's preference for gradual change, the Australian government was keen to press ahead more swiftly. In February 1975 Charteris complained to the permanent undersecretary at the Foreign Office that 'As is often the case with Mr Whitlam, matters concerning the institution of an Australian system of Awards are moving with break neck speed.'[20] Indeed, later that month the establishment of the Order of Australia was announced. This subsequently became a matter of party political controversy, very much as the Palace had feared. In a pointedly egalitarian move, the Order instituted by the Whitlam government had only three grades: Companion, Officer, and Member. In May 1976, on the advice of Malcolm Fraser, who had replaced Whitlam as prime minister following his dismissal the previous November, the Queen introduced three additional categories: Knight, Dame, and Medal of the Order of Australia. With the return of Labor to power in the 1980s, the categories of Knight and Dame were revoked (although not for existing recipients).[21]

Another of Whitlam's innovations was to seek to introduce a new national anthem. The purpose of this, he explained, was 'to foster a fresh and distinctive reputation for Australia overseas and to encourage in our domestic affairs a shared purpose in national unity'.[22] He maintained, however, that 'God Save the Queen' would continue to be played when the Queen was present or 'when it is especially important to acknowledge our links with the Crown'. A competition was held to find a set of lyrics for a new national anthem. In July 1973, it was announced that six had been selected from around 2,500 entries. It did not go unnoticed in the FCO that one of the shortlisted set of lyrics, written by Bob Ellis, contained the exhortation:

> Lift your head Australia;
> The hour to stand alone
> *Without the proud regalia*
> *Of kingdoms not our own*
> Approaches every minute
> And bids us speak the right; [author's italics][23]

This period of reform and innovation came to an abrupt end on 11 November 1975, when Whitlam was dismissed from office by the Governor General, Sir John Kerr.[24] The pretext for this action was that Whitlam's government 'could not obtain supply'. The death of a Queensland Labor Senator in June 1975 had tipped the balance of power in the Senate in favour of the Liberal Opposition, giving it a bare majority. In October, following the latest revelation in a scandal over investment funds from the Middle East, the Senate announced that it would block the government's appropriation bills until a general election had been held. Having failed to secure any agreement on the question of an election, and with the government's supply likely to run out within weeks, Kerr made the decision to remove Whitlam from office and replace him with the leader of the Liberal Party, Malcolm Fraser, as caretaker prime minister. The election, which took place the following month, was comfortably won by a coalition under Fraser's leadership.

Kerr took the decision to dismiss Whitlam without consulting the Queen, and only informed the Palace retrospectively. In the early hours of 11 November, Sir William Heseltine, the Queen's assistant private secretary, received a telephone call in London from Kerr's private secretary, David Smith, informing him of the news.[25] Heseltine attempted to rouse Martin Charteris without success, and he decided against waking the Queen. Before Heseltine had the opportunity to pass on the news, Charteris took a call from Whitlam, and greeted him as 'Prime Minister'. Although initially irritated at having been caught out in this way, Charteris later agreed with Heseltine, when they spoke for the first time at about 8.00am, that his innocent mistake might actually have proved helpful in demonstrating to Whitlam that the Palace was not engaged in plotting the downfall of the Labor government. Heseltine and Charteris then went and jointly conveyed the news to the Queen so that she would not learn about the matter from the morning's news.

Kerr was to claim that Whitlam's dismissal had been necessary to enable Australia to be governed effectively. Yet, purely on constitutional grounds, many questioned why he had felt it necessary to respond so suddenly, without giving Whitlam any warning that he was contemplating such an extreme course of action.[26] There was also a strong case that Whitlam's difficulties arose from the fact that his political opponents had acted in defiance of constitutional precedent. The Opposition had only obtained its majority in the Senate because two state premiers in quick succession had ignored the well-established convention that casual vacancies in the Senate would be filled on the recommendation of the party to which the previous senator had belonged. Hence, in June 1975, on the death of Labor Senator Milliner, the premier of Queensland, Joh Bjelke-Peterson, appointed in his place a Labor Party member who had made clear that he would not support the Whitlam government in the Senate. The decision by the Senate to deny supply was itself a further breach of tradition.

Many of Whitlam's sympathizers in Australia and around the world saw something far more sinister at work than the poor judgement of the Governor General. They pointed to the fact that a Labor government—the first to be elected in twenty-three years—had set about implementing a series of radical measures, both at home and abroad, only to be ejected from office without reference to the electorate. There were claims that Whitlam had been the victim of a right-wing 'establishment', possibly in league with the Western intelligence community that he had done so much to alienate.[27] Public opprobrium tended to focus on the figure of Kerr himself, rather than that of the Queen. Yet Kerr also came powerfully to symbolize an 'alien' aristocratic imposition on the Australian people. As McKenna notes, 'With his top hat, tails, imperial honours and warnings about republicanism, Kerr's appearance was a constant reminder to Australians that their "republic" was disguised by a portly, champagne-soaked Governor-General who seemed to represent the British aristocracy more than the Australian people.'[28]

Kerr's actions undoubtedly contributed to making the Crown a politically divisive institution in a way it had not previously been in post-war Australian politics. One direct consequence of the affair was the establishment in November 1975 of Citizens for Democracy (CFD), which provided the rallying point for Australian republicanism, drawing contributions from leading figures in the arts and academia as well as politics.[29]

Kerr himself was keen to point out that he had acted without reference to the Palace.[30] On the question of whether he had been right to do so, the Palace publicly supported him. Responding to the request from the Speaker of the Australian House of Representatives for the Queen to restore Whitlam to office, her private secretary wrote:

> As we understand the situation here the Australian Constitution firmly places the prerogative powers of the Crown in the hands of the Governor General as the representative of the Queen of Australia. The only person competent to commission an Australian Prime Minister is the Governor General, and the Queen has no part in decisions which the Governor General must take in accordance with the Constitution.[31]

Privately, on the broader question of whether Kerr had acted wisely in not consulting the Queen, officials at the Palace appear to have had some doubts. Interviewed on Australian television in 2001, Sir William Heseltine commented, 'I'm very surprised myself that he, Kerr, didn't take the advantage of the Queen's long experience and consult her about what he intended to do. . . . my own feeling is that she would have advised him to play out the situation a little longer.'[32]

Whitlam passed his own verdict on the affair in a letter he wrote to Harold Wilson at the end of 1975. He accused Kerr of having deceived him and of having 'connived' with the Chief Justice and indirectly with the leader of the Opposition and 'the Establishment'. Whitlam continued, 'If the Crown in Australia has reserve powers such as the Governor-General used, no elected government, particularly a reforming government, can be safe under it. The upshot is that republicanism has received a very significant boost in Australia.'[33] Significantly, Whitlam suggested the events that had led to his removal from office 'could never have happened in Britain, and as I said more than once "the Queen would never have done it"—a feeling I know you will share'. Wilson declined to confirm or deny that this was the case. Indeed, in line with the British government's determination throughout the affair not to become involved, his office judged it better not to reply at all.

If Whitlam did not believe that such a thing could have happened in Britain, some inside Harold Wilson's own party were not so confident. In March 1976, *The Times* reported the details of a Labour Party policy document on the machinery of government which was about to be discussed by the party's home policy committee. The document recommended a review of the prerogative powers of the Crown, citing 'the recent dismissal of the Prime Minister of Australia and the appointment of a new one by the Governor General' as a case that 'raised a serious question [about] whether prerogative powers were at present appropriately placed with the Crown or its representatives'.[34] It suggested that the power to dissolve Parliament might more appropriately be vested in the Speaker of the House of Commons. There was also pressure for the clarification of the use of prerogative powers in the Queen's other realms. It was suggested by Mr Justice Evatt in Australia that a special expert Commonwealth conference might be convened for this purpose, and his call was taken up in the April 1976 edition of *Round Table* in an article by H. V. Hodson. Characteristically, there was no appetite in the Foreign Office for a clarification of the situation, with one official warning, 'it would open not one but a whole series of Pandora's boxes, and I cannot see any Commonwealth politicians welcoming the idea'.[35]

In July 1976, with no sign that the controversy over Kerr was diminishing, the suggestion was raised publicly that Prince Charles might be appointed as Kerr's replacement as Governor General. The idea was not a new one. It had been floated in the 1960s. Indeed, writing in *Round Table* in 1970, Dermot Morrah claimed that it was no longer politically advisable for Charles to be appointed Governor General of a Commonwealth nation. Instead, he suggested, that the reverse might be attempted: the Queen might spend a year in Australia, taking the place of the Governor General, allowing Charles and any future Princess of Wales to gain experience of the duties of the monarch of the United Kingdom.[36]

The idea of Charles becoming Governor General was revived in October 1973 by R. R. Southey, the federal president of the Australian Liberal Party (in the course of a speech in which he also suggested that the Queen should have a permanent residence in Australia).[37] The notion was again aired during Charles's visit to Australia a year later.[38] At around that time he apparently raised the idea of buying property in Australia so that he would have some permanent base there, but this was vetoed by Harold Wilson's government on the grounds that it might seem extravagant at a time of austerity.[39]

In July 1976 the issue was raised, first by the Australian *Nation Review,* and then by an editorial in *The Times. The Times* noted that protest still attended Kerr's public appearances and expressed concern that his unpopularity might rebound on the Queen herself when she next visited Australia. It suggested that the appointment of Prince Charles as Governor General, as someone who was outside the Australian political arena and yet 'an integral part of the Australian constitution', might 'strengthen the Australian monarchy' while at the same time restoring 'impartiality to Government House'.[40]

The editorial caused some alarm within the Foreign Office. Although one of his colleagues pointed out that any such appointment would be made by the Queen on the advice of her Australian ministers, R. W. H. du Boulay of the Protocol and Conference Department saw the possibility of Britain being drawn into the row over Kerr. He noted the advice of the outgoing British high commissioner to Australia, Sir Morrice James, that the UK should avoid any action that would involve it in Australian politics. Du Boulay continued:

> The appointment of a member of the Royal Family as suggested by *The Times* would have just this effect and in addition embroil the Royal Family directly in controversy. The whole trend of our policy has been the exact opposite of this and it would be a great mistake to reverse the process on the basis of the otherwise attractive, but specious, argument that as the Prince of Wales may one day be King of Australia, it would be reasonable for him to have a 'dummy run' first.[41]

Du Boulay's fears can hardly have been allayed when, early the following month, Whitlam himself weighed into the debate, claiming publicly that, while there were many other suitable candidates, Prince Charles would certainly make a better Governor General than Kerr.[42] In the circumstances, any indication of British support for the idea of Charles becoming Governor General was likely to be perceived in Australia as an intervention in the debate about whether Kerr had been right to act as he did. Yet Charles himself only seems to have abandoned hope of becoming Governor General following a visit to Australia in April 1981. While Malcolm Fraser and his government apparently supported the idea, what *The Times* described as 'vigorous lobbying by the Prince and his staff' failed to persuade leaders of the Australian Labor Party to drop their opposition.[43] Having initially believed that his personal popularity, on the eve of his marriage to Lady Diana Spencer, would overcome Australian resistance, he was ultimately forced to concede that this was too deep-seated. Fraser, however, continued to hint that Charles's appointment might still be a possibility. In a television interview in August 1981, he spoke of the Prince's desire to be 'more involved in a permanent way with Australians' and dismissed opinion polls which pointed to growing opposition to the idea of Charles being Governor General.[44] It was Fraser's defeat in the March 1983 general election and his replacement as prime minister by the republican Labor leader Bob Hawke that effectively spelled the end for any hope of Charles being offered the governor generalship. Hawke would later confirm publicly that the idea had been put to him when he entered office, but he had rejected it on the grounds that, with the Queen as Australian Head of State, this would represent a 'double dose' of the monarchy.[45]

REPUBLICANISM BY STEALTH? TRUDEAU'S CANADA

Canada in the 1970s also seemed ripe for republicanism. As the decade progressed, Pierre Trudeau's barely disguised republican sympathies, combined with his determination to 'patriate' the Canadian constitution, aroused concerns within Whitehall and the Palace. French Canadian separatism further exposed the Crown to political controversy. The issue overshadowed the Queen's Jubilee visit to Canada in 1977. Acting on Trudeau's advice, the Queen made a speech appealing for national unity, a move that drew criticism from the premier of Quebec, René Lévesque. Lévesque, who was campaigning for a negotiated departure of Quebec from the confederation, accused Trudeau of exploiting the Queen's visit for political ends.[46] Trudeau also drew criticism from monarchists for what Paul Martin, the Canadian high commissioner in London, described as his 'flippancy' in relation to the royal visit. Martin complained, 'Trudeau's off-the-cuff remarks on the monarchy reach the royal ears as they have others', and he noted the Duke of Edinburgh's irritation at the Canadian prime minister's behaviour.[47]

Trudeau was conspicuously keen to distance himself from the Crown as an institution, while expressing his personal admiration for the Queen. His speech at the state dinner at Government House during the visit of 1977 omitted any reference to her as 'Queen of Canada', while her speech in reply, which had been drafted by Trudeau, referred to 'the Government' of Canada rather than to 'my Government'. Trudeau had already attracted criticism from Canadian monarchists by advising the Queen to confine her visit to the national capital so as not to antagonize Quebec separatist sensibilities. All these features of the visit attracted comment from the British high commissioner in Ottawa, J. B. Johnston, in an assessment of the state of health of the monarchy in Canada written in October 1977.[48] From his time in the CRO and his posting to Australia, Johnston was familiar with the strains upon the Crown in the 'Old Dominions', and his despatch on the monarchy had a distinctly 'Lintottian' flavour. It noted 'a growing volume of thoughtful concern' in Canada about the 'drawbacks of having a non-resident, non-Canadian Head of State', including familiar problems such as the awkward complications of Governors General conducting state visits, widespread ignorance within Canada about the constitutional position of the Queen, and the tendency of even enthusiastic monarchists to think of her as the 'Queen of England' rather than the 'Queen of Canada'. Johnston judged that while Trudeau had no personal commitment to the monarchy he recognized that it would currently be too politically divisive to make any move against it. In the longer term, however, Johnston speculated that he could, at some point in the future, see the abandonment of the monarchy as a means of preserving national unity.

At least at an official level, the Palace maintained a more optimistic view of the future of the monarchy in Canada while remaining distinctly wary of Trudeau. Commenting on Johnston's despatch, the Queen's private secretary Philip Moore noted:

> We have followed very closely Trudeau's attitude to the Monarchy ever since he became Prime Minister. I would have thought he started by being a Republican and he may still be one at heart. From the time however when, accompanied by his young bride, he received the Queen in British Columbia in 1971 and found to his surprise that she drew crowds far greater than himself, Trudeau, as a shrewd politician, seems to have changed his attitude towards the Monarchy.[49]

On the basis of this and subsequent visits, Moore suggested, Trudeau had realized that a republic was not a realistic prospect in the foreseeable future. As for the distinctly downbeat tone of Johnston's despatch, Moore presciently commented, 'Observers have been prophesying that Canada will become a Republic in the next few years ever since I started work here. They may prove to be right one day but I do not believe it is near at hand.'

Trudeau's attitude to the monarchy added a further layer of sensitivity to his move in 1978 to initiate the patriation of the Canadian constitution. A significant symbolic step in that direction had already been taken at the end of 1977, when the Queen's powers to approve letters of credence, commission, and recall to Canada's overseas representatives were transferred to the Canadian Governor General.[50] The Queen herself regretted this, and in an audience with Trudeau proved unexpectedly keen to impress on him her objections to what she regarded as a weakening of her personal capacity to keep up with Canadian affairs.[51] The constitutional proposals published the following year further defined and strengthened the powers of the Governor General. In the Queen's absence he or she would act on behalf of the Crown, but would do so by virtue of the powers granted to them by the Canadian constitution rather than simply as the Queen's representative. The Governor General would also personally assent to legislation rather than doing so in the name of the Queen.[52]

When in June 1978 Trudeau published his proposals, he took the unusual step of sending his Minister of Justice, Ronald Basford, and special constitutional adviser Donald Thorson to brief the Queen in person. In addition to their visit, Trudeau wrote his own letter to the Queen to reassure her that he had no intention of altering the Crown's essential relationship to Canada. He justified the new constitution as an essential means of maintaining the unity of the Federation.[53] There was clearly some concern on the part of the Canadians about how the Queen would react, and they were relieved when, in the words of Paul Martin, she 'sought information rather than imposing any impediment in [*sic*] the government's decision to present the bill'.[54] While requesting the advice of Foreign Office legal advisers on the bill, the Queen's private secretary expressed satisfaction at its affirmation that the Queen was 'the sovereign head of Canada . . . whose sovereignty as such shall pass to her heirs and successors in accordance with law' and also with its treatment of the office of Governor General.[55] Martin did his best to provide further reassurance to the Palace, passing on to Moore a record of a telephone conversation he had had with Trudeau in which the prime minister had explicitly stated, 'Canada would remain a constitutional monarchy and the Queen of Canada will remain the head of this constitutional monarchy'.[56] The Palace was not perturbed by subsequent criticism in Canada that, in enhancing the status of the Governor General, the position of the Queen would be downgraded, or indeed that, in giving the Governor General, the title of 'First Canadian', the Queen would in some sense be rendered a foreigner in Canada. Moore claimed to be able to see no problem in styling the Governor General as First Canadian 'since The Queen of Canada, as the fountain of precedence, stands above precedence and it seems perfectly proper for her to accord precedence to the Governor-General as the First Canadian'.[57]

The difficulty the Palace faced was not that it opposed the provisions of the bill dealing with the Crown, but that the monarchy was inevitably drawn into the political controversy surrounding the constitution. The principal factor provoking opposition to Trudeau's constitutional proposals was the fear that they would strengthen the powers of the Federal government against those of the provinces. Indeed, the bill faced unanimous opposition from Federal premiers. In this context, the question of Trudeau's attitude towards the Crown became a useful rallying point for the bill's opponents. When the Queen arrived in Edmonton at the end of July 1978 to open the Commonwealth Games, she found herself in the middle of a growing political storm. The former Canadian prime minister John Diefenbaker, one the most vocal opponents of the constitutional proposals, exploited Trudeau's absence on holiday in Morocco to accuse him of having slighted the Queen.[58] He claimed that Trudeau's ultimate ambition was to have a political pawn as head of state.

During an audience with the Queen on a visit to London in December 1978, Trudeau took the opportunity to stress that his proposed legislation for the first time enshrined in statute the position of the monarchy in Canada. The Queen, for her part, appears to have refrained from raising a significant point of ambiguity— the designation of the Governor General in Trudeau's bill as 'Head of State'.[59] Nevertheless, behind the polite exchanges, significant tensions remained. Speaking to Paul Martin after the audience, while affirming her 'indispensability as monarch . . . on purely personal grounds', Trudeau appears to have expressed doubts about the future for her successor.[60] For her part, the Queen seems to have been upset by the way in which Trudeau used the audience on 7 December to advise her of his decision that Edward Schreyer should be the new Governor General. She was taken by surprise by the decision and was clearly annoyed that he had not at least gone through the motions of 'consulting' her.

In July 1979, by which time Trudeau was safely out of office, Philip Moore was prepared to brief Paul Martin more frankly than he had hitherto felt able to do about the Queen's irritation about this and other indiscretions. According to Martin: 'He brought up some of Trudeau's antics—e.g., dancing after the Queen had moved on at a Palace reception. She had read of his sliding down the banister. What worried the Palace more were Trudeau's ambiguities in a speech to Oxford students two years ago. His references to the Crown suggested it had little meaning for him.'[61]

It was against the background of tensions between Trudeau and Canadian monarchists that Sir John Ford, the recently appointed British high commissioner in Ottawa, sent a despatch to London in September 1978. Ford described what would now be termed a process of 'De-Dominionisation' under which successive Liberal administrations in Canada had gradually weakened the presence of the Crown: 'One by one, whether it be in the flag, insignia on letter boxes or names of regiments, the symbols and reminders of the Royal connection have been steadily and quietly reduced in number; and no encouragement is given to those who seek to maintain the Royal connection or encourage new links between the Royal family and the Canadian public'.[62] On the other hand, he pointed to 'a vast reserve of goodwill towards the Queen' among the majority of Canadians. Ford argued that, as part of the broader objective of strengthening transatlantic ties, the maintenance of the Canadian monarchy was in Britain's interests, and he was critical of what he implied had been a policy of 'benign neglect' towards that goal. He issued a direct plea to the Foreign Office 'for any ways you can indicate in which I and my team out here can work to strengthen [the Canadian monarchy]'.

This elicited a distinctly nervous response from officials at the FCO. G. E. Hall pointed to the danger of the British government appearing to take sides on what might develop into a divisive issue within Canada, and questioned the strength of support for the monarchy there. He argued that any attempts to strengthen the monarchy by the UK high commission could prove counterproductive, giving rise to 'extraneous accusations about British meddling'. His proposed advice to Ford was therefore 'hands off'. More significantly, he suggested that there was 'very little evidence that the continuation of the monarchy in Canada is a significant means of strengthening UK/Canada relations'.[63] Given the range of other, more important factors that bound the two countries together, there was, he argued, 'no reason to believe that relations with a republican Canada would necessarily be any less close than they are with republican USA'. Michael Palliser wrote to Philip Moore, reiterating Hall's suggestion that a proactive policy towards the Canadian monarchy might prove counterproductive. Moore agreed, suggesting 'The main obstacle we are up against all the time is that so many Canadians think of the Queen as the British Queen and we have always agreed as a matter of policy that the British High Commission in Canada should adopt a low profile. Jack Johnson was very sensible about this and my advice to John Ford would be to proceed with great caution.'[64] The question of how far British officials should become directly involved in efforts to counter the rise of republicanism in the Commonwealth realms would, as we shall see, become even more pressing in years to come.

CONFLICTING TRENDS: MALTA, TRINIDAD AND TOBAGO, AND PAPUA NEW GUINEA

To what extent, then, was there a broader trend towards republicanism in the Commonwealth during the 1970s? The cases of Malta and Trinidad and Tobago certainly suggested so, although that of Papua New Guinea pointed in the opposite direction. Yet they all demonstrate that both the move to republican status and, conversely, the birth of an independent monarchy could present the British government with a potentially embarrassing situation. This was particularly true of Malta, which became a republic in December 1974. Its prime minister, Dom Mintoff, had long been unhappy with a number of aspects of the Maltese constitution—including the role of the Crown—and by the beginning of 1974 appeared impatient to make changes. The problem he faced was that the entrenched clauses in the constitution could only be overturned by a two-thirds majority of the Maltese House of Representatives, and Mintoff's party had a majority of only three.[65] The monarchical clause was doubly entrenched, requiring, in addition to the vote in the House of Representatives, a separate referendum in order to overturn it.[66] It seemed quite possible that Borg Olivier's Nationalist Party would oppose Mintoff's proposed reforms, thus denying him the necessary two-third majority. This raised what were for the British government and the Palace two disturbing possibilities. The first was that Mintoff would force through a package of reforms—including the introduction of a republic—by unconstitutional means. As one official at the Foreign Office pointed out, 'The Queen could be faced with what would amount to a coup d'état which would depose Her.'[67] There was little appetite in the FCO for taking a stand on this issue as 'this could easily open up a wrangle about The Queen's Commonwealth title which could have very serious repercussions'.[68] The second possibility was that Mintoff would force through a number of reforms unconstitutionally, while stopping short of abolishing the monarchy. This raised the prospect of the Queen being petitioned, in her capacity as Queen of Malta, to restore the constitution and thus being involved even more directly in a political row. The view of the Foreign Office was that, of the two scenarios, the second was potentially more serious and that 'if Mintoff did precipitate a serious constitutional crisis, it would probably cause less embarrassment to The Queen in the long run if he went the whole way and declared a Republic'.[69] This was also the view of Martin Charteris at the Palace. Indeed, in the light of the Maltese prime minister's notoriously volatile behaviour, Charteris conjured up a further scenario, with distinct echoes of the Rhodesian situation. He told the permanent undersecretary at the Foreign Office, Thomas Brimelow, 'On the grounds that when dealing with Mintoff nothing is impossible, I have had the fantasy that he might leave the Commonwealth but wish to keep Malta as a Monarchy. The idea is, I am sure, too fanciful to be worth considering, but I thought you might be entertained by my nightmares.'[70]

Once it became clear in September 1974 that a move by Mintoff on the republican issue was imminent, Charteris was keen he should appreciate 'that Her Majesty will not be *personally* embarrassed by Malta becoming a Republic if that is what the Maltese as a whole desire, but only by being asked to do something unconstitutional'.[71] As always in these situations, the British government was limited in the extent to which it could manage this issue, despite it having potentially had repercussions for the UK's foreign relations. Strictly speaking, it was a matter for the Palace and the Maltese government alone to settle. Charteris, when seeking advice from the Foreign Office, was careful to stress that this was of a purely informal nature, and that Mintoff was likely to resent any suggestion of British interference.

On a visit to London by the Maltese Governor General, Sir Anthony Mamo, Charteris took the opportunity to repeat to him the point that the Queen would only be embarrassed by the move to a republic if it was achieved unconstitutionally and against the general wishes of the Maltese people. He also stressed that 'the worst course from the point of view of the Queen' would be if Mintoff forced through a series of reforms in violation of the constitution, but left Malta as a monarchy.[72] Charteris promised to consult with the Queen and then to write to Mamo in terms the Governor General could show Mintoff. Mamo, for his part, explained Mintoff's actions in terms that would have been thoroughly familiar to the Palace. He claimed they were motivated not by any lack of respect and affection for the Queen but rather by the confusing nature of the monarchical relationship: 'it was simply not understood at home or abroad that "The Queen of Malta" was something different from "The Queen of the United Kingdom"'. Following this meeting, Charteris discussed with the FCO the terms of the letter he was to send to the Governor General.[73] The Foreign Office recommended that the letter rehearse the points put to Charteris by Mamo, ending with the 'punch line' that 'For a Constitutional Monarch, the only possible cause of embarrassment is to be asked to act unconstitutionally'.[74]

Great care was taken to observe constitutional conventions, with Charteris stressing that he was seeking the advice of the Foreign Office on a purely informal basis and the FCO, in turn, worrying about the nature of the advice the British high commissioner could properly give to Mintoff. Yet, ironically, following Mintoff's introduction of three bills on 12 November to amend the constitution, the British felt no compunction about actually spying on Maltese leaders to discover the state of their negotiations over the republican issue. Towards the end of November, Brimelow passed on to Charteris a report based on information 'from secret and vulnerable sources' (Whitehall code for material from the intelligence agencies).[75] This suggested that, following private talks between the two major parties, the Nationalist Opposition was likely to cooperate with Mintoff in passing a package of reforms. The report was shown to the Queen, and Charteris commented, with some satisfaction, that it looked 'as if this business may be [e]ffected without too much of a rumpus'.[76]

With the process of transition reaching its climax, Mamo approached the Palace, asking what formal advice he was required to offer to the Queen. He was told 'that no formal advice was required. In all previous instances, the action necessary to transform the Monarchy into a republic had been taken locally, and the Queen had been kept informed by her representative.'[77] On 10 December, three days before Malta became a republic, Mamo wrote to Charteris, enclosing a letter from Mintoff to the Queen informing her of the constitutional changes that were about to take effect.[78] Mintoff took the opportunity to thank the Queen for her 'understanding response', and stressed the continuing strength of the association between Britain and Malta.

In the case of Trinidad and Tobago, there had long been, as we have seen, rumblings of discontent at the country's monarchical constitution. The move towards a republic only really gained momentum, however, following the abortive 'Black Power' revolt of 1970. This drew support from a variety of sources, including students, trades unionists, and some members of the armed forces. While Prime Minister Eric Williams succeeded in suppressing the immediate challenge to his authority, the Black Power movement had a more pervasive radicalizing influence. It served to focus attention on the institution of the monarchy, portraying it as a symbol of colonial oppression. On a more personal level, Williams found himself being characterized by leading radicals as nothing more than a black puppet of white economic interests.[79] His country's continuing allegiance to an absentee European monarch could only serve to lend credence to such accusations.

A more immediate spur to constitutional reform was, however, the boycott of the 1971 elections by the country's main opposition parties, which allowed Williams' People's National Movement (PNM) to return to power unopposed. While Williams was keen both to bolster the questionable legitimacy of his new administration and to move his country towards republican status, he was less enthusiastic about the prospect of more significant reforms.[80] He therefore played for time, announcing a review of the existing constitution, to be chaired by a former chief justice, Sir Hugh Wooding, and urging Wooding not to hurry. The commission worked in a suitably leisurely fashion, only releasing its findings in January 1974. These proved unacceptable to the PNM, which feared that elements of the report might undermine its hold on power, particularly the recommendation that proportional representation be introduced. Instead, Williams established a joint select committee of both houses of parliament to make fresh constitutional recommendations. A constitution bill, based upon the committee's findings and heavily influenced by Williams' own views, was finally passed into law in March 1976. This retained the Senate, the first-past-the-post system, and appeals to the Privy Council, all of which would have been abolished under the constitution recommended by Wooding. Two elements which both sets of constitutional proposals shared, however, were the proposal to lower the voting age from 21 to 18, and the introduction of a republic. The transition to a republic took place on 1 August 1976.

The response of British officials to the ending of the monarchical link with Trinidad and Tobago was characteristically sanguine. The British High Commissioner C. E. Diggines raised some familiar points about the unhelpful confusion the previous arrangements had caused. He noted that Williams had tended to play down his country's association with the royal family: the Queen's birthday was not celebrated and 'God Save the Queen' was rarely played. 'This', Diggines suggested:

> has hardly enhanced Her Majesty's dignity in Trinidad and Tobago and has made it even more difficult than it would otherwise have been for many Trinidadians to understand her separate status as Queen of Trinidad and Tobago as distinct from Queen of the UK. So the Republic, when it comes, will have the advantage of defining more clearly the relationship which was becoming increasingly blurred.[81]

He thought it unlikely that the move towards a republic would have any harmful repercussions for relations with the UK. Indeed, he suggested that 'if anything, I believe that, with this final severance of even a symbolic colonial umbilical cord (apart from the continuation of appeals to the Privy Council) there is every possibility that the relationship, already generally good, could even become better'. The Caribbean Department of the FCO warmly endorsed this verdict, telling Diggines, 'We were interested to see your assessment (with which we agree) that this change is likely to have little effect on British-Trinidadian relations, but that any effect it may have will probably be for the better.'[82]

Defying the trend for Commonwealth countries to move towards republican status, Papua New Guinea (PNG) specifically opted to become a monarchy on independence in 1975. Although this might have been heartening for the Palace, the process was complicated by the fact that the territory was governed by Australia and communications with the Palace over the issue had to go through the Australian government. At the end of the First World War, Australia had been granted what had been German New Guinea as a League of Nations mandate. It had already taken control of Papua during the war, and governed it as an external territory of the Australian Commonwealth. In March 1975, shortly before formal independence, the elected government of PNG assumed responsibility for foreign affairs. Later that month, the Foreign Office was concerned to learn that PNG ministers wished to use the British government as an intermediary with the Palace in negotiations over becoming a Commonwealth realm. Their reason for wanting to do so appeared to be suspicion that republican sentiments within the Whitlam administration would make it unsympathetic to PNG's desire to become a monarchy. Its chief minister, Michael Somare, had apparently been offended by an anti-monarchist remark by the Australian minister responsible for PNG, Bill Morrison.[83] These suspicions were confirmed when Whitlam wrote to Somare about arrangements to mark independence. Britain's representative in PNG was told in confidence by the Chairman of the Independence Celebrations Organisation that Whitlam's letter 'was couched in terms implying that the Prime Minister did not consider that Papua New Guinea should opt for a monarchical form of government'.[84] The Foreign Office, however, was not willing to be drawn into this matter, fearing that it might damage the UK's relations with Australia. It told its representative in Canberra that its understanding was that the Queen's position in relation to PNG derived from her status as Queen of Australia, and that any request from the PNG government about her future role as Head of State should be channeled through the Australian authorities.[85] Papua New Guinea's independence as a Commonwealth realm was marked by a ceremony in September 1975, with Prince Charles in attendance as the Queen's representative. Also there were Sir John Kerr and Gough Whitlam. It would not be long before the idea of the three of them posing together in a single photograph would be unthinkable.

10

'On Her Own': The Queen and the Commonwealth in the 1980s

SOUTHERN AFRICA AND TENSIONS WITH THE THATCHER GOVERNMENT

As we have already seen in relation to the Lusaka CHOGM, Mrs Thatcher came to power in 1979 with relatively little experience of the Commonwealth and very limited sympathy for the policies of some of its more radical members, particularly over Southern Africa. There was reportedly a joke among Mrs Thatcher and her closest advisers that the acronym CHOGM stood for 'Compulsory Hand-Outs for Greedy Mendicants'.[1] It is unlikely that the Queen would have been amused by this, and their very different attitudes towards the Commonwealth always threatened to bring them into conflict. In the early years of the Thatcher government, the Commonwealth proved of genuine value to the UK not only over the transfer of power in Zimbabwe in 1979–80, but also in rallying diplomatic support for Britain over the granting of independence to Belize in 1981 and during the Falklands crisis the following year. Nevertheless, by the beginning of Mrs Thatcher's second term, signs had begun to appear of a rift between the Conservative Party and the Palace over the Commonwealth.

The monarch's 1983 Christmas broadcast seemed to many Conservative commentators a case of the Queen championing Commonwealth interests against the policy of her own government. The broadcast came in the aftermath of the Queen's visit to Delhi for the 1983 CHOGM. She noted that, despite the progress that had been made on the subcontinent, 'the greatest problem in the world today remains the gap between rich and poor countries and we shall not begin to close this gap until we hear less about nationalism and more about interdependence. One of the main aims of the Commonwealth is to make an effective contribution towards redressing the economic balance between nations.' The Queen suggested that technological advance was serving to obscure basic human needs: 'Electronics cannot create comradeship; computers cannot create compassion; satellites cannot transmit tolerance.' W. David McIntyre detected in these phrases, the 'alliterative style' of Commonwealth Secretary-General Sonny Ramphal.[2] Others suspected the influence of India's prime minister, Indira Gandhi, footage of whom speaking to the Queen about technology appeared in the broadcast.

Enoch Powell, by then Ulster Unionist MP for South Down, cast himself in the familiar role of tribune of the Right and guardian of the constitution.[3] In a speech on 20 January 1984 Powell accused ministers of putting into the Queen's mouth words suggesting she had 'the interests and affairs of other countries in other continents as much or more at heart than those of her own people'.[4] Powell claimed that there ought to be 'unique and exclusive sympathy' between the Crown and the people of the United Kingdom. On its own, Powell's speech might well have been dismissed by the Palace as a predictable criticism from an equally predictable source. Indeed, its public response, that the Queen had 'all her people at heart, irrespective of their race, creed or colour', was a graceful tilt against the Powellite bogeyman.[5] What must have caused far greater consternation is that the following day *The Times* in a major editorial took Powell's criticisms a stage further. It noted the standard doctrine that the headship of the Commonwealth had no constitutional character: 'It has no formal responsibilities. It is not endowed with any repository of ministerial advice. It has no statutory foundation and is not recognised in any of the Parliaments of the Commonwealth.' It suggested that Powell's reference to ministers having put words into the Queen's mouth was disingenuous, as the Queen's Christmas Day broadcast, to which he was clearly referring, was 'the only formal speech she makes without the constitutional backing of advice from any minister in any of the Commonwealth monarchies'. She was, in effect 'on her own'. *The Times* attacked the Queen's assertions that there was a 'gap' between rich and poor nations and that a major aim of the Commonwealth should be to redress the balance between these countries, accusing her of having fallen victim to 'an insidious kind of global egalitarianism'. Her claims, *The Times* suggested, were both 'questionable' and 'quite legitimately open to direct criticism rather than to the circuitous method pursued by Mr Powell'.

On 26 January Powell returned to the attack with an article in *The Times*, which recalled his anonymous 1964 pieces. He outlined a familiar set of dilemmas which confronted the Queen when acting as Head of the Commonwealth, suggesting that they arose because the Commonwealth itself was 'not a political entity, or indeed an entity at all except in make-believe'.[6] He linked this issue to mass immigration into the UK, suggesting that the British Nationality Act of 1948 had paved the way for both by breaking the link between citizenship and loyalty to the Crown. Powell placed the blame and the solution for this firmly at the door of the British government:

> It was upon the advice of the Crown's United Kingdom ministers that the chimera of the Commonwealth was invented and installed ... There is equally little room for doubt who is responsible for its continuance and who alone could end the constitutional contradiction in which the Sovereign has been caught up. It is Her Majesty's ministers in the United Kingdom—who else?

The historian and constitutional expert Lord Blake stepped into the debate with a set of clear definitions which he clearly hoped would close down the discussion: the Christmas Day and Commonwealth Day messages were the only times the Queen spoke without ministerial advice. In Britain and on visits to Commonwealth republics she spoke on the advice of British ministers. In the other Commonwealth realms she spoke on the advice of their prime ministers. This did not, however, satisfy Powell, who demanded to know when the convention about the two annual messages was declared and which ministers were responsible for it, 'remembering that advice that advice is not requisite is also advice'.[7] This bizarre exchange was brought to a suitably surreal end by Blake, who replied, 'If ministerial advice is not needed, ministerial advice that it is not needed is also not needed.'

If this debate was conducted at a fairly esoteric level, a more personal and potentially damaging clash came in 1986, at a point when a number of countries were threatening to boycott the Commonwealth Games in protest over the Thatcher government's resistance to sanctions against South Africa.[8] The previous year's CHOGM in Nassau had seen Mrs Thatcher isolated over the issue. Sonny Ramphal claimed that the Queen had avoided taking Britain's side against the other Commonwealth members. He recalled, 'Not for one moment did anyone suspect that she might enter the arena or do anything else but try to bridge the divide which existed, in the interests of the Commonwealth.'[9] He also later claimed that, not for the first time, her presence at the CHOGM proved decisive in holding the Commonwealth together during a major crisis: 'If the Queen hadn't been there we might have gone on the rocks... Mrs Thatcher became an aberration, and added to that by not caring.'[10]

The year 1986 witnessed a series of articles in the British press pointing to a rift between the Palace and Downing Street over the Commonwealth and other issues. The then editor of the *Sunday Times* would later claim that this was the product of a 'whispering campaign' inspired by a 'faction' within the Palace intended to 'distance the Royal Family from the policies of Margaret Thatcher and undermine her government in the process'.[11] The articles included a profile of Prince Charles in *The Economist* by Simon Jenkins, based on an extensive off-the-record interview, which suggested that his views were considerably to the left of those of Mrs Thatcher. An article in the *Today* newspaper on 7 June, which was largely dismissed at the time, suggested that the Queen was concerned that the issue of sanctions would break up the Commonwealth, and had urged Mrs Thatcher to change her views. Less easy to dismiss were pieces along similar lines that appeared subsequently in *The Times* and *Daily Telegraph*. Finally, on 20 July, alongside a report on the growing tally of countries boycotting the Commonwealth Games, the *Sunday Times* carried on its front page the headline 'Queen dismayed by "uncaring" Thatcher'. Both the front-page story and a longer feature article inside entitled 'The African Queen: At odds with No 10' were written by Simon Freeman and by the paper's political correspondent, Michael Jones. The stories contained what they claimed to be an 'unprecedented disclosure of the Monarch's political views'. Freeman suggested that over the Commonwealth, over foreign policy issues such as the decision to allow the USA to bomb Libya from British bases (about which she was described as having been 'furious'), and over domestic issues such as the 1984 Miners' Strike, the Queen regarded Mrs Thatcher's policies as 'uncaring, confrontational and socially divisive'. He identified Mrs Thatcher's deputy prime minister, Lord Whitelaw, as the source of the story carried by the press the previous week that 'senior cabinet ministers' were concerned 'that the Queen might be involved in a constitutional crisis because of the conflicting loyalties imposed on her three roles as Head of State of the United Kingdom, monarch of 17 other Commonwealth countries and head of the Commonwealth'.[12] According to his biographers, Whitelaw, who had close links with the Palace, 'knew the Queen was deeply troubled'.[13] Enoch Powell had already denounced this leak, claiming that it was a serious breach of a Privy Councillor's oath to attribute to the Queen views that were at odds with those of her prime minister.[14] Yet, citing as his sources 'friends' and 'advisors' of the Queen, Freeman claimed that the Palace had been 'privately delighted' by this coverage, hoping it would persuade Mrs Thatcher to pursue a more conciliatory line on the issue of sanctions against South Africa. Meanwhile, Jones' section of the feature gave an all too plausible account of the Thatcher administration's frustration with the Commonwealth. It suggested that Downing Street blamed some of the rumours of a rift between the Queen and Mrs Thatcher on the Commonwealth Secretary-General, Sonny Ramphal, whom it regarded as 'a meddler in matters beyond his authority, a bureaucrat—earning £53,029 a year Downing Street points out—who wrongly incites controversy by his agitation for stiff economic sanctions against South Africa'.

The Queen's press secretary, Michael Shea, issued an 'unqualified denial' of Freeman's story. Yet Andrew Neil, the editor of the *Sunday Times*, insisted it came from 'a highly placed source in Buckingham Palace'.[15] The following weekend the *Sunday Times* provided further details of the background to Freeman's piece without directly naming his 'highly placed' source.[16] It claimed that the informant at the Palace had, among other things, spoken of the Queen's affection for the Commonwealth, her view that she was 'able to take a wider view of international problems than any national leader', and that 'her intervention in the Lusaka summit of 1979 had helped resolve the Rhodesian crisis'. It had also been suggested that she did not share Downing Street's concerns about Ramphal, whom she regarded as 'very wise'. The piece claimed that both the Queen's private secretary, Sir William Heseltine, and Mrs Thatcher's private secretary had known the previous day that the articles of 20 July were likely to be published. While the *Sunday Times* still refrained from naming its source in the Palace, that day's *Observer* suggested it had been Michael Shea. The *Daily Mirror*'s royal correspondent, James Whitaker, later claimed that he had realized Shea had been Freeman's source as soon as he had read the article, as he had heard 'all the expressions, all the phrases' from Shea's own mouth in the weeks before.[17]

In a clear attempt to manage a deteriorating situation, Heseltine wrote a letter to *The Times*, which was published on 28 July. He provided the first official acknowledgement that Shea had indeed had 'several' exchanges with Freeman before the *Sunday Times* articles were published, but claimed that he had 'said nothing which could reasonably bear the interpretation put upon it by the writers of the article on the front page in the edition of July 20'.[18] Heseltine also admitted that parts of the story had been read back to Shea prior to publication, but claimed that not all of them had been. He implied that the reason no attempt had been made to stop the article was that this would simply have generated greater publicity. Neil responded indignantly to these claims the following day, claiming that the story had been read to Shea in full prior to publication. Following the appearance of the articles, Neil suggested, Shea had made no complaint that he had been 'duped', merely that the front page story had drawn 'unwarranted' conclusions from the more detailed feature inside. Neil also claimed that, had the Palace made any representation to him about the story prior to publication, he would have responded with changes. He added:

> It is difficult to avoid the conclusion that those in the Palace who knew about *The Sunday Times* articles before their publication, who provided guidance for them and who failed to use the ample opportunity they had to undo the damage were playing with fire and did not have the wit to blow it out before it burned them, and more grievously, reflected upon her Majesty's constitutional position.[19]

When, during the 1990s, Ben Pimlott spoke to both Shea and Freeman about the affair he received, unsurprisingly, two quite different versions of events. Shea implied that he had been presented with a series of leading questions designed to elicit evidence of a rift between Downing Street and the Palace. Others close to the Palace went so far as to suggest that Shea had been 'tricked' into indiscretion by Freeman.[20] This was also the impression that Nicholas Soames, a close friend of Prince Charles, had apparently sought to give to the maverick journalist and former politician Woodrow Wyatt.[21] There were, however, a number of problems with this. Shea was a highly experienced press secretary who appeared to have the confidence of the Queen. For their part, Freeman and Jones were experienced and respected journalists, who were unlikely to have wished to endanger relations with such a valuable source by misrepresenting his words.

While it is far from easy to reconcile these various accounts, they probably need to be placed within the context of the febrile atmosphere generated by the threatened mass boycott of the Commonwealth Games. It is difficult to imagine that this did not lead to serious concerns within the Palace both that the Commonwealth was in danger of splitting apart and that Downing Street was not doing enough to avert this threat. In the circumstances, Shea may have felt an unusual degree of licence to signal these concerns, less as a means of undermining Mrs Thatcher than of seeking to mollify the feelings of her critics within the Commonwealth. Certainly, according to Neil, there was a view within the Foreign Office that the *Sunday Times* stories had helped to persuade African leaders to remain within the Commonwealth.[22] Whatever the truth, Shea retained his post for only a few months longer before leaving the Palace, ostensibly at his own volition, to take up a post in the private sector.

Peregrine Worsthorne, writing in the *Sunday Telegraph*, provided an imaginative updating of the criticisms voiced of the Queen in the 1950s by John Grigg and Malcolm Muggeridge to the effect that she was surrounded by a circle of friends and advisers drawn from a narrow and unrepresentative social clique. Her current predilection for mixing with dignitaries from the Commonwealth meant that she had in effect, Worsthorne suggested, 'replaced one unrepresentative and undemocratic lot of sycophants with another, simply ending up even more isolated in an ivory tower than she was before'.[23] Ramphal, who was clearly one of the targets of Worsthorne's jibe and who had clearly been briefed against by Downing Street, was, unsurprisingly, convinced that Freeman had accurately represented the Queen's views. He later recalled, 'I was very glad about the Thatcher row. What was in the *Sunday Times*, what Michael Shea was saying to the press, was what we knew to be the reality, and it needed to be said.'[24]

It has been suggested that the affair conformed to a broader republican agenda on the part of the Australian-born entrepreneur Rupert Murdoch, whose News International group had acquired both *The Times* and the *Sunday Times* in 1981. While it would probably be unwise to place too much weight on this source, corroborative evidence can certainly be found in the diaries of Woodrow Wyatt. Wyatt records a conversation with Murdoch about possible sources of the Freeman and Jones story. Murdoch commented that Prince Philip was 'mad keen about the Commonwealth. It's something that makes them feel different from other Royal families.' Wyatt continues,

> I said 'Well they still have Australia, New Zealand and Canada.' He [Murdoch] said, 'They won't last for ever.' 'But you are not going to push them out of Australia are you?' 'Oh no. No government would do that, it will just fade away in fifty years' time.'[25]

Murdoch's republican views are unlikely to have driven the affair. Yet he certainly appears to have defended Neil against a move by some national directors of Times Newspapers (at least one of whom was close to the Palace) to have him sacked.[26] In January 1988 in an editorial entitled 'Modernising the Monarchy', the *Sunday Times* itself made the link between republicanism in Australia and the row within the Commonwealth over South Africa:

> If Australia were to become a republic it would undoubtedly upset royalist sentiment in Britain... But there would be some advantages. The Queen's personal role in Commonwealth affairs reinforces the myth that Britain has a special obligation to pay heed to what the Commonwealth, particularly some of its more vociferous Third World members, think... but propping up an imperial heritage is no way to foster relationships which need to be based on contemporary realities.[27]

Neil's belief that his newspaper had stumbled upon a 'conspiracy' against the Thatcher government by some within the Palace was only strengthened by a conversation he had in October 1989 with another Tory 'grandee' with close links to the royal family, Norman St John-Stevas. St John-Stevas had publicly refuted the story of a rift between the Queen and Mrs Thatcher over the Commonwealth when it had appeared three years earlier. Neil recalls,

> [I asked] 'Why did you attack me, Norman... when you must have known the story was true?' He looked very hard at me: 'Yes Andrew, it was true—which is precisely why I had to deny it.' Then he added with a smile: 'It was more true, Andrew, than you'll ever know.'[28]

GRENADA AND FIJI

If the Queen's role as Head of the Commonwealth appears to have brought her into conflict with Mrs Thatcher, developments in two of her Commonwealth realms also fostered divisions between the Palace and Downing Street. In October 1983 US President Ronald Reagan ordered the invasion of the Commonwealth realm of Grenada, where a violent coup had overthrown the government leading to the murder of the prime minister, Maurice Bishop. Since itself seizing power in 1979, Bishop's People's Revolutionary Government (PRG) had received aid from Cuba and the Eastern bloc, creating a growing rift with the United States. Following Reagan's election as president in 1980, there were clear signs that the US government would expect Britain to fall into line behind a tougher policy towards Grenada. One of Mrs Thatcher's closest advisers, Alfred Sherman, visited Washington in January 1981 and offered her some extremely shrewd advice on possible points of tension with the Reagan administration over foreign policy issues. He correctly predicted a harder line over countering the spread of Communism in Central America and the Caribbean, adding 'They now expect Britain to see Caribbean problems in terms of America's strategic interests and not in terms of Britain's residual commitments in the area ("A rocket base in Grenada would not be aimed at London.")'[29] While the Foreign Office was keen not to alienate the USA, there was considerable sympathy in the UK towards the socialist programme of Bishop's government, as was witnessed by a report on the Caribbean and Central America by the House of Commons Foreign Affairs Select Committee, which spoke of the 'considerable degree of success' Grenada had achieved.[30] The situation changed radically when, following a power struggle within Bishop's own administration, he was placed under house arrest by his deputy prime minister on 13 October 1983 and murdered six days later.

    The USA feared that Bishop's killing was the prelude to a much closer alignment of Grenada with the Eastern bloc. The decision on 21 October by the Organisation of Eastern Caribbean States (OECS) to call for a multinational force to overthrow the new regime in Grenada provided the USA with the diplomatic cover it required for military action. The following day, the prime minister of Barbados, Grantley Adams, made a request for UK involvement in an invasion of Grenada to the British high commissioner to the West Indies, Giles Bullard (whose responsibilities included Grenada). The British government, however, was cautious, believing military action could be counterproductive.[31] A Cabinet meeting on 24 October raised numerous objections to military intervention, and it was decided that any request for the UK to join a multinational force should be refused. Later that day, the British Foreign Secretary, Geoffrey Howe, told the House of Commons he had 'no reason to think that American military intervention is likely'.[32] He suggested that Britain had been in the 'closest possible touch' with the USA over the issue of Grenada. In fact, the Reagan administration had been making plans for an invasion and had taken the decision not to inform the British government until the last possible moment. Shortly before midnight on 24 October, Mrs Thatcher learned from Reagan that he had decided to 'respond positively' to the OECS request. The invasion began early the following morning. In the House of Commons, Howe came under fierce attack from MPs not merely from the Opposition benches but from his own. The government was accused of incompetence in its handling of the affair and of a craven failure to condemn a violation of international law which the

Labour Shadow Foreign Secretary, Denis Healey, compared to the Soviet invasion of Czechoslovakia in 1968.[33] The issue of Grenada provided a rallying point for opponents of the Thatcher government's close relationship with the Reagan administration, particularly over the deployment of nuclear weapons. An assessment by the US State Department in early November expressed concern on this point, noting that Thatcher and Howe had been 'hurt domestically by what appears to many in the UK to have been our failure to consult adequately with Her Majesty's Government'. It also noted a recent poll which 'showed that three-quarters of the British people would not trust the United States to consult before pulling the nuclear trigger on dual-key systems'.[34]

If Howe faced a rough ride in the House of Commons, it appears that the Queen was extremely upset at the invasion of one of her realms, and that she focused some of that anger on Mrs Thatcher. We have a series of vivid, if not necessarily mutually consistent, accounts of Mrs Thatcher's frosty encounter with Her Majesty in the wake of the invasion.[35] Yet there was another side to this particular coin: the actions of the Queen's own representative on Grenada, Sir Paul Scoon. On seizing power in 1979 the PRG had retained the Queen as Grenada's Head of State, seeing this as an important means of signalling its constitutional legitimacy.[36] Scoon, who had been appointed as Governor General under the previous government, retained his post. On 26 October 1983, in the wake of the invasion, he was taken into protective custody aboard a US warship. On his return to the island the following day he found himself at the centre of a controversy over his own role in the invasion. The prime minister of Dominica, Eugenia Charles, who had supported the invasion, claimed that Scoon had sent word to the OECS meeting requesting military action.[37] The British government denied having known of any such request. The Palace itself was also drawn into the row. In a statement, it confirmed that the Queen had been in contact with Sir Paul up to the time of the invasion; but it also denied knowing of any request for military action. The fact that the sole document from Scoon requesting foreign intervention was only signed by him *after* the invasion had taken place merely served to fuel accusations that the USA had used Scoon as a viceregal fig leaf to conceal the essential illegality of their intervention.[38]

In his memoirs, published in 2003, however, Scoon reiterated the claim that he had called for outside support and provided further details. He noted that on 22 October he received telephone calls from both the Commonwealth Secretary-General, Sonny Ramphal, and from the Queen's assistant private secretary, Robert Fellows, but claimed that he neither sought nor received advice from either.[39] The following morning, Scoon received a visit from the deputy British high commissioner in Barbados, David Montgomery. Scoon's account of their conversation was subsequently corroborated by Montgomery.[40] Montgomery noted that there was a possibility of joint military action involving the OECS and the USA, although he was not aware of any imminent moves. He told Scoon that his 'views on military action as an option to restore my country to normality would be crucial to any decision on that score'.[41] When Scoon indicated that it would have his support, Montgomery asked whether he would be prepared to provide this in writing. Scoon proved reluctant to do so, given the need for secrecy. Scoon claimed that Montgomery then

> suggested that I could perhaps authorize him to pass on the gist of my views to, say, Prime Minister Adams, adding that I would not wish military action by friendly states to be inhibited by the absence of a formal request by me. That being so and having regard to the paramount need for secrecy, I would be content for the message being conveyed (by Montgomery) to be regarded *pro tem*, as such a request with a formal written request from me to follow as soon as a secure, practicable means of communication became available.[42]

Scoon authorized him to speak to Adams in these terms.

Scoon's account is unlikely to settle the controversy around his role. At the very least, however, it suggests that the indignation not only of the Palace, but also of Downing Street, might have been somewhat misplaced. Scoon and Montgomery agree that an experienced British diplomat effectively encouraged the Queen's representative on Grenada to call for an invasion of the island, and acted as a secret conduit for communications with Caribbean leaders. Their account suggests how the constitutional status of the realms could complicate and confuse British foreign policy. Scoon's role also raises important questions about the legality of the invasion and the residual powers of the Crown. Did Scoon have the right effectively to request the foreign invasion of his country? Although he would normally be obliged to act on ministerial advice, he could plausibly argue that the October coup had both deprived him of that advice and imposed upon him a duty to act in order to restore law and order. The recent precedent of Whitlam's dismissal by Kerr in 1975 might also have suggested that he had the right to act without consulting the Palace (indeed, he could plausibly claim that he had spared the Queen from embarrassment by failing to consult her). Nevertheless, given that, in this case, he was inviting foreign powers to invade one of the Queen's realms, surely he had a duty to inform her in advance? An examination of this issue in *The Times*, shortly after the invasion, which drew on the views of Professor L. H. Leigh of the LSE, noted:

> The Governor-General may well be able to do acts in the Queen's name of which she thoroughly disapproves and in respect of which she has no status to act. This but illustrates an unforeseen problem in relation to the anachronistic governor-general system.[43]

Fiji presented a quite different scenario, but an almost equally uncomfortable one for Downing Street and the Palace. The country achieved independence in 1970 as a constitutional monarchy with a complex electoral system that provided separate communal representation for the territory's ethnic Fijian and Indian populations. For the next seventeen years, Fijian politics were dominated by the National Alliance Party, under the leadership of Ratu Kamisese Mara. His administration espoused a multiracial policy, but drew its core support from the Fijian and 'General' constituencies (the latter representing the other non-Indian races).[44] Following a general election in 1987, the recently formed Fiji Labour Party under the leadership of Timoci Bavandra took power with the support of the Indian-based

National Federal Party. This challenge to ethnic Fijian political hegemony was met on 14 May 1987 by the first of two coups carried out that year by Colonel Sitiveni Rabuka. With the public support of the Palace, the Governor General, Sir Penaia Ganilau (a senior Fijian chief), used his authority in an attempt to guide Fiji back to constitutional government. In July, Ganilau established a Constitutional Review Committee, which included members nominated by Mara and Bavandra. In what can only be interpreted as an attempt to avert the declaration of a republic, the British high commissioner in Fiji, Roger Bartrop, issued a press release noting that '[w]ere Fiji to become a republic it would be necessary to obtain the unanimous agreement of all other Commonwealth countries for her membership to continue'.[45]

Yet, just as the Constitutional Review Committee seemed about to achieve consensus between the main parties, on 25 September 1987 Rabuka carried out a second coup in the name of securing ethnic Fijian political supremacy. The reaction of the Governor General initially appeared rather equivocal. Various parties sought to persuade him to adopt a firmer position against the coup, including, it seems, the Queen's private secretary, Sir William Heseltine, who was in regular contact with him in the wake of the coup.[46] Certainly, the Palace responded immediately to the September coup by issuing a message from the Queen declaring that the Governor General remained the 'sole legitimate source of the executive authority in Fiji' and expressing the hope that 'the process of restoring Fiji to constitutional normality might be resumed'.[47] None of this escaped Enoch Powell's ever vigilant eye. In an article in *The Times* published at the beginning of October, he noted that the Crown—represented in the realms by the Governor General—was required to act only on ministerial advice. If a revolutionary situation had deprived it of ministers, its constitutional duty was to remain aloof from the situation. The notion that either the Queen personally or 'some curious entity called "Buckingham Palace"' could, without advice, make statements designed to influence events was one Powell described as 'constitutionally unsound and fraught with disagreeable consequences'.[48]

Despite the intervention from the Palace, Rabuka declared himself head of state on 1 October and a week later issued a decree formally proclaiming Fiji a republic. There was still no response from Ganilau. The British government was reluctant to press matters in a way that might lead to Fiji's departure from the Commonwealth. Yet the Palace appears to have decided that the position was no longer tenable and pressed Genilau to offer his resignation. It then effectively settled matters on 15 October, while the Queen was in Vancouver for the 1987 CHOGM. It published the Governor General's letter of resignation to the Queen, along with a message claiming that the Queen was 'sad to think that the ending of Fijian allegiance to the Crown should have been brought about without the people of Fiji being given an opportunity to express their opinion on the proposal'.[49] This appears to have come as a surprise to Mrs Thatcher, who had made a statement of her own expressing her hope that Fiji would remain in the Commonwealth, claiming that the country was 'much more likely to come back to democracy and back to the standards we know if we keep the Commonwealth links'.[50] In the retreat at the Vancouver CHOGM, Nigeria (itself under military rule) appears to have supported Mrs Thatcher's position, but India, Australia, and New Zealand did not. In the absence of consensus, Fiji's membership of the Commonwealth was deemed to have 'lapsed'.[51]

Speaking to the journalist Robert Hardman, Heseltine has subsequently admitted that the Queen acted on her own initiative and against the wishes of the British government. He noted:

> The Governor-General had been sort of pretending to be in charge of Fiji. But after the second coup happened he really couldn't pretend to go on doing that. So the Queen took the initiative to suggest to him that the time had come for him to accept that Fiji was now a republic. It was no use pretending any longer that Fiji was a realm. Mrs Thatcher was quite opposed to the idea of the Queen, as it were, abdicating. But it wasn't up to her because it was as Queen of Fiji that she had come to this conclusion.[52]

In a letter to *The Times*, published in the wake of the Governor General's resignation, Powell again questioned the Queen's right to intervene as Queen of Fiji in the absence of Fijian ministerial advice, and pointed to the danger that the Palace and the British government were effectively operating different policies.[53]

One of the striking things about Fiji was that the declaration of a republic was not immediately followed by an attempt to erase symbols of the link to the Crown. As Barltrop noted in 1996, 'The Queen still features on Fiji's currency notes and coins; her Official Birthday is still a public holiday; and the flag remains unchanged, with the "Union Jack" still in the corner.' This raised the possibility that Fiji might one day not merely return to the Commonwealth, but might do so as a Commonwealth realm. As Barltrop suggested, 'Transition from realm to republic is a familiar feature in the history of the Commonwealth. But reversion to realm would be a route not trodden.' An alternative course that was also canvassed was that, while remaining a republic, Fiji might invite the Queen to take the supreme chiefly title of *Tui Viti*, which had been conferred on Queen Victoria and her successors since the Deed of Cession in 1874. Indeed, although Fiji officially rejoined the Commonwealth in 1997 under a new republican constitution, in 2002 the chairman of Fiji's Great Council of Chiefs declared that the title of *Tui Viti* had never actually lapsed and continued to apply.[54] In 2009, a few months before Fiji was suspended from the Commonwealth for failing to hold fresh elections, the Fijian prime minister, Frank Bainimarama, was quoted as saying that he still saw himself as a 'Queen's man' and that he would like to see the Queen 'restored as our monarch'.[55]

THE CANADIAN AND AUSTRALIAN CONSTITUTION ACTS

The 1980s also witnessed the culmination of 'De-Dominionisation' in the form of a series of constitution acts which removed Westminster's remaining legislative powers over Canada (1982), Australia (1986), and New Zealand (1986). Of these, the first proved by far the most troublesome and controversial from the point of view of the British government, although this had very little to do with disagreements about the position of the monarchy. In the case of the Australian Constitution Act of 1986, the position of the Crown was more central, but the process of passing the British bill through Parliament was considerably smoother.

In June 1980 Pierre Trudeau told Mrs Thatcher that his government wished to make a renewed attempt to 'patriate' the Canadian constitution, and that this would require the UK parliament to pass legislation. Mrs Thatcher indicated that her own position was that Britain would do this if it was the wish of the Canadian government, whether or not the Canadian provinces agreed with the legislation.[56] When, however, she and the British Foreign Secretary, Lord Carrington, met Carrington's Canadian counterpart in October 1980, Mrs Thatcher had to explain that, although her own position had not changed, legislation in the UK was likely to be controversial, leading to possible delays in the passage of any bill.[57] The reason for the controversy was the opposition of the majority of Canadian provinces to Trudeau's new constitution.

Unlike Trudeau's previous efforts at constitutional reform, this opposition did not relate in any significant degree to changes relating to the Crown or suspicions of a hidden republican agenda. Indeed, Trudeau effectively ring-fenced the issue of the monarchy, in the process erecting a formidable constitutional barrier to republicanism. Section 41(a) of the 1982 Constitution made provision for amendments relating to 'the office of the Queen, the Governor General and the Lieutenant Governor of a province'. Yet, as the consequence of negotiations between Trudeau and the premiers of Canada's provinces in November 1981, any such amendments would require resolutions from the Canadian Senate and House of Commons, as well as the unanimous backing of all the provincial legislative assemblies.[58] While section 41(a) would allow, in theory, for the abolition of the monarchy, in practice the fact that any province could exercise a veto over such legislation would make it extremely difficult to pass legislation of this kind. During the committee stage of the passage of the bill in the British Parliament, this section was criticized by the Labour MP Michael English for depriving Canadians of the ability to make constitutional amendments in this area. English, who had himself introduced a bill on the laws of succession to the throne, noted that Canadian legislation on this subject might fall foul of section 41.[59]

The controversy surrounding the legislation proposed by Trudeau derived largely from his decision to introduce a bill of rights as part of the package. Provincial governments feared that this would undermine their powers, and in October 1980 the Attorneys General of the six provinces that dissented most strongly from the legislation agreed to launch actions in three provincial courts as a preliminary to a reference to the Supreme Court. Among the issues these actions sought to explore was whether it was constitutional for the Federal government to ask the UK parliament to pass legislation which would alter the balance of power between the Federal and provincial governments without the support of the provincial administrations. In the circumstances, the British government was reluctant to press ahead with legislation that might subsequently be ruled illegal in the Canadian courts. At that point only one province—Ontario—unequivocally supported Trudeau's proposals.

Provincial objections to the legislation made a strong impression on MPs in Westminster. In January 1981 a report by the Commons Foreign Affairs Committee concluded that it would be wrong for the UK parliament to enact the proposals in the face of this opposition. They based this on the principle that under section 7 of the 1931 Statute of Westminster, the British parliament was a guarantor of the rights of the provinces. The British Lord Chancellor, Lord Hailsham, disagreed with this reading of the Statute. Like many of his senior colleagues, however, his main argument was political rather than constitutional. He wrote, 'I cannot conceive any advantage accruing to the UK by disregarding a "request and consent" properly passed by the established machinery in Ottawa which could possibly compensate for the infinite damage which would accrue to the UK interests in Canada, to our relations with Canada, bilaterally, in the Commonwealth, in NATO, in the UNO.'[60] He compared any decision to exercise a veto over the Canadian government's legislation to the House of Lords' rejection of the Liberal government's 'People's Budget' of 1909 (a blunder which ultimately resulted in the emasculation of the House of Lords by the 1911 Parliament Act). The Thatcher government therefore faced a dilemma: either to damage relations with the Canadian government by refusing to introduce legislation enacting the reforms or to face opposition and possible defeat from a strong cross-party lobby within parliament. This lobby, incidentally, included many of the opponents of decolonization in the 1960s who still retained their seats, as well—inevitably—as the Ulster Unionist MP for South Down, J. Enoch Powell.

The British government's dilemma was ostensibly not eased by the Canadian Supreme Court's ruling in September 1981 that the Trudeau government's intended course of action was legal but against constitutional conventions. British parliamentarians who regarded themselves as the ultimate arbiters of this dispute between the Federal and provincial governments would inevitably be able to draw support from the judgement.[61] This, in turn, however, helped to force Trudeau back into negotiations with the provinces. The provinces themselves were less than certain that they would ultimately prevail, and were also prepared to talk. These negotiations in November 1981, during which Trudeau proved willing to dilute the provisions of his Charter of Rights, radically changed the arithmetic, such that by the end only Quebec was standing out against a deal. Issues surrounding aboriginal rights continued to fuel passionate and eloquent opposition to the bill in Westminster. But Trudeau's deal with the provinces in November effectively spared the Thatcher government from a potentially highly embarrassing parliamentary struggle, and ensured the bill's passage in March 1982. It is a strange irony that the rather belated grant of full independence to Canada in 1982, which has gone largely unnoticed in standard histories of decolonization, proved more troublesome to party managers in the UK than the independence bills passed during the supposedly more controversial period of withdrawal from Empire in the 1950s and 1960s.

The 1986 Australia Act again involved two separate bills passed by the British and Australian Parliaments which had the effect of removing any residual powers of the British Parliament over the Australian states, and of abolishing appeals and references to the Privy Council by state courts. As we have seen, one of the constitutional anomalies that survived the passing of the Statute of Westminster was that the British government continued to be formally responsible for advising the monarch on the appointment of the governors of the Australian states (based on recommendations from state premiers). Despite being a rather bizarre relic of colonial rule, it helped to preserve the balance of power between the state and federal governments, which would have been disrupted had the federal prime minister performed this task. The package of reforms which the Labor Government of Bob Hawke introduced in the mid-1980s sought to address this long-standing oddity by allowing state premiers direct access to the Queen on the selection of governors. This part of the package, however, encountered resistance from the Palace. It suited the Palace that there should be only one channel for advice from Australia itself. The Palace also feared that any change in the existing arrangements might result in the Queen receiving conflicting advice from the state and federal governments.

When the suggestion had been made by the Whitlam government in the mid-1970s that state premiers might be given the right to advise the Queen on the appointment of state governors, the Palace had made clear its opposition to the idea. The Queen's private secretary, Martin Charteris, had written that 'As things stand at the moment, State Premiers have no rights to advise The Queen on anything and this is a satisfactory state of affairs which I think it would be dangerous to alter.'[62] In discussions with Whitlam in December 1974, the then British prime minister, Harold Wilson, and Foreign Secretary, James Callaghan, had also questioned the proposal, arguing that state premiers did not have the necessary constitutional status to advise the Queen.[63] Following these discussions, the Attorney General's office in Canberra admitted that while 'the present procedures are plainly anachronistic... awkward implications could arise out of the development of a system enabling State Ministers to advise The Queen directly'.[64]

Faced with a determined attempt by the federal government in the 1980s to abolish the last remnants of colonial subordination to the UK, the Thatcher government proved quite happy to be relieved of its remaining responsibilities. It was concerned, however, that it should not find itself in the middle of a constitutional row between the Commonwealth government and the states. As such, its principal concern was that a solution should be found that would command general support in Australia. Mrs Thatcher's own view was that it would be 'too colonial for words' if the UK sought to interfere in matters that were essentially for the Australians to decide.[65] Yet the British government was also adamant that it had a constitutional right to advise the Queen on the proposed reforms by virtue of the relationship between UK ministers, the Crown, and the states.[66] Indeed, should the proposals have implications for her functions as Queen of the UK or as Head of the Commonwealth, the British government would have a strong interest in doing so. Accordingly, the Thatcher administration became concerned when it appeared that the key negotiations were taking place on a bilateral basis between the federal government of Australia and the Palace. In March 1985 (incidentally providing powerful evidence for A. G. Hopkins' argument that such constitutional tussles need to be seen within the broader context of decolonization), an official at the Foreign Office wrote:

> A moment's reflection leads to the thought that we are engaged in Australia's inde-
> pendence negotiations. Typically, these should be conducted by the British Govern-
> ment of the day with the dependent territory in question and with British Ministers
> taking into their brief the concerns of the Palace. But in this instance, the extraordinary
> situation has arisen where it is the Palace that is now in direct negotiations with
> representatives of the dependent territory.[67]

More specifically, the memorandum appears to point to a familiar sense of unease on the part of the FCO at the Palace's ability to pursue, in effect, an independent policy with another Commonwealth government. By this stage, a clear divergence of opinion had opened up between the British government and the Palace. The former tended to support the Australian government's view that the Queen would not be placed in an embarrassing situation by the right of state premiers to advise her, so long as that advice was confined to the appointment of state governors, and the federal government refrained from offering advice on that subject. The Palace continued to see dangers in allowing state premiers to offer advice, and was particu-larly concerned that when the Queen was physically present in a state she might be advised by its premier to make a speech criticizing the federal government.[68]

When Sir Geoffrey Yeend, representing the Hawke government, discussed this matter with the Palace in May 1985, he apparently sought to overcome royal objections by raising the ultimate threat: that Hawke would formally advise the Queen in favour of the proposal that state premiers should have direct access to her. Faced with this prospect, the Palace relented, allowing Hawke to offer informal advice on the legislation at the end of May. In his letter to Hawke the following month, telling the Australian prime minister that the Queen was 'pleased to accept' his advice, her private secretary, Sir Philip Moore, made it plain that she was doing so with considerable reluctance. He told Hawke:

> As you are aware, The Queen has been very chary about accepting any arrangement
> under which she has to receive formal advice from more than one set of Ministers of
> one country. This will not only establish a new constitutional principle for the Queen
> but will also expose Her Majesty to the risk of having to accept formal advice from the
> Premier of an Australian State when she is fully aware that what is proposed is
> unpalatable to the Government of Australia.[69]

Moore added that the Queen understood Australia's federal system made it unacceptable for state premiers to channel advice to her through the federal government, and in these circumstances accepted Hawke's approach. Yet Moore's letter sent an unmistakable message that the Queen was far from reassured that the new arrangements would work.

One point that puzzled British officials during these negotiations was why the Australians had made no attempt to repeal section 2 of their 1900 Constitution Act as part of the package of reforms. Section 2 stated that those provisions of the Constitution referring to the Crown 'shall extend to Her Majesty's heirs and successors in the sovereignty of the United Kingdom'.[70] According to some interpretations, this would mean that British legislation would continue to apply to Australia in respect of any changes to the laws of succession passed in Westminster. British officials regarded this as incompatible with the intentions behind the 1986 Act, but were reluctant to go on record suggesting its repeal. One noted,

> I am sure we do not want to suggest a change to the Bill to allow this to be done, since this would, I fear, be construed as our facilitating the possible future transformation of Australia into a Republic. Not something, I think, which would be looked upon favourably by our Ministers and certainly not by the Palace.[71]

The Australia Act of 1986 set the seal on what Brian Galligan has described as an essentially republican constitution disguised by monarchical forms.[72] This situation might have offered few practical incentives for undertaking the complex planning necessary to achieve formal republican status. Yet, as we shall see in the following chapter, the Australia Act did not succeed in taking the momentum from the republican movement in Australia.

11

The Fall and Rise of the Royal Commonwealth

ANNUS HORRIBILIS

Between the initial appearance of Tom Nairn's classic republican rallying call, *The Enchanted Glass*, in 1988 and the publication of its revised edition in 1994, something very remarkable happened to the domestic fortunes of the British royal family. The year 1992, which was to have provided an opportunity to celebrate the fortieth anniversary of the Queen's accession to the throne, became instead her *annus horribilis*. She herself deployed this memorable phrase (coined by her former assistant private secretary, Edward Ford) in a speech made at the Guildhall on 23 November 1992. She used it to characterize a year which she claimed—with no risk of overstatement—she would not recall 'with undiluted pleasure'. It had seen the publication in June of Andrew Morton's *Diana: Her True Story*, which laid bare the troubled marriage of the Prince of Wales and his wife, something that was already becoming painfully apparent to anyone who observed their public appearances together. Indeed, tours of Commonwealth countries by Charles and Diana had been incorporated into the campaign of psychological warfare the couple were increasingly conducting against one another via the press. A notorious example came during their visit to India in February 1992. Arriving without her husband at the Taj Mahal, to which Charles had many years before pledged to take her, Diana obliged press photographers by posing wistfully against this most romantic of backgrounds, the very image of a neglected wife.[1]

In March 1992 the Queen's second son, Prince Andrew, Duke of York, announced that he was separating from his wife. Shortly afterwards, newspaper readers were treated to intimate photographs of the Duchess of York relaxing with her 'financial adviser', Johnny Bryan.[2] If none of this was calculated to enhance the dignity of the monarchy, there was a potentially even more damaging publication in 1992. This was Philip Hall's *Royal Fortune*, which focused unprecedented attention on the Queen's personal wealth and her exemption from taxation. When on 20 November 1992 a fire gutted parts of Windsor Castle, there was public outrage when a British minister suggested the government would cover the costs of restoration. The Queen responded by announcing that both she and the Prince of Wales would voluntarily begin paying income tax.

The British author A. N. Wilson caught the mood of the time when he entitled his 1993 study of the royal family *The Fall of the House of Windsor*. A year later, in the revised edition of *The Enchanted Glass*, Nairn confidently labelled sections of his new introduction 'After the Fall' and 'The Shattered Glass'. Yet the fortunes of the Windsors still had some way to fall. In 1994, the Prince of Wales gave what to some seemed an excruciatingly self-revelatory television interview to the journalist Jonathan Dimbleby, in which he admitted to adultery. Charles's willingness to air his personal troubles so publicly represented for some of his critics an error of equal if not greater magnitude to his infidelity. Writing in *The Round Table* in 1995, in one of his last interventions on Commonwealth affairs, the veteran academic and journalist H. V. Hodson noted that Charles's suitability for the Crown had been called into question not so much by his personal life as by his self-exposure, suggesting a 'restless, insecure and self-centred character'.[3]

Finally, of course, there was the tragedy of Diana's death in a car crash in Paris on 31 August 1997. The hysterical popular reaction, whipped up by the media, created a particularly dangerous moment for the royal family. An unqualified public-relations disaster was narrowly averted when the Queen was persuaded to make a live television broadcast, speaking both as Queen and (in a phrase inserted at the suggestion of Tony Blair's press secretary, Alastair Campbell) 'as a grandmother'. It was a carefully crafted and remarkably effective speech, one that managed to dispel the immediate air of tension surrounding her reaction to the tragedy. Yet, while she acknowledged that Diana's death had provoked 'an overwhelming expression of sadness', the Queen herself remained characteristically composed. She saved her tears for a later occasion.

In terms of Commonwealth affairs, the fortunes of the House of Windsor were far more mixed. The 1990s was by no means a comfortable decade for the Queen. As we shall see, she lost her beloved yacht *Britannia*, which had played such an important part in facilitating her peripatetic role as Head of the Commonwealth; a couple of accident-prone Commonwealth visits suggested that royal tours might be losing some of their magic; and the impending Australian republican referendum cast a broader question mark over the future of the Commonwealth realms. Ironically, however, given what was happening in the UK, the Queen actually emerged from the 1990s with her prestige within Commonwealth circles enhanced. While this undoubtedly owed something to her record of devotion to the organization over previous decades, it was probably also a product of the Commonwealth's own identity crisis, as the advent of majority rule in South Africa robbed it of the issue that since the 1960s had given it a sense of purpose and mission.

DARK CLOUDS (I): THE ROYAL YACHT

The final incarnation of the royal yacht *Britannia* (in a tradition that dated back to the days of Charles II) came into service in 1954. Over the subsequent decades it became an essential instrument in efforts to project the monarchy on a global stage. By providing what was in effect a floating palace, it addressed concerns on the part of courtiers and officials that 'embarrassment' might in some sense be caused by the accommodation provided for the Queen by some of her less prosperous hosts.

Conversely, it offered her a mobile base from which to entertain on a suitably regal scale. National prestige would thereby not only be preserved but enhanced. This was of particular importance in the context of the Commonwealth, which contained some of the world's poorest nations. Such considerations were spelled out explicitly in 1974 by the Secretary of State of Defence, Roy Mason, when, at a time of departmental retrenchment, he was asked to comment on the 'presentational advantages' of *Britannia*. Mason explained:

> From the representational point of view, the Royal Yacht contributes significantly to the cohesion of the Commonwealth, and to United Kingdom interests by enabling Her Majesty, as Head of the Commonwealth, to be present when Heads of Government meet in maritime capitals; and to receive Prime Ministers individually . . . In the smaller maritime capitals, such as Kingston, it might be difficult for The Queen and her suite to be suitably accommodated ashore at the same time as all the visiting Prime Ministers, and if the Yacht were not available, the Governments might feel obliged to make it known that, for administrative reasons, they would prefer Her Majesty not to attend. The Royal Yacht also enables The Queen to visit many poor countries, whether Commonwealth or foreign, without putting her hosts to expenses and trouble which might embarrass them.[4]

Nevertheless, the royal yacht was vulnerable to Whitehall's periodic exercises in cost cutting, despite increasing efforts to deploy it as a floating ambassador for British trade. While the other Commonwealth realms could hardly object to the British government—which entirely funded the *Britannia*—using it for this purpose, the prospect of UK firms busily touting their wares on the decks of the royal yacht was hardly in the spirit of the divisible monarchy. None of this, however, was enough to save the *Britannia*. John Major, who moved to 10 Downing Street from the Treasury in 1990, was sympathetic to the argument that the yacht had value, but was not convinced that a compelling economic case could be made for its retention. Meanwhile, Major's Chancellor of the Exchequer, Norman Lamont, was worried about the precedent a decision to replace the *Britannia* might set for the other spending departments.[5] In 1994 his government announced that the yacht would be decommissioned when the time came for its next overhaul. No undertaking was made about a replacement. Such was the low ebb of the royal family's fortunes at the time that ministers clearly believed any announcement of a successor vessel would simply focus further adverse publicity on the Palace, and the Palace itself was in no position to press the matter.

Yet, in a move that ultimately endeared neither major party to the Palace, shortly before the 1997 general election the abrasive Secretary of State for Defence, Michael Portillo, won Cabinet approval for an announcement that if the Conservatives were returned to power, they would commission a new royal yacht. As we have seen, when early in 1959 Harold Macmillan sought to reach an agreement with the Palace over the future of Marlborough House, he made a point of bringing the leaders of the Labour and Liberal parties into the discussion. In 1997 John Major's government appears to have had no similar conversation with the Opposition. Indeed, the issue seems to have been identified by the Conservatives, who were floundering in the opinion polls, as one that might embarrass their Labour opponents. In the process, they could reasonably be accused of having politicized not just the specific issue of the *Britannia*, but the monarchy as a whole. The Labour Party had no compunction about criticizing the Conservative government's commitment to replace the yacht and, following Labour's landslide victory in May 1997, the new Treasury team comprehensively squashed the idea. At the decommissioning ceremony for the yacht in December, the normally impassive Queen appeared to shed a very public tear. While the new prime minister, Tony Blair, had to face the ill-concealed resentment of members of the royal family at this move, it is clear that some residents of the Palace felt that the blame should be spread more evenly. Prince Philip provided a characteristically blunt synopsis to the former politician and broadcaster Giles Brandreth: 'Major was blocked by Lamont and didn't get the Opposition on board. And then Portillo got involved and made a complete bollocks of it. Absolutely idiotic.'[6] There were suspicions in the Palace that, had the Major government made a sustained, low-key attempt to persuade Blair of the value of the *Britannia* rather than politicizing the issue, it might have succeeded. Indeed, according to his press secretary, Alastair Campbell, having seen the yacht in action during the handover of Hong Kong in June 1997, Blair was converted. According to Campbell, 'T[ony]B[lair] said as we drove away "We must keep *Britannia*." I knew he would. "What an asset," he said.'[7] By then, however, it was too late.

DARK CLOUDS (II): TURBULENT TOURS

The sense that the fortunes of the House of Windsor had turned in a fairly decisive fashion appeared to be confirmed by two turbulent and controversial tours of the Commonwealth in the early years of the Blair government. The first of these—a visit to the Indian subcontinent in October 1997—took on something of the quality of a nightmare. The death of Diana at the end of August 1997 inevitably cast a shadow over the Queen's visit to South Asia, which was her first overseas engagement since the tragedy. In the wake of what was generally judged to have been the Palace's clumsy response to Diana's death, the press was in no mood to forgive further royal blunders. The British high commissioner in Delhi during the Queen's 1997 visit was David Gore-Booth, whose father had been high commissioner at the time of the Queen's first tour of India in 1961. Gore-Booth studied the itinerary of her two earlier Indian tours and identified some different locations for the Queen to visit. These included Amritsar and Cochin, which she had never visited, and Madras, which had been part of her programme in 1961 but not on her later tour in 1983.[8] At Amritsar, her visit would take in the Golden Temple, an important focus of pilgrimage for Sikhs, something Gore-Booth believed would go down well with the Sikh community in the UK. It would also include Jallianwala Bagh, the site of a notorious massacre of many hundreds of unarmed Indians in April 1919 by troops under the command of Brigadier-General Reginald Dyer. This was something of a gamble given the sensitivity of the site and the mixed signals from the Indian government about whether it would welcome Amritsar being added to the royal itinerary. Gore-Booth opposed any suggestion that the Queen should apologize for the Jallianwala Bagh massacre, but believed that the very fact of her going to the site and honouring the dead would be appreciated by the Indians as a conciliatory gesture. Nevertheless, he recognized the danger that offence might be caused by her failure to make a clear apology. Ironically, this was to be one of the more successful parts of the Queen's visit.

The tour of India was preceded by what was generally considered to be a successful state visit to Pakistan. The Queen was accompanied by the Foreign Secretary, Robin Cook. Although by that stage there was an expectation that the Foreign Secretary should accompany the Queen on visits to Commonwealth republics on some such occasions, the Palace's own preference had been that the Queen should not be accompanied by a minister. When she had visited India and Pakistan in 1961 it had been decided that it would not be appropriate for a British minister to be in attendance.[9] On her tour of Africa in 1979 at the time of the Lusaka CHOGM, her private secretary, Philip Moore, had advised that it would be preferable if the Queen's party did not include a minister. With the issue of Rhodesia continuing to generate divisions within the Commonwealth, Moore had explained that the Palace wanted the visit 'to be as uncontroversial as possible and I imagine it would be very difficult for a British Minister to be in attendance on the Queen without giving the tour a political flavour'.[10] In short, it was feared that the presence of a British minister could exacerbate or even generate political controversy. This certainly proved to be the case during the 1997 tour of Pakistan and India.

Cook had come to this post following the Labour Party victory early in the year, publicly committed to the notion that Britain, as the former Imperial power, had a responsibility to help resolve the Kashmir dispute between India and Pakistan. As the director for South and South East Asia at the Foreign Office, Hilary Synnott had warned Cook to avoid the issue of Kashmir during the 1997 trip for fear of offending Indian sensibilities.[11] Cook, however, not only felt strongly about this particular issue but was also apparently impatient with the largely passive role usually adopted by foreign secretaries on state visits. During talks in Islamabad, he reportedly agreed to a request from the Pakistani prime minister, Nawaz Sharif, that Britain should lend a hand in seeking to resolve the Kashmir issue.[12] This offer was promptly leaked by the Pakistanis (for whom external mediation was an important objective), to the fury of the Indian government and press. The leak seemed all the more plausible in the light of a speech the Queen herself had delivered in Islamabad in which she urged India and Pakistan to settle their differences over Kashmir. India's prime minister, Inder Kumar Gujral, reportedly told a private meeting in Egypt that Britain was a 'third rate power' which 'has no business to play any role in this issue in any form, since in any case it was responsible for the partition of the country'.[13] His subsequent claim that his words had been misreported was no more convincing than Cook's disavowal of the leaks from Pakistan.

The Queen's visit to Amritsar, at which she and the Duke of Edinburgh laid a wreath at Jallianwalla Bagh, proved relatively successful in setting the tone of reconciliation Gore-Booth had desired. The *New York Times* described the visit as 'an act of contrition for Britain's colonial past'.[14] Her actual words stopped considerably short of a conventional apology. Speaking the evening before her visit, she described the massacre as 'a distressing example' of 'difficult episodes in our past', but went on to assert that 'history cannot be rewritten, however much we might sometimes wish otherwise'. The good impression created by the visit was, however, undermined somewhat by the Duke, who chose the occasion to question the figure of 2,000 deaths on a memorial plaque at Jallianwalla Bagh, reportedly suggesting to his guide that it was a 'bit exaggerated' and must have included the wounded. It did not help that the Duke cited as his own source an account by General Dyer's son, whom he had known in the navy.[15]

While this gaffe was treated less indulgently than some of the Duke's other off-the-cuff remarks, it was far from being the most embarrassing part of the tour. A serious row erupted over plans for the Queen to deliver a toast at a banquet at Madras. The Indian government objected to this on the grounds that she had already delivered one in Delhi. This led to mutual recriminations. Gore-Booth was quoted as blaming 'incompetent bunglers' within the Indian government.[16] In response, India's Foreign Ministry spokesman blamed 'British ineptitude', suggesting that the UK government had scheduled the speech in Madras in the belief they could 'bully the Indians into acceptance of something completely without precedent'.[17] The Indians were to pursue their vendetta against Gore-Booth once the visit was over, with officials briefing the British media that the Indian government wanted his recall because of his 'rude and haughty behaviour'.[18] They warned that his continued presence could jeopardize trade between the two countries. In fact, Gore-Booth was recalled a few months later following a separate row over Indian nuclear testing. Cook conspicuously declined to offer him another senior diplomatic post and Gore-Booth resigned from the service.[19] Even the Queen's departure from India descended into farce when the Indian police jostled members of the royal entourage at Madras airport. The Queen reportedly 'looked on in disbelief' as police attempted to prevent her press secretary boarding the plane and manhandled a female British diplomat.[20]

In December 1997, in a damage-limitation operation clearly aimed at distracting attention from Cook's own patent culpability in the matter, the Foreign Office provided a briefing to the press in which it showered blame in a variety of different directions. It claimed that the Queen's tour of India had prompted the government to carry out a major overhaul of royal visits, as part of which the Foreign Secretary's senior media adviser would in future accompany the royal party.[21] The briefing also blamed the previous Conservative government for having arranged the visit to coincide with the fiftieth anniversary of India's independence, a decision it claimed Cook had questioned. Finally, with an authentically New Labour touch, it suggested Cook felt the focus of royal tours should be 'on the future rather than the past'. It claimed that Cook had been frustrated that the Queen's recent tour of India had 'harked back to the days of the Empire rather than looking to build trade relations', and that he hoped in future 'to promote a more "modern" approach to state visits with less emphasis on imperial heritage'. None of this could fail to evoke memories of some of the criticisms aired following Diana's death: that the Palace itself was 'out of touch'.

The press briefing mentioned that the Foreign Secretary was anxious to avoid any repeat of the kind of problems that had been encountered in India when he accompanied the Queen on a state visit to Malaysia the following year. In the event, the trip to Malaysia, timed to coincide with the 1998 Commonwealth Games in Kuala Lumpur, was to prove that even the best media machine could not insulate the royal party from the impact of unexpected events.

Despite maintaining generally good relations with the West, Malaysia's long-serving prime minister, Dr Mahathir Mohamad, was known for his strident anti-British rhetoric. In the 1980s he had threatened to withdraw Malaysia from the Commonwealth, and he had been enraged by coverage in the British press in 1994 of corruption allegations surrounding the construction of the Pergau Dam.[22] Ahead of the Queen's visit in September 1998, the signals coming from the Malaysian government were hardly reassuring. Somewhat to the dismay of British officials, Prince Edward, the Queen's representative at the opening of the Commonwealth Games, was treated to a pageant which showed peaceful Malays being cowered into submission by British and Portuguese imperialists, represented by inflatable plastic dragons.[23] Yet it transpired that Dr Mahathir's wrath would be reserved not for the British but for his former colleague, Anwar Ibrahim, whom he had recently sacked as deputy prime minister and minister of finance. Anwar, a potential political rival to the prime minister, was subjected to a lurid series of accusations including adultery, sodomy, and treason. Shortly after his sacking, in what many regarded as a show trial, his adopted brother pleaded guilty to being sodomized by Anwar. Perhaps emboldened by the influx of foreign press that accompanied the Games and the Queen's impending visit, and confident that he would be safe while Malaysia remained in the spotlight, on 20 September, the day the Queen flew into Kuala Lumpur, Anwar organized a mass rally in the city's Freedom Square, close to where the Queen would be attending a service in the Anglican cathedral. In front of a crowd of up to 40,000, which was cordoned off by the police from the area around the cathedral, he criticized the government's record on human rights, described the prime minister as a dictator, and called for his resignation. The police responded to this challenge by arresting him and his wife on charges of sexual indecency amid scenes of escalating violent unrest.[24]

In a sign of the concerns of the Foreign Office at the deteriorating situation, Robin Cook, who had accompanied the Queen to Malaysia, announced that he had cancelled plans to fly on to New York for a meeting of the United Nations General Assembly, and that he would, instead, remain with the Queen.[25] Yet, despite the best efforts of the Foreign Office, it proved difficult to avoid some of the popular anger against Dr Mahathir being deflected towards the Queen. It was reported that as her Bentley drove past the magistrates court in Kuala Lumpur there were boos from a crowd of supporters of Anwar which had assembled in anticipation of his appearance there.[26] The crowd itself was later brutally dispersed by the Malaysian security forces, by which stage the Queen herself was paying a 'courtesy call' on Dr Mahathir. In a leading article, *The Guardian* speculated that the unrest which had accompanied the visit would be 'very troubling for the monarch who usually gets more respectful coverage abroad than at home' and suggested that 'she should be more careful about her host's domestic set-up before she starts out'.[27]

DARK CLOUDS WITH SILVER LININGS: THE AUSTRALIAN REFERENDUM

Within the Commonwealth realms, perhaps the major threat hanging over the House of Windsor in the 1990s was posed by Australian republicanism. The Australian Labor Party's 1991 national conference endorsed the aim of a republic by 2000 and, following Labor's victory in the December 1991 general election, the new prime minister, Paul Keating, pursued the matter vigorously. Worryingly for London, Keating's pro-republican rhetoric was peppered with attacks on the British legacy.[28] Keating appointed a Republic Advisory Committee under the chairmanship of Malcolm Turnbull, which recommended in 1994 a 'minimalist' form of republican constitution under which the president would not be directly elected but would be nominated by the prime minister in consultation with the leader of the Opposition and elected by a two-thirds majority of both houses of parliament. This was also the model broadly adopted by the Constitutional Convention which Keating's successor, John Howard, held in February 1998. The issue was put to a referendum in November 1999.

British representatives in Canberra were keen to distance themselves as far as possible from the issue. The approach of Sir John Coles, who served as Britain's deputy high commissioner from 1988 to 1991, echoed sentiments expressed within the Foreign Office in the late 1970s over the Crown in Canada, namely, that the UK should studiously steer clear of the republican issue.[29] This was also the position of Sir Brian Barder, who served as British high commissioner from 1991 to 1994. Yet, as the republican issue gathered momentum, it proved more difficult for British representatives to remain aloof. The notion of a divided Crown was poorly understood, and many in Britain and Australia believed that the republican movement had the potential to damage relations between the two countries. Barder recalled that some within the Foreign Office believed public opinion in the UK would expect British representatives to support the monarchist cause. He therefore came under some pressure to abandon his neutral stance.[30] This pressure only ceased after the Foreign Secretary, Douglas Hurd, made a visit to Canberra and concluded for himself, on the basis of conversations with Australian ministers, that the republican issue was one Britain should keep out of. When Sir Roger Carrick succeeded Barder as UK high commissioner in 1994, he was directed by Hurd to maintain the stance of neutrality. Carrick's successor, Sir Alexander Allan, whose period in Canberra coincided with the referendum, continued this policy.[31]

As Barder recalled, however, UK representatives were faced with a fine balancing act between, on the one hand, wishing to reassure Australians that the relationship with Britain was strong enough to withstand any change in the status of the Crown and, on the other, not wanting to appear to be offering support to the republican camp.[32]

Meanwhile, as Allan later noted, many in the monarchist camp simply assumed that the UK high commission would be on their side.[33] Yet there were undoubtedly those on the British side whose instinctive sympathies lay with the republicans. Sir John Coles, who by the time Keating left office was permanent undersecretary at the Foreign Office, later confessed that he suspected that had he been an Australian he would have voted for a republic.[34] More than a hint of this attitude emerged in 1998, when the FCO sponsored a conference in Canberra alongside the Australian Institute of International Affairs. According to Peter Boyce, 'the FCO seemed confident that the Australian electorate would shortly endorse the proposal for a republic, and several senior participants at the conference argued that within a republican framework relations with the United Kingdom, far from being weakened, would be purged of irritations and misunderstandings generated by real or imagined British condescension, or by public controversy surrounding the Royal Family'.[35] As we have already seen, such sentiments would not have been out of character with the views privately expressed by British officials over many years. Indeed, the surprising thing about the FCO's approach earlier in the 1990s is that Whitehall's long experience of the issue of republicanism in the Commonwealth realms should not have produced a more settled policy.

The result of the Australian referendum would by no means be a foregone conclusion. John Howard, the leader of a Liberal–National Party coalition which had ousted Labor from power following the general election of February 1996, was a staunch monarchist who was able to exploit republican divisions over the form of the new constitution. Voters in 1999 were simply asked whether they supported a bill to 'alter the Constitution to establish the Commonwealth of Australia as a republic with the Queen and Governor-General being replaced by a President appointed by a two-thirds majority of the members of the Commonwealth Parliament'. In voting 'no' they would be supporting the status quo. Although opinion polls indicated a clear republican majority in the country, many republicans were prepared to vote against the motion rather than accept the form of republic that was on offer. The 'minimalist' republic presented an easy target to the monarchy's Australian defenders. They were able to portray it as a recipe for a 'politicians' president' who would inevitably act in the interests of the political class.[36] By extension, they also attempted to portray the movement for republicanism as something that was being driven by a narrow left-wing elite.[37]

With the republican campaign faltering, there were worrying signs that, whatever the result of the referendum, the prestige of the monarchy might be damaged in both Australia and the Queen's other realms. The monarchist camp had tended to focus attention away from the royal family itself. One of the arguments made by the pressure group 'Australians for Constitutional Monarchy' was that Australia already had an indigenous 'head of state' in the form of the Governor General, and that the Queen was merely the 'sovereign'. Buckingham Palace duly obliged in mid-1999 by removing from its website a statement that the Queen was 'head of state' in her overseas realms.[38] Perhaps frustrated by the apparent success of this strategy, members of the republican movement threatened to launch a more personal and aggressive campaign confronting voters with the prospect of 'King Charles III and

Queen Camilla'.[39] There were also signs that the campaign was taking on a sectarian dimension, with the Catholic archbishop of Melbourne, George Pell, urging his flock to vote 'yes' in the referendum.

Against this background, whatever disappointments it contained, the overall result of the referendum must, at least initially, have come as a source of relief for the Palace. In order to win, the 'yes' camp needed an overall majority of the votes cast and a majority in four of the six Australian states. In the event, it achieved neither. Only 45.3 per cent of Australian voters supported the motion for a republic while 54.7 per cent rejected it. Of the six states there was a narrow majority for the motion in only one: Victoria.[40]

One can imagine that the 1999 referendum result was not greeted with unmitigated satisfaction in the FCO. From the point of view of the Palace, if there was initial relief, the considered reaction may also have been ambivalent. The fact that, at the very least, the monarchy had been spared the humiliation of a decisive rejection by Australian voters was a rare piece of good news in a dismal decade. While the Queen's senior advisers were aware that it would be unwise to regard the result as a vote of confidence for the monarchy, the fact remained this this was widely *perceived* as a victory for the Palace. Indeed, one 'insider' saw the referendum as a turning point in the fortunes of the House of Windsor which served to enhance the monarchy's prestige in the UK itself.[41] He might have taken comfort from some of the press coverage of the time. Matthew Engel, writing in *The Guardian*, speculated that the Australian referendum result might 'well mark the start of a new era, and a formal end to years of royal defensiveness that began with the *annus horribilis* of 1992, when the Waleses' marital traumas became public, and reached a peak after Diana's death in 1997'.[42]

At the same time, there were some who shared the view that, in the longer term, the monarchy might have benefited from a 'clean break' with a country that contained a clear republican majority. Robert Lacey claims that Prince Philip's reaction was 'What's the matter with these people? Can't they see what's good for them?'[43] Whatever credence one places on this story, there was a clear acknowledgement in the statements subsequently released by the Palace of the ambiguous message the referendum result had sent, and of the continuing strength of republican sentiment. The immediate response of the Palace in November 1999 noted that 'For some while it has been clear that many Australians wanted constitutional change. Much of the debate has been what that change should be.' Speaking on a visit to Australia in March the following year, the Queen said, 'I have always made it clear that the future of the monarchy in Australia is an issue for you, the Australian people, and you alone to decide by democratic and constitutional means. It should not be otherwise.'[44]

With the Australian referendum result ringing in her ears, the Queen commenced a tour of Africa. The visit began in Ghana and from there moved to South Africa, where the Queen attended the opening of the Durban CHOGM and made a carefully measured expression of regret for the losses of life during the second Boer War. It ended with a brief, twelve-hour stopover in Mozambique, which had joined the Commonwealth four years earlier.

The visit to Ghana, the Queen's first since her tour of the country in 1961, bore the unmistakable fingerprints of the Blair government. Once again, the Queen was accompanied by Robin Cook. Ghana's president, Jerry Rawlings, had come to power in a military coup in 1979. After a brief experiment with civilian rule, he again seized power again in 1981. In line with the democratic winds blowing through Africa at the time, Rawlings had stood for election in 1992. He had been returned to power and successfully stood for office again in 1996. By 1999, however, he was coming to the end of his second period as a democratically elected head of state, and under the terms of the constitution was formally barred from seeking re-election. Many feared, however, that the attractions of office would overcome any scruples he might have about tearing up the constitution. In the circumstances, the purpose of the Queen's visit was clear in respect to Rawlings. As one British journalist covering the visit wrote, 'The Queen is here to hold his hand, to give him credit for the journey he has made so far and ensure that he remains on the path of righteousness. The fact that she can still be used for this purpose, and even be welcomed, is another sign that there is life in the old dog of the Windsor dynasty yet.'[45] The Foreign Office made no secret of the fact that this was the UK's agenda. A representative told *The Times*, 'We want to demonstrate to other States on the continent that the more they behave themselves at home, the more they are likely to attract foreign help. With the state visit we are saying to President Rawlings, "Well done, keep it up."'[46]

In case there was any doubt about the matter, the Queen gave a remarkably pointed speech when she addressed Ghana's parliament. Craig Murray, who was then Britain's deputy high commissioner in Ghana, claims to have drafted the part of the address that attracted particular attention. The text was subsequently cleared with the FCO and the Palace.[47] The Queen commended the Ghanaian people for having been 'in the forefront of the renaissance in Africa of democratic values'. She went on, 'Next year, your president, who has led you through the implemented changes, will reach the end of his second term.'[48] This nicely understated but finely calculated entreaty to Rawlings to honour his constitutional obligation caused uproar in the parliament building. The Queen, who was clearly not used to having her speeches interrupted in this way, had to halt temporarily. In her subsequent remarks she noted, 'An open society of free media, a truly independent judiciary and a democratically chosen, accountable executive provides the conditions under which equality of opportunity, initiative and a stable society can flourish.' Whatever the specific impact of the Queen's visit might have been, Rawlings stood aside in the 2000 presidential elections and endorsed his vice-president. It seemed that there was, indeed, life in the old dog of the Windsor dynasty.

THE APOTHEOSIS OF A CEREMONIAL HEADSHIP

It was not without irony that, at the very moment the royal family was struggling to maintain public confidence in the UK, the Commonwealth secretariat under Chief Emeka Anyaoku moved to formalize the Queen's ceremonial role within the organization. There even seems to have been a surreptitious attempt to settle the question of the future of the headship in favour of the 'British' monarchy. A number of factors may have fed into this strange divergence between the Queen's standing within the Commonwealth and her more troubled position 'at home'. In both a positive and a negative sense, some of these related to the position of South Africa. Political negotiations of the sort that the Commonwealth had long encouraged led in February 1990 to the unbanning of the ANC and the release from prison of its most prominent activist, Nelson Mandela. The following year, Mandela was elected as president of the ANC. The movement went on to win power in April 1994 in South Africa's first universal franchise elections and two months later the country rejoined the Commonwealth after an absence of thirty-three years.

As we have seen, the Queen was generally perceived as having been critical of the Thatcher government's intransigent position over the issue of sanctions against South Africa, and sympathetic towards the objective of black majority rule. That perception was underlined by an incident charged with symbolism which took place at the Harare Heads of Government Meeting in 1991. As was by then traditional at CHOGMs, the Queen held a banquet for Commonwealth leaders. A delegation from the ANC, which included Mandela, was present in Harare, but it enjoyed only observer status. As such, Mandela was not invited to the dinner. Owing to a misunderstanding on the part of one of his aides, however, he arrived at the old Government House where the banquet was taking place, in full view of the world's press, clearly expecting to attend. Both the Queen's press secretary, Charles Anson, and her private secretary, Robert Fellowes, recognized that it would be a public relations disaster if Mandela was turned away. When the situation was explained to the Queen she immediately understood its potential significance, and directed that a place should be found for Mandela near to her own table. The Head of the Commonwealth and the world's most famous former political prisoner conversed and established an instant rapport. As Anson recalls:

> The Queen and Nelson Mandela got on like a house on fire from the start. That first time they talked about sport, the huge worldwide interest in cricket and rugby and how sport had helped to break down racial divisions and unify people across national boundaries.[49]

In 1995 the Queen made a triumphant visit to South Africa, disembarking from the royal yacht *Britannia* in Cape Town to be greeted by President Mandela. Anson was impressed by the warmth of the reception, with even the roads leading out of the towns on the Queen's route being lined with cheering crowds of up to five to ten deep. The tour had its own profound symbolism. It was her first visit to South Africa since 1947 when she had famously pledged her life to the service of her 'Imperial family'. The empire had now completed its metamorphosis into the modern Commonwealth and, in encouraging and nurturing this process, the Queen had established for herself an unassailable position within the organization. She took the opportunity of the 1995 visit to present Mandela with the Order of Merit. Yet, as Steve Bell shrewdly suggested in a cartoon in *The Guardian*, it may have been the British monarchy that was basking in Mandela's reflected glory rather than vice versa (see Illustration 16).

The advent of majority rule in South Africa was a bittersweet moment for the Commonwealth. It represented the ultimate proof of the organization's utility in the post-war world. With the struggle against apartheid over, however, the Commonwealth lost the issue that had for decades provided it with a sense of purpose. An attempt to refocus its activities around the promotion of democracy and human rights witnessed a number of admirable statements of values, beginning with the Harare Declaration of 1991, and the creation in 1995 of the Commonwealth Ministerial Action Group to respond to serious violations of its principles. In practice, however, the Commonwealth's record in dealing with member states that have been guilty of significant abuses has been less than impressive.[50] Various initiatives to reform the organization failed to revive the sense of momentum it enjoyed in the 1970s and 1980s, and doubts have increasingly been raised about its continuing value. As such, far from being seen as a slightly embarrassing relic of the Imperial past, as might have been the case in the Ramphal era, the link to the royal family has arguably become an important means by which the Commonwealth can ensure that senior ministers—particularly in the UK—continue to engage with it.

If the notion of a ceremonial rather than a purely symbolic head of the Commonwealth was controversial in the 1950s, it was clearly a far less divisive issue by the 1990s. The gradual accumulation of public functions connected with the headship, which is outlined in Chapter 7, had paved the way for the acceptance of a formal ceremonial role. The Commonwealth itself had changed out of all recognition in the intervening decades. It had become an organization predominantly composed of republics, the foreign policies of which had taken radically different courses. Meanwhile, in Canada, Australia, and New Zealand, the process of 'De-Dominionisation', outlined in Chapter 10, had helped foster a more confident sense of nationhood within the larger Commonwealth realms. As such, the idea of the Queen playing a formal role within the Commonwealth could hardly be regarded as any kind of constitutional threat to the sovereignty of its member states.

The first stage of the process of giving the headship a formal ceremonial role came at the Harare CHOGM in 1991, when heads of government unanimously approved a proposal from the Royal Anniversary Trust to present the Queen with a special Commonwealth Mace to mark the fortieth anniversary of her accession to the throne in 1992. The Trust had been established in 1990 as a privately funded registered charity, at the instigation of the businessman Sir Robin Gill. Its initial purpose was to arrange celebrations to mark the fortieth anniversary. The Queen was presented with the mace at a gala event in Earl's Court in October 1992, at which she was accompanied by Anyaoku.[51] She also received 52 silver gilt toasting goblets, one for each of the then members of the Commonwealth. The mace itself was designed by the London-based goldsmith Gerald Benney (see Illustration 14).[52] It contains five kilos of eighteen carat gold, and is decorated with the royal coat of arms, the Commonwealth symbol, and the enamelled flags of the member states. It has subsequently been in regular use when the Queen, or a member of the royal family representing her, is present as Head of the Commonwealth, including the

Multi-Faith Observance and the Commonwealth Day reception at Marlborough House. It has also been carried in procession on other special Commonwealth occasions, including the service in Westminster Abbey in July 1994 to celebrate South Africa's return to the Commonwealth.[53] In 1997 Anyaoku took a further step in cementing the Queen's ceremonial role within the Commonwealth by giving her a formal part in opening the Edinburgh CHOGM. This neo-tradition was maintained at subsequent CHOGMs, and the Commonwealth Mace has accompanied the Queen to the opening ceremonies.

There was another significant development in relation to the Queen at the Edinburgh CHOGM, one that some Commonwealth 'insiders' have linked to Anyaoku's monarchist sympathies. It emerged out of the debate about the requirements for Commonwealth membership, a subject on which the organization had long avoided proper codification. A review in 1991 led to the publication of a memorandum on Commonwealth membership. This set out two key conditions: that there needed to have been some constitutional link between the applicant and either the United Kingdom or another Commonwealth state; and that the applicant accepted the principles set out in the Harare Declaration of 1991.[54] The entry of Mozambique in 1995 raised the prospect of further applications from countries with no constitutional links with Great Britain, and led to the establishment of an Inter-governmental Group on Criteria for Commonwealth Membership (IGCCM), chaired by John Collinge, New Zealand's high commissioner in the UK and an avowed monarchist. The group's report was 'received and endorsed' by the Edinburgh CHOGM in 1997.[55] It recommended that applicants should be obliged to acknowledge 'the role of the British monarch as a symbol of the free association and as such Head of the Commonwealth'.[56] The implications of the term 'British monarch' seem to have been lost on some of the key players at Edinburgh, including the British prime minister, Tony Blair, who was asked about it at the final press conference and apparently failed to grasp the significance of the question. The Commonwealth secretariat, by contrast, seems to have been fully aware of what it implied, namely, that Queen Elizabeth II was Head of the Commonwealth by virtue of being the British monarch, and the role would therefore pass automatically to her successor. If the intention had been to effect a permanent change in Commonwealth doctrine, however, the impact of the IGCCM report was undermined by the fact that the Edinburgh CHOGM did not formally discuss it, and the Edinburgh communiqué made no specific mention of the requirement to acknowledge the British monarch as Head of the Commonwealth.

In 2005 a further committee on Commonwealth membership was established under the chairmanship of P. J. Patterson, prime minister of Jamaica from 1992 to 2006. Its report, published in September 2007, was considered by that year's CHOGM in Kampala. The report had spoken of the 'acknowledgement of the Queen as Head of the Commonwealth' by new members.[57] In their communiqué, however, the heads of government at Kampala were even more specific. They stipulated that applicants would be formally required 'to acknowledge Queen Elizabeth II as the head of the Commonwealth'.[58] At the very least, this made no attempt to foreclose the question of whether the Queen was head of the Commonwealth in a personal capacity, or by virtue of being the British monarch. As such, it represented a distinct retreat from the position taken at the Edinburgh meeting during Anyaoku's period as Secretary-General.

The communiqué of the Kampala meeting also made clear that countries which became republics would no longer be required to apply to remain in the Commonwealth, provided they continued to meet all the criteria for membership. Campaigners for a republic in Australia had expressed indignation at the notion that their country might have to reapply for Commonwealth membership if a republic was achieved. The Kampala communiqué removed this potential point of friction.[59]

A ROYAL COMMONWEALTH?

Anyone observing the contemporary Commonwealth might find it difficult to believe that the organization had ever been uneasy about its relationship with the monarchy, or that the notion of a ceremonial headship was ever considered controversial. Indeed, for much of the international media, the Commonwealth appears to be of interest almost entirely by virtue of its connection with the royal family. The Queen's preeminent position within this troubled institution was plainly apparent at the 2011 CHOGM in Perth. The main item for discussion at Perth was the report of an Eminent Persons Group (EPG) chaired by the former prime minister of Malaysia, Tun Abdullah Ahmad Badawi, which had been mandated by the 2009 CHOGM to suggest means by which the Commonwealth could be revitalized. The most controversial of its 106 recommendations was for the creation of a Commissioner for Democracy, the Rule of Law and Human Rights.[60] The release of the report was poorly handled by the secretariat, and the debate around the proposed commissioner split along familiar lines, with the UK and some of the other more prosperous members of the Commonwealth supporting it, while many developing nations dismissed the emphasis on human rights and political reform as peculiarly Western fixations. In her speech at the opening ceremony of the Perth CHOGM, the Queen pointedly wished the assembled leaders well in

> agreeing further reforms that respond boldly to the aspirations of today and that keep the Commonwealth fresh and fit for tomorrow. In these deliberations we should not forget that this is an association not only of governments but also of peoples. That is what makes it so relevant in this age of global information and communication.

Given that the title of the EPG report was *A Commonwealth of the People—Time for Urgent Reform*, the Queen appeared to be sending a far from subtle message to her audience. Had Enoch Powell still been alive he would no doubt have written to *The Times* demanding to know whether the Queen had spoken on the advice of British ministers and, if not, on what basis she had felt able to intervene in a matter touching on UK foreign policy. In his absence, those questions still deserved to be asked.

The British press paid little attention to the EPG controversy. In so far as they considered the Perth CHOGM newsworthy at all, it was because of the agreement reached on the fringes of the meeting by the prime ministers of the Commonwealth realms about changes to the laws of succession. The sense that the Commonwealth had largely ceased to interest the British public unless it could be tied to the royal family was powerfully underlined by the events of 2012—the year of the Queen's Diamond Jubilee. In the UK, the Jubilee celebrations almost certainly generated more media interest in the specific issue of the Commonwealth than did the 2011 CHOGM. They also led to a number of initiatives that explicitly linked the Commonwealth with the monarchy. These included the Royal Commonwealth Society's on-line Jubilee Time Capsule. People from around the Commonwealth were invited to 'Share Your Story with the Queen' by submitting an anecdote about a particular day in the Queen's reign. Many of the recollections that appeared on the website related to a meeting with the Queen herself or another member of the royal family. The capsule was presented to the Queen at a ceremony in November 2012. The photograph of the event, which appeared on the RCS website, was of a Malawian orphan, John Samson, on bended knee before a seated Queen, offering her an electronic tablet from which she could access the capsule (see Illustration 20). One wonders whether Commonwealth leaders in earlier decades would have been altogether comfortable with the iconography of this image.[61]

Another initiative was the announcement at the 2011 CHOGM of the establishment of the Queen Elizabeth Diamond Jubilee Trust chaired by former prime minister Sir John Major and including among its trustees the Commonwealth Secretary-General Kamalesh Sharma. The purpose of the Trust is to invest in charitable causes across the Commonwealth organized around six broad themes, one for each decade of the Queen's reign. In February 2012, on the exact anniversary of the Queen's accession, David Cameron confirmed that the British government would make a contribution of up to £50 million to the Trust, with the hope that contributions would also be secured from other Commonwealth states and from private sources.[62] The sort of gravitational pull that such a well-financed organization could exert over the rest of the administrative machinery of the Commonwealth can be illustrated in relation to discussions about the future of the Commonwealth Foundation. The Foundation had been brought into existence in 1966 with the aim of 'increasing interchanges between Commonwealth organizations in professional fields throughout the Commonwealth'. A particularly troubled period in the Foundation's existence was brought to an end in April 2011 when an acting director was seconded to the organization with a mandate to carry out reform. One of the options under consideration was apparently that the Foundation should be folded entirely into the planned Jubilee Trust. The principal organization supporting the non-governmental Commonwealth would thus have been explicitly linked to the British royal family. Although this idea was eventually rejected, the fact that it was seriously contemplated reflects the extent to which the Commonwealth has come to be associated with the Queen.[63]

This close association between the Commonwealth and the royal family may well appear to serve the interests of both parties. Yet it carries with it serious problems. The first relates to the position of the Head of the Commonwealth. It is generally accepted as a central tenet of Britain's unwritten constitution that in political matters the monarch only speaks or acts on ministerial advice. As we have seen in the course of this study, and as was again apparent in Perth, Commonwealth affairs have become an area in which the Palace expects a certain freedom of action without ministerial direction. While the Queen's extraordinary discretion and self-control has meant this this has rarely posed any serious constitutional problems, there is no guarantee this would be the case were her successor as monarch to occupy the headship.

This in turn raises a related problem: the uncertain future of the headship beyond the current reign. Under Anyaoku's successor, Don McKinnon, the secretariat appears to have moved decisively to a position that the role of Head of the Commonwealth was not hereditary. A remark to that effect by McKinnon provoked criticism in the British press, but was endorsed by the Foreign Office minister in the House of Lords, Baroness Amos.[64] Until recently, the website of the Commonwealth Secretariat stated explicitly that 'Queen Elizabeth II's heir will not automatically become Head of the Commonwealth. It will be up to the Commonwealth Heads of Government to decide what they want to do about this symbolic role.'[65] There were clear signs that the secretariat under McKinnon expected Charles in some sense to 'run' for the post of head, and he confirms in his memoirs that he felt the heir to the throne should be more fully involved in Commonwealth affairs and therefore decided to pull Charles 'closer into the fold'.[66] Charles visited Uganda at the time of the Kampala CHOGM in 2007, officially on an entirely separate visit at the invitation of President Museveni, although he attended a reception in Kampala for Commonwealth leaders. The *Daily Telegraph*'s diplomatic correspondent David Blair suggested that this visit was part of a programme to 'introduce' Charles to the Commonwealth and to prepare the way for him to become its head on his mother's death.[67] How, then, was the succession to be managed? It appears to have been decided that, on the death of the Queen, her successor as the British monarch should not be described as 'Head of the Commonwealth' in their accession proclamation.[68] The reason for this was apparently McKinnon's belief that there had to be proper consultations with Commonwealth leaders about the matter, initiated by the Secretary-General. If a consensus in favour of her successor as monarch emerged before their coronation, the headship could be included in the sovereign's titles. If not, the matter would have to be decided at the next heads of government meeting.[69]

The outpouring of affection which is bound to accompany the death of the Queen might well ensure that the succession of the headship is quickly resolved in favour of Charles. Indeed, the former Commonwealth Secretary-General, Emeka Anyaoku, has recently suggested that on the Queen's passing, his own latest successor should simply inform Commonwealth heads of government that in keeping with the London Declaration, the new monarch should become Head of the Commonwealth.[70] This would essentially be to lay down a challenge to member states to exercise a veto and block such a move. Yet, in an organization of over fifty states, there could be no guarantee that such a veto would not be deployed, or that the matter would not prove controversial. In July 2009 the Royal Commonwealth Society issued the results of a YouGov opinion poll it had commissioned, which had been carried out in seven Commonwealth countries. The poll revealed little popular enthusiasm for the prospect of Charles becoming Head of the Commonwealth. In India, only 15 per cent of those questioned supported this option, compared with around 50 per cent who favoured a rotating headship. Even in Australia, where Charles's support was greatest, only 27 per cent wished to see him become Head of the Commonwealth.[71] As we have seen in the course of this study, the role of the Head of the Commonwealth has been moulded around the functions and resources of the monarch to such an extent that it would be almost impossible to detach one from the other. We have also seen the difficulties that would be entailed by a rotating headship. In the circumstances, the best solution might be, as was suggested recently in a pamphlet issued by the Institute of Commonwealth Studies, the abolition of the position of Head of the Commonwealth at the end of the Queen's reign.[72] Whatever the case, if the monarchy, through the headship, has become a central prop of the contemporary Commonwealth, it is one with a very uncertain future.

A further element of difficulty in the relationship between the monarchy and the Commonwealth is provided by the Commonwealth realms. On the fringes of the Perth CHOGM of 2011, British prime minister David Cameron and the leaders of the other realms reached agreement in principle to two significant changes to the laws of succession: an end both to the male primogeniture rule for all descendants of the Prince of Wales and to the rule that anyone marrying a Catholic would be barred from succession to the throne.[73] The issue had been given a sense of urgency by the marriage earlier in the year of the second in line to the throne, Prince William.

The Perth agreement came after a number of years during which successive British governments had expressed sympathy for a change to the law of succession but had pointed to the practical difficulties of implementing reform. The Secretary of State for Justice, Jack Straw, claimed in March 2008 that any alteration to the laws of succession would involve amending scores of ancient statutes and 'would among other things require the consent of member nations of the Commonwealth'.[74] Straw's reference to 'member nations of the Commonwealth' pointed to the confusion around the requirement for Commonwealth consultation. A number of commentators pointed to the Statute of Westminster of 1931 as the basis for this obligation. Certainly, as we have seen, the preamble to the Statute articulated the convention that 'any alteration in the law touching the Succession to the Throne or the Royal Style and Titles' should require the assent of 'the Parliaments of all the Dominions' as well as that of the UK parliament. Although the preamble did not have legal force, it was, in the words of Robert Blackburn, 'a powerful political convention', one that was 'equivalent to a treaty' for the Commonwealth countries concerned.[75] Vernon Bogdanor also cited the convention, which had been confirmed in the preamble to the Statute of Westminster, as the basis for claiming that 'it would be unconstitutional, although not illegal, for the British government unilaterally to alter the rule of succession.'[76]

Yet, as Anne Twomey has pointed out, of the parties to the Statute, in addition to Britain itself, the preamble could no longer be considered to apply in any respect to more than two: Australia and Canada.[77] Of the other four parties, Newfoundland had become part of the Canadian Confederation in 1949, Ireland and South Africa had both become republics, and New Zealand had repealed the Statute of Westminster. Even in the case of Australia and Canada it was doubtful whether the preamble effectively remained active. At the time of the 1999 referendum, there had been no suggestion that Australia might have to seek the assent of other Commonwealth parliaments if it abolished the monarchy altogether.[78] In practice, then, even Australia regarded the preamble as obsolete. Of the other Commonwealth realms that had achieved statehood since 1931, none had adopted the Statute of Westminster on independence. The confusion around this issue may in itself have inhibited the governments of the realms from embracing reform. They may also have been reluctant to act because of the sensitive issues that could be raised by legislation relating to the succession, particularly in the federal states of Australia and Canada. In Australia, there was the question of whether the 1986 Australia Act (which, as we have seen, recognized the right of state premiers to advise the Queen directly on state matters) actually created a series of separate Australian crowns. If it did, then the states could plausibly claim the right to pass their own legislation on the law of succession as the Queen was part of the state constitutions. In an article published in April 2011, Twomey presciently noted that, in the case of Canada, section 41(a) of the 1982 constitution could provide the basis of a challenge to any federal legislation that was not also endorsed by all the provincial legislatures.[79] In the event, at the time of the birth of Prince William's first child in July 2013, although legislation in the UK changing the laws of succession had already received royal assent, it had yet to come into effect because not all of the other realms had managed to pass legislation of their own. Indeed, only hours after William's wife, the Duchess of Cambridge, had gone into labour, the government of Quebec announced that it was associating itself with a legal challenge to Canadian legislation, citing section 41(a) of the 1982 constitution.[80] As it turned out, the baby was a boy, and as such his place in line to the throne was already assured. Had the baby been a girl, however, the delay caused by the need to coordinate legislation with the other Commonwealth realms might have generated far more critical comment in the UK. This recent incident recalls a number of themes of this book and points to their continuing relevance. At one level it demonstrates the byzantine structure of laws and conventions that have developed around the monarchy's relationship with Commonwealth countries. Their complexity is such that they are open to misinterpretation even by ministers. This, in turn, opens the possibility that they might lead to misunderstandings or even friction between the member states involved. A more specific problem, certainly in the case of the UK, is that they have the capacity to inhibit reforms that might enhance the acceptability of the monarchy by making it more attuned to contemporary attitudes. Customizing constitutional monarchy to fit into the modern world is a difficult enough task. It becomes all the more so if a country feels that it does not have exclusive ownership of its monarchy.

There is the further problem that the realms pose to the British government which has been identified in the course of this study, and which was illustrated again during the Diamond Jubilee Year. A visit to Jamaica by William's brother, Prince Harry—intended to celebrate the Queen's dedication to the Commonwealth during her sixty years on the throne—was overshadowed by the announcement by the country's prime minister, Portia Simpson Miller, that she intended to introduce a republican constitution. This announcement was partly justified in terms of Jamaica distancing itself from the Imperial past. Simpson Miller suggested that Britain might want to apologize for the 'wicked and brutal' years of slavery. She told reporters, 'No race should have been subjected to what our ancestors were subjected to,' adding, 'We gained our freedom through the sweat, blood and tears of our ancestors and we are now free. If Britain wishes to apologise, fine with us, no problem at all.'[81] The incident posed a familiar dilemma: the survival of the monarchy in the Commonwealth realms is a historical anomaly which has already lasted far longer than many British officials thought likely. Yet while its eventual abandonment is an almost inevitable process, it is one that has the potential to damage relations with the UK through the deployment of the sort of rhetoric used by Simpson Miller. From both a constitutional and a pragmatic point of view, however, the British government is virtually powerless to intervene. If the Commonwealth realms are indeed a legacy of Imperialism, this is one aspect of decolonization over which the UK long ago lost control. In the process, it also—arguably—lost the ability to 'patriate' its own constitution.

Recent events in Jamaica remind us that, rather than acting as a symbol of unity, the monarchy has frequently been a symbolic battleground upon which underlying conflicts around power and status are fought out. This is another reason why the Commonwealth should, perhaps, be wary of maintaining a royal headship beyond the end of the current reign. Yet the Commonwealth also needs to look to its own record over the previous two decades. If the monarchy increasingly appears to be the life-support machine for a dying organization, that is hardly the fault of the Palace. Nor would the Commonwealth be wise to become dependent upon royal patronage. In May 2013 the Palace announced that, as part of a general review of her long-haul travel, the Queen would not be going to that year's CHOGM. This would be the first time she had missed one of these meetings since 1971. The deeply misguided decision to allow Sri Lanka to host the 2013 CHOGM had led to protests from a range of human rights and Commonwealth civil society organizations. The prime minister of Canada, Stephen Harper, made clear that his absence from the meeting in November was a protest against the Sri Lankan government's human rights record. As such, her presence at the 2013 CHOGM would have caused considerable embarrassment, and it is telling that the Palace subsequently announced her intention to attend the 2015 meeting in Malta. In the longer term, it is difficult to see how the Commonwealth will manage without her. Nevertheless, the history of the organization provides clues as to how it might do so. The monarchy has undoubtedly played an important role in shaping the modern Commonwealth, but so too have the wit, courage and imagination of its leaders. Perhaps it is time for the Commonwealth to rediscover these characteristics.

Endnotes

CHAPTER 1: THE HOLY FAMILY

1. For a much broader survey of the historiography of the British monarchy than the one attempted here see Andrzej Olechowicz, 'Historians and the Modern British Monarchy', in Andrzej Olechowicz (ed.), *The Monarchy and the British Nation 1780 to the Present* (Cambridge: Cambridge University Press, 2007), 6–44.
2. Walter Bagehot, *The English Constitution* ([1867]; London: Fontana, 1963), 117.
3. Bagehot, *English Constitution*, 85.
4. Bagehot, *English Constitution*, 111.
5. Tom Nairn, *The Enchanted Glass: Britain and its Monarchy* (London: Vintage, 1994), xvii.
6. Nairn, *Enchanted Glass*, 350.
7. David Cannadine, *History in Our Time* (London: Penguin, 2000), 4.
8. Attlee to Nehru, 20 March 1949, The National Archives, Kew, CAB 21/3374.
9. Philip Williamson, 'The Monarchy and Public Values 1910–1953', in Olechowicz (ed.), *The Monarchy and the British Nation*, 223–57.
10. Lecture by Dr David Starkey at the Institute of Historical Research, Senate House, London, 25 June 2012: ' "Head of our Morality": Why the Twentieth Century British Monarchy Matters'. A podcast of the lecture is available at <https://historyspot.org.uk/podcasts/marc-fitch-lectures/head-our-morality-why-twentieth-century-british-monarchy-matters> (accessed 3 July 2012).
11. *The Times*, 14 December 1936.
12. Ian Bradley, *God Save the Queen: The Spiritual Heart of the Monarchy* (London: Continuum, 2012), 177.
13. Dermot Morrah, 'The British Monarchy', in *The Queen's Visit: Elizabeth II in India and Pakistan* (London: Asia Publishing House, 1961), 25.
14. Williamson, 'Monarchy and Public Values', 223–57.
15. Duff Hart-Davis (ed.), *King's Counsellor: Abdication and War: The Diaries of Sir Alan Lascelles* (London: Weidenfeld and Nicolson, 2006), 399.
16. Hart-Davis (ed.), *King's Counsellor*, 124.
17. Thomas R. Metcalf, *Ideologies of the Raj* (Cambridge: Cambridge University Press, 1995), 192–3.
18. David Cannadine, *Ornamentalism* (Penguin: London, 2001), 101 and 120.
19. David Cannadine, 'The Context, Performance and Meaning of Ritual: The British Monarchy and the "Invention of Tradition", c. 1820–1977', in E. J. Hobsbawm and T. O. Ranger (eds), *The Invention of Tradition* (Cambridge: Cambridge University Press, 1983), 101–38.
20. Minute by Thomas, 11 March 1953, CO 1021/9.
21. Minute by Smith, 10 February 1953, CO 1021/9.
22. Cannadine, *Ornamentalism*, 153–4.
23. See, for example, Chandrika Kaul, 'Monarchical Display and the Politics of Empire: Princes of Wales and India 1870–1920s', *Twentieth Century British History*, 17/4 (2006), 464–88.

24. Donal Lowry, 'The Crown, Empire Loyalism and the Assimilation of Non-British White Subjects in the British World: An Argument against "Ethnic Determinism" ', in Carl Bridge and Kent Fedorowich (eds), *The British World: Diaspora, Culture and Identity* (London: Frank Cass, 2003), 96–120.

25. A. G. Hopkins, 'Rethinking Decolonization', *Past and Present*, 200 (2008), 211–47. The term 'De-Dominionisation' was coined in 1979 by Jim Davidson.

26. Cannadine, *Ornamentalism*, 90.

27. Cannadine, *Ornamentalism*, 145.

28. Cannadine, *Ornamentalism*, 168.

29. David Estep, 'Losing Jewels from the Crown: Considering the Future of the Monarchy in Australia and Canada', *Temple International and Comparative Law Journal*, 7/2 (1993), 218.

30. Claudio Kullmann, 'Attitudes towards the Monarchy in Australia and New Zealand Compared', *Commonwealth and Comparative Politics*, 46/4 (2008), 454.

31. Peter Boyce, *The Queen's Other Realms: The Crown and Its Legacy in Australia, Canada and New Zealand* (Sydney: Federation Press, 2008), 227–8.

32. Boyce, *The Queen's Other Realms*, 114–15.

33. Two highly influential volumes by John MacKenzie are *Propaganda and Empire: The Manipulation of British Public Opinion, 1880–1960* (Manchester: Manchester University Press, 1984) and (ed.) *Imperialism and Popular Culture* (Manchester: Manchester University Press, 1986).

34. See Bernard Porter, *The Absent-Minded Imperialists: Empire, Society and Culture in Britain* (Oxford: Oxford University Press, 2004). For the ensuing debate see Antoinette Burton's vitriolic review of Porter's book in *Victorian Studies*, 47/4 (2005), 626–8; Bernard Porter, 'Further Thoughts on Imperial Absent-Mindedness', *Journal of Imperial and Commonwealth History*, 36/1 (2008), 101–17; John M. MacKenzie, 'Comfort and Conviction: A Response to Bernard Porter', *Journal of Imperial and Commonwealth History*, 36/4 (2008), 659–668.

35. Tom Nairn, *The Break-Up of Britain: Crisis and Neo-Nationalism* (London: Verso, 1977 and 1981), 259.

36. Nairn, *Break-Up of Britain*, 266.

37. Philip Murphy, *Party Politics and Decolonization: The Conservative Party and British Colonial Policy in Tropical Africa 1951–1964* (Oxford: Clarendon Press, 1995), 227.

38. John Ramsden, *The Making of Conservative Party Policy: The Conservative Research Department since 1929* (London, 1980), 213.

39. The speech is quoted in full in A. N. Porter and A. J. Stockwell, *British Imperial Policy and Decolonization*, vol. 2: *1951–64* (London: Macmillan 1989), 508–13.

40. Murphy, *Party Politics and Decolonization*, 227–8.

41. Arnold Smith (with Clyde Sanger), *Stitches in Time: The Commonwealth in World Politics* (Ontario: General Publishing, 1981), 267.

42. Bill Schwarz, *Memories of Empire*, vol. 1: *The White Man's World* (Oxford: Oxford University Press, 2011), 12.

43. Peter Hennessy, *The Hidden Wiring: Unearthing the British Constitution* (London: Victor Gollancz, 1995), 49–72.

44. 'Cabinet Office Precedent Book: Relations with Buckingham Palace', CAB 181/7.

45. 'Cabinet Office Precedent Book: Relations with Buckingham Palace', CAB 181/7, para. 10.

46. Dorothy Thompson, *Queen Victoria: Gender and Power* (London: Virago, 1990), 139–40.

47. Thompson, *Queen Victoria*, 141–3.

48. Antony Taylor, *'Down with the Crown': British Anti-monarchism and Debates about Royalty since 1790* (London: Reaktion Books, 1999), 28.

49. Frank Prochaska, *Royal Bounty: The Making of a Welfare Monarchy* (New Haven, CT: Yale University Press, 1995).

50. Prochaska, *Royal Bounty*, 280.

51. Prochaska, *Royal Bounty*, 275.

52. Robert Lacey, *Royal: Her Majesty Queen Elizabeth II* (London: Little Brown, 2002), 256.

53. Robert Hardman, *Our Queen* (London: Hutchinson, 2011), 301.

54. Ewan Morris, 'Forty Years On: Australia and the Queen, 1954', *Journal of Australian Studies*, 4 (March 1994), 3.

55. See, for example, Vernon Bogdanor, *The Monarchy and the Constitution* (Oxford: Oxford University Press, 1995); Nicholas Mansergh, *The Commonwealth Experience* (Basingstoke: Macmillan, 1982); Sir William Dale, *The Modern Commonwealth* (London: Butterworths 1983); David Adamson, *The Last Empire: Britain and the Commonwealth* (London: Tauris, 1989). See also W. David McIntyre's articles, 'The Strange Death of Dominion Status', *Journal of Imperial and Commonwealth History*, 27/2 (1999), 193–212; 'Commonwealth Legacy', in Judith Brown and Wm. Roger Louis (eds), *The Oxford History of the British Empire: The Twentieth Century* (Oxford: Oxford University Press, 1999), 693–702; and 'The Commonwealth', in Robin Winks (ed.), *The Oxford History of the British Empire: Historiography* (Oxford: Oxford University Press, 1999), 558–70.

56. David Fieldhouse, 'Decolonization, Development and Dependence: A Survey of Changing Attitudes', in Prosser Gifford and Wm. Roger Louis (eds), *The Transfer of Power in Africa: Decolonization, 1940–1960* (New Haven, CT: Yale University Press, 1982), 491.

57. Wm. Roger Louis and Ronald Robinson, 'The Imperialism of Decolonization', *Journal of Imperial and Commonwealth History*, 22/3 (1994), 462–511.

58. Tony Chafer, *The End of Empire in French West Africa: France's Successful Decolonization?* (Oxford: Berg, 2002), 12–13.

59. Minute by Lintott, 3 March 1960, DO 35/7566.

60. See, for example, 'Nigeria: Possibility of Nigeria Becoming a Republic', Head to Sandys, 27 May 1961, PRO, DO 177/57.

CHAPTER 2: 'THE PIVOT OF EMPIRE'

1. John Wheeler-Bennett, *King George VI: His Life and Reign* (London: Macmillan, 1958), 160–1.

2. Wheeler-Bennett, *King George VI*, 160.

3. W. David McIntyre, *The Britannic Vision: Historians and the Making of the British Commonwealth of Nations, 1907–48* (Basingstoke: Palgrave, 2009), 161.

4. Lorna Lloyd, *Diplomacy with a Difference: The Commonwealth Office of High Commissioner, 1880–2006* (Leiden: Martinus Nijhoff, 2007), 47–8.

5. *Imperial Conference, 1926: Inter-Imperial Relations Committee Report*, Section II.

6. *Imperial Conference, 1926: Inter-Imperial Relations Committee Report*, Section IV c).

7. Anne Twomey, 'Responsible Government and the Divisibility of the Crown', University of Sydney Law School, Legal Studies Research Paper 08/137, 11.

8. *Imperial Conference, 1926: Inter-Imperial Relations Committee Report*, Section IV b).

9. Lloyd, *Diplomacy with a Difference*, 23.

10. Lloyd, *Diplomacy with a Difference*, 52–3.

11. Harold Nicolson, *King George the Fifth: His Life and Reign* (London: Constable, 1952), 478.

12. J. R. Mallory, 'The Appointment of the Governor-General: Responsible Government, Autonomy, and the Royal Prerogative', *Canadian Journal of Economics and Political Science*, 26/1 (1960), 97 and 100.

13. Nicolson, *King George the Fifth*, 480.

14. Nicolson, *King George the Fifth*, 481–2.

15. Mallory, 'The Appointment of the Governor-General', 100.

16. Bogdanor, *The Monarchy and the Constitution*, 283.

17. Bogdanor, *The Monarchy and the Constitution*, 284–5.

18. Mallory, 'The Appointment of the Governor-General', 104.

19. Sir William Heseltine, 'I Did But See Him Passing By': The Second Menzies Lecture, Institute of Commonwealth Studies, University of London, 7 November 1989.

20. Harshan Kumarasingham, *Onward with Executive Power: Lessons from New Zealand 1947–57* (Wellington: Institute of Policy Studies, 2009), 51.

21. Kumarasingham, *Onward*, 49.

22. Mallory, 'The Appointment of the Governor-General', 107.

23. Harshan Kumarasingham, *A Political Legacy of the British Empire: Power and the Westminster System in Post-Colonial India and Sri-Lanka* (London: Tauris, 2012), 213.

24. R. F. Holland, *Britain and the Commonwealth Alliance 1918–1939* (London: Macmillan, 1981), 61.

25. Holland, *Britain and the Commonwealth Alliance*, 59–60.

26. D. P. O'Connell, 'The Crown in the British Commonwealth', *International and Comparative Law Quarterly*, 6/1 (January 1957), 112.

27. Holland, *Britain and the Commonwealth Alliance*, 61.

28. Holland, *Britain and the Commonwealth Alliance*, 60.

29. Dixon to Brook, 5 August 1948, DO 35/2167.

30. S. A. de Smith, 'The Royal Style and Title', *International and Comparative Law Quarterly*, 2/2 (April 1953), 263.

31. Tom Fleming, *Voices Out of the Air: The Royal Christmas Broadcasts 1932–1981* (London, Heinemann, 1981), 11.

32. Fleming, *Voices Out of the Air*, 12.

33. Fleming, *Voices Out of the Air*, 14.

34. Fleming, *Voices Out of the Air*, 10.

35. Thomas Hajkowski, *The BBC and National Identity in Britain, 1922–53* (Manchester: Manchester University Press, 2010), 86.

36. Hajkowski, *BBC and National Identity*, 87.

37. Hajkowski, *BBC and National Identity*, 26.

38. Philip Ziegler, *King Edward VIII: The Official Biography* (London: Collins, 1990), 114.

39. Ziegler, *King Edward VIII*, 114.

40. Hart-Davis (ed.), *King's Counsellor*, 104.

41. Hart-Davis (ed.), *King's Counsellor*, 105.

42. Piers Brendon and Philip Whitehead, *The Windsors: A Dynasty Revealed 1917–2000* (London: Pimlico, 2000), 53.

43. Williamson, 'Monarchy and Public Values', 244.

44. *Papers Relating to the Demise of the Crown*, Dominions no. 165, 1936, p. 3, DO 114/73.

45. Mary Kenny, *Crown and Shamrock: Love and Hate between Ireland and the British Monarchy* (Dublin: New Island, 2009), 188–9.
46. Kenny, *Crown and Shamrock*, 196.
47. *Papers Relating to the Demise of the Crown*, pp 21–3. For a fuller treatment of the politics surrounding Dublin's relations with the Crown during this period see Deirdre McMahon, *Republicans and Imperialists: Anglo-Irish Relations in the 1930s* (New Haven, CT: Yale University Press, 1984) and Paul Canning, *British Policy towards Ireland 1921–1941* (Oxford: Oxford University Press, 1985).
48. Susan Williams, *The People's King: The True Story of the Abdication* (London: Allen Lane, 2003), 130.
49. Williams, *The People's King*, 101.
50. Williams, *The People's King*, 117.
51. This issue arose in the context of discussions within the Commonwealth Relations Office over whether Commonwealth members had the right to advise the Queen on her visit to Ghana in 1961. See Dixon, 6 October 1961, DO 161/80.
52. Williams, *The People's King*, 130.
53. Williams, *The People's King*, 131.
54. 'Memorandum by Sir Harry Batterbee on talks in Dublin with Eamon de Valera, Joseph P. Walshe, John Dulanty and John Hearne, 29 November 1936', CAB 127/156; reproduced in Catriona Crowe and Dermot Eogh (eds), *Documents on Irish Foreign Policy*, vol. IV: *1932–1936* (Dublin: Royal Irish Academy, 2004), Doc. 383.
55. Notes by the Department of External Affairs on the Constitutional Crisis in Great Britain, undated, December 1936, UCDA P67/115; reproduced in *Documents on Irish Foreign Policy*, vol. IV: *1932–1936*, Doc. 384.
56. Memorandum by the Department of External Affairs on the Abdication Crisis, 7 December 1936, no. 390 NAI DFA Secretary's Files S57; reproduced in *Documents on Irish Foreign Policy*, vol. IV: *1932–1936*, Doc. 390.
57. McIntyre, *Britannic Vision*, 226–7.
58. McIntyre, *Britannic Vision*, 228.
59. British High Commissioner in South Africa to Dominions Office, telegram 149 (part 2), 6 December 1936, PREM 1/462.
60. British High Commissioner in South Africa to Dominions Office, telegram 149 (part 1), 6 December 1936, PREM 1/462.
61. British High Commissioner in South Africa to Dominions Office, telegram 148, 5 December 1936, PREM 1/462.
62. Floud to MacDonald, 22 December 1936, DO 35/531/2/2.
63. Despatch by Sir Gerald Campbell, 27 June 1939, DO 35/639.
64. Campbell to Hardinge, 9 March 1939, DO 35/638.
65. Hardinge to Stephenson, 8 March 1939, DO 35/638.
66. Keith Jeffery, 'The Second World War', in Brown and Louis (eds), *Oxford History of the British Empire*, 307–9.
67. Andrew Stewart, *Empire Lost: Britain, the Dominions and the Second World War* (London: Continuum, 2008), 77.
68. Hajkowski, *BBC and National Identity*, 95.
69. Wheeler-Bennett, *King George VI*, 680.
70. Wheeler-Bennett, *King George VI*, 681.
71. Hart-Davis (ed.), *King's Counsellor*, 168.
72. Ziegler, *King Edward VIII*, 420–36.

73. Ziegler, *King Edward VIII*, 426–7.
74. Ziegler, *King Edward VIII*, 450.
75. Ziegler, *King Edward VIII*, 480–3.
76. Hart-Davis (ed.), *King's Counsellor*, 359.
77. Hart-Davis (ed.), *King's Counsellor*, 359.
78. Wheeler-Bennett, *King George VI*, 696.
79. Wheeler-Bennett, *King George VI*, 698–9.
80. Wheeler-Bennett, *King George VI*, 700–2.
81. Robert Rhodes James, *A Spirit Undaunted: The Political Role of George VI* (London: Abacus, 1999), 241–4. This has echoes of the occasion following the 1945 general election when the King expressed far more vehement opposition to a proposal that Hugh Dalton be appointed Foreign Secretary (Rhodes James, *Spirit Undaunted*, 275–6).

CHAPTER 3: 'A COMMON ACT OF WILL'

1. Wheeler-Bennett, *King George VI*, 703.
2. Wheeler-Bennett, *King George VI*, 710–11.
3. Wheeler-Bennett, *King George VI*, 703.
4. Wheeler-Bennett, *King George VI*, 716.
5. Cannadine, *Ornamentalism*, 114–15.
6. Entry for 26–7 April 1952, John Colville, *The Fringes of Power: Downing Street Diaries*, vol. 2: *1941–April 1955* (London: Sceptre, 1987), 301.
7. Kumarasingham, *Onward*, 44.
8. 'Dominions and King', *The Spectator*, 19 April 1946.
9. Hart-Davis (ed.), *King's Counsellor*, 333–4.
10. Kumarasingham, *Onward*, 43–4.
11. Rhodes James, *Spirit Undaunted*, 290.
12. Telegram from British High Commission, Pretoria to the Dominions Office, 21 March 1946, DO 35/1131.
13. Ronald Hyam and Peter Henshaw, *The Lion and the Springbok: Britain and South Africa since the Boer War* (Cambridge: Cambridge University Press, 2003), 278.
14. Hart-Davis (ed.), *King's Counsellor*, 368.
15. *The Times*, 21 February 1947.
16. Hyam and Henshaw, *The Lion and the Springbok*, 278.
17. Charles Douglas-Home, *Evelyn Baring: The Last Proconsul* (London: Collins, 1978), 153.
18. Hilary Sapire, 'African Loyalism and Its Discontents: The Royal Tour of South Africa, 1947', *Historical Journal*, 24/1 (2011), 227.
19. Sapire, 'African Loyalism and Its Discontents', 228.
20. Sapire, 'African Loyalism and Its Discontents', 232.
21. Hyam and Henshaw, *The Lion and the Springbok*, 279.
22. Sapire, 'African Loyalism and Its Discontents', 234.
23. Hyam and Henshaw, *The Lion and the Springbok*, 280.
24. Sapire, 'African Loyalism and Its Discontents', 225.
25. Tait to Machtig, 16 June 1946, DO 35/1131.
26. Dermot Morrah, *The Royal Family in Africa* (London: Hutchinson, 1947).
27. Quoted in Rhodes James, *Spirit Undaunted*, 294.

28. Wheeler-Bennett, *King George VI*, 687.
29. Douglas-Home, *Evelyn Baring*, 154.
30. William Shawcross, *Queen Elizabeth the Queen Mother: The Official Biography* (London: Macmillan, 2009), 618–19.
31. Baring to Addison, 16 May 1947, FO 371/65575.
32. Kate Williams, *Young Elizabeth: The Making of Our Queen* (London: Weidenfeld and Nicolson, 2012), 209–10. There is an interesting puzzle around the way in which this speech is regularly cited. Williams gives an accurate rendering. Some recent works, however (for example, Wendy Webster, *Englishness and Empire, 1939–1965* (Oxford: Oxford University Press, 2005), 93), suggest that Princess Elizabeth used the phrase 'Imperial Commonwealth' rather than 'Imperial family', thus losing an important element of the speech's iconography. The BBC archive recording of the speech leaves no doubt that she actually said 'Imperial family'. The error may date back to Dermot Morrah's rendering of the speech (*The Royal Family in Africa*, 124). Morrah uses the phrase 'Imperial Commonwealth' earlier in the book. Elizabeth begins her speech by referring to the 'peoples of the British Commonwealth and Empire', but then uses 'Empire' and 'Commonwealth' as almost interchangeable terms. Morrah's 'error' may have been an attempt to promote the term 'Imperial Commonwealth'. That, however, is pure speculation.
33. Note by Blackburne, June 1948, CO 875/50/3.
34. Note by Chandos, undated 1948, CO 875/50/3.
35. Minute by Lloyd, 5 August 1948, CO 875/50/3.
36. Minute by Blackburne, 29 September 1948, CO 875/50/3.
37. Minute by Blackburne, 29 September 1948, CO 875/50/3.
38. Lloyd to Lascelles, 30 September 1948, CO 875/50/3.
39. Lloyd to Lascelles, 8 December 1948, CO 875/50/3.
40. *West Africa*, 17 April 1948.
41. Lloyd to Burns, 30 September 1948, CO 875/50/3.
42. McIntyre, *Britannic Vision*, 149.
43. *Imperial Conference, 1926: Inter-imperial Relations Committee Report*, Section V a).
44. Rance to Listowel, 9 June 1947, PREM 8/412.
45. MacDonald to Creech Jones, 27 June 1947, PREM 8/412.
46. Minutes of the India and Burma Committee, 1 July 1947, PREM 8/412.
47. McIntyre, *Britannic Vision*, 238–40.
48. Kenny, *Crown and Shamrock*, 258–9.
49. Kenny, *Crown and Shamrock*, 260.
50. Chris Reeves, ' "Let Us Stand By Our Friends": British Policy towards Ireland 1949–59', *Irish Studies in International Affairs*, 11 (2000), 91.
51. 'Record of Conversation between the Secretary of State for Commonwealth Relations and the Irish Minister for External Affairs on Monday, 27th October 1952', PREM 11/3021. Perhaps because of the views expressed by Salisbury, this file remained closed until July 2012 and was only opened after a Freedom of Information request by the author.
52. Reeves, ' "Let Us Stand By Our Friends" ', 92.
53. 'The Link with India', note by Gordon Walker, 31 December 1949, CAB 134/119.
54. Entry for 7 January 1949, Edward Pearce (ed.), *Patrick Gordon Walker: Political Diaries 1932–1971* (London: Historians' Press, 1991), 183.
55. 'The Link with India', note by Gordon Walker, 31 December 1949, CAB 134/119.

56. Minute by Gordon Walker, 7 February 1949, DO 121/73.
57. See Abnita Inder Singh, 'Imperial Defence and the Transfer of Power in India, 1946–1947', *International History Review*, 4/4 (1982), 568–88; and 'Keeping India in the Commonwealth: British Political and Military Aims, 1947–49', *Journal of Contemporary History*, 20 (1985), 469–81.
58. Entry for 7 January 1949, Pearce (ed.), *Patrick Gordon Walker: Political Diaries*, 182.
59. Wheeler-Bennett, *King George VI*, 724.
60. Lloyd, *Diplomacy with a Difference*, 130–1.
61. R. J. Moore, *Making the New Commonwealth* (Oxford: Clarendon Press, 1987), 172–81.
62. Moore, *Making the New Commonwealth*, 185.
63. 'Tactics on India', note by Gordon Walker, 6 April 1949, CAB 134/119.
64. 'The King's Title', note by Brook, 2 April 1949, CR (49) 10, CAB 134/119.
65. Minutes of Prime Ministers' Meeting, PMM (49) 1st meeting, 22 April 1949, CAB 133/89.
66. 'Statement by the Prime Minister of South Africa', 22 April 1949, CAB 133/89.
67. Minutes of Prime Ministers' Meeting, PMM (49) 4th meeting, 27 April 1949, CAB 133/89.
68. Frank Bongiorno, 'Commonwealthmen and Republicans: Dr H. V. Evatt, the Monarchy and India', *Australian Journal of Politics and History*, 46/1 (2000), 33–50.
69. See Harshan Kumarasingham, 'The "New Commonwealth" 1947–49: A New Zealand Perspective on India joining the Commonwealth', *Round Table*, 95/385 (2006), 441–54.
70. W. David McIntyre, *The Significance of the Commonwealth, 1965–90* (Basingstoke: Palgrave, 1991), 247.
71. McIntyre, *Britannic Vision*, 252.
72. Bogdanor, *The Monarchy and the Constitution*, 263.
73. Minute by Sayers, 1 June 1949, CO 121/73.
74. Minute by Sayers, 9 June 1949, CO 121/73.

CHAPTER 4: 'A PERSONAL AND LIVING BOND'

1. Wheeler-Bennett, *King George VI*, 769.
2. Wheeler-Bennett, *King George VI*, 792.
3. Wheeler-Bennett, *King George VI*, 801.
4. Williamson, 'Monarchy and Public Values', 245.
5. De Smith, 'The Royal Style and Title', 266.
6. Commonwealth Relations Office note, 'The King's Title', 11 February 1952, DO 121/193.
7. Extract from *The Accession Proclamation*, Commonwealth Relations no. 21, DO 161/334.
8. *Papers Relating to the Demise of the Crown*, p. 3.
9. 'Form of Accession Proclamation: Note by the Cabinet Secretary', C (52) 22, 6 February 1952; Cabinet Conclusions, CC (52) 12, min. 1, 6 February 1952, PREM 11/39.
10. Clive Ponting, *Churchill* (London: Sinclair-Stevenson, 1994), 762.
11. Brook to Churchill, 9 February 1952, PREM 11/39.
12. 'The Imperial Crown: Note by the Prime Minister', 14 February 1952, C (52) 34, CAB 129/49.

13. Extract from *The Accession Proclamation*.
14. De Smith, 'The Royal Style and Title', 268.
15. Minute by Liesching, 26 February 1952, DO 121/193.
16. 'The Royal Style and Titles: Results of Consultation with other Commonwealth Governments', 19 September 1952, DO 121/193.
17. De Smith, 'The Royal Style and Title', 272.
18. 'The Royal Style and Titles: Results of consultation with other Commonwealth Governments'.
19. De Smith, 'The Royal Style and Title', 278.
20. HC Deb, vol. 512, 3 March 1953, col. 195.
21. Robert Shepherd, *Enoch Powell: A Biography* (London: Random House, 1996), 112.
22. HC Deb, vol. 512, 3 March 1953, col. 245.
23. HC Deb, vol. 512, 3 March 1953, col. 247.
24. Shepherd, *Enoch Powell*, 114, Simon Heffer, *Like the Roman: The Life of Enoch Powell* (London: Weidenfeld and Nicolson, 1998), 185.
25. John Hall, *Queen Elizabeth II and Her Church: Royal Service at Westminster Abbey* (London: Continuum, 2012), 9–10.
26. Pimlott, *The Queen*, 207.
27. Webster, *Englishness and Empire*, 93.
28. Webster, *Englishness and Empire*, 97–8.
29. Pimlott, *The Queen*, 205–6. John Colville subsequently claimed that the Queen herself had been responsible for overturning the Cabinet's original decision to exclude the cameras, although there seems to be no trace of this in the written records.
30. Anon., 'The Coronation and the Commonwealth', *Round Table*, 168 (September 1952), 297–304.
31. The first signed articles appeared in July 1966. Morrah also seems likely to have been the author of a subsequent leader in *The Times* on the same subject and a follow-up anonymous letter to the newspaper (Liesching to Lloyd, 26 November 1952, CO 1021/12).
32. Anon., 'The Coronation and the Commonwealth', 303–4.
33. Liesching to Lloyd, 19 September 1952, CO 1021/11.
34. Commonwealth Relations Office note, 'The Coronation Oath and the Coronation Service', July 1952, CO 1021/11.
35. Note by C. W. Dixon, 23 October 1952, CO 1021/12. The delegation included G. F. Sayers, the imperial affairs specialist at the Conservative Research Department.
36. Peter Trepanier, 'Some Visual Aspects of Monarchical Tradition', *Canadian Parliamentary Review*, (Summer 2004), 27–31.
37. Jeffries to Knox, 11 February 1953, CO 1021/11.
38. Creasy to Lloyd, 28 August 1952; Lloyd to Creasy, 8 September 1952, CO 1021/5.
39. Creasy to Lloyd, 11 September 1952, CO 1021/5.
40. 'Memorandum on Arrangements for Representation of Colonial Territories at the Coronation of Her Majesty Queen Elizabeth II', CO 885/127.
41. 'Memorandum on Arrangements for Representation of Colonial Territories'.
42. Acting governor to Martin, 3 May 1953, CO 1021/5.
43. Minute by Morris, 12 June 1953, CO 1021/6.
44. Note by Norman Brook, 19 May 1953, DO 35/5022; minute by Morris, 12 June 1953, CO 1021/6.
45. Note by Colville, 19 May 1953, PREM 11/475.
46. Personal telegram from Olivier, 21 May 1953, PREM 11/475.

47. Churchill to Lyttelton, 28 May 1953, PREM 11/475.
48. Minutes by Smith, 17 September 1952, and Williams, 22 September 1952, CO 1021/4.
49. Minutes by Smith, 17 September 1952, CO 1021/4.
50. Minute by Williams, 22 September 1952, CO 1021/4.
51. Arden-Clarke to Lloyd, 23 October 1952, CO 1021/4.
52. Minute by A. R. Thomas, 3 March 1953, CO 1021/2.
53. Baring to Lyttelton, 28 February 1953, CO 1021/3.
54. Lloyd to Baring, 5 March 1953, CO 1021/3.
55. Christian to the Secretary of the Governor of Fiji, 26 July 1953, CO 1021/9.
56. Governor of Fiji to Secretary of State for the Colonies, 2 September 1953, CO 1021/9.
57. Pain to Elford, 9 February 1953, BBC Written Archives, N1/36.
58. Script for the South African contribution to 'The Queen's Commonwealth', N1/36.
59. Pain to Elford, 18 March 1953, N1/36.
60. Pain to Elford, 18 March 1953, N1/36.
61. Boland to Nunan, 10 June 1953, National Archives of Ireland, DFA/408/191/6.
62. Klaus Dodds, David Lambert, and Bridget Robison, 'Loyalty and Royalty: Gibraltar, the 1953–54 Royal Tour and the Geopolitics of the Iberian Peninsula', *Twentieth Century British History*, 18/3 (2007), 365–90.
63. Dodds, Lambert, and Robison, 'Loyalty and Royalty', 372.
64. Anne Spry Rush, *Bonds of Empire: West Indians and Britishness from Victoria to Decolonization* (Oxford: Oxford University Press, 2011), 213–14.
65. Rush, *Bonds of Empire*, 217.
66. Kumarasingham, *Onward*, 71.
67. 'Report on the Visit of the Queen', DO 35/5141, cited in Kumarasingham, *Onward*, 72–3.
68. Fleming, *Voices Out of the Air*, 72–4.
69. Jane Connors, 'The 1954 Royal Tour of Australia', *Australian Historical Studies*, 25 (1993), 371–82.
70. Connors, 'The 1954 Royal Tour', 371–2.
71. Connors, 'The 1954 Royal Tour', 378.
72. David Lowe, '1954: The Queen and Australia in the World', *Journal of Australian Studies*, 46 (1995), 6–7.
73. Lowe, '1954', 6.
74. Ewan Morris, 'Forty Years On: Australia and the Queen, 1954', *Journal of Australian Studies*, 40 (1994), 10.
75. Lowe, '1954', 7.
76. Cabinet Conclusions, CC (54) 19, 16 March 1954; Cabinet Secretary's notebook, CAB 195/12, 13th to 78th conclusions 1954.
77. CRO inward telegram 344, 2 September 1953, PREM 11/743.
78. Swinton to Senanayake, 4 September 1953, PREM 11/743.
79. CRO inward telegram 357, 8 September 1953, PREM 11/743.
80. Garner to Lascelles, 16 September 1953, PREM 11/743.
81. Note for Prime Minister, 29 September 1953, PREM 11/743.
82. CRO inward telegram 437, 14 October 1953, PREM 11/743.
83. *The Times*, 7 and 10 November 1953.
84. *The Times*, 10 November 1953.
85. *The Times*, 13 November 1953.
86. Kumarasingham, *A Political Legacy of the British Empire*, 127.

87. Cabinet Memoranda, C (54) 64, 'Royal Tour of Uganda: Memorandum by the Secretary of State for the Colonies', 19 February 1954.
88. *The Times*, 18 January 1954.
89. Dodds, Lambert, and Robison, 'Loyalty and Royalty', 386.
90. *The Times*, 1 February 1954.
91. Dodds, Lambert, and Robison, 'Loyalty and Royalty', 383.
92. Cabinet Memoranda, C (54) 80, 'The Royal Tour: Gibraltar', 1 March 1954.
93. Cabinet Secretary's Notebook, CC (54) 11, 24 February 1954.
94. *The Times*, 18 March 1954.
95. *The Times*, 8 May 1954.
96. Dodds, Lambert, and Robison, 'Loyalty and Royalty', 374.
97. Dodds, Lambert, and Robison, 'Loyalty and Royalty', 385.

CHAPTER 5: WINDS OF CHANGE AND THE ROYAL FAMILY

1. Sarah Bradford, *Elizabeth: A Biography of Her Majesty the Queen* (London: Heinemann, 1996), 233.
2. For a recent account of Mountbatten's involvement in the affair see Adrian Smith 'Rewriting History? Admiral Lord Mountbatten's Efforts to Distance Himself from the 1956 Suez Crisis', *Contemporary British History*, 26/4 (2012), 489–508.
3. Robert Rhodes James, *Anthony Eden* (London: Weidenfeld, 1986), 495.
4. Pimlott, *The Queen*, 254.
5. Hugh Thomas, *The Suez Affair* (Harmondsworth: Penguin, 1970), 150.
6. Pimlott, *The Queen*, 253–5.
7. Monckton Papers, Bodleian Library, Oxford, dep. Monckton 7, fols 175–7.
8. Anthony Montague Browne, *Long Sunset: Memoirs of Winston Churchill's Last Private Secretary* (London: Cassell, 1995), 214.
9. Philip Ziegler, *Mountbatten: The Official Biography* (London: Collins 1985), 546.
10. Bradford, *Elizabeth*, 233.
11. Rhodes James, *Eden*, 619–20.
12. Brendon and Whitehead, *The Windsors*, 147.
13. Peter Hennessy, 'What the Queen Knew', *The Independent*, 21 December 1994.
14. Pimlott, *The Queen*, 255.
15. Bradford, *Elizabeth*, 233.
16. Hennessy, 'What the Queen Knew'. Hennessy is quoting the contents of file PREM 11/1163, which had just been released to the UK National Archives.
17. Philip Murphy, 'Telling Tales out of School: Nutting, Eden and the Attempted Suppression of *No End of a Lesson*', in Simon C. Smith (ed.), *Reassessing Suez 1956: New Perspectives on the Crisis and its Aftermath* (Aldershot: Ashgate, 2008), 203–4.
18. W. Scott Lucas, *Divided We Stand* (London: Hodder and Stoughton, 1991), 244.
19. Cabinet conclusions, CAB 128/30, CM 74 (56), 25 October 1956.
20. Lucas, *Divided We Stand*, 248.
21. Murphy, 'Telling Tales', 206.
22. Zulueta to Bligh, 4 February 1960, PREM 11/3073.
23. Philip Murphy, *Alan Lennox-Boyd: A Biography* (London: Tauris, 1999), 216.
24. Macmillan Papers, Bodleian Library, Oxford, Ms Macmillan Dep d. 36, f. 17, 15 June 1959.
25. Ms Macmillan Dep d. 36, f. 124, 22 August 1959.

26. Salisbury to Macmillan, 13 December 1958, PREM 11/3507.

27. Undated note by Dixon, June 1959, DO 35/9208.

28. David Rooney, *Kwame Nkrumah: The Political Kingdom in the Third World* (London: Tauris, 1988), 142.

29. Undated note by Dixon, June 1959, DO 35/9208.

30. Undated note by Dixon, June 1959, DO 35/9208.

31. Minute by Snelling, 11 June 1959, DO 35/9208.

32. Pimlott, *The Queen*, 305.

33. Rooney, *Kwame Nkrumah*, 152.

34. 'Proposed Visit of the Queen to the Federation of Rhodesia and Nyasaland, and Visit of the Queen Mother, May 1960', undated draft, May 1960, DO 35/7719.

35. Home to Macmillan, 29 May 1959, PREM 11/3090.

36. Macmillan to Welensky, 11 August 1959, DO 161/206.

37. Welensky to Home, 13 August 1959, DO 161/206. Interestingly, this section of Welensky's telegram is redacted and closed in the copy that appears in PREM 11/3090.

38. *The Times*, 10 May 1960.

39. Ms Macmillan Dep d. 39, f. 7, 13 May 1960.

40. *The Times*, 18, 20, and 31 May 1960.

41. Colin Baker, *State of Emergency: Nyasaland 1959* (London: Tauris, 1997), 241.

42. Note for the record by Bligh, 14 December 1959, PREM 11/3073.

43. Hunt to Clutterbuck, DO 35/10570, 8 February 1960, reproduced in Ronald Hyam and Wm Roger Louis (eds), *The Conservative Government and the End of Empire, 1957–1964*, British Documents on the End of Empire Series A (London: The Stationery Office, 2000), Part II, 394–8.

44. Maud to Home, 23 January 1960, PREM 11/3070.

45. Minute by Macmillan, 4 February 1960, reproduced in Hyam and Louis (eds), *Conservative Government and End of Empire*, Part II, 392–4; Harold Macmillan, *Pointing the Way, 1959–1961* (London: Macmillan, 1972), 154.

46. Macmillan, *Pointing the Way*, 483.

47. Frank Hayes, 'South Africa's Departure from the Commonwealth, 1960–1961', *International History Review*, 2/3 (1980), 472.

48. Hayes, 'South Africa's Departure from the Commonwealth', 479–80.

49. CRO Confidential Print, UK High Commissioner in India to the Lord Chancellor, 5 April 1961, CAB 21/5955.

50. Memorandum by Dixon, 26 October 1961, DO 161/80.

51. Memorandum by Dixon, 26 October 1961, DO 161/80.

52. Adeane to Bligh, 20 December 1960, PREM 11/3507.

53. Macmillan, *Pointing the Way*, 459–72.

54. Minute by Stacey, 13 October 1961, DO 161/80.

55. Pimlott, *The Queen*, 305–9.

56. Martin Gilbert, *Never Despair: Winston S. Chuchill 1945–1965* (London: Heinemann, 1988), 1330.

57. Simon Ball, *The Guardsmen* (London: HarperCollins, 2004), 358.

58. Memorandum by Dixon, 26 October 1961, DO 161/80.

59. Adeane to Garner, 19 March 1962, DO 161/80.

60. Memorandum by Dixon, 26 October 1961, DO 161/80.

61. Draft memorandum by C. W. Dixon, March 1962, DO 161/80.

62. *The Times*, 8 November 1961.

63. Jackson to Sandys, 20 November 1961, Papers of Duncan Sandys, Churchill College, Cambridge, DSND 15/6.

64. Harold Evans, *Downing Street Diary: The Macmillan Years, 1957–1963* (London: Hodder and Stoughton, 1981), 171.

65. Ms Macmillan Dep d. 37, f. 67, 11 November 1959.

66. 'Memorandum for Private Secretaries to Members of the Royal Family about Visits Overseas', May 1954, DO 35/7921.

67. Garner to Nye, 19 June 1954, DO 35/7921.

68. Nye to Garner, 28 June 1954, DO 35/7921.

69. Adeane to Brook, 15 June 1959, CAB 21/3899.

70. Cabinet Committee on Royal Visits Overseas and Visits by Foreign Heads of State, GEN 693/1, 20 July 1959, CAB 21/3899.

71. Adeane to Brook, 20 October 1959, CAB 21/3899.

72. Hawkins to Lennox-Boyd, 3 February 1959, CO 967/338.

73. Notes by the Duke of Edinburgh forwarded by Reid (Downing Street) to Henderson (Foreign Office), 30 November 1964, CO 1031/4961.

74. Minute by Williams, 7 March 1966, CO 1031/5194.

75. Duke of Edinburgh to Lord Longford, 3 March 1966, CO 1031/5194.

76. See, for example, Richard Rathbone, 'Things Fall Apart: The Erosion of Local Government, Local Justice and Civil Rights in Ghana, 1955–60', in Martin Lynn (ed.), *The British Empire in the 1950s: Retreat or Revival?* (London: Palgrave, 2005), 122–43.

77. Adeane to Macmillan, 13 February 1963, PREM 11/4445.

78. Minute by Poynton, 18 May 1966, CO 1032/496.

79. Lennox-Boyd to Home, 12 February 1957, DO 35/9747.

80. *The Times*, 1 April 1960.

81. Pearson to Macleod, 4 July 1961, CAB 21/4962.

82. Minute by Williams, 7 July 1966, CO 1031/5179.

83. MacDonald to Sandys, 3 August 1963, CO 822/3238.

84. Minute by Milton, 12 August 1963, CO 822/3238.

85. Minute by Poynton, 24 January 1966, CO 1031/5179.

86. Minute by Fairlie, 12 January 1966, CO 1031/5179.

87. Home and Lennox-Boyd to Eden, 9 November 1956, PREM 11/1859.

88. Minute by Terry, 10 February 1957, CO 554/1390.

89. Draft letter from Sir John Macpherson to Sir Donald MacGillivray, forwarded Macpherson to Laithwaite, 11 December 1956, DO 35/9747.

90. Lennox-Boyd to Home, 12 February 1957, DO 35/9747.

91. Salisbury to Adeane, 8 March 1957, DO 35/9747.

92. Minute by Gilmore, 8 July 1963, CO 822/3238.

93. Zulueta to Macmillan, 22 June 1962, PREM 11/3851.

94. Zulueta to Macmillan, 25 June 1962, PREM 11/3851.

95. Bligh to Macmillan, 9 July 1962, PREM 11/3851.

96. Shepherd to Secretary of State, 6 March 1968, FCO 32/337.

97. Macleod to Macmillan, 17 April 1961, CO 554/2529.

98. Adeane to Poynton, 18 April 1961; Adeane to Poynton, 19 April 1961, CO 554/2529.

99. Colonial Office to Bligh, 18 April 1961, CO 554/2529.

100. Poynton to Garner, 21 February 1962, PREM 11/3851.

101. Pearson to Macleod, 4 July 1961, CAB 21/4962.

102. Pearson to Macleod, 4 July 1961, CAB 21/4962.
103. Pearson to Martin, 4 July 1961, CAB 21/4962.
104. Minute by Dalton, 2 January 1979, FCO 107/69.
105. FCO telegram to Tarawa, 16 January 1979, FCO 107/69.
106. Minute by Snodgrass, 8 May 1979, FCO 107/73.
107. Wall to Carrington, 8 May 1979, FCO 107/73.
108. Minute by Snodgrass, 8 May 1979, FCO 107/73.
109. Minute by Deputy Commissioner, 8 June 1973, MEPO 10/29.
110. Minute by Perkins, 17 June 1973, MEPO 10/29.
111. Minute by Deputy Commissioner, 18 June 1973, MEPO 10/29.
112. *Daily Telegraph*, 23 February 2006.

CHAPTER 6: 'A POOR SORT OF COURTESY TO HER MAJESTY'

1. 'Head of the Commonwealth: Note prepared by the Commonwealth Relations Office', July 1955; memorandum by Churchill, 4 February 1955, DO 35/5134.
2. See Roger Kershaw, *Monarchy in South-East Asia: The Faces of Tradition in Transition* (London: Routledge, 2001).
3. 'Nigeria: Possibility of Nigeria Becoming a Republic', Head to Sandys, 27 May 1961, DO 177/57.
4. Internal minute by Wakely, 13 July 1961, DO 177/57.
5. Internal minute by Dixon, 30 June 1961, DO 177/57.
6. Poynton to Snelling, 16 April 1962, CO 1032/390.
7. Extract from annex to despatch no. 8 from Lagos, 5 May 1961, DO 177/57.
8. Talk between the Secretary of State and Dr Azikiwe at Chatsworth, 29 July 1961, DO 177/57.
9. Poynton to Snelling, 16 April 1962, CO 1032/390.
10. Minute by W. B. L. Monson, 2 April 1962, CO 1032/390.
11. Poynton to Snelling, 16 April 1962, CO 1032/390.
12. Mansergh, *The Commonwealth Experience*, 161–2.
13. Poynton to Stallard, 11 December 1962, CO 1032/390.
14. Minute by N. B. J. Huijsman, 9 October 1962, CO 1032/390.
15. For further details see PREM 11/3814.
16. Butler had, of course, served as Undersecretary of State in the India Office, an experience he was to recall when dealing with some of the more thorny aspects of his responsibilities as Secretary of State for Central Africa.
17. See, for example, Baker, *State of Emergency*, 184.
18. Baker, *State of Emergency*, 197.
19. Jones to Butler, 9 August 1963, DO 183/59.
20. Jones to Butler, 8 August 1963, DO 183/59.
21. Baker, *State of Emergency*, 198–9.
22. Jones to Butler, 8 August 1963, DO 183/59.
23. Chadwick to Bass, 9 August 1963, DO 183/59.
24. Sandys to Colonial Office, 14 September 1963, DO 181/136.
25. Cabinet Conclusions, CC (63) 57, min. 3, 24 September 1963, CAB 128/37.
26. Garner to Poynton, 22 March 1962, CO 1032/390.
27. Garner to Poynton, 22 March 1962, CO 1032/390.

28. The earlier letter is mentioned in unidentified to Aden, 7 November 1963, CO 822/3117.
29. MacDonald to Sandys, 7 June 1963, cited in Hyam and Louis (eds), *Conservative Government and End of Empire*, Part I, 538–40.
30. Cabinet Conclusions, CC (63) 41, 24 June 1963, CAB 128/37, cited in Hyam and Louis (eds), *Conservative Government and End of Empire*, Part I, 540–2.
31. Colonial Office [unidentified] to Adeane, 7 November 1963; MacDonald to Sandys, 18 September 1963, CO 822/3117.
32. Hickman to Webber, 14 August 1963, CO 822/3117.
33. MacDonald to Webber, 17 August 1963, CO 822/3117.
34. MacDonald to Sandys, 18 August 1963, CO 822/3117.
35. A similar complaint was made by the Foreign Minister of Mauritius, Gaetan Duval, in February 1971. He told the visiting British politician Humphry Berkeley of his concerns about the forthcoming conference of the Organization Commune Africaine et Malgache (OCAM), of which Mauritius was the only Commonwealth state, and which it was due to host. Duval was worried that if the Governor General, Sir Leonard Williams, were to receive guests as the Queen's representative, it might give the impression that Mauritius was still a colonial dependency (Berkeley to Adeane, 9 February 1971, Commonwealth Secretariat Archives, MH 2000/130).
36. Colonial Office [unidentified] to Adeane, 7 November 1963, CO 822/3117.
37. Thomas to Whitley, 4 March 1964, DO 183/70.
38. Minutes by Jamieson and Whitley, 11 March 1964, DO 183/70.
39. Christopher Andrew, *The Defence of the Realm: The Authorized History of MI5* (London: Allen Lane, 2009), 478–9.
40. S. R. Ashton and David Killingray (eds), *The West Indies, British Documents on the End of Empire*, series B, vol. 6 (London: The Stationery Office, 1999), 571–86.
41. Selwyn Ryan, *Eric Williams: The Myth and the Man* (Jamaica: University of the West Indies Press, 2009), 309.
42. Costar to Atkins, 3 May 1963, DO 200/67.
43. Poynton to Adeane, 11 November 1965, CO 1031/4425.
44. Undated draft letter, Poynton to Adeane, CO 1031/4425.
45. Poynton to Adeane, 11 November 1965, CO 1031/4425.
46. Adeane to Poynton, 16 November 1965, CO 1031/4425.
47. Note by Poynton, 22 November 1965, CO 1031/4425.
48. Lintott to Garner, 30 June 1964, DO 161/209.
49. Garner to Lintott, 31 July 1964, DO 161/209.
50. Pimlott, *The Queen*, 339.
51. 'The Queen's Visit to Canada, October 1964', DO 161/223.
52. Lintott to Garner, 13 April 1966, DO 161/209.
53. Minute by Johnston, 2 May 1966, DO 161/209.
54. Minute by Shannon, 4 May 1966, DO 161/209.
55. Lintott to Secretary of State, 1 March 1967, FCO 49/68.
56. 'The Queen's Visit to Canada', Sir Henry Lintott's despatch no. 8, 18 July 1967, FCO 49/68.
57. Lintott to Garner, 15 November 1967, FCO 49/107.
58. Note by Garner for Secretary of State, 17 November 1967, FCO 49/107.
59. Note by Lintott 'of a conversation between Mr Wilson and Mr Pearson after lunch on 10 February 1968', PREM 13/1960.
60. Minute by Hunt, 14 February 1968, PREM 13/1960.

61. Minute by Hunt, 23 February 1968, PREM 13/1960.
62. Minute by Lintott, 28 June 1968, PREM 13/1960.
63. Crowe to Stewart, 24 February 1970, DO 127/140.
64. Quoted in Crowe to Stewart, 24 February 1970, DO 127/140.
65. Johnston to Stewart, 13 May 1970, DO 127/140, recalling his earlier letter of 26 January 1967.
66. Johnston to Stewart, 13 May 1970, DO 127/140.
67. Minute by McConville, 22 June 1970, DO 127/140.
68. Bligh to Huijsman, 7 February 1964, DO 183/269.
69. For an overview of the situation see Richard Coggins, 'Wilson and Rhodesia: UDI and British Policy towards Africa', *Contemporary British History*, 203 (2006), 363–81.
70. Philip Murphy (ed.), *Central Africa*, Part II: *Crisis and Dissolution, 1959–1965*, British Documents on the End of Empire, series B, vol. 9 (London: The Stationery Office, 2005), 546.
71. Pimlott, *The Queen*, 347.
72. J. R. T. Wood, *'So Far and No Further!' Rhodesia's Bid for Independence during the Retreat from Empire 1959–1965* (Victoria, BC: Trafford, 2006), 412.
73. Pimlott, *The Queen*, 347.
74. Manuele Facchini, 'The "Evil Genius": Sir Hugh Beadle and the Rhodesian Crisis, 1965–1972', *Journal of Southern African Studies*, 33/3 (2007), 675.
75. A longer account of this incident can be found in J. R. T. Wood's article (unfortunately lacking references) ' "Four Tall NCOs of the Life Guards": Lord Mountbatten, Harold Wilson, and the Immediate Aftermath of UDI: The Proposed Mountbatten Mission', available at <http://www.jrtwood.com/article_guardsmen.asp>.
76. Wood, *So Far and No Further!*, 390.
77. Ziegler, *Mountbatten*, 648.
78. Note for the record by D. J. Mitchell, 18 November 1965, PREM 13/553.
79. Note for the record by D. J. Mitchell, 18 November 1965, PREM 13/553.
80. Further note for the record by D. J. Mitchell, 18 November 1965, PREM 13/553.
81. Mitchell to Adeane, 20 November 1965, PREM 13/553.
82. Pimlott, *The Queen*, 350.
83. Pimlott, *The Queen*, 351.
84. Ken Flower, *Serving Secretly—An Intelligence Chief on Record: Rhodesia into Zimbabwe, 1964–81* (London: John Murray, 1987), 94–5.
85. O'Neill to Wilson, 1 October 1966, PREM 13/1762.
86. Forster to Reid, 7 October 1966, PREM 13/1762.
87. Wilson to O'Neill, 7 October 1966, PREM 13/1762. When O'Neill raised this again early the following year Wilson spoke to O'Neill and 'killed the idea' (Pallister to Mackilligin, 13 January 1967, PREM 13/1762).
88. Facchini, 'The "Evil Genius" ', 684.
89. Minute by Steel, 4 October 1968, FCO 36/593.
90. Minute by Steel, 4 October 1968, FCO 36/593.
91. J. R. T. Wood, *A Matter of Weeks Rather than Months* (Victoria, BC: Trafford, 2008), 647.
92. Brighty to Youde, 18 April 1969, FCO 36/593.
93. Brighty to Youde, 18 April 1969, FCO 36/593.
94. Minute by Ling, 11 April 1969, FCO 36/593.
95. 'Rhodesia: The Royal Connection', Note by the Minister of State for Foreign and Commonwealth Affairs, 30 May 1969, FCO 36/593.

96. Youde to McCluney, 14 July 1969, FCO 36/393.
97. Bradford, *Elizabeth*, 383.
98. Note by George Thomson, 24 June 1969, FCO 36/393.
99. Youde to McCluney, 14 July 1969, FCO 36/393.

CHAPTER 7: 'A FRAGILE FLOWER'

1. See W. David McIntyre, 'The Admission of Small States to the Commonwealth', *Journal of Imperial and Commonwealth History*, 24/2 (1996), 244–77.
2. Brook to Macmillan, 7 December 1959, PREM 11/2910.
3. 'Evolution of the Commonwealth', note by Brook, 24 April 1962, reproduced in Hyam and Louis (eds), *Conservative Government and End of Empire*, Part II, 670.
4. Lorna Lloyd, 'Britain and the Transformation from Empire to Commonwealth: The Significance of the Immediate Post-war Years', *Round Table*, 343 (1997), 333–60.
5. Trevor Reese, 'Keeping Calm about the Commonwealth', *International Affairs*, 41/3 (1965), 455.
6. See W. David McIntyre, 'Britain and the Creation of the Commonwealth Secretariat', *Journal of Imperial and Commonwealth History*, 28/1 (2000), 135–58.
7. S. R. Ashton, 'British Government Perspectives on the Commonwealth, 1964–71: An Asset or a Liability?', *Journal of Imperial and Commonwealth History*, 35/1 (2007), 88.
8. For a contemporary account of this process see J. D. B. Miller, 'Britain and the Commonwealth', *South Atlantic Quarterly*, 69/2 (Spring 1970). See also Philip Murphy, *Party Politics and Decolonization: The Conservative Party and British Colonial Policy in Tropical Africa 1951–1964* (Oxford: Oxford University Press, 1995), 223–8, and most recently Schwarz, *Memories of Empire*, 384–438.
9. 'Patriotism Based on Reality Not on Dreams', *The Times*, 2 April 1964. Although Powell was widely assumed to be the author of the piece, he refused to confirm this until shortly before his death when he told his biographer, Simon Heffer, that he had indeed written the three articles (Heffer, *Like the Roman*, 351).
10. Minutes by Garner and Halliley, 2–6 April 1964, DO 194/44.
11. Minute by Sandys, 2 April 1964, DO 194/44.
12. See Philip Murphy, 'By Invitation Only: Lord Mountbatten, Prince Philip and the attempt to Create a Commonwealth Bilderberg Group, 1964–1966', *Journal of Imperial and Commonwealth History*, 33/2 (May 2005), 245–65.
13. Draft letter from Mountbatten to Wilson, 5 October 1965, CAB 21/5505. This claim was checked and confirmed by the CRO (Garner to Brockman, 22 October 1965, CAB 21/5505).
14. Record of a meeting between the British and Canadian Prime Ministers at the Prime Minister's residence, 9 December 1964, DO 193/69.
15. Mountbatten to Wilson, 17 January 1965, Mountbatten Archive, University of Southampton, MB1/J28A.
16. Record of an informal meeting between Sir Robert Menzies and Lord Mountbatten, 3 March 1965, CAB 21/5505.
17. Brockman had performed this role since 1943, first as Admiral's Secretary to Lord Mountbatten in all appointments and then, from 1959 to 1965, as principal staff officer to the Chief of the Defence Staff.

18. 'A New Type of Commonwealth Conference', undated, May 1965, CAB 21/5505. Mountbatten told Prince Philip that the document had been drafted jointly by himself and Brockman (Mountbatten to Prince Philip, 24 May 1965, MB1/J28A).

19. For example, in place of the reference to 'the danger of interminable speeches', the revised paper stated '[t]hese meetings will be of a strictly private nature, so that participants can express themselves freely and in a completely confidential atmosphere without running the risk of indiscretions in the press'.

20. 'Head of the Commonwealth', CRO note April 1953, DO 35/5134.

21. Minute by Duggan, undated late October/early November 1969, FCO 68/27.

22. Adeane to Clutterbuck, 26 September 1959. DO 35/5134. This letter was not, in fact, posted, but was presented to Clutterbuck by Adeane in October following a discussion between them.

23. 'Title of His Royal Highness, the Duke of Edinburgh', note by C. W. Dixon, July 1958, DO 35/5131.

24. Adeane to Clutterbuck, 3 November 1959, DO 35/5134.

25. Adeane to Clutterbuck, 26 September 1959, DO 35/5134.

26. 'Head of the Commonwealth: Note prepared by the Commonwealth Relations Office', July 1955; memorandum by Churchill, 4 February 1955, DO 35/5134.

27. Macleod to Foot, 14 December 1959, PREM 11/2910.

28. Minute by Rogers, 1 July 1965, DO 193/81, reproduced in S. R. Ashton and Wm Roger Louis (eds), *East of Suez and the Commonwealth 1964–1971*, *Race*, Part II: *Europe, Rhodesia, Commonwealth*, British Documents on the End of Empire series (London, The Stationery Office, 2004), 340–3.

29. Minute by Walker, 17 November 1966, DO 193/81.

30. McIntyre, *Britannic Vision*, 255.

31. CRO outward telegram no. 361 to British High Commissions, 10 September 1959, PREM 11/2910.

32. 'Commonwealth Representation at the Investiture of the Prince of Wales, Summer 1969: Brief for meeting in the Welsh Office—14 September 1967', FCO 49/161.

33. Hughes to Wilson, 10 October 1967, FCO 49/161.

34. Minute by Wakely, 15 March 1961, DO 161/178.

35. Minute by Dixon, 23 May 1961, DO 161/178.

36. One recently declassified file on arrangements for the Queen's death (HO 290/95) is not particularly helpful on this matter.

37. Minute by Storar, 24 March 1972, FCO 68/450.

38. Undated paper entitled 'Head of the Commonwealth' forwarded by Reith to Storar, 14 November 1973, FCO 68/518.

39. Minute by Storar, 9 May 1972, FCO 68/450.

40. Smith to Brimelow, 10 December 1974, FCO 9/2027.

41. FCO to British High Commission, Port of Spain, 30 March 1976, FCO 6/143. For the Maltese case, see Smith to Brimelow, 10 December 1974, FCO 9/2027.

42. Eaton to Paterson, 11 March 1976, FCO 6/143.

43. Minute by McEntee, 1 June 1971, FCO 68/330.

44. Minute by Reith, 20 July 1973, FCO 68/518.

45. Bottomley to Wilson, 31 August 1965, PREM 13/1365.

46. 'Commonwealth Day: Memorandum by the Government of Canada', March 1975, 2007/159.

47. *Daily Express*, 1 June 1976.

48. Smith, *Stitches in Time*, 274.

49. Minute by Hewitt for Prime Minister, PREM 13/1365.
50. Smith, *Stitches in Time*, 275.
51. Donald Simpson, 'Thirty Years of the Commonwealth Day Observance', *Round Table*, 86/341 (1997), 28.
52. Minute by Barltrop, 30 October 1978, FCO 68/776.
53. Simpson, 'Thirty Years', 28–9.
54. Hall, *Queen Elizabeth II and Her Church*, 75.
55. As H. V. Hodson pointed out, however, the objective is literally meaningless: 'Latin, the language in which the title was granted, has no definite article, and it is open to anyone of an ecumenical turn of mind to render *Fidei Defensor* as "Defender of Faith"' ('Crown and Commonwealth', *Round Table*, 84/333 (January 1995), 91).
56. Bradley, *God Save the Queen*, 230–1.
57. Bradley, *God Save the Queen*, 262.
58. Bradley, *God Save the Queen*, 263.
59. Smith, *Stitches in Time*, 278.
60. Derek Bateman and Derek Douglas, *Unfriendly Games—Boycotted and Broke: The Inside Story of the 1986 Commonwealth Games* (Glasgow: Mainstream Publishing, 1986), 71.
61. Bateman and Douglas, *Unfriendly Games*, 83–8.
62. Available at <http://www.royal.gov.uk/MonarchAndCommonwealth/QueenandCommonwealth/TheCommonwealthGames.aspx> (accessed 27 July 2013).
63. Minute by Smallman, 22 December 1969, FCO 68/60.
64. Minute by Smallman, 22 December 1969, FCO 68/60.
65. Minute by Johnston, 30 December 1969, FCO 68/60.
66. *The Guardian*, 31 May 2010.
67. *The Independent*, 28 September 2010.
68. Available at <http://www.royal.gov.uk/MonarchAndCommonwealth/QueenandCommonwealth/TheCommonwealthGames.aspx> (accessed 27 July 2013).
69. *The Guardian*, 27 September 2010.
70. *The Independent*, 2 October 2010.
71. Undated note, 'The Queen's Christmas Message Broadcasts', FCO 68/27. The 1957 televised message was delivered live. Thereafter, a pre-recorded message was used each year.
72. Armstrong to Charteris, 4 December 1972, PREM 15/1880.
73. Halls to Wilson, 16 October 1969, PREM 13/2899.
74. Minute by Collins, 28 January 1971, FCO 68/330.
75. Charteris to Armstrong, 7 December 1972, PREM 15/1880.
76. Armstrong to Heath, 1 December 1972, PREM 15/1880.
77. Halls to Wilson, 5 December 1968, PREM 13/2899.
78. Gore-Booth to Halls, 9 December 1968, PREM 13/2899.
79. Halls to Wilson, 16 October 1969, PREM 13/2899.
80. Memorandum by Booker, 21 October 1969, FCO 68/27.
81. Memorandum by Smallman, 27 October 1969, FCO 68/27.
82. *The Observer*, 26 October 1969.
83. *Daily Express*, 27 October 1969.
84. McIntyre, 'Britain and the Creation of the Commonwealth Secretariat', 138.
85. McIntyre, 'Britain and the Creation of the Commonwealth Secretariat', 139.
86. Note for the record by D. R. J. Stephen, 23 January 1959, PREM 11/4102.

87. Macmillan to Brook, 3 February 1959, PREM 11/4102.
88. Adeane to Brook, 12 February 1959, PREM 11/4102.
89. Hope to Sandys, 21 February 1961, PREM 11/4102.
90. Note for the record by D. R. J. Stephen, 23 January 1959, PREM 11/4102.
91. Brook to Macmillan, 29 January 1959, PREM 11/4102.
92. McIntyre, 'Britain and the Creation of the Commonwealth Secretariat', 146.
93. McIntyre, 'Britain and the Creation of the Commonwealth Secretariat', 147.
94. Smith, *Stitches in Time*, 268–9.
95. Minute by Coombs, 19 September 1969, FCO 69/27.
96. Minute by Coombs, 19 September 1969, FCO 68/27.
97. Minute by Walker, 22 June 1966, FCO 68/27.
98. Minute by Walker, 22 June 1966, FCO 68/27.
99. Memorandum by Wade, 16 May 1972, Archives of the Commonwealth Secretariat, Marlborough House (hereafter 'MH'), 2005/130.
100. 'Secretary-General's Call on the Queen', 24 July 1973, MH 2005/130.
101. Lloyd, *Diplomacy with a Difference*, 286.
102. Bradley, *God Save the Queen*, 190.
103. Lloyd, *Diplomacy with a Difference*, 286.

CHAPTER 8: A ROYAL 'DUTY'

1. Memorandum by Trend for Wilson, 1 May 1970, PREM 13/3110.
2. The controversy surrounding the resumption of arms sales to South Africa was exacerbated by its premature announcement (see John Campbell, *Edward Heath: A Biography* (London: Jonathan Cape, 1993), 299).
3. Memorandum by Armstrong for Heath, 18 September 1970, PREM 15/627.
4. Adeane to Armstrong, 24 September 1970, PREM 15/627.
5. Memorandum by Armstrong for Heath, 18 September 1970, PREM 15/627.
6. Adeane to Armstrong, 24 September 1970, PREM 15/627.
7. Douglas-Home to Heath, 5 October 1970, PREM 15/627.
8. Campbell, *Edward Heath*, 338.
9. Heath to the Queen, 15 October 1970, PREM 15/627.
10. This advice had been recently reiterated in Adeane to Greenhill, 17 July 1970, PREM 15/627.
11. Adeane to Heath, 20 October 1970, PREM 15/627.
12. Lacey, *Royal*, 256.
13. Campbell, *Edward Heath*, 338–9.
14. *The Times*, 23 June 1971.
15. Prince Philip to Heath, 22 June 1971, PREM 15/633.
16. Heath to Prince Philip, 2 July 1971, PREM 15/633.
17. Note by Heath, 29 October 1972, PREM 15/1348.
18. Smith, *Stitches in Time*, 272.
19. Lacey, *Royal*, 256.
20. Smith, *Stitches in Time*, 272–3.
21. Storar to Murray, 27 June 1973, FCO 68/550.
22. Overton to Watson, 21 December 1972, FCO 57/526.
23. Mark Curtis, *Unpeople: Britain's Secret Human Rights Abuses* (London: Vintage, 2004), 249.

24. Curtis, *Unpeople*, 253.
25. Curtis, *Unpeople*, 254.
26. Note by Bridges, 4 December 1972, PREM 15/1348.
27. Douglas-Home to Heath, 11 December 1972, PREM 15/1348.
28. *Daily Telegraph*, 15 March 1973.
29. Storar to Murray, 27 June 1973, FCO 68/550.
30. Minute by Reith, 20 July 1973, FCO 68/518.
31. Smith, *Stitches in Time*, 272–3.
32. James Callaghan, *Time and Chance* (London: Collins, 1987), 380.
33. Callaghan, *Time and Chance*, 380–1.
34. Hunt to Wilson, 29 March 1974, PREM 16/316.
35. Hunt to Wilson, 29 March 1974, PREM 16/316.
36. Smith, *Stitches in Time*, 273–4.
37. Smith, *Stitches in Time*, 274.
38. Minute by Storar, 16 July 1975, FCO 68/672.
39. Minute by Storar, 16 July 1975, FCO 68/672.
40. Minute by Watson, 17 October 1975, FCO 68/672.
41. Wright to Weston, 27 November 1975, FCO 68/672.
42. Minute by Storar, 2 September 1975, FCO 68/672.
43. Lord Thomson's views of President Amin's possible attendance at the CHGM, FCO minute, 11 May 1977, available at <http://webarchive.nationalarchives.gov.uk/97801992142352/http://cabinetoffice.gov.uk/foi/pdf/amin35.pdf>. This is one of a series of files released in September 2006 following a Freedom of Information request and posted on the National Archives website.
44. Callaghan to Amin, 22 May 1977; 'Note of a Discussion after the Prime Minister's Lunch for the First Deputy Prime Minister of Saudi Arabia at Chequers on Sunday 22 May 1977', available at <http://webarchive.nationalarchives.gov.uk/97801992142352/http://cabinetoffice.gov.uk/foi/pdf/amin34.pdf>.
45. 'Operation "Bottle", 23 May 1977', available at <http://webarchive.nationalarchives.gov.uk/97801992142352/http://cabinetoffice.gov.uk/foi/pdf/amin33.pdf>.
46. Philip Ziegler (ed.), *From Shore to Shore: The Final Years: The Diaries of Earl Mountbatten of Burma, 1953–1979* (London: Collins, 1989), 366–7.
47. *The Times*, 8 June 1977.
48. Pimlott, *The Queen*, 448.
49. Record of a conversation between the Prince of Wales and the Secretary-General, 23 June 1970, Commonwealth Secretariat Archives, MH, 2005/130.
50. *The Times*, 9 June 1977.
51. *The Times*, 8 June 1977.
52. 'Text of the first Focus lecture delivered by His Royal Highness the Prince of Wales on Monday 20 June 1977 in the Commonwealth Hall', Commonwealth Secretariat Archives, SG 145/10.
53. *The Times*, 21 June 1977. The headline was 'Criticism of Amin's Rule Approved by Prince'.
54. *The Times*, 29 July 1977.
55. *The Times*, 3 August 1977.
56. Harry M. Miller, *Confessions of a Not-So-Secret Agent* (Sydney: Hachette Australia, 2009), 167.
57. Cabinet conclusions, CAB/128/58/8, CC (76) 8th, 4 March 1976.
58. Callaghan, *Time and Chance*, 378.

59. Callaghan, *Time and Chance*, 380–1.
60. Cabinet conclusions, CAB/128/58/8, CC (76) 8th, 4 March 1976.
61. Murphy, *Lennox-Boyd*, 253–6.
62. Downing Street record of discussions with the German Chancellor, 11 May 1979, PREM 19/106.
63. Lord Carrington, *Reflect on Things Past* (London: Collins, 1988), 290.
64. Memorandum by Hunt, 4 May 1979, PREM 19/106.
65. Cartledge to Wall, 6 June 1979, PREM 19/107.
66. Cartledge to Wall, 15 June 1979, PREM 19/107.
67. Interview with Sir Walter Leonard Allinson in 1996, DOHP 6.
68. Interview with Sir Walter Leonard Allinson in 1996, DOHP 6.
69. Moore to du Boulay, 14 September 1979, FCO 105/26.
70. Pimlott, *The Queen*, 467–8.
71. Carrington, *Reflect on Things Past*, 276–7.
72. Sally Bedell Smith, *Elizabeth the Queen: The woman behind the throne* (London: Penguin, 2012), 293.
73. Lacey, *Royal*, 257.

CHAPTER 9: 'DE-DOMINIONISATION' IN THE 1970s

1. Transcript of the editorial in telegram from Wellington to London, 10 January 1974, FCO 24/1882.
2. Memorandum by Kelley, 17 January 1974, FCO 24/1882.
3. Pimlott, *The Queen*, 418–19.
4. *The Times*, 20 February 1974.
5. *The Times*, 1 March 1974.
6. Note for the record by Sir Robert Armstrong on 'Events Leading to the Resignation of Mr Heath's Administration on 4 March 1974', 16 March 1974, PREM 16/231. This document was retained when the file was originally opened in 2005, and was only released subsequently following a Freedom of Information request by the Thatcher Foundation. Even then, however, two sections of the document—apparently relating to conversations between Charteris and Armstrong—remained closed.
7. *The Times*, 8 March 1974.
8. Charteris to Palliser, 30 May 1976, FCO 57/681.
9. 'Value of State Visits: Memorandum by the Foreign and Commonwealth Office', November 1976, FCO 57/681.
10. Mark McKenna, *The Captive Republic: A History of Republicanism in Australia 1788–1996* (Cambridge: Cambridge University Press, 1996), 227.
11. McKenna, *The Captive Republic*, 228.
12. McKenna, *The Captive Republic*, 229.
13. Minute by Watts, 26 March 1973, FCO 24/1672.
14. Charteris to Acland, 12 April 1973, FCO 24/1672.
15. Minute by Storar, 28 March 1973, FCO 24/1672.
16. 'Text of a Letter from Sir Martin Charteris to Mr Roberts', undated April 1973, FCO 24/1672.
17. Charteris to Acland, 12 April 1973, FCO 24/1672.
18. S. R. Ashton, Carl Bridge, and Stuart Ward, *Documents on Australian Foreign Policy: Australia and the United Kingdom 1960–1975* (Australian Department of Foreign

Affairs and Trade, 2010), 1093, record by Wright of Meeting of Prime Ministers, 20 December 1974.

19. Ashton, Bridge, and Ward, *Documents on Australian Foreign Policy*, 1094–5, Charteris to Yeend, 30 December 1974.

20. Ashton, Bridge, and Ward, *Documents on Australian Foreign Policy*, 1105, Charteris to Brimelow, 10 February 1975.

21. Ashton, Bridge, and Ward, *Documents on Australian Foreign Policy*, 1094–5 and 1105, note 1.

22. Whitlam's statement of 26 January 1973, repeated in Neilson to Clark, 3 July 1973, FCO 24/1672.

23. Neilson to Clark, 3 July 1973, FCO 24/1672. A press report containing the lyrics was enclosed. The two lines in italics in the text were underlined in pen.

24. For an account of this episode see D. A. Low, 'The Dismissal of a Prime Minister: Australia, 11 November 1975', in D. A. Low (ed.), *Constitutional Heads and Political Crises: Commonwealth Episodes, 1945–85* (Basingstoke: Macmillan, 1988), 90–106.

25. Interview with Sir William Heseltine, Perth, 20 August 2008.

26. Low, 'The Dismissal of a Prime Minister', 104.

27. For allegations of CIA involvement see William Blum, *Killing Hope: US Military and CIA Interventions since World War II* (London: Zed Books, 2003), 245–6.

28. McKenna, *The Captive Republic*, 231.

29. McKenna, *The Captive Republic*, 231–5.

30. Zelman Cowen, 'The Office of Governor-General', *Daedalus*, 114/1, Australia: Terra Incognita? (Winter, 1985), 133.

31. Quoted in Cowen, 'The Office of Governor-General', 132–3.

32. *The Age*, 10 March 2001.

33. Whitlam to Wilson, 31 December 1975, FCO 24/2200. Interestingly, while Whitlam's letter is openly available in this file, it has been closed in another National Archives file, presumably because of its reference to the personal views of the Queen.

34. *The Times*, 6 March 1976.

35. Minute by P. G. de Courcy-Ireland, 14 June 1976, FCO 24/2200.

36. Dermot Morrah, 'The Monarchy in The Commonwealth: from King Emperor to Head of the Commonwealth', *Round Table*, 60, 240 (1970), 493–502.

37. *The Times*, 30 October 1973.

38. *The Times*, 30 October 1974.

39. Private information. This account appears to be corroborated by the existence in the National Archives of a closed file from March–June 1974 entitled 'ROYAL FAMILY: Purchase by the Prince of Wales of Farming Property in Australia' (PREM 16/269).

40. 'The Monarchy in Australia', *The Times*, 24 July 1976.

41. Memorandum by du Boulay, 28 July 1976, FCO 24/2254.

42. *Daily Telegraph*, 6 August 1976.

43. *The Times*, 4 May 1981.

44. *The Times*, 3 August 1981.

45. *The Times*, 30 June 2007.

46. *The Times*, 19 October 1977.

47. Paul Martin, *The London Diaries, 1975–1979*, ed. William R Young (Ottawa: University of Ottawa Press, 1988), 301.

48. Johnston to Palliser, 25 October 1977, FCO 82/815.

49. Moore to Palliser, 22 November 1977, FCO 82/815. The reference to Trudeau's 'young bride' is perhaps revealing. His marriage to Margaret Trudeau, thirty years his

junior, seems to have exerted a particular fascination on British politicians and officials, which bordered in some cases on *Schadenfreude* as the relationship collapsed. See, for example, the reference in a diary entry in March 1977 by the Callaghan aide Bernard Donoughue to Trudeau's 'hippy wife' having spent 'two wild nights' with one of the Rolling Stones (Bernard Donoughue, *Downing Street Diary*, vol. 2: *With James Callaghan in No. 10* (London: Jonathan Cape, 2008), 162–3).

50. Lloyd, *Diplomacy with a Difference*, 286.
51. Martin, *London Diaries*, 336. Account by Ivan Leigh Head in Deborah Hart Strober and Gerald S. Strober, *The Monarchy: An Oral Biography of Elizabeth II* (New York: Broadway Books, 2002), 322–3.
52. *The Times*, 26 August 1978.
53. Moore to Palliser, 15 June 1978, FCO 82/815.
54. Martin, *London Diaries*, 387.
55. Moore to Palliser, 15 June 1978, FCO 82/815. The Foreign Office subsequently confirmed that it saw no difficulties in the current wording of the bill relating to the Queen and the Governor General (Palliser to Moore, 5 July 1978, FCO 82/815).
56. Martin, *London Diaries*, 389.
57. Moore to Palliser, 20 July 1978, FCO 82/815.
58. *The Times*, 2 August 1978.
59. Martin, *London Diaries*, 445.
60. Martin, *London Diaries*, 445.
61. Martin, *London Diaries*, 535.
62. Ford to Palliser, 6 September 1978, FCO 82/815.
63. Note by Hall, 21 September 1978, FCO 82/815.
64. Moore to Palliser, 6 September 1978, FCO 82/815.
65. Minute by Goodison, 16 April 1974, FCO 9/2027.
66. 'Note on Sir Martin Charteris' meeting with Sir Anthony Mamo', 7 October 1974, FCO 9/2027.
67. Minute by Goodison, 16 April 1974, FCO 9/2027.
68. Minute by Goodison, 16 April 1974, FCO 9/2027.
69. Brimelow to Charteris, 26 March 1974, FCO 9/2027.
70. Charteris to Brimelow, 28 March 1974, FCO 9/2027.
71. Charteris to Brimelow, 29 September 1974, FCO 9/2027.
72. 'Note on Sir Martin Charteris' meeting with Sir Anthony Mamo', 7 October 1974, FCO 9/2027.
73. Minute by Thomas, 10 October 1974, FCO 9/2027.
74. Brimelow to Charteris, 21 October 1974, FCO 9/2027.
75. Brimelow to Charteris, 29 November 1974, FCO 9/2027.
76. Charteris to Brimelow, 2 December 1974, FCO 9/2027.
77. Heseltine to Curle, 9 December 1974, FCO 9/2027.
78. Charteris to Brimelow, 11 December 1974, enclosing Mamo to Charteris, 10 December 1974, and Mintoff to the Queen, 9 December 1974, FCO 9/2027.
79. Colin A. Palmer, *Eric Williams and the Making of the Modern Caribbean* (Chapel Hill, NC: University of North Carolina Press, 2006), 302.
80. Ryan, *Eric Williams*, 441–54.
81. C. E. Diggines, 'Constitutional Change in Trinidad and Tobago and the New Republic', 10 June 1976, FCO 6/1431.
82. Preston to Diggines, 30 June 1976, FCO 6/143.
83. Baker to de Courcy, 20 March 1975, FCO 24/2138.

84. Baker to de Courcy, 11 April 1975, FCO 24/2138.
85. FCO telegram to Canberra, 4 April 1975, FCO 24/2138.

CHAPTER 10: 'ON HER OWN'

1. Piers Brendon, *The Decline and Fall of the British Empire 1781–1997* (London: Jonathan Cape, 2007), 596.
2. McIntyre, *Significance of the Commonwealth*, 258.
3. Bogdanor, *The Monarchy and the Constitution*, 263.
4. McIntyre, *Significance of the Commonwealth*, 258.
5. *The Times*, 23 January 1984.
6. 'What Commonwealth?', *The Times*, 26 January 1984.
7. McIntyre, *Significance of the Commonwealth*, 259.
8. For Pimlott's account of the affair see *The Queen*, 503–15.
9. Pimlott, *The Queen*, 504.
10. Brendon and Whitehead, *The Windsors*, 209.
11. Andrew Neil, *Full Disclosure* (London: Macmillan, 1996), 202.
12. 'The African Queen: At Odds with No 10', *Sunday Times*, 20 July 1986.
13. Mark Garnett and Ian Aitken, *Splendid, Splendid: The Authorized Biography of Willie Whitelaw* (London: Jonathan Cape, 2002), 315.
14. *The Times*, 17 July 1986.
15. 'Rebel Tories Accused of Thatcher Plot', *The Times*, 21 July 1986.
16. 'The Story They Couldn't Kill', *Sunday Times*, 27 July 1986.
17. James Whitaker interviewed for 'The Queen: The Rivals', broadcast on Channel 4, 1 December 2009. Shea himself had died in October 2009.
18. *The Times*, 28 July 1986.
19. *The Times*, 29 July 1986.
20. Pimlott, *The Queen*, 511–12.
21. Sarah Curtis (ed.), *The Journals of Woodrow Wyatt*, vol. 1 (London: Macmillan, 1998), 195–6 (diary entry for 23 September 1986).
22. Neil, *Full Disclosure*, 206.
23. Pimlott, *The Queen*, 507.
24. Pimlott, *The Queen*, 510–11.
25. Curtis, *Unpeople*, 180.
26. Neil, *Full Disclosure*, 198.
27. Nairn, *The Enchanted Glass*, 350.
28. Neil, *Full Disclosure*, 206.
29. Memo by Sherman, 8 February 1981, Margaret Thatcher Papers, Churchill Archives Centre, Cambridge, THCR 1/10/19 f. 3.
30. Gary Williams, ' "A Matter of Regret": Britain, the 1983 Grenada Crisis and the Special Relationship', *Twentieth Century British History*, 12/2 (2001), 212.
31. Sir Paul Scoon, *Survival for Service: My Experiences as Governor General of Grenada* (London: Macmillan, 2003), 130.
32. Williams, ' "A Matter of Regret" ', 218.
33. *The Times*, 27 October 1983.
34. Reagan Library, NSC Country File Box 91331, 'The Allies and Grenada', 2 November 1983.
35. Pimlott, *The Queen*, 497, Brendon and Whitehead, *The Windsors*, 207. Perhaps the most colourful account comes from Michael Cole, who was the BBC's royal

correspondent in the 1980s. Cole suggests that, hours after she first heard of the invasion of Grenada, Mrs Thatcher held an emergency Cabinet meeting. During this, 'the message came through that the Queen wanted to discuss the crisis with Thatcher. Downing Street sent a message back saying that Thatcher would go to the Palace when the Cabinet meeting was over but the reply from the Palace was unequivocal. Her Majesty wished to see her prime minister *now* and so Maggie had to get up, leave the meeting, go straight to Buckingham Palace because the Queen was extremely put out that her realm had been invaded by our ally' (*Daily Express*, 1 December 2009).

36. Peter Fraser, 'A Revolutionary Governor-General? The Grenada Crisis of 1983', in D. A. Low (ed.), *Constitutional Heads and Political Crises: Commonwealth Episodes, 1945–85* (Basingstoke: Macmillan, 1988), 154.
37. *The Times*, 28 October 1983.
38. Fraser, 'A Revolutionary Governor-General?', 156.
39. Scoon, *Survival for Service*, 126.
40. CCBH/LSE IDEAS, Witness Seminar 'Britain and the Grenada Crisis, 1983: Cold War in the Caribbean', 29 May 2009. I am grateful to Michael Kandiah for making an uncorrected transcript available to me.
41. Scoon, *Survival for Service*, 135.
42. Scoon, *Survival for Service*, 135–6. When in 2013 documents from the Prime Minister's Office on the invasion (PREM 19/1048–9) were released to the National Archives, they contained a telegram from Montgomery recording this meeting but making no mention of the suggestion that he should pass on a message from Scoon. Indeed, Montgomery suggested that, because of the risks involved, Scoon 'doubted ... that he could ask for outside help', but would otherwise be sympathetic towards a foreign intervention. It remains a matter of supposition how this can be reconciled with subsequent accounts by Scoon and Montgomery.
43. 'Legal Aspect of Governor's Role: Appeal for Troops Might Be Justified', *The Times*, 29 October 1983.
44. McIntyre, *Significance of the Commonwealth*, 93.
45. Roger Barltrop, 'Fiji, Crown and Commonwealth', *Round Table*, 337/1 (1996), 83–9.
46. Boyce, *The Queen's Other Realms*, 37.
47. Bogdanor, *The Monarchy and the Constitution*, 287; Pimlott, *The Queen*, 516.
48. 'Danger for Her Majesty', *The Times*, 2 October 1987.
49. Pimlott, *The Queen*, 516.
50. *Glasgow Herald*, 16 October 1987.
51. McIntyre, *Significance of the Commonwealth*, 40.
52. Hardman, *Our Queen*, 309.
53. Pimlott, *The Queen*, 517.
54. *Sydney Morning Herald*, 20 November 2002.
55. *The Australian*, 1 May 2009.
56. Frédéric Bastien, 'Britain, the Charter of Rights and the Spirit of the 1982 Canadian Constitution', *Commonwealth and Comparative Politics*, 48/3 (2010), 324.
57. 'The Canadian Constitution', Memorandum by the Secretary of State for Foreign and Commonwealth Affairs, 11 November 1980, C (80) 69, CAB 129/210/19.
58. David Estep, 'Losing Jewels from the Crown: Considering the Future of the Monarchy in Australia and Canada', *Temple International and Comparative Law Journal*, 217 (1993), 230.
59. HC Deb, 3 March 1982, vol. 19, cols 296–300.
60. Hailsham to Thatcher, 23 February 1981, FCO 82/1042.
61. Bastien, 'Britain, the Charter of Rights', 339–42.

62. Ashton, Bridge, and Ward, *Documents on Australian Foreign Policy*, 1095–6, Charteris to Wright, 31 December 1974.
63. Ashton, Bridge, and Ward, *Documents on Australian Foreign Policy*, 1098, 'The Prime Minister's Discussions in London Concerning Constitutional Matters, 20 and 24 December 1974'.
64. Ashton, Bridge, and Ward, *Documents on Australian Foreign Policy*, 1098, 'The Prime Minister's Discussions in London Concerning Constitutional Matters, 20 and 24 December 1974'.
65. Anne Twomey, *The Chameleon Crown: The Queen and Her Australian Governors* (Annandale: The Federation Press, 2006), 249.
66. Twomey, *The Chameleon Crown*, 235.
67. Twomey, *The Chameleon Crown*, 251.
68. Twomey, *The Chameleon Crown*, 250–1.
69. Twomey, *The Chameleon Crown*, 254.
70. Anne Twomey, 'Changing the Rules of Succession to the Throne', *Public Law* (April 2011), 390.
71. Twomey, 'Changing the Rules', 392.
72. Brian Galligan, 'Regularising the Australian Republic', *Australian Journal of Political Science*, 28 (1993), 56–66.

CHAPTER 11: THE FALL AND RISE OF THE ROYAL COMMONWEALTH

1. Sally Bedell Smith, *Diana: The Life of a Troubled Princess* (London: Aurum, 1999), 220–1.
2. Brendon and Whitehead, *The Windsors*, 230.
3. H. V. Hodson, 'Crown and Commonwealth', *Round Table*, 84/333 (January 1995), 91.
4. Mason to Wilson, 19 November 1974, PREM 16/267.
5. Hardman, *Our Queen*, 176–7.
6. Hardman, *Our Queen*, 177.
7. Alastair Campbell, *The Alastair Campbell Diaries*, vol. II: *Power and the People 1997–1999* (London: Hutchinson, 2011), 76.
8. Interview with Sir David Gore-Booth in 1999, The Diplomatic Oral History Project (hereafter DOHP), Churchill College, Cambridge, DOHP 49.
9. Moore to Palliser, 22 March 1979, FCO 105/24.
10. Moore to Palliser, 22 March 1979, FCO 105/24.
11. Interview with Sir Hilary Synnott in 2008, DOHP 114.
12. *The Economist*, 18 October 1997.
13. *The Independent*, 14 October 1997.
14. *New York Times*, 15 October 1997.
15. *Frontline*, 14/22 (1–14 November 1997).
16. *The Observer*, 26 October 1997.
17. *The Observer*, 19 October 1997.
18. *The Observer*, 26 October 1997.
19. Obituary of Sir David Gore-Booth, *The Times*, 2 November 2004.
20. *The Observer*, 19 October 1997.
21. *The Times*, 24 December 1997.

22. *The Independent*, 20 September 1998.
23. *The Independent*, 18 September 1998.
24. *The Independent*, 21 September 1998.
25. *The Guardian*, 21 September 1998.
26. *The Independent*, 22 September 1998.
27. *The Guardian*, 22 September 1998.
28. Boyce, *The Queen's Other Realms*, 213.
29. Sir John Coles interviewed in 2000, DOHP 46.
30. Sir Brian Barder, speaking at a witness seminar at the Foreign and Commonwealth Office on 'The Role and Functions of the British High Commission in Canberra' (hereafter 'FCO witness seminar'), 8 November 2012.
31. Sir Roger Carrick and Sir Alexander Allan speaking at FCO witness seminar, 8 November 2012.
32. Sir Brian Barder interviewed in 1997, DOHP 22.
33. Sir Alexander Allan speaking at FCO witness seminar, 8 November 2012.
34. Sir John Coles interviewed in 2000, DOHP 46.
35. Boyce, *The Queen's Other Realms*, 241.
36. *The Guardian*, 5 November 1999.
37. Boyce, *The Queen's Other Realms*, 217.
38. Boyce, *The Queen's Other Realms*, 216.
39. *The Guardian*, 25 October 1999.
40. Oxford Analytica Brief, 8 November 1999.
41. Private information.
42. *The Guardian*, 8 November 1999.
43. Lacey, *Royal*, 387.
44. Lacey, *Royal*, 388.
45. *The Guardian*, 8 November 1999.
46. *The Times*, 8 November 1999.
47. Craig Murray interviewed on 'Your World: The Royal Visit', broadcast by the BBC World Service, 26 May 2012.
48. *The Independent*, 9 November 1999.
49. Interview with Charles Anson, 20 November 2012.
50. For a recent assessment of the Commonwealth's record see Kwadwo Afari-Gyan, Asma Jahangir, and Tim Sheehy, *Democracy in the Commonwealth* (London: Commonwealth Policy Studies Group and Electoral Reform International Services, 2009), 56–95.
51. *The Times*, 27 October 1992.
52. *The Times*, 20 August 1994.
53. *The Times*, 21 July 1994.
54. Memorandum by the Royal Commonwealth Society on Commonwealth Membership. Submission to the Working Committee on Commonwealth Membership, November 2006.
55. Victoria te Velde-Ashworth, 'The Future of the Modern Commonwealths: Widening vs Deepening?', Aide mȳmoire from a seminar at the Institute of Commonwealth Studies, 10 October 2005.
56. Report of the Committee on Commonwealth Membership, September 2007, 2.
57. Report of the Committee on Commonwealth Membership, September 2007, vii.
58. Communiqué of the 2007 Commonwealth Heads of Government Meeting, para. 87.
59. Communiqué of the 2007 Commonwealth Heads of Government Meeting, para. 88.
60. Philip Murphy, 'A Gigantic Farce?', *The Spectator Australia*, 19 November 2011.

61. For the author, at least, the scene has troubling echoes of Thomas Jones Barker's mid-nineteenth-century painting *The Secret of England's Greatness*.
62. HC Debs, 6 February 2012, Written Ministerial Statement, col. 5WS.
63. Daisy Cooper, *A Five-Point Plan to Make the Commonwealth Foundation's Re-launch Transformational* (Commonwealth Advisory Bureau (CA/B) Opinion, October 2012), 3. Available at <http://events.sas.ac.uk/icws/publications/972> (accessed 18 November 2012).
64. Don McKinnon, *In the Ring: A Commonwealth Memoir* (London: Elliott and Thompson, 2013), 32.
65. Available at <http://www.thecommonwealth.org/Internal/191086/150757/head_of_the_commonwealth/> (accessed 25 July 2012). The appearance on the website in July 2013 of a less emphatic statement fuelled speculation that the Palace might be seeking to secure Charles's succession to the headship.
66. McKinnon, *In the Ring*, 31.
67. *Daily Telegraph*, 3 November 2007. The article also provided some details about secret plans for the succession, the accuracy of which are largely confirmed by McKinnon's memoir.
68. Private information from two highly placed sources.
69. McKinnon, *In the Ring*, 37–9.
70. Anyaoku was speaking at the Institute of Commonwealth Studies on 11 January 2012. For a recording of the event see <http://www.sas.ac.uk/videos-and-podcasts/history/diamond-jubilee-seminar-series-monarchy-and-commonwealth-opening-event> (accessed 20 December 2012).
71. *The Observer*, 2 August 2009.
72. Philip Murphy and Daisy Cooper, *Queen Elizabeth II Should Be the Final Head of the Commonwealth* (CA/B, Opinion, July 2012). Available at <http://www.commonwealthadvisorybureau.org/fileadmin/CPSU/documents/Publications/Queen_Elizabeth_II_should_be_the_final_head_of_the_Commonwealth.pdf> (accessed 20 July 2012).
73. Available at <http://www.number10.gov.uk/news/prime-minister-unveils-changes-to-royal-succession/>. Downing Street website, accessed 28 December 2011.
74. Lucinda Maer, 'The Act of Settlement and the Protestant Succession', House of Commons Library research paper, 24 January 2011, 12.
75. Robert Blackburn, *King and Country: Monarchy and the Future King Charles III* (London: Politico's, 2006), 126, cited by Maer, 'The Act of Settlement and the Protestant Succession', 13.
76. Bogdanor, *The Monarchy and the Constitution*, 45, cited in Maer, 'The Act of Settlement and the Protestant Succession', 13.
77. *Montreal Gazette*, 23 July 2013.
78. Twomey, 'Changing the Rules', 378–401.
79. The report of a 2003 Commission by the Fabian Society on the future of the monarchy, which was also sceptical about the continued relevance of the Statute of Westminster, made a similar point about the 1999 referendum, citing Peter Harry of the Commonwealth Institute.
80. Maer, 'The Act of Settlement and the Protestant Succession', 14.
81. *The Guardian*, 6 March 2012.

Bibliography

UNPUBLISHED MANUSCRIPTS

The National Archives, Kew (TNA)
The following abbreviations are used for TNA files:

CAB   Cabinet Office
CO   Colonial Office
DO   Dominions Office/Commonwealth Relations Office
FCO   Foreign and Commonwealth Office
FO   Foreign Office
MEPO Metropolitan Police
PREM Prime Minister's Office

BBC Written Archives Centre, Caversham
Commonwealth Secretariat Archives, Marlborough House, London
Diplomatic Oral History Project interviews, Churchill College Archives Centre, Cambridge
Macmillan Papers, Bodleian Library, Oxford
Monckton Papers, Bodleian Library, Oxford
Mountbatten Papers, University of Southampton
National Archives of Ireland, Dublin
Powell Papers, Chuchill College Archives Centre, Cambridge
Sandys Papers, Churchill College Archives Centre, Cambridge
Thatcher Papers, Churchill College Archives Centre, Cambridge

PAMPHLETS, BRIEFING PAPERS, AND OTHER UNPUBLISHED PAPERS

Cooper, Daisy, *A Five-Point Plan to Make the Commonwealth Foundation's Re-launch Transformational* (Commonwealth Advisory Bureau (CA/B) Opinion, October 2012).

Heseltine, William, 'I Did But See Him Passing By', The Second Menzies Lecture, Institute of Commonwealth Studies, University of London, 7 November 1989.

Maer, Lucinda, 'The Act of Settlement and the Protestant Succession', House of Commons Library research paper, 24 January 2011.

Murphy, Philip, and Cooper, Daisy, *Queen Elizabeth II Should Be the Final Head of the Commonwealth* (CA/B Opinion, July 2012).

Royal Commonwealth Society, Memorandum on Commonwealth Membership. Submission to the Working Committee on Commonwealth Membership, November 2006.

Te Velde-Ashworth, Victoria, 'The Future of the Modern Commonwealths: Widening vs Deepening?', Aide mȳmoire from a seminar at the Institute of Commonwealth Studies, 10 October 2005.

Twomey, Anne, 'Responsible Government and the Divisibility of the Crown', University of Sydney Law School, Legal Studies Research Paper 08/137.

Wood, J. R. T., ' "Four Tall NCOs of the Life Guards": Lord Mountbatten, Harold Wilson, and the Immediate Aftermath of UDI: The Proposed Mountbatten Mission', available at <http://www.rhodesia.nl/mountbat.htm>.

NEWSPAPERS AND PERIODICALS

The Economist
The Guardian
The Independent
New Statesman
New York Times
The Observer
The Spectator Australia
Sunday Times
Sydney Morning Herald
The Times
West Africa
The Spectator

DOCUMENTARY COLLECTIONS

Ashton, S. R., Bridge, Carl, and Ward, Stuart (eds), *Documents on Australian Foreign Policy: Australia and the United Kingdom 1960–1975* (Australian Department of Foreign Affairs and Trade, 2010).

Ashton, S. R. and Killingray, David (eds), *The West Indies, British Documents on the End of Empire*, series B, vol. 6 (London: The Stationery Office (TSO), 1999).

Ashton, S. R. and Louis, Wm. Roger (eds), *East of Suez and the Commonwealth 1964–1971, Race*, Part II: *Europe, Rhodesia, Commonwealth*, British Documents on the End of Empire series (London: TSO, 2004).

Crowe, Catriona and Eogh, Dermot (eds), *Documents on Irish Foreign Policy*, vol. IV: *1932–1936* (Dublin: Royal Irish Academy, 2004). Available at <http://www.difp.ie/browse-volumes/display.asp?VolumeID=4>.

Hyam, Ronald and Louis, Wm. Roger (eds), *The Conservative Government and the End of Empire, 1957–1964*, British Documents on the End of Empire, series A (London: TSO, 2000).

Murphy, Philip (ed.), *Central Africa*, Part II: *Crisis and Dissolution, 1959–1965*, British Documents on the End of Empire, series B, vol. 9 (London: TSO, 2005).

Porter, A. N. and Stockwell, A. J., *British Imperial Policy and Decolonization*, vol. II: *1951–64* (London: Macmillan, 1989).

BIOGRAPHIES, MEMOIRS, AND DIARIES

Bedell Smith, Sally, *Diana: The Life of a Troubled Princess* (London: Aurum, 1999).

Bedell Smith, Sally, *Elizabeth the Queen: The Woman Behind the Throne* (London: Penguin, 2012).

Bradford, Sarah, *Elizabeth: a Biography of Her Majesty the Queen* (London: Heinemann, 1996).

Callaghan, James, *Time and Chance* (London: Collins, 1987).

Campbell, Alastair, *The Alastair Campbell Diaries*, vol. II: *Power and the People 1997–1999* (London: Hutchinson, 2011).

Campbell, John, *Edward Heath: A Biography* (London: Jonathan Cape, 1993).

Carrington, Peter, *Reflect on Things Past* (London: Collins, 1988).

Colville, John, *The Fringes of Power: Downing Street Diaries*, vol. II: *1941–April 1955* (London: Sceptre, 1987).

Donoughue, Bernard, *Downing Street Diary*, vol. II: *With James Callaghan in No. 10* (London: Jonathan Cape, 2008).

Douglas-Home, Charles, *Evelyn Baring: The Last Proconsul* (London: Collins, 1978).

Earl Mountbatten of Burma, ed. Philip Ziegler, *From Shore to Shore: The Final Years:. The Diaries of Earl Mountbatten of Burma, 1953–1979* (London: Collins, 1989).

Flower, Ken, *Serving Secretly—An Intelligence Chief on Record: Rhodesia into Zimbabwe, 1964–81* (London: John Murray, 1987).

Garnett, Mark and Aitken, Ian, *Splendid, Splendid: The Authorized Biography of Willie Whitelaw* (London: Jonathan Cape, 2002).

Gordon Walker, Patrick, ed. Edward Pearce, *Patrick Gordon Walker: Political Diaries 1932–1971* (London: The Historians' Press, 1991).

Hardman, Robert, *Our Queen* (London: Hutchinson, 2011).

Heffer, Simon, *Like the Roman: The Life of Enoch Powell* (London: Weidenfeld & Nicolson, 1998).

Howard, Anthony, *RAB: The Life of R. A. Butler* (London: Macmillan, 1987).

Lacey, Robert, *Royal: Her Majesty Queen Elizabeth II* (London: Little Brown, 2002).

Lascelles, Sir Alan, ed. Duff Hart-Davis, *King's Counsellor: Abdication and War: The Diaries of Sir Alan Lascelles* (London: Weidenfeld & Nicolson, 2006).

McKinnon, Don, *In the Ring: A Commonwealth Memoir* (London: Elliot, and Thompson, 2013).

Marr, Andrew, *The Diamond Queen: Elizabeth II and Her People* (London: Macmillan, 2011).

Martin, Paul, *The London Diaries, 1975–1979*, ed. William R. Young (Ottawa: University of Ottawa Press, 1988).

Miller, Harry M., *Confessions of a Not-So-Secret Agent* (Sydney: Hachette Australia, 2009).

Montague Browne, Anthony, *Long Sunset: Memoirs of Winston Churchill's Last Private Secretary* (London: Cassell, 1995).

Murphy, Philip, *Alan Lennox-Boyd: A Biography* (London: Tauris, 1999).

Neil, Andrew, *Full Disclosure* (London: Macmillan, 1996).

Nicolson, Harold, *King George the Fifth: His Life and Reign* (London: Constable, 1952).

Palmer, Colin A., *Eric Williams and the Making of the Modern Caribbean* (Chapel Hill, NC: University of North Carolina Press, 2006).

Pimlott, Ben, *The Queen: A Biography of Elizabeth II* (London: HarperCollins, 1996).

Ponting, Clive, *Churchill* (London: Sinclair-Stevenson, 1994).

Rhodes James, Robert, *Anthony Eden* (London: Weidenfeld & Nicolson, 1986).

Rhodes James, Robert, *A Spirit Undaunted: The Political Role of George VI* (London: Abacus, 1999).

Rooney, David, *Kwame Nkrumah, The Political Kingdom in the Third World* (London: Tauris, 1988).

Ryan, Selwyn, *Eric Williams: The Myth and the Man* (Jamaica: University of the West Indies Press, 2009).

Scoon, Paul, *Survival for Service: My Experiences as Governor General of Grenada* (London: Macmillan, 2003).

Shawcross, William, *Queen Elizabeth the Queen Mother: The Official Biography* (London: Macmillan, 2009).

Shepherd, Robert, *Enoch Powell: A Biography* (London: Random House, 1996).

Smith, Arnold (with Clyde Sanger), *Stitches in Time: The Commonwealth in World Politics* (Ontario: General Publishing Co., 1981).

Thompson, Dorothy, *Queen Victoria: Gender and Power* (London: Virago, 1990).

Wheeler-Bennett, John, *King George VI: His Life and Reign* (London: Macmillan, 1958).

Williams, Kate, *Young Elizabeth: The Making of Our Queen* (London: Weidenfeld & Nicolson, 2012).

Wyatt, Woodrow, ed. Sarah Curtis, *The Journals of Woodrow Wyatt*, vol. I (London: Macmillan, 1998).

Ziegler, Philip, *Mountbatten: The Official Biography* (London: Collins, 1985).

Ziegler, Philip, *King Edward VIII: The Official Biography* (London: Collins, 1990).

MONOGRAPHS AND COLLECTED ESSAYS

Adamson, David, *The Last Empire: Britain and the Commonwealth* (London: Tauris, 1989).

Andrew, Christopher, *The Defence of the Realm: the Authorized History of MI5* (London: Allen Lane, 2009).

Bagehot, Walter, *The English Constitution* ([1867]; London: Fontana, 1963).

Baker, Colin, *State of Emergency: Nyasaland 1959* (London: Tauris, 1997).

Blackburn, Robert, *King and Country: Monarchy and the Future King Charles III* (London: Politico's, 2006).

Bogdanor, Vernon, *The Monarchy and the Constitution* (Oxford: Oxford University Press, 1995).

Boyce, Peter, *The Queen's Other Realms: The Crown and Its Legacy in Australia, Canada and New Zealand* (Sydney: Federation Press, 2008).

Bradley, Ian, *God Save the Queen: The Spiritual Heart of the Monarchy* (London: Continuum, 2012).

Brendon, Piers, *The Decline and Fall of the British Empire 1781–1997* (London: Jonathan Cape, 2007).

Brendon, Piers and Whitehead, Philip, *The Windsors: A Dynasty Revealed 1917–2000* (London: Pimlico, 2000).

Cannadine, David, *History in Our Time* (London: Penguin, 2000).

Cannadine, David, *Ornamentalism* (London: Penguin, 2001).

Canning, Paul, *British Policy towards Ireland 1921–1941* (Oxford: Oxford University Press, 1985).

Chafer, Tony, *The End of Empire in French West Africa: France's Successful Decolonization?* (Oxford: Berg, 2002).

Curtis, Mark, *Unpeople: Britain's Secret Human Rights Abuses* (London: Vintage, 2004).

Dale, William, *The Modern Commonwealth* (London: Butterworths, 1983).

Fleming, Tom, *Voices Out of the Air: The Royal Christmas Broadcasts 1932–1981* (London: Heinemann, 1981).

Hajkowski, Thomas, *The BBC and National Identity in Britain, 1922–53* (Manchester: Manchester University Press, 2010).

Hall, John, *Queen Elizabeth II and Her Church: Royal Service at Westminster Abbey* (London: Continuum, 2012).

Hennessy, Peter, *The Hidden Wiring: Unearthing the British Constitution* (London: Victor Gollancz, 1995).

Holland, R. F., *Britain and the Commonwealth Alliance 1918–1939* (London: Macmillan, 1981).

Hyam, Ronald and Henshaw, Peter, *The Lion and the Springbok: Britain and South Africa since the Boer War* (Cambridge: Cambridge University Press, 2003).

Kenny, Mary, *Crown and Shamrock: Love and Hate between Ireland and the British Monarchy* (Dublin: New Island, 2009).

Kershaw, Roger, *Monarchy in South-East Asia: The Faces of Tradition in Transition* (London: Routledge, 2001).

Kumarasingham, Harshan, *Onward with Executive Power: Lessons from New Zealand 1947–57* (Wellington: Institute of Policy Studies, 2009).

Kumarasingham, Harshan, *A Political Legacy of the British Empire: Power and the Westminster System in Post-colonial India and Sri Lanka* (London: Tauris, 2012).

Lloyd, Lorna, *Diplomacy with a Difference: the Commonwealth Office of High Commissioner, 1880–2006* (Leiden: Martinus Nijhoff, 2007).

Lucas, W. Scott, *Divided We Stand* (London: Hodder and Stoughton, 1991).

McIntyre, W. David, *The Significance of the Commonwealth, 1965–90* (Basingstoke: Palgrave, 1991).

McIntyre, W. David, *The Britannic Vision: Historians and the Making of the British Commonwealth of Nations, 1907–48* (Basingstoke: Palgrave, 2009).

MacKenzie, John M., *Propaganda and Empire: The Manipulation of British Public Opinion, 1880–1960* (Manchester: Manchester University Press, 1984).

MacKenzie, John M. (ed.) *Imperialism and Popular Culture* (Manchester: Manchester University Press, 1986).

McMahon, Deirdre, *Republicans and Imperialists: Anglo-Irish Relations in the 1930s* (New Haven, CT: Yale University Press, 1984).

Mansergh, Nicholas, *The Commonwealth Experience*, vol. II: *From British to Multi-racial Commonwealth* (Basingstoke: Macmillan, 1982).

Metcalf, Thomas R., *Ideologies of the Raj* (Cambridge: Cambridge University Press, 1995).

Moore, R. J., *Making the New Commonwealth* (Oxford: Clarendon Press, 1987).

Morrah, Dermot, *The Royal Family in Africa* (London: Hutchinson, 1947).

Murphy, Philip, *Party Politics and Decolonization: The Conservative Party and British Colonial Policy in Tropical Africa 1951–1964* (Oxford: Oxford University Press, 1995).

Nairn, Tom, *The Break-Up of Britain: Crisis and Neo-Nationalism* (London: Verso, 1977 & 1981).

Nairn, Tom, *The Enchanted Glass: Britain and its Monarchy* (London: Vintage, 1994).

Olechowicz, Andrzej (ed.), *The Monarchy and the British Nation 1780 to the Present* (Cambridge: Cambridge University Press, 2007).

Porter, Bernard, *The Absent-Minded Imperialists: Empire, Society and Culture in Britain* (Oxford: Oxford University Press, 2004).

Prochaska, Frank, *The Making of a Welfare Monarchy* (New Haven, CT: Yale University Press, 1995).

Ramsden, John, *The Making of Conservative Party Policy: The Conservative Research Department since 1929* (London: Prentice Hall Press, 1980).

Rush, Anne Spry, *Bonds of Empire: West Indians and Britishness from Victoria to Decolonization* (Oxford: Oxford University Press, 2011).

Schwarz, Bill, *Memories of Empire*, vol. 1: *The White Man's World* (Oxford: Oxford University Press, 2011).

Stewart, Andrew, *Empire Lost: Britain, the Dominions and the Second World War* (London: Continuum, 2008).

Taylor, Anthony, *'Down with the Crown': British Anti-monarchism and Debates about Royalty since 1790* (London: Reaktion Books, 1999).

Thomas, Hugh, *The Suez Affair* (Harmondsworth: Penguin, 1970).

Twomey, Anne, *The Chameleon Crown: The Queen and Her Australian Governors* (Annandale: The Federation Press, 2006).

Ward, Stuart, *Australia and the British Embrace* (Melbourne: Melbourne University Press, 2001).

Webster, Wendy, *Englishness and Empire, 1939–1965* (Oxford: Oxford University Press, 2005).

Williams, Susan, *The People's King: The True Story of the Abdication* (London: Allen Lane, 2003).

Wood, J. R. T., *'So Far and No Further!' Rhodesia's Bid for Independence during the Retreat from Empire 1959–1965* (Victoria, BC: Trafford, 2006).

Wood, J. R. T., *A Matter of Weeks Rather than Months* (Victoria, BC: Trafford, 2008).

ARTICLES AND ESSAYS

Aldrich, Richard J., 'Did Waldegrave Work? The Impact of Open Government upon British History', *Twentieth Century British History*, 9/1 (1998), 111–26.

Anon., 'The Coronation and the Commonwealth', *Round Table*, 168 (September 1952), 297–304.

Anon., 'The Coronation and the Commonwealth III: Retrospect and Prospect', *Round Table*, 172 (September 1953), 306–15.

Barltrop, Roger, 'Fiji, Crown and Commonwealth', *Round Table*, 337/1 (1996), 83–9.

Bastien, Frédéric, 'Britain, the Charter of Rights and the Spirit of the 1982 Canadian Constitution', *Commonwealth and Comparative Politics*, 48/3 (2010), 320–47.

Bongiorno, Frank, 'Commonwealthmen and Republicans: Dr H. V. Evatt, the Monarchy and India', *Australian Journal of Politics and History*, 46/1 (2000), 33–50.

Buckner, Phillip, 'The Last Great Royal Tour: Queen Elizabeth's 1959 Tour to Canada', in Philip Buckner (ed.), *Canada and the End of Empire* (Toronto: University of British Columbia Press, 2005), 66–93.

Cannadine, David, 'The Context, Performance and Meaning of Ritual: The British Monarchy and the "Invention of Tradition", *c*.1820–1977', in E. J. Hobsbawm and T. O. Ranger (eds), *The Invention of Tradition* (Cambridge: Cambridge University Press, 1983), 101–38.

Coggins, Richard, 'Wilson and Rhodesia: UDI and British Policy towards Africa', *Contemporary British History*, 20/3 (2006), 363–81.

Connors, Jane, 'The 1954 Royal Tour of Australia', *Australian Historical Studies*, 25 (1993), 371–82.

Dodds, Klaus, Lambert, David, and Robison, Bridget, 'Loyalty and Royalty: Gibraltar, the 1953–54 Royal Tour and the Geopolitics of the Iberian Peninsula', *Twentieth Century British History*, 18 (2007), 365–90.

Estep, David, 'Losing Jewels from the Crown: Considering the Future of the Monarchy in Australia and Canada', *Temple International and Comparative Law Journal*, 7/2 (1993), 217–42.

Facchini, Manuele, 'The "Evil Genius": Sir Hugh Beadle and the Rhodesian Crisis, 1965–1972', *Journal of Southern African Studies*, 33/3 (2007), 673–89.

Fieldhouse, David, 'Decolonization, Development and Dependence: A Survey of Changing Attitudes', in Prosser Gifford and Wm. Roger Louis (eds), *The Transfer of Power in Africa: Decolonization, 1940–1960* (New Haven, CT: Yale University Press, 1982), 483–514.

Fraser, Peter, 'A Revolutionary Governor-General? The Grenada Crisis of 1983', in D. A. Low (ed.), *Constitutional Heads and Political Crises: Commonwealth Episodes, 1945–85* (Basingstoke: Macmillan, 1988), 142–62.

Galligan, Brian, 'Regularising the Australian Republic', *Australian Journal of Political Science*, 28 (1993), 56–66.

Hayes, Frank, 'South Africa's Departure from the Commonwealth, 1960-1961', *International History Review*, 2/3 (1980), 453–84.

Hodson, H. V., 'Crown and Commonwealth', *Round Table*, 84/333 (1995), 89–95.

Hopkins, A. G., 'Rethinking Decolonization', *Past and Present*, 200 (2008), 211–47.

Jeffery, Keith, 'The Second World War', in Judith M. Brown and Wm. Roger Louis (eds), *Oxford History of the British Empire: The Twentieth Century* (Oxford: Oxford University Press, 1999), 306–28.

Kaul, Chandrika, 'Monarchical Display and the Politics of Empire: Princes of Wales and India 1870–1920s', *Twentieth Century British History*, 17/4 (2006), 464–88.

Kullmann, Claudio, 'Attitudes towards the Monarchy in Australia and New Zealand Compared', *Commonwealth and Comparative Politics*, 46/4 (2008), 442–63.

Kumarasingham, Harshan, 'The "New Commonwealth" 1947–49: A New Zealand Perspective on India Joining the Commonwealth', *Round Table*, 95/385 (2006), 441–54.

Lloyd, Lorna, 'Britain and the Transformation from Empire to Commonwealth: The Significance of the Immediate Post-war Years', *Round Table*, 343 (1997), 333–60.

Louis, Wm. Roger and Robinson, Ronald, 'The Imperialism of Decolonization', *Journal of Imperial and Commonwealth History*, 22/3 (1994), 462–511.

Low, D. A., 'The Dismissal of a Prime Minister: Australia, 11 November 1975', in D. A. Low (ed.), *Constitutional Heads and Political Crises: Commonwealth Episodes, 1945–85* (Basingstoke: Macmillan, 1988), 90–106.

Lowe, David, '1954: The Queen and Australia in the World', *Journal of Australian Studies*, 46 (1995), 1–10.

Lowry, Donal, 'The Crown, Empire Loyalism and the Assimilation of Non-British White Subjects in the British World: An Argument against "Ethnic Determinism"', in Carl Bridge and Kent Fedorowich (eds), *The British World: Diaspora, Culture and Identity* (London: Frank Cass, 2003), 96–120.

McIntyre, David W., 'The Admission of Small States to the Commonwealth', *Journal of Imperial and Commonwealth History*, 24/2 (1996), 244–77.

McIntyre, David W., 'Commonwealth Legacy', in Judith Brown and Wm. Roger Louis (eds), *The Oxford History of the British Empire: The Twentieth Century* (Oxford: Oxford University Press, 1999), 693–702.

McIntyre, David W., 'The Strange Death of Dominion Status', *Journal of Imperial and Commonwealth History*, 27/2 (1999), 193–212.

McIntyre, David W., 'The Commonwealth' in Robin Winks (ed.), *The Oxford History of the British Empire: Historiography* (Oxford: Oxford University Press, 1999), 558–70.

McIntyre, David W., 'Britain and the Creation of the Commonwealth Secretariat', *Journal of Imperial and Commonwealth History*, 28/1 (2000), 135–58.

MacKenzie, John M., ' "Comfort" and Conviction: A Response to Bernard Porter', *Journal of Imperial and Commonwealth History* 36/4 (2008), 569–668.

Mallory, J. R., 'The Appointment of the Governor-General: Responsible Government, Autonomy, and the Royal Prerogative', *Canadian Journal of Economics and Political Science*, 26/1 (1960), 96–107.

Mansergh, Nicholas, 'The Commonwealth at the Queen's Accession', *International Affairs*, 29/3 (July 1953), 277–91.

Morris, Ewan, 'Forty Years On: Australia and the Queen, 1954', *Journal of Australian Studies*, 40 (1994), 1–13.

Murphy, Philip, 'The African Queen? Republicanism and Defensive Decolonization in British Tropical Africa, 1958–64', *Twentieth Century British History*, 14/3 (2003), 243–63.

Murphy, Philip, 'By Invitation Only: Lord Mountbatten, Prince Philip and the Attempt to Create a Commonwealth Bilderberg Group, 1964–1966', *Journal of Imperial and Commonwealth History*, 33/2 (May 2005), 245–65.

Murphy, Philip, 'Breaking the Bad News: Plans for Announcement to the Commonwealth of the Death of Elizabeth II, 1952–69', *Journal of Imperial and Commonwealth History*, 34/1 (2006), 139–54.

Murphy, Philip, 'Independence Day and the Crown', *Round Table*, 97/398 (2008), 667–76.

Murphy, Philip, 'Telling Tales out of School: Nutting, Eden and the Attempted Suppression of *No End of a Lesson*', in Simon C. Smith (ed.), *Reassessing Suez 1956: New Perspectives on the Crisis and its Aftermath* (Aldershot: Ashgate, 2008), 195–214.

Murphy, Philip, 'Censorship, Declassification and the History of End of Empire in Central Africa', in Andrew Finn and Harriet Jones (eds), *Freedom of Information: Open Access or Empty Archives?* (London: Routledge, 2009), 155–68.

O'Connell, D. P., 'The Crown in the British Commonwealth', *International and Comparative Law Quarterly*, 6/1 (1957), 109–10.

Olechowicz, Andrzej, 'Historians and the Modern British Monarchy', in Andrzej Olechowicz (ed.), *The Monarchy and the British Nation 1780 to the Present* (Cambridge: Cambridge University Press, 2007), 6–44.

Porter, Bernard, 'Further Thoughts on Imperial Absent-Mindedness', *Journal of Imperial and Commonwealth History*, 36/1 (2008), 101–17.

Rathbone, Richard, 'Things Fall Apart: The Erosion of Local Government, Local Justice and Civil Rights in Ghana, 1955–60', in Martin Lynn (ed.), *The British Empire in the 1950s: Retreat or Revival?* (Basingstoke: Palgrave, 2005), 122–43.

Reese, Trevor, 'Keeping Calm about the Commonwealth', *International Affairs*, 41/3 (1965), 451–62.

Reeves, Chris, ' "Let Us Stand By Our Friends": British Policy Towards Ireland 1949–59', *Irish Studies in International Affairs*, 11 (2000), 85–102.

Sapire, Hilary, 'African Loyalism and Its Discontents: The Royal Tour of South Africa, 1947', *Historical Journal*, 24/1 (2011), 215–40.

Simpson, Donald, 'Thirty Years of the Commonwealth Day Observance', *Round Table*, 86/341 (1997), 27–36.

Singh, Abnita Inder, 'Imperial Defence and the Transfer of Power in India, 1946–1947', *International History Review*, 4/4 (1982), 568–88.

Singh, Abnita Inder, 'Keeping India in the Commonwealth: British Political and Military Aims, 1947–49', *Journal of Contemporary History*, 20 (1985), 469–81.

Smith, Adrian, 'Rewriting History? Admiral Lord Mountbatten's Efforts to Distance Himself from the 1956 Suez Crisis', *Contemporary British History*, 26/4 (2012), 489–508.

Smith, S. A. de, 'The Royal Style and Title', *International and Comparative Law Quarterly*, 2/2 (April 1953), 263–74.

Trepanier, Peter, 'Some Visual Aspects of Monarchical Tradition', *Canadian Parliamentary Review*, (Summer 2004), 27–31.

Twomey, Anne, 'Changing the Rules of Succession to the Throne', *Public Law*, (April 2011), 378–401.

Williams, Gary, ' "A Matter of Regret": Britain, the 1983 Grenada Crisis and the Special Relationship', *Twentieth Century British History*, 12/2 (2001), 208–30.

Williamson, Philip, 'The Monarchy and Public Values 1910–1953', in Andrzej Olechowicz (ed.), *The Monarchy and the British Nation 1780 to the Present* (Cambridge: Cambridge University Press, 2007), 223–57.

Index

Index

Printed and bound by CPI Group (UK) Ltd, Croydon, CR0 4YY